Thesaurus Musicarum Latinarum
Canon of Data Files

The *Thesaurus Musicarum Latinarum* (TML) is a full-text database of music theory written in Latin, extending from Augustine's *De musica* through treatises of the sixteenth century. Including nearly 5,000,000 words arranged in 665 separate texts accompanied by more than 4,000 graphics, the TML is available to students and scholars worldwide on the Internet. This new edition of the *TML Canon of Data Files* (the seventh in the series and the first with the University of Nebraska Press) includes full instructions on the various ways in which users can access the database, as well as the "Principles of Orthography" and "Table of Codes for Noteshapes …," both of which provide essential explanations of the special ways in which the texts have been encoded to facilitate searching and the widest possible use within various computer environments. This edition also includes a table of contents for the major series of texts found in the TML, with each treatise within these series keyed to its corresponding version in the TML.

Following the prefatory material, the Canon provides for each separate edition a bibliographic record of the name of the author; title of the treatise; incipit; source of the text; the names of the individuals responsible for entering, checking, and approving the data; the name and location of the data file as it appears within the TML; the size of the file; and annotations identifying accompanying graphics (if any) and various other types of pertinent data. The Canon is in turn followed by a full alphabetical index of incipits, keyed to both the Canon itself through author and title and to the database through the name of the data file as it appears within the TML.

Thomas J. Mathiesen is David H. Jacobs Distinguished Professor of Music and Director of the Center for the History of Music Theory and Literature at Indiana University.

Publications of the
Center for the History of Music Theory
and Literature

Thomas J. Mathiesen,
Director
Indiana University

volume 1

CANON OF DATA FILES

Including
Introduction to the TML,

Principles of Orthography
and Table of Codes for Noteshapes,

Table of Contents of Major Series and
Their Location in the TML,

and Index of Incipits

Edited by

Thomas J. Mathiesen

University of Nebraska Press
Lincoln and London

Library of Congress Cataloging-in-Publication Data
Thesaurus musicarum Latinarum : canon of data files : including
introduction to the TML, principles of orthography and table of
codes for noteshapes, table of contents of major series and their
location in the TML, and index of incipits / edited by Thomas J.
Mathiesen.
   p. cm. — (Publications of the Center for the History of
Music Theory and Literature, vol. 1)
ISBN 0-8032-8233-8 (pbk. : alk. paper)
1. Thesaurus musicarum Latinarum (Computer file)—Handbooks,
manuals, etc.   2. Music—Theory—Early works to 1800—Databases—
Handbooks, manuals, etc.   I. Mathiesen, Thomas J. II. Series.
MT5.5.T45   1999   99-10606
781—dc21   CIP

∞

CONTENTS

PREFACE

In the Spring of 1989, a small group of scholars active in textual criticism, codicology, editing early music, cataloguing manuscripts, and the general history of music theory began casual conversations about the possibility of forming a database that would eventually contain the entire corpus of Latin music theory—printed and manuscript—written during the Middle Ages and the early part of the Renaissance. A larger representative group was invited to convene for discussion of the project at the annual meeting of the American Musicological Society in Austin, Texas on 26 October 1989. A general commitment to see the project to its conclusion was made and preliminary editorial and technical committees were established, with Thomas J. Mathiesen (Indiana University) as Project Director. Indiana University provided some substantial funding to establish the principal TML Center, and the Department of Music at Princeton University hosted a subsequent and extended planning conference, 17–21 January 1990. At this time, the project was officially established and designated as the *Thesaurus Musicarum Latinarum*. Both meetings included musicologists, specialists in computer applications, and librarians. By the end of the January conference, unanimous agreement emerged on matters of coverage, organization, access, medium, file structure, and similar sorts of technical decisions, and a general plan of work was adopted. Participants in the conferences and other interested scholars remained in close contact through the mails, regular telephone conversations, and a TML distribution list on Bitnet and Internet. From the first, the TML has been a consortium project involving universities from all regions of the United States.

In November of 1990, free of charge, the TML began public distribution of its database, which initially consisted of only a few texts, general instructions for accessing the database, and basic applications for decoding files and viewing graphic material. In approximately eight years, the TML has grown to include nearly five million words of text with more than four thousand accompanying graphics for the figures, musical examples, and other sorts of images that appear in Latin music theory. All the Latin texts of the Coussemaker and Gerbert *Scriptores, Greek and Latin Music Theory, Divitiae musicae artis*, the series of the Colorado College Music Press, the first thirty-five volumes of the *Corpus scriptorum de musica*, and the bulk of all individual editions separately published, as well as a substantial number of manuscript sources are included in the database, which is accessible around the world twenty-four hours a day through various Internet resources and in other forms. Thus, the TML has made it possible for scholars to locate and display in a matter of minutes on their personal computers—whether Macintosh, Windows, MS-DOS, or other machines—every occurrence of a particular term, a phrase or passage, or a group of terms in close proximity in more than 650 separate editions and manuscript sources.

In order to assist users of the database over the years, the TML published six periodic soft cover editions of the *TML Canon of Data Files*, which were distributed free of charge at meetings of the American Musicological Society and in response to letters of request. This was a reasonable practice when the database was growing rapidly and many elements were in a state of flux. But as the TML reached a level of maturity and stability in the mid-1990s, it seemed advisable to publish more formal periodic editions, of which the present edition is the first. When sufficient growth in the database warrants, new editions will be issued, but probably no more often than every three or four years. In the interim between editions, subscribers to the TML[1] will always be kept informed of new texts as soon as they have been added to the database.

The present edition of the *TML Canon of Data Files* includes full instructions on the various ways in which users can access the database, as well as the "Principles of Orthography" and "Table of Codes for Noteshapes ...," both of which provide essential explanations of the special ways in which the texts have been encoded to facilitate searching and the widest possible use within the various computer environments. For the first time, this edition also includes a table of contents for the major series of texts found in the TML, with each treatise within these series keyed to its corresponding version in the TML.

The Canon itself follows all this prefatory material and provides for each separate edition a bibliographic record of the name of the author; title of the treatise; incipit; source of the text; the names of the individuals responsible for entering, checking, and approving the data; the name and location of the data file as it appears within the TML; the size of the file; and annotations identifying accompanying graphics files (if any) and various other types of pertinent data.[2] The Canon is in turn followed by a full alphabetical index of incipits, keyed to both the Canon itself through author and title and to the database through the name of the data file as it appears within the TML.

---

[1]Full instructions appear on p. xvi below.

[2]In keeping with the TML's policy of representing the sources as accurately as possible, the author's name, the title of the treatise, and the chronological period to which it is assigned follow in all cases the source from which the data has been derived. On this matter, see pp. xi and xxvi–xxvii below.

A project such as the TML relies very heavily on the cooperative efforts of the many individuals who work on it over the years. The TML has been most fortunate from the first to have had two excellent committees, a Project Committee and an Editorial Committee. The names of the members of these committees appear regularly throughout the Canon, because in addition to providing valuable guidance and advice, they also established centers for the TML at their own institutions, from which they and their student assistants—who are also named throughout the Canon—created, checked, and approved countless numbers of data files that now form a part of the TML. Every one of these individuals has been central to the success of the TML, and as Director of the project, I take great pleasure in expressing my most sincere appreciation for their efforts. In addition, I must extend an extra measure of appreciation to Professors Oliver B. Ellsworth (University of Colorado–Boulder) and Peter M. Lefferts (University of Nebraska–Lincoln), both of whom spent countless hours far above and beyond the call of duty testing and re-testing the technical aspects of the TML, reading drafts of material (including this version of the Canon), and providing the TML with an almost uninterrupted stream of data of the highest quality from the very beginning of the project to the present day. Finally, it is a pleasure to acknowledge most especially my colleague Andreas Giger, Associate Director of the Center for the History of Music Theory and Literature and TML Project Assistant since 1994. Without his unfailingly cheerful work on every aspect of the TML—entering and checking data, creating hundreds of graphics and converting literally thousands of files in the course of developing the TML Web site, managing the project office, making suggestions for improvements, and just generally taking care of whatever needed to be done—the TML would not have flourished.

For all that is good in the TML, credit is most assuredly due all these individuals. For whatever shortcomings may be found in the TML and in this publication, I alone bear the responsibility.

Thomas J. Mathiesen
Director
Center for the History of
Music Theory and Literature
School of Music
Indiana University

October 1998

Thesaurus Musicarum Latinarum
Project and Editorial Committees

Project Committee:

Charles M. Atkinson
(Ohio State University)

Margaret Bent
(Oxford University)

Oliver Ellsworth
(University of Colorado)

Jan Herlinger
(Louisiana State University)

Sergei Lebedev
(Moscow Conservatory)

Peter Lefferts
(University of Nebraska)

Peter Jeffery
(Princeton University)

Tom Ward
(University of Illinois—Urbana)

Editorial Advisory Committee:

André Barbera
(St. John's College, Annapolis)

Calvin Bower
(University of Notre Dame)

Walter Kreyszig
(University of Saskatchewan)

Dolores Pesce
(Washington University)

Sandra Pinegar
(Columbia University)

Benito Rivera
(Indiana University)

Edward Roesner
(New York University)

Albert C. Rotola, S.J.
(St. Louis University)

John Snyder
(University of Houston)

Jeremy Yudkin
(Boston University)

INTRODUCTION TO THE
THESAURUS MUSICARUM LATINARUM
AND ITS USE

The *Thesaurus Musicarum Latinarum* (TML) is an evolving database that will eventually contain the entire corpus of Latin music theory written during the Middle Ages and the Renaissance. It complements but does not duplicate the *Thesaurus Linguae Graecae* (TLG), *Thesaurus Linguae Latinae* (TLL), *Lexicon musicum Latinum medii aevi* (LmL), and similar projects such as those of the Center for Computer Analysis of Texts (CCAT). Originally developed as the project of a consortium of universities, the TML is maintained by the Center for the History of Music Theory and Literature at Indiana University—Bloomington, in consultation with the TML Project and Editorial Committees. Work on the TML has been partially supported by generous grants from The National Endowment for the Humanities, an independent federal agency.

The TML Project Committee agreed from the outset on two fundamentals. First, the TML should enable users to locate and retrieve the text of the source, just as it stands and without editorial intrusions. For example, an author attribution appearing in the Coussemaker *Scriptores* that modern scholarship might consider erroneous would still be retained in the data file (although annotations clarifying attributions and providing other information about the data file are included in the *TML Canon*). The only exceptions to the rule of representing the text exactly as it appears in the source are governed by the "Principles of Orthography" and the "Table of Codes for Noteshapes ...."[1] Second, the TML should contain every printed edition, even if an earlier edition might seem to have been supplanted by a more modern one. These earlier editions can be excluded from database searches, but their presence in the database enables comparison of editions, among the many other possible uses of the database. The number of editions is large, but as the treatises are fairly short in general, the overall quantity of data at present amounts to approximately 157 megabytes. In the longer range, the TML aims to include as many manuscript sources as possible so that scholars will be able to retrieve not only published material but also readings that appear in the source material itself.

At present, the entire TML database may be viewed and searched online or downloaded to a scholar's personal computer (MS-DOS, Macintosh, or Win-

---

[1]Described below under the heading "TML Text Files."

dows) from several Internet resources. It may also be obtained on a CD-ROM.[2] When downloaded to a personal computer or read from the CD-ROM, even more sophisticated searching—including proximity and "fuzzy" searches—can be accomplished in a matter of minutes and displayed through a special program, *GOfer*™, available from the TML at a minimal cost. The database can also be tailored to the individual's particular interests. Any part of the TML, text and graphics, will run separately or together. With *GOfer*, searches of the TML can be endlessly configured: earlier editions of the same treatise can be included or excluded, treatises of specified centuries or a certain special group of texts ranging across many centuries can be marked for search, an individual treatise can be searched, and so on.

The TML can be accessed on the Internet in three ways: (1) through the TML LISTSERV, operated by the LISTSERV program running on a Windows NT server at Indiana University; (2) through the File Transfer Protocol (FTP) at a TML-FTP address (with the TCP/IP number 129.79.5.189); or (3) by means of a World Wide Web (hereafter WWW) client connecting to a Web server at theme.music.indiana.edu (with the TCP/IP number 129.79.184.104). All three systems will be described later in this Introduction. Although they may at first appear complex (especially if one is not used to Internet communications), the TML has been designed for quick and easy access in a large number of ways, most of which should require little, if any, investment in new computer hardware or software.

The steps for accessing the TML on the Internet are simple and straight-forward (instructions for each step are provided below):

1. Subscribe to the TML by sending a message to LISTSERV. (This should be done before using any part of the TML. Instructions are provided below, under the heading "LISTSERV's Commands." Subscriptions to the TML are necessary in order to receive the periodic notifications of new files, which are distributed only through the TML-L.)

2. Examine the list of available files by requesting one or more of the indexes from the TML LISTSERV or from the TML-FTP, or by viewing the

---

[2]For further information on this option, send the following one-line e-mail message:

>get cd ordrform tml-l

to:

>listserv@listserv.indiana.edu

or retrieve the order form from the TML-FTP. Full instructions for communicating with LISTSERV and the TML-FTP are provided below. Order forms may also be requested by calling or writing to the Center for the History of Music Theory and Literature (the address and telephone numbers appear on p. xxxi below).

indexes online from the TML Web. The TML is comprised of eight basic types of files: filelist, index, text, manuscript, graphics, stack, data, and HQX or UUE (for applications distributed by the TML). Each file has a "name" comprised of a file name (hereafter **fn**) and a file type (hereafter **ft**). Together, these indicate the content of the file and the type of data.

3. If the WWW is available at a user's site, the text and graphics files can be viewed and searched online in order to determine which files may be most pertinent to the user's interests. The TML Web, however, includes only files of the index, text, manuscript, and graphics types; filelist, stack, data, HQX, and UUE types can be retrieved only from the TML LISTSERV or the TML-FTP.

Then,

4a. Tell the TML LISTSERV which files to send by e-mail; or, retrieve them from the TML-FTP to a local mainframe.

5a. Download the files from the local mainframe to a personal computer.

Or,

4b. If a user's personal computer is connected directly to the Internet through a local network of some sort, FTP and WWW clients may already reside on the personal computer; consequently, the personal computer can connect directly to the TML-FTP and the TML Web without going through an intermediate machine such as a mainframe or e-mail server.

5b. In that case, files can be transferred from the TML-FTP directly to the personal computer or can be saved from the TML Web.

6. Read the files in any word processor or search them for various terms or text strings by using any of several available programs.

The first five steps are preliminary; it is in the sixth step where the TML reveals its full potential. The instructions for the first few steps are rather long and a bit involved because the TML must address many different operating systems around the world. But the first step is taken only once, and within the context of each individual's Internet system, the second, third, fourth, and fifth steps should be easy to master.

Communication with the TML LISTSERV

If a user's system supports only Internet, most—though not all—files can be retrieved from the TML LISTSERV; nevertheless, it will probably be more efficient for them to be retrieved from the TML-FTP or the TML Web.[3] The following paragraph pertains primarily to users whose e-mail is handled by a mainframe server. If, as is increasingly common, a user's personal computer is con-

---

[3]These operations are described below under the appropriate headings.

nected directly to the Internet and employs one of the many e-mail programs that reside on individual machines, e-mail messages can usually be saved directly to the personal computer.

Files requested from the TML LISTSERV will normally be sent as mail messages. Before a mail message can be downloaded to a personal computer, it must be extracted as a file to a user's directory on the mainframe. Every system handles mail files in a somewhat different way, and this brief introduction cannot supply detailed information. In VMS, it is usually a simple matter of issuing the command EXTRACT at the mail prompt. The user is then prompted to assign a name to the new file, after which the mail message, with all of its headers, is copied out of the mail utility and into the individual directory. In CMS, issuing the command LOG would copy the mail message into the directory. Mail files, however, must subsequently be edited to remove the various headers and other material that is not a part of the actual TML file (some systems support the command EXTRACT/NOHEADER, which will extract the TML file while automatically deleting the mail headers). Moreover, many mail systems will not accept more than eighty characters per line, and files with the **ft** DATA therefore cannot be effectively received in this manner. In general, users will be better advised to retrieve files from the TML-FTP or capture them from the TML Web rather than requesting them from the TML LISTSERV. Nevertheless, as some subscribers to the TML still find it more efficient to request and receive files by e-mail, this option has been retained.

A Brief Introduction to LISTSERV

LISTSERV, a product of L-Soft International, is a Mailing Lists Manager originally designed to run on mainframes operating under VM/CMS but now also running on mainframes operating in VMS and Unix environments and as a server on Windows NT and Windows 95. The program is flexible and powerful, and it has various complex options. Nevertheless, only a very few commands are needed to use the TML LISTSERV.

LISTSERV will accept commands in two forms: as mail, and as "Batch Jobs" in any of several transmission formats. Because there are various sorts of confusions that can arise in electronic addresses, it will generally be best if commands are sent as mail; this will insure that LISTSERV recognizes the electronic address and observes the best path to use in responding to commands.

Mail utilities differ widely, both on the various types of mainframes and in the popular mail servers residing on personal computers. If one is uncertain about the procedure for sending mail messages, computer consultation is generally available from educational institutions, Internet Service Providers, and public libraries.

Once the mail utility has been instructed to send a message, it will normally issue a prompt for an address. Commands intended for the TML LISTSERV must be addressed to:

listserv@listserv.indiana.edu [or, listserv@129.79.5.189]

In some mail utilities, addresses will need to be placed within quotation marks and prefixed with some indication telling the mailer which network to use (for example, IN%"listserv@listserv.indiana.edu"); the managers of the local computer system should be able to provide the exact combination of characters needed for the individual user's system.

When all the necessary information has been provided for a valid address, the mail utility will normally issue a prompt for a subject (and perhaps other header information such as cc:, attachments, etc.); all these fields should be left blank. Then, the mailer will ask for the message to be entered, which in this case will be a command or a series of commands. In other words, the message following the address and other fields in the mail header is treated by LISTSERV as a file of commands, with each line considered as a separate command. This feature enables the user to send several requests in a single message. The commands are very simple and easy to use, but it is important to note the following: because LISTSERV reads each line of a message as a command, absolutely nothing other than a specified command may be placed in the message. If extraneous material **follows** a command or set of commands (some mail utilities have been configured to do this automatically), LISTSERV may send an error message because it will not recognize this material. Nevertheless, any commands preceding this material will still be properly executed and the error message may be safely disregarded. On the other hand, if too many lines of extraneous material **precede** a command or set of commands (some mail utilities have been configured to do this automatically), LISTSERV may, once again, send an error message; in this case, however, any commands following this material will probably **not** be executed. If this problem arises, commands must be sent as "batch jobs," the second method of communicating with LISTSERV.[4]

Within a short period of time after commands have been sent to the TML LISTSERV (the exact period depends on network traffic), mail will arrive from LISTSERV confirming that the commands have been executed and providing the requested files. Communicating with LISTSERV in this way is very simple; the basic procedure is identical to that used for sending any ordinary piece of e-mail.

Fuller information is available in the general LISTSERV documentation, especially the General Introduction. Instructions for obtaining this guide are pro-

---

[4]Further information on communicating with LISTSERV "batch jobs" may be obtained by calling or writing to the Center for the History of Music Theory and Literature.

vided at the beginning of the message sent by LISTSERV in response to a subscription request to the TML-L.

LISTSERV's Commands

LISTSERV has an abundance of commands, but the ones generally needed
for the TML LISTSERV are the commands for subscribing, unsubscribing, and
requesting files or filelists. Any and all of the following commands must be sent
to listserv@listserv.indiana.edu [or, listserv@129.79.5.189].

Subscribing to the TML. To subscribe to the TML, send the command:
        SUBSCRIBE TML-L <the subscriber's full—and real—name here>
As an example, a subscription message might look like this:
                SUBSCRIBE TML-L Hugo Riemann
            [but the subscriber's real name must be used]
All subscription requests are forwarded by LISTSERV to the Project Director, who in turn sends a request for a short statement of interest in the TML (this
has become necessary to exclude those who would use the TML for mass mail-
ings or similar purposes: "spams," in the common parlance). Once the subscriber's statement has been received, the subscription is processed by the Project
Director (normally within a day), and LISTSERV sends two introductory mail
messages: one providing general information on communications with
LISTSERV, the other providing information specific to the TML.

To cancel a subscription to the TML and sign off the TML-L, send the
command:
                SIGNOFF TML-L

Requesting filelists, indexes, and other files from the TML. As noted above, the
TML contains eight basic types of files: filelist, index, text, manuscript,
graphics, stack, data, and HQX or UUE (the latter two for applications distributed by the TML), each file with a "name" comprised of a **fn** and a **ft**.

All the treatises contained in the TML are listed in various filelists according to the century to which the treatise has been attributed. The set of filelists
includes:
                4TH-5TH FILELIST
                6TH-8TH FILELIST
                9TH-11TH FILELIST
                12TH FILELIST
                13TH FILELIST
                14TH FILELIST
                15TH FILELIST
                16TH FILELIST
                17TH FILELIST

Each filelist also includes an Index, providing full bibliographic records for the sources of the treatises and other pertinent information. Users can see which treatises are currently available in the TML by asking LISTSERV to send any or all of the filelists or indexes. The following command will cause the appropriate file to be sent as an e-mail message:

GET 14TH FILELIST

or:

GET 14TH INDEX[5]

A series of GET commands can be enclosed in a single message, as long as each command appears on its own line. Be sure, therefore, to press the return or enter key at the end of each command.

Any of the files listed in the filelists can be requested by sending the command (for example):

GET VITARSN TEXT

VITARSN is the **fn** for one edition of de Vitry's *Ars nova*; TEXT, the **ft**, indicates that this is an ASCII text file derived from a printed source (the 14TH INDEX or *TML Canon* provide a full bibliographic record). Or, for another example:

GET HANREG MLBL4909

HANREG is the **fn** for Robertus de Handlo's *Regule*; MLBL4909, the **ft**, indicates that this is an ASCII text file derived from a manuscript source (the 14TH INDEX or *TML Canon* provide a full bibliographic record). Thus, as the examples illustrate, any file can be requested by issuing a command in the form:

GET **fn ft**

Further information on more advanced LISTSERV commands, written in language intended for the general user, is available in the "LISTSERV User Guide." The guide can be viewed online or retrieved in various formats from L-Soft International's Web site (http://www.lsoft.com/manuals/userindex.html) or FTP site (ftp.lsoft.com).

TML-FTP

If an individual's mainframe or personal computer supports FTP, the Internet system for transferring files from one computer to another, TML files can also be retrieved through the TML-FTP. FTP can be very fast (depending on the network), and it avoids the step of receiving files from the mail utility.

The TML-FTP is merely a different point of access to the same files distributed by the TML LISTSERV. Files can be requested from the TML-FTP by any subscriber using standard FTP commands. When using FTP, files are trans-

---

[5]The number "14" in this command may, of course, be replaced by any of the other numbers.

ferred directly from the TML-FTP to the machine originating the FTP session, whether another mainframe or a personal computer. The files do not need to be subsequently received from a mail utility as will normally be the case with files sent by LISTSERV.

To start FTP in VMS or CMS (or in a Telnet session originating from a personal computer), type:

ftp 129.79.5.189   [and press return]

After a few moments, an FTP connection will be opened, and a prompt will be issued for the account to which one wishes to connect. Type "TML-FTP" (always omitting the quotation marks) at this point. When asked for a password, type "themulat." A connection to the TML-FTP directory will then be opened in read-only mode. On the computer screen, a sample session to this point might appear as:

```
$ ftp 129.79.5.189
Connected to 129.79.5.189.
220 piano Microsoft FTP Service (Version 3.0).
Name (129.79.5.189:[your user name will appear here]):
tml-ftp
331 Password required for tml-ftp.
Password: themulat
230-Welcome to the LISTSERV server at IUB.
230 User tml-ftp logged in.
Remote system type is Windows_NT.
```

A prompt (either an asterisk or a word or abbreviation [e.g., Command: or ftp>) will appear on the following line. To retrieve any text or graphics files, the user must first move to the appropriate subdirectory filelist. As in LISTSERV, the filelists are arranged as various subdirectories of the TML-FTP. For example, to move down to a subdirectory from which a user wishes to retrieve files, "cd 12th"[6] would be entered. To move back up to the main TML-FTP directory, "cd .." would be entered (the two dots tell the system to move up one directory); from this point, the user can then move down into another subdirectory.

If the user already knows which files to request at this point, the commands may simply be entered at the prompt within the appropriate subdirectory; for example, in the 15th subdirectory, the user might enter:

---

[6]"12th" is the name of one of the subdirectories; if a user wished to retrieve a file from the 14th filelist, "14th" would be used; from the 9th-11th filelist, "9th-11th"; and so on.

GET ANO5ARS.TEXT[7]

FTP will indicate that it is opening the connection and transferring the file. When it has finished, a new prompt will await instructions. If this was the only file a user wished to transfer, the command "close" (some systems may require "disconnect") would then be entered, and at the next prompt, "quit" (some systems may require "exit"). At this point, the user is returned to the operating system of the mainframe or the Telnet session on a personal computer.

On the other hand, a user may need to see a list of all the files contained in one of the subdirectories before deciding which ones to request. Such a list is retrieved by typing (always within the appropriate subdirectory) "dir" at the prompt. On the computer screen, a sample session to this point might appear as:

```
cd 6th-8th
250 CWD command successful.
dir
200 PORT command successful.
150 Opening ASCII mode data connection for /bin/ls.
226 Transfer complete.
10-22-97   02:41AM     6421 6TH-8TH.INDEX
10-22-97   02:12AM     5638 6TH-8TH.CATALOG
07-25-97   11:49PM     2413 ALCMUS.TEXT
07-25-97   11:49PM    31466 BEDMUST.TEXT
02-20-97   06:37PM    14717 BOEDIM1.01GF
02-20-97   06:37PM    23151 BOEDIM1.02GF
02-20-97   06:37PM    35940 BOEDIM1.03GF
02-20-97   06:37PM    27231 BOEDIM1.04GF
02-20-97   06:37PM    28506 BOEDIM1.05GF
02-20-97   06:37PM    23140 BOEDIM1.06GF
07-25-97   11:49PM    67688 BOEDIM1.TEXT
02-20-97   06:38PM    19506 BOEDIM2.01GF
02-20-97   06:38PM    12907 BOEDIM2.02GF
02-20-97   06:38PM    15077 BOEDIM2.03GF
02-20-97   06:38PM    11137 BOEDIM2.04GF
02-20-97   06:38PM    15119 BOEDIM2.05GF
02-20-97   06:38PM     9639 BOEDIM2.06GF
02-20-97   06:38PM    15413 BOEDIM2.07GF
02-20-97   06:38PM    11202 BOEDIM2.08GF
02-20-97   06:38PM     8024 BOEDIM2.09GF
```

---

[7]In the TML-FTP, the **fn** and **ft** must be separated by a period rather than by a space, as in LISTSERV commands. In FTP commands, upper-case letters must be used for the **fn** and **ft**.

```
07-25-97  11:49PM     64368 BOEDIM2.TEXT
```
 [all the other files available will be listed here,
  one after the other]

Separate "get" commands can then be issued for whichever files the user wishes to retrieve.

Some users will want to transfer many or all the TML files. In this case, the "mget" command should be used (in FTP syntax, "mget" means that multiple "get" commands are being issued). Before issuing any mget commands, however, the command "interactive" should be entered at the first prompt, unless one wishes to retrieve every file in the subdirectory.[8] The "interactive" mode, which is normally set as the default for FTP servers, will cause the server to issue a separate confirmation query prior to sending each file, to which the user simply responds by typing "y" or "n." If the system responds to the command "interactive" that this is an invalid command, the command "status" should be sent, which will in most cases cause the system to display the default settings for the FTP transfer; one of these will normally (though not always) state either "Prompt: on" or "Confirm: on." If the status indicates that "prompt" (or "confirm") is off, sending the command "prompt" (or "confirm") will turn the function back on (see sample session below). To test the setting, one might, for example, send the command (in the 6th-8th subdirectory) "mget BOEDIM1.*"; in this command, the asterisk functions as a wild card, indicating that the TML-FTP should send all files with the **fn** BOEDIM1, regardless of the **ft**. If the system supports the mget option and "interactive" mode is on, this command will cause the TML-FTP to send the BOEDIM1 text file with all its graphics, each file preceded by a prompt asking for confirmation before it is sent.

If it has been determined that a system supports the mget option and that all the files in a given subdirectory are to be transferred, two wild cards should be used with the command: mget *.* will cause the TML-FTP to send every file in the subdirectory. If interactive mode is on, each file will be preceded by a confirmation prompt; otherwise, the files will be sent one after another without further prompts.

On the computer screen, a sample session to this point might appear as follows (this sample also demonstrates the final commands for closing the FTP session):

```
ftp> interactive
?Invalid command
ftp> prompt
Interactive mode off.
```

_____

[8]Some systems may not support interactive mode.

XX

```
ftp> prompt
Interactive mode on.
ftp> cd 4th-5th
250 CWD command successful.
ftp> mget *.*
mget 4TH-5TH.INDEX? n
mget 4TH-5TH.CATALOG? n
mget AUGDEM1.TEXT? y
200 PORT command successful.
150 Opening ASCII mode data connection for
AUGDEM1.TEXT(49410 bytes).
226 Transfer complete.
49410 bytes received in 0.43 seconds (1.1e+02 Kbytes/s)
mget AUGDEM2.TEXT? y
200 PORT command successful.
150 Opening ASCII mode data connection for
AUGDEM2.TEXT(44806 bytes).
226 Transfer complete.
44806 bytes received in 0.18 seconds (2.4e+02 Kbytes/s)
mget AUGDEM3.TEXT? y
200 PORT command successful.
150 Opening ASCII mode data connection for
AUGDEM3.TEXT(34831 bytes).
226 Transfer complete.
34831 bytes received in 0.15 seconds (2.2e+02 Kbytes/s)
mget AUGDEM4.TEXT? y
200 PORT command successful.
150 Opening ASCII mode data connection for
AUGDEM4.TEXT(55060 bytes).
226 Transfer complete.
55060 bytes received in 0.27 seconds (2e+02 Kbytes/s)
mget AUGDEM5.TEXT? y
200 PORT command successful.
150 Opening ASCII mode data connection for
AUGDEM5.TEXT(42937 bytes).
226 Transfer complete.
42937 bytes received in 0.27 seconds (1.5e+02 Kbytes/s)
                [etc.]
ftp> close [some systems may require "disconnect" instead]
221 Thank you!
ftp>quit [some systems may require "exit" instead]
```

Special FTP programs designed to simplify this process are available for certain models of personal computers. Macintosh users who have their computers connected directly to the Internet, for example, may prefer to use the program *Fetch*, rather than remembering and typing all the commands noted above.[9] Once *Fetch* has been started, it is only necessary to click on the button "Open Connection ..." to bring up a box in which the host name or IP number (i.e., listserv.indiana.edu or 129.79.5.189), the user ID (i.e., TML-FTP), and the password (i.e., themulat) are entered. Once these have been entered, the information is sent by clicking on the button marked "OK." *Fetch* will then connect and begin receiving the TML-FTP directory, showing the various subdirectories and other files. Double-clicking on a subdirectory will open it and display all its files. Once the contents of a subdirectory have been received, transfers are effected simply by selecting any or all of the files and clicking on the button marked "Get File ...." If one wishes to retrieve several but not subsequent files, these can be selected while pressing the command key. Clicking on the button marked "Close Connection"[10] concludes the session.

TML Web

The text, graphics, and index files of the TML can also be viewed online or retrieved by means of a WWW client. This Internet option is configured in a wide variety of different ways at each site, and an introduction of this sort cannot attempt to describe the exact process one needs to follow to use the TML Web. Users should first consult with their local specialists about the best means for connecting to their "Web home page." Once this connection has been made, the following instructions should present no difficulty.

When connected to a Web page, an individual's machine is running a Web client that can link to other types of servers, which are identified by means of a

---

[9]This program is licensed free of charge for use in educational and non-profit organizations and is commonly available from university computing services.

[10]Most subscribers will find that their FTP systems are set to transfer data as ASCII text. In a few cases (especially at European sites), the data may arrive in some unrecognizable form because the default for the site has been set to something other than ASCII. If in doubt, at the FTP prompt, type "status" and press return; FTP will then display its current settings (if this does not work, typing "type" should cause FTP to respond with "a" [for "ascii"] or "i" [for "binary"]). If the transfer type is something other than ASCII, it can be easily changed. At the FTP prompt (and prior to transferring the files), type "ascii" (some users may need to type "type ascii") and press return. This will set FTP's file transfer type to the form needed for TML files. Checking to be sure the change has been made is accomplished by once again typing "status" or "type" (and pressing return) at the next FTP prompt.

URL (Uniform Resource Locator). The URL indicates the type of server (e.g., gopher, ftp, or http), the location, and the path to the data. The URL for the TML is:

http://www.music.indiana.edu/tml

When a Web client is directed to load this URL, it will make the necessary connection and then display a Copyright Notice, followed by the highlighted link "Continue." Clicking on this link will cause the "TML home page" to be displayed, from which users can in turn connect to a page for searching the TML files (instructions for using the search engine are included on the page) or to the various indexes of files, corresponding to the indexes contained in the TML LISTSERV and TML-FTP. The TML Web indexes, however, are linked to each file and function as bibliographic tables of contents. Within the Web client, users can search the files of each index (or all the files in all the indexes), view the texts or graphics themselves, and save to their personal machines any or all files of interest.

TML Text Files

Unlike other types of texts commonly studied by scholars in fields such as classics, literature, or philosophy, Latin music theory includes abundant figures and musical notation for which no ASCII equivalents exist. This material cannot simply be omitted. Musical notation included within sentences is entered as codes in the text file, while full musical examples or figures are scanned and saved in GIF format and keyed to locations within the text files themselves. If the example includes text, this is given in the ASCII file within brackets (e.g., [Berkeley, 86; text: E-la, D-la-sol, C-sol-fa, B-fa-B-mi, A-la-mi-re, G-sol-re-ut, F-fa-ut, E-la-mi, D-la-sol-re, C-sol-fa-ut, D-sol-re, C-fa-ut, B-mi, A-re, Gamma-ut, 5 superacute, 7 acute, 8 graves, Declaracio manus secundum usum]), thereby enabling search engines to locate and display text strings that appear within figures as well as those within the treatise proper. The text, of course, also appears in the graphics file storing the figure, table, or musical example itself.

The treatises in the TML have been entered following specific rules of orthography and notation codes. These will need to be consulted in order to make the fullest use of the data files. The tables of orthography and notation codes are not distributed on the TML LISTSERV or TML-FTP, but they may be viewed from links on the TML Web; they are also included in this publication on pp. xxxii–xxxv.[11]

---

[11]They have also been published in: Thomas J. Mathiesen, "Transmitting Text and Graphics in Online Databases: The *Thesaurus Musicarum Latinarum* Model," *Computing in Musicology* 9 (1993–94): 33–48 (the tables appear on pp. 43–47).

Graphics Files

The graphics files, by their nature, are somewhat more complex. The GIF format was selected in preference to any other format for several reasons: first, GIF files are quite small, and thus they can be downloaded very quickly; second, the format can be read on any of the major hardware configurations with simple conversion programs available as free- or shareware; and third, the graphics files can be displayed directly online by WWW clients.

The TML's graphics files may be displayed on a Macintosh by using any program that interprets GIF files; DOS computers must be properly configured to display graphics, and depending on the configuration, the GIF file may either be displayed directly or readily translated into a compatible format. In general, DOS users will either need to be running some version of Windows or have at the very least a graphics monitor with the appropriate card.

In an effort to make the use of graphics files as convenient as possible, the TML LISTSERV and TML-FTP offer two necessary programs for Macintosh subscribers: *GIFConverter* and *UUTool*. Both are stored in binhex encoding to insure that they can be transferred to any remote system without corruption. A number of GIF viewers and UU decoders are also available for DOS and Windows. There is no single common program for all these machines, but the TML LISTSERV and TML-FTP offer the shareware program *CompuShow* in UU encoded form.[12]

Macintosh subscribers interested in viewing graphics should first request (as described in the previous section) the following files from the TML LISTSERV or TML-FTP: GIFCON HQX, GIFCODOC HQX, and UUMAC HQX. These files are fairly long, but they need only be requested and transferred once.[13] GIFCON HQX is a binhex-encoded version of the program *GIFConverter*, an excellent shareware program that enables GIF files to be viewed as well as translated into formats that can be used in word processing programs or other contexts; GIFCODOC HQX is the binhex-encoded user's manual for the program; and UUMAC HQX is a binhex-encoded version of the program *UUTool*, a simple but essential program that enables the graphics files to be decoded so they can be viewed with *GIFConverter*.

After these three files have been received and downloaded to a Macintosh, they must be decoded with a binhex program (*Fetch* automatically decodes binhexed files as it transfers them to an individual machine; programs such as *StuffIt* and *Compact Pro* feature a binhex decoder, and other programs are also

---

[12]See further information below on UU encoding. The Center for the History of Music Theory and Literature will also assist TML subscribers in recommending other viewers and in providing a UU decoder on disk.

[13]Described below under the heading "Downloading Files."

common among Macintosh owners). When decoded, GIFCON HQX and UUMAC HQX become self-extracting archives that contain *GIFConverter* and *UUTool* (together with a short instruction manual for *UUTool*); GIFCODOC becomes a Microsoft *Word* file. The two self-extracting archives show little icons like filing cabinets; when these are double-clicked, a prompt will appear asking where the programs should be saved; following the user's response, the files are extracted and saved. *GIFConverter* and *UUTool* will then operate like any other Macintosh program.[14]

DOS users interested in viewing graphics should request the following file from the TML LISTSERV or TML-FTP: CSHOWA UUE. This file is fairly long but will only need to be requested and transferred once.[15] If a user's mainframe has a UU decoding utility (as many of them do), the file can be decoded prior to downloading. If the file has been decoded on a mainframe, it must be downloaded to a personal computer with the file transfer protocols set for "Binary." On the other hand, if a user's mainframe does not have a UU decoding utility—or the user is uncertain about the process for downloading anything other than a text file—the file can be downloaded in its UU encoded form and then decoded with an individual UU decoder.[16] When decoded, CSHOWA UUE will become CSHOWA.EXE, a self-extracting archive. The files are extracted by typing CSHOWA at the DOS prompt and following the subsequent prompts.[17]

Users wishing to transfer the TML's graphics by means of a WWW client running on their personal computers need only select and save them. The programs take care of insuring the settings to enable the files to be properly transferred.

Transferring graphics from the TML LISTSERV and TML-FTP is somewhat more complex. The graphics files on the TML LISTSERV and TML-FTP are stored in UU encoded format to insure that they can be transmitted by e-mail or FTP without being corrupted. UU encoding has been used (rather than bin-

---

[14]Macintosh subscribers who prefer to be sent these programs on disk may request them from the Center for the History of Music Theory and Literature.

[15]Described below under the heading "Downloading Files."

[16]Available from the Center for the History of Music Theory and Literature on disk upon request.

[17]The TML makes *GIFConverter* and *CompuShow* available to subscribers with the permission of their authors, but the programs are shareware programs. Users who decide to use either of them must send the authors their very reasonable fees. The programs themselves provide full information. *UUTool* is offered free of charge to TML subscribers, with the kind permission of its author, Bernie Wieser.

hexing) because it offers greater standardization and can be readily decoded on any hardware platform, including many mainframes.

The procedure for retrieving and viewing a graphics file on the TML LISTSERV or TML-FTP is as follows. After the file has been received and downloaded to a personal computer, it must first be decoded with *UUTool* or a comparable UU decoder for DOS (or some other system). Once the graphics file has been decoded, it can be opened by a GIF viewer such as *GIFConverter* and displayed on the computer's screen.[18] Users with computers capable of running text and graphics programs simultaneously can view the graphic material on screen while reading the text of the treatise.

However viewed or retrieved, the graphics files are in each case coordinated with specific treatises. Thus, the file's **fn** matches that of the corresponding treatise and the **ft** is 01GF, 02GF, 03GF, etc. Approximately 4,000 graphics for the treatises are now available, and TML subscribers are notified as new texts and accompanying graphics go online.

The TML will continue to adapt its treatment of the graphics portion of the database to maintain the broadest and easiest access. Users with graphics capabilities on their machines are able to search and retrieve text as well as musical notation and figures, while those without graphics capabilities are still able to search the text database.

The TML Canon

In addition to the data and graphics files for each treatise, other sorts of documents are contained in the TML: informational files, such as a general introduction to the TML (INTRO TEXT), from which the material printed here has been adapted; and the TMLCANON STACK, a binhex-encoded version of a template for the HyperCard stack that indexes all the treatises, and the TMLCANON DATA, a tab-separated-variable version of the data that can be imported into the TMLCANON STACK or any database program, or viewed in a word processing program (the TML Canon is not available on the TML Web).[19] This data is published periodically in print editions, such as the present edition of the *TML Canon of Data Files*.

Each entry in the Canon includes the following fields: the name of the author of the treatise, as given in the source from which the data was taken; the title of the treatise; the incipit; the filename; the filetype; the source and type

---

[18]When opening files for the first time with *GIFConverter*, select the option "Look inside all files" in the "Open ..." dialogue box; then click on the button marked "Fix file types for shown files."

[19]Information for retrieving the TMLCANON STACK and TMLCANON DATA is included in the INTRO TEXT.

(i.e., manuscript or print) of the data file; the filelist; the size of the file in kilobytes; the names of the persons responsible for entering, checking, and approving the data; and annotations (including specific details on manuscripts, if the file is not derived from a printed source).

Downloading Files

Users whose personal computers are connected directly to the Internet, either through a hardwire, SLIP, or PPP connection, will most probably have retrieved TML files directly to their individual machine and need not peruse this section, which applies only to users who make use of a modem to effect a dial-up connection to a mainframe (or some similar intervening machine).

After the data files of the TML have been transferred to a local system, they are ready to be read and searched. Although most mainframes do have some sort of searching capabilities within their text viewers or editors, and these may be suitable for certain users, the TML assumes that most users will want to download the files to their personal computers in order to take advantage of the search engine described in the next section.

Mainframes have differing selections of error-correction protocols available, which help insure that data transferred over telephone lines through low-speed asynchronous connections is not corrupted in the process of transmission. Most mainframes have at least Kermit and Xmodem. Each communications program and modem addresses these protocols in different ways, and this Introduction is not intended to substitute for individual instruction manuals. There are, however, a few points to keep in mind when one prepares to download files for searching.

Subscribers with DOS computers. Users will not need to do anything special when they download the files or search them using the TML's recommended search program, *GOfer*™, described below. They have been configured with the necessary carriage returns and line feeds to display properly on any DOS machine (users may, however, need to adjust the font size and margins to fit their monitors or printers). Users should set their communications programs so that they do **not** filter out any characters.

Subscribers with Macintosh computers. Users interested simply in displaying texts to read on screen or search for single words need only filter out the line feeds (ASCII 10) that will appear at the beginning of each line of text. Some communications programs allow this to be done in the course of downloading, but it can also be easily accomplished by using the "search and replace" utility that exists in most word processors (the manual should explain the procedure for entering an ASCII code in the utility). Users wishing to convert the files to pure Macintosh files (i.e., with a carriage return [ASCII 13] only at the ends of full paragraphs) can do this in the following fashion:

1. Remove all the line feeds at the beginning of each line (if not already done).

2. Using the word processor's "search and replace" utility, instruct it to find all double carriage returns and replace them with ASCII 30. Sometimes the process of downloading a file will add a space between the double carriage returns, and if the "search and replace" utility does not find any double carriage returns, this has probably occurred. In such a case, repeat the process with a space between the two ASCII codes.
3. Using the word processor's "search and replace" utility once again, instruct it to find all single carriage returns and replace them with a space.
4. Finally, use the word processor's "search and replace" utility to find all instances of ASCII 30 and replace them with single carriage returns.

Note: The graphics, canon, and program files, which are encoded with binhex or UU encoding, must be downloaded without any filtering or paragraph conversion.

Searching the TML

As noted above, the TML files can be searched on the TML Web, and while such searches may be sufficient for many purposes, even more sophisticated searching is possible when the data files of the TML reside on a personal computer. Although the files may be searched or otherwise manipulated using any one of a number of programs, at present the TML recommends *GOfer*™ as the engine to be used for searching the database when it resides on a personal computer.[20]

GOfer provides both simple and Boolean structures, as well as retrieving information even in unspecified variant spellings—an important advantage when searching texts in medieval and Renaissance Latin. *GOfer* also allows for nested searches and for searches to be scripted. Scripts can be exchanged among subscribers over the TML-L (see below), thereby providing a ready opportunity for scholars to review word lists or text strings in various groups of treatises. Finally, *GOfer* runs in either DOS or Macintosh environments and thus ensures a ready utility without investment in expensive new or specialized equipment. Users who may not need all the powerful searching capabilities of *GOfer* can, of

---

[20]The TML has made a special arrangement with Microlytics, Inc. (formerly of Two Tobey Village Office Park, Pittsford, N.Y. 14534), which originally produced and sold *GOfer*, to distribute the product for a minimal charge. Persons interested in purchasing a copy of *GOfer* should retrieve the order form, either from the link on the TML Web, by sending the normal GET command for the file GOFER ORDRFORM to the TML LISTSERV or TML-FTP, or by requesting a form from the Center for the History of Music Theory and Literature.

course, use other programs or the search utilities included in most word processors.

GOfer provides a thorough manual with instructions for its use and configuration, and these instructions need not be repeated here. A few recommendations, however, may be helpful.

1. The files of the TML should first be grouped in a single folder (on the Macintosh) or in a single subdirectory (in DOS) to aid the program in searching them most efficiently.

2. Below this, the files might be grouped in additional folders or subdirectories according to their century (rather like the TML's filelists) or some other configuration that would enable *GOfer* to be directed to examine only certain types of treatises rather than the entire database; this will considerably increase the speed of searches by eliminating unnecessary data files.

3. Best results will always be obtained if only individual words are placed in one or more of *GOfer*'s search fields; this will ensure that the program finds every occurrence according to the specifications. It is possible to place a phrase in a single *GOfer* search box, but in that case, *GOfer* will only find this phrase if there is an exact match. For example, if "frustra fit" is entered as a phrase in a single box, *GOfer* will **not** find this if it should happen that "frustra" and "fit" are separated by, perhaps, a page-break mark (e.g., "frustra [-32-] fit"), a musical example code, or an entry of marginalia. In addition, on a Macintosh, if the carriage return and line-feed characters that accompany every line in the texts as they are sent from the TML LISTSERV or TML-FTP are not removed, and if "frustra" appears at the end of one line and "fit" at the beginning of another, the Macintosh version of *GOfer* will not find this phrase because it will see the passage as "frustra^13^10fit," even though these control codes (^13 and ^10) do not appear on the screen. This problem does not exist in the DOS version of *GOfer*: it pays no attention to these ASCII characters unless directed to do so.

4. When a sequence of letters (a "string") is entered in *GOfer*'s search boxes, it will find matches within words and as whole words. That is, the entry "dia" will find not only every occurrence of that word but also "dia" in the middle of "Indiana." If this is not desirable, entering a space before the string will prevent *GOfer* from finding internal strings; the sequence of letters will only be found if it appears with a preceding space (i.e., only when it is the beginning of a word or an entire word itself).

After the desired material has been located, any number of further actions are possible: a detailed report may be printed, showing the number of "finds" and their location (in as large or small a context as may be specified); nested searches may be initiated to narrow the focus; passages located may be readily imported into a word processing document; the entire text of the treatise containing the passage may be printed; and so on.

Because the TML is composed of ASCII text and GIF graphics, it can be used by any machine with its own search program. This structure also makes it possible to adapt the files to other systems of delivery that may become feasible or popular in the coming decades.

Exchanging Mail with Other Subscribers to the TML

In addition to its function as a file server, the TML LISTSERV also supports the exchange of mail among subscribers through the TML-L. Questions or other communications that one may wish to share with all TML subscribers should be sent to:

TML-L@listserv.indiana.edu

Communications sent to this address are immediately forwarded to all other subscribers to the TML.

Mail intended for distribution to everyone subscribing to the TML must be addressed to:

TML-L@listserv.indiana.edu

By contrast, requests for the TML LISTSERV to send information or data files must be addressed to:

listserv@listserv.indiana.edu

because these are commands to LISTSERV and not mail for distribution.

All messages distributed by the TML-L are retained in annual logs. These list archives can be readily viewed or searched on the Web by connecting to the following URL:

http://listserv.indiana.edu/archives/index.html

This Web page lists in alphabetical order all the archives stored at this site. When the TML-L is selected from the list, a subsequent page will appear, listing all the TML-L logs by year. Within each year, the messages can be sorted by author, date, or topic; all the messages in all the TML-L logs can also be searched with various options explained on the search pages. Any of the messages in the TML-L logs can be viewed online and saved to an individual machine.

Contributions to the TML

Text files of treatises are regularly contributed to the project by scholars from around the world, and the TML very much welcomes contributions from individual scholars as well as from the members of its Project and Editorial Committees. Contributions of this sort should be sent to the Center for the History of Music Theory and Literature, either over the mainframe or by mail. Treatises or other data files for distribution must **not** be sent as mail on the list.

Problems with the TML or suggestions for its improvement should be sent to Thomas J. Mathiesen, Director, Center for the History of Music Theory and Literature, School of Music, Indiana University, Bloomington, IN 47405, USA (telephone: [812] 855-5471 or 855-6889; INTERNET: mathiese@indiana.edu; CompuServe: 74040,37).

PRINCIPLES OF ORTHOGRAPHY FOR THE TML

① Text

Text data files produced from printed or manuscript sources will retain as exactly as possible the original spelling, punctuation, and capitalization, with the following exceptions.

1. In manuscript sources (but not in printed material), i/j, u/v, c/t before i plus vowel will be normalized.
2. In printed material, small caps will be converted to upper- or lower-case letters as the context requires (Roman numerals will always be entered as upper-case letters).
3. In printed material, corrigenda published as a part of the book itself should be entered (but note ¶1e below).
4. Accented letters are entered without accents.
5. Suspensions and abbreviations will be expanded.[1]
6. Periods, commas, colons, or *paragraphi* will always be placed on the baseline.
7. Proper nouns will be capitalized.
8. Initial letters of titles and true *incipits* will be capitalized, but initial letters of obvious or apparent fragments will not be capitalized.
9. Non-roman letters, which are not part of the standard ASCII character set, will be entered as capitalized letter-names between brackets (e.g., Γ will be entered as [Gamma]); words written in non-roman letters will be transliterated according to the standards of the *Chicago Manual of Style*, 13th edition.
10. In order to preserve the lining of poetry, a return (ASCII code 13) will be entered at the end of each line.
11. Double letters set one above the other (e.g., $\overset{e}{e}$) are entered side by side (e.g., ee).

Various types of symbols are available and will be used in data files that will be stored as ASCII files readable on any machine.[2]

1. Single brackets ([= ASCII code 91;] = ASCII code 93) will enclose six types of material.
(a) Codes showing the beginning of each page or folio side, surrounded by hyphens. For example, [-2-] will indicate the beginning of page 2 in text drawn from a published (or paginated) work; [-f.22v-] will indicate the beginning of the verso of folio 22 in text drawn from a manuscript (or foliated) work.
(b) Codes for musical notation appearing within a sentence (see Table of Codes and ② below).
(c) Editorial notes indicating the presence of figures, tables, or a musical example. For each example, a separate line will exhibit a reference to the source (e.g., [Berkeley, 88] or [Madrid, Biblioteca Nacional, 6486, f.22v]). If the example is accompanied by text, this will be included within the brackets (e.g., [Berkeley, 86; text: E-la, D-la-sol, C-sol-fa, B-fa-B-mi, A-la-mi-re, G-sol-re-ut, F-fa-ut, E-la-mi, D-la-sol-re, C-sol-fa-ut, D-sol-re, C-fa-ut, B-mi, A-re, Gamma-ut, 5 superacute, 7 acute, 8 graves, Declaracio manus secundum usum]) to enable the search program to locate and display text strings within figures as well as within the text proper. The text, of course, will also appear in the graphics file that will store the figure, table, or musical example itself.[3]

(d) Text added by later hands[4] (noted following the text: m.sec. or m.alt. or m.rec.), especially marginal hands (noted following the text: in marg.).

(e) Corrections added to the base text, either above the line (noted: corr. supra lin.) or in the margin (noted: corr. in marg.).

(f) Non-Roman letter-names.

2. Double brackets ([[ ]]) will enclose letters or words cancelled in the manuscript itself.

3. Angle brackets (< = ASCII code 60; > = ASCII code 62) will enclose (a) letters, words, or passages read by conjecture; or (b) if a short passage cannot be certainly transcribed, dots indicating the approximate number of letters. In the very few cases where an entire passage may be illegible, the number of lines followed by "legi non potest" will be noted within the angle brackets.

4. Braces ({ = ASCII code 123; } = ASCII code 125) will surround an interpolated passage to show the appropriate transposition.

5. The asterisk (ASCII code 42) will be used as equivalent to the obelus (†).

② Musical notation

All musical symbols or notation that appear within sentences of the text will be entered as codes. In general, single-line examples—especially examples with no specific pitch content—should also be encoded. See "Table of Codes for Noteshapes, Rests, ..." Polyphonic or other more complex musical examples, charts, figures, graphs, and similar sorts of material that cannot be easily keyed as ASCII text (which may, of course, include the use of tabs to lay out simple tables) will be scanned, saved in GIF format, and keyed to its original location in the printed or manuscript source.

----

[1] Abbreviated cardinal or ordinal numbers (e.g., 2ª, 4ª, 3ᵘˢ, etc.) should be expanded when the result can be expressed as a single word (e.g., secunda, quarta, tritus, etc.) but otherwise should be left in abbreviated form (e.g., 1343o). Numerals (Roman or Arabic), of course, should be left as numerals.

[2] I.e., alphanumeric codes 32–126.

[3] The figures themselves will be stored and retrievable as GIF files.

[4] Including glosses and scholia.

TABLE OF CODES FOR NOTESHAPES, RESTS, LIGATURES, MENSURATION SIGNS, CLEFS, AND MISCELLANEOUS FIGURES

Noteshape codes are placed between brackets and must appear in the order given in this table. Each group of symbols under N, P, L, or M appears together with no spaces or punctuation; each noteshape, rest, ligature, mensuration sign, clef, or miscellaneous figure is separated from the following one by a comma.

NOTESHAPES

N1. Multiples[1]

Quadruplex	4
Triplex	3
Duplex	2

N2. Shapes

Maxima		MX
Longa		L
Brevis		B
Semibrevis		S
Minima		M
Semiminima		SM
Addita		A
Fusa		F

N3. Coloration

nigra[2]	b
vacua	v
rubea	r
semivacua	sv
semirubea	sr

N4. Tails[3]

cauda	c
plica	p
cauda yrundinis	cy

N5. Direction[4]

sursum	s
deorsum	d
dextre	dx
sinistre	sn
oblique	o

N6. Flags[5]

vexilla [preceded by number[6]]	vx
retorta	vxrt
dextre	vxdx
sinistre	vxsn

RESTS

P1. Multiples (optional)

Quadruplex	4
Triplex	3
Duplex	2

P2. Shapes

Maxima	MXP
Longa	LP[7]
Brevis	BP
Semibrevis	SP
Minima	MP
Semiminima	SMP
Addita	AP
Fusa	FP

LIGATURES[8]

L1. Ligatures are indicated by "Lig" followed (in this order and as applicable) by: (1) the number of notes in the ligature; (2) coloration (see N3 above);[9] (3) cs or cd and the side on which the tail appears (see N4–5 above); and (4) the intervals in order, with "a" for ascending and "d" for descending, with additional tails indicated in the order in which they appear.[10] If a subsequent note in a ligature is turned back over the preceding note (as in the podatus, porrectus, liquescent neumes, plicas, etc.), the letter indicating the interval is followed by "rt." For example:

would equal [M,M,M,M,S,B,pt,Lig2cssnod, Lig4cssnaodacddx,pt,Lig5aadd,MX]

MENSURATION AND PROPORTION SIGNS

M1. Shape

Circle	O
Semicircle open on the right	C
Semicircle open on the left	CL
Semicircle open on the top	CT
Semicircle open on the bottom	CB
Rectangle	R
Triangle	TR

M2. Internal marks

dot (preceded by a number if more
   than one)   d
descending vertical line (preceded by
   a number if more than one)   rvd
ascending vertical line (preceded by
   a number if more than one)   rvs
horizontal line extending right
   (preceded by a number if more
   than one)   rhdx
horizontal line extending left
   (preceded by a number if more
   than one)   rhsn

M3. Proportions

The presence of the line of *diminutio* is indicated by "dim" following the symbols of M1 and M2. Fractional proportions are simply indicated by the two numbers separated by a virgule (e.g., 3/2).

Clefs

If the clef is shown on a staff, a number is appended indicating the line on which the clef appears (counting from the bottom of the staff), with two numbers separated by a hyphen indicating that the clef appears in the space between the two lines (for example, ClefG2 or ClefC3-4).

C clef   ClefC
F clef   ClefF
G clef   ClefG

etc.

Miscellaneous

square b   sqb
round b   rob
punctus (of whatever type)   pt
a small line extending above and
below a staff line **not** functioning
as one of the rests   r
double letters set one above the other

(e.g., ȩ) are entered side by side
(e.g., ee).
   A vacant staff is indicated by "staff," followed by a number indicating the number of lines in the staff (e.g., staff4 or staff5); "on staff" following a set of notation codes indicates that all the preceding notation appears on a staff; if additional codes follow, this indicates that the staff ended while the notation continues.

Barlines or multiple examples on a single staff

If several illustrative passages appear in a single example, a semicolon (;) followed by a space indicates the presence of a single or double bar separating one passage from another. If a single passage includes barlines, these may also be indicated by a semicolon followed by a space. Here is an example of such a case:

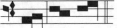

encoded as: [ClefF3,Lig2MXcddxaMXcddx; Lig2MXdMX,Lig2MXaMXcddx on staff4]

---

[1] Optional. May only be applied to the maxima and longa.

[2] The symbol "b" is to be used only in ligatures exhibiting more than one color as specified in n. 9 *infra*. In all other cases, black is the color assumed unless otherwise noted.

[3] Indicated only if the tail varies from the basic shape pictured in N2.

[4] Always indicated in ligature codes; otherwise, only if direction differs from the basic shape pictured in N2.

[5] Flags are assumed to be drawn on the oblique to the right side of the tail, unless otherwise indicated. In this section, dx and sn mean that the flag appears at a right angle to the tail and points left or right.

[6] Indicated by numeral only if greater than one.

[7] If the context calls for differentiating between perfect and imperfect longa rests, this may be done by using 2LP and 3LP.

[8] All notes are assumed to be square, unless the reference to the interval is preceded by "o" (for oblique) or "cu" (for *conjuncturae* or *currentes*).

[9] If the ligature exhibits more than one color, "r," "v," or "b" precede the codes of (3) and (4) to indicate the point at which the color changes.

[10] Except in the case of a longa or a maxima **within** a ligature (this exception does not apply to the **final** note of the ligature), which is indicated as "L" or "MX" following the interval that precedes it or following the codes of (1), (2), and (3) if it is the first note of the ligature. In ligatures, MX is assumed to refer only to the extended rectangular notehead; if it also has a tail, the location and direction are indicated. Note the example under "Barlines or multiple examples on a single staff."

TABLE OF CONTENTS OF MAJOR SERIES AND THEIR LOCATION IN THE TML

Scriptores ecclesiastici de musica sacra potissimum, 3 vols., ed. Martin Gerbert (St. Blaise: Typis San-Blasianis, 1784)

Page	Author	Title	Filename[1]
1:4–5	Anonymous	Monacho qua mente sit psallendum	MONPSAL
1:5–8		Instituta patrum de modo psallendi sive cantandi	PATPSAL
1:9–14	Nicetius, episcopus	De laude et utilitate spiritualium canticorum, quae fiunt in ecclesia Christiana; seu de psalmodiae bono	NICLAU
1:15–19	Cassiodorus, Aurelius	Institutiones musicae, seu excerpta ex eiusdem libro, de artibus ac disciplinis liberalium litterarum	CASINS
1:20–25	Isidorus Hispalensis	Sententiae de musica	ISISEN
1:26–27	Alcuinus, Flaccus	Musica	ALCMUS
1:27–63	Aurelianus Reomensis	Musica disciplina	AURMUS
1:63–69	Remigius Altisiodo-rensis	Musica	REMMUS
1:95–102	Notker	De musica	NOTDEM
1:103–25	Hucbald	De harmonica institutione	HUCHAR
1:125–52	Anonymous	Alia musica	ALIMUS
1:152–73	Anonymous	Musica enchiriadis	MUSENC
1:173–212	Anonymous	Scholia enchiriadis de arte musica	SCHENC
1:213–29	Anonymous	Commemoratio brevis de tonis et psalmis modulandis	ANOCOMB
1:230–47	Regino Prumiensis	Epistola de harmonica institutione	REGHAR
1:247–50	Odo	Tonarium	ODOTON

---

[1]The filetype is TEXT throughout.

1:251–64	Odo	Dialogus de musica	ODODIA
1:265–84	Odo	De musica	ODOMUS
1:285–95	Odo	Regulae de rhythmimachia	ODORHY
1:296–302	Odo	Regulae super abacum	ODOREG
1:303	Odo	Quomodo organistrum construatur	ODOORG
1:303–12	Adelboldus	Musica	ADEMUS
1:312–30	Bernelinus	Cita et vera divisio monochordi in diatonico genere	BERNDIV
1:330–38	Anonymous I	Musica	ANO1MUS
1:338–42	Anonymous II	Tractatus de musica	ANO2TDM
1:343–44	Anonymous III	Fragmentum musices	ANO3FRA
1:344–48	Anonymous	Mensura monochordi Boetii	ANOMEN
2:2–24	Guido d'Arezzo	Micrologus	GUIMIC
2:25–34	Guido d'Arezzo	Regulae rhythmicae in antiphonarii sui prologum prolatae	GUIRR
2:34–42	Guido d'Arezzo	Prologus in antiphonarium	GUIPRAN
2:43–50	Guido d'Arezzo	Epistola Guidonis Michaeli monacho de ignoto cantu directa	GUIEPI
2:50–55	Guido d'Arezzo [Ps.]	Tractatus Guidonis correctorius multorum errorum, qui fiunt in cantu gregoriano in multis locis	ANOTRA2
2:55–61	Anonymous	Quomodo de arithmetica procedit musica	ANOQUO
2:62–79	Berno Augiensis	Musica seu Prologus in Tonarium	BERNPRO
2:79–91	Berno Augiensis	Tonarius	BERNTON
2:91–114	Berno Augiensis	De varia psalmorum atque cantuum modulatione	BERNVAR
2:114–24	Berno Augiensis	De consona tonorum diversitate	BERNDEC

2:125–49	Hermannus Contractus	Musica	HERMUSG
2:149–53	Hermannus Contractus	Versus ad discernendum cantum	HERVER
2:154–82	Willehelmus Hirsaugensis	Musica	WILMU
1:183–96	Theogerus Metensis	Musica	THEMUS
1:197–230	Aribo	Musica	ARIMUS
2:230–65	Johannes Afflige-mensis	Musica	JOHMUS
2:265–77	Anonymous	Tonale Sancti Bernardi	BERTON
2:277–78	Gerlandus	Fragmenta de musica	GERFRA
2:279–82	Eberhardus Frisingensis	Tractatus de mensura fistularum	EBETRA
2:283–87	Anonymous	De mensura fistularum in organis	ANOFIS
2:287–98	Engelbertus Admontensis	De musica, tractatus primus	ENGDEM1
2:298–320	Engelbertus Admontensis	De musica, tractatus secundus	ENGDEM2
2:320–38	Engelbertus Admontensis	De musica, tractatus tertius	ENGDEM3
2:338–69	Engelbertus Admontensis	De musica, tractatus quartus	ENGDEM4
2:370–93	Aegidius Zamorensis	Ars musica	ZAMLAM
3:1–16	Franco	Ars cantus mensurabilis	FRAARSC
3:16–64	Salomo, Elias	Scientia artis musicae	SALSCI
3:64–70	Marchetus de Padua	Lucidarium, tractatus primus	MARLU1
3:70–76	Marchetus de Padua	Lucidarium, tractatus secundus	MARLU2
3:76–78	Marchetus de Padua	Lucidarium, tractatus tertius	MARLU3
3:78–80	Marchetus de Padua	Lucidarium, tractatus quartus	MARLU4

3:80–83	Marchetus de Padua	Lucidarium, tractatus quintus	MARLU5
3:83–87	Marchetus de Padua	Lucidarium, tractatus sextus	MARLU6
3:87–88	Marchetus de Padua	Lucidarium, tractatus septimus	MARLU7
3:88–92	Marchetus de Padua	Lucidarium, tractatus octavus	MARLU8
3:92–100	Marchetus de Padua	Lucidarium, tractatus nonus	MARLU9
3:100	Marchetus de Padua	Lucidarium, tractatus decimus	MARLU10
3:101–17	Marchetus de Padua	Lucidarium, tractatus undecimus	MARLU11
3:117–19	Marchetus de Padua	Lucidarium, tractatus duodecimus	MARLU12
3:119	Marchetus de Padua	Lucidarium, tractatus decimustertius	MARLU13
3:120	Marchetus de Padua	Lucidarium, tractatus decimusquartus	MARLU14
3:120	Marchetus de Padua	Lucidarium, tractatus decimusquintus	MARLU15
3:121	Marchetus de Padua	Lucidarium, tractatus decimussextus	MARLU16
3:121–88	Marchetus de Padua	Pomerium	MARPOM
3:190–248	Johannes de Muris	Summa	MURSUM
3:249–83	Johannes de Muris	Tractatus de musica	MURMUS
3:284–86	Johannes de Muris	De numeris, qui musicas retinent consonantias, secundum Ptolomaeum de Parisius	MURDEN
3:286–91	Johannes de Muris	Tractatus de proportionibus	MURDEP
3:292–301	Johannes de Muris	De practica musica, seu de mensurabili	MURPRA
3:301–8	Johannes de Muris	Quaestiones super partes musicae	MURQUAE
3:308–12	Johannes de Muris	De tonis	MURTON
3:312–15	Johannes de Muris	Ars discantus data a Magistro Iohanne de Muris abbreviando	MURAD

3:316–18	Arnulphus de Sancto Gilleno	Tractatulus de differentiis et generibus cantorum	ARNTRA
3:319–29	Keck, Ioannes	Introductorium musicae	KECKINMU
3:329–41	Adamus de Fulda	Musica, pars prima	FULMUS1
3:341–58	Adamus de Fulda	Musica, pars secunda	FULMUS2
3:359–66	Adamus de Fulda	Musica, pars tertia	FULMUS3
3:367–81	Adamus de Fulda	Musica, pars quarta	FULMUS4
3:382–96	Anonymous	Constitutiones capellae pontificiae	ANOCON

Scriptorum de musica medii aevi nova series a Gerbertina altera, 4 vols., ed. Edmond de Coussemaker (Paris: Durand, 1864–76)

Page	Author	Title	Filename[2]
1:1–89	Ieronimus de Moravia	Tractatus de musica	IERTRA1
1:89–94; 1:139–54	Ieronimus de Moravia	Tractatus de musica	IERTRA2
1:94–97	Anonymous	Discantus positio vulgaris	DISPOS
1:97–117	Johannes de Garlandia	De musica mensurabili positio	GARDEMP
1:117–36	Franco	Ars cantus mensurabilis	FRAARS
1:136–39	Petrus Picardus	Musica mensurabilis	PETMUS
1:154–56	Franco	Compendium discantus	FRACOM
1:157–75	Magister de Garlandia	Introductio musice	GARINT
1:175–82	Johannes de Garlandia	De musica mensurabili	GARDEM
1:182–250	Odington, Walter	De speculatione musice	ODIDES

---

[2]The filetype is TEXT throughout.

1:251–81	Aristotle	Tractatus de musica	ARITRA
1:282–92	Petrus de Cruce Ambianensis	Tractatus de tonis	PETTRA
1:292–96	Johannes dictus Ballox	Abreviatio Magistri Franconis	BALABR
1:296–302	Anonymous 1	Tractatus de consonantiis musicalibus	ANO1TRA
1:303–19	Anonymous 2	Tractatus de discantu	ANO2TRA
1:319–27	Anonymous 3	De cantu mensurabili	ANO3DEC
1:327–64	Anonymous 4	De mensuris et discantu	ANO4DEM
1:364–65	Anonymous	De sinemenis	ANODES
1:366–68	Anonymous 5	De discantu	ANO5DED
1:369–77	Anonymous 6	Tractatus de figuris sive de notis	ANO6TRA
1:378–83	Anonymous 7	De musica libellus	ANO7DEM
1:383–403	Robertus de Handlo	Regulae	HANREGU
1:403–48	Hanboys, Johannes	Summa	HANSUMA
2:1–73	Regino Prumiensis	Tonarius	REGTON
2:74–78	Hucbald	De organo	HUCORG
2:78–115	Guido d'Arezzo	De modorum formulis et cantuum qualitatibus	GUIMOD
2:115–16	Guido d'Arezzo	De sex motibus vocum ad se invicem et dimensione earum	GUISEX
2:117–49	Odo	Intonarium	ODOINT
2:150–92	Abbot Guido	Regulae de arte musica	ABGURAM
2:193–279	Jacobus Leodiensis	Speculum musicae, Liber sextus	JACSM6A
2:279–383	Jacobus Leodiensis	Speculum musicae, Liber sextus	JACSM6B

2:383–433	Jacobus Leodiensis	Speculum musicae, Liber septimus	JACSM7
2:434–83	Monachus Carthusiensis	Tractatus de musica plana	CARTRA
2:484–98	Anonymous	Tractatus de musica plana et organica	ANOMUPO
3:1–12	Marchetus de Padua	Brevis compilatio in arte musicae mensuratae	MARBRE
3:12–13	Johannes de Garlandia	Optima introductio in contrapunctum pro rudibus	GAROPT
3:13–22	Philippe de Vitry	Ars nova	VITARSN
3:23–27	Philippe de Vitry	Ars contrapunctus	VITARSC
3:28–35	Philippe de Vitry	Ars perfecta in musica	VITARSP
3:35–46	Philippe de Vitry	Liber musicalium	VITLIBM
3:46–58	Johannes de Muris	Libellus cantus mensurabilis	MURLIB
3:59–68	Johannes de Muris	Ars contrapuncti	MURARSC
3:68–113	Johannes de Muris	Ars discantus	MURARSD
3:113–15	Henricus de Zelandia	Tractatus de cantu perfecto et imperfecto	ZELTRA
3:116–18	Phillipotus Andrea	De contrapuncto quaedam regulae utiles	ANDCON
3:118–24	Philippus de Caserta	Tractatus de diversis figuris	CASTRA
3:124–28	Aegidius de Murino	Tractatus cantus mensurabilis	AEGTRA
3:129–77	Johannes Verulus de Anagnia	Liber de musica	VERLIB
3:177–93	Theodoricus de Campo	De musica mensurabili	CAMDEM
3:193–99	Prosdocimo de' Beldomandi	Tractatus de contrapuncto	PROTRAC
3:200–228	Prosdocimo de' Beldomandi	Tractatus practice de musica mensurabili	PROTRAP1

3:228–48	Prosdocimo de' Beldomandi	Tractatus practice de musica mensurabili ad modum italicorum	PROTRAP2
3:248–58	Prosdocimo de' Beldomandi	Libellus monocordi	PROLIB
3:258–61	Prosdocimo de' Beldomandi	Brevis summula proportionum	PROBRE2
3:262–64	Weyts, Carmelite	Regule	WEYREG
3:264–73	Sadze de Flandria, Christianus	Tractatus modi, temporis et prolationis	FLATRA
3:273–307	Guilielmus monachus	De preceptis artis musice et pratice compendiosus libellus	MONPRE
3:307–27	De Leno, Antonius	Regulae de contrapunto	LENREG[3]
3:328–30	Hothby, Johannes	Regulae super proportionem	HOTREGP
3:330–32	Hothby, Johannes	De cantu figurato	HOTDEC
3:333–34	Hothby, Johannes	Regulae supra contrapunctum	HOTREGC
3:334–64	Anonymous I	De musica antiqua et nova	ANO1DEM
3:364–70	Anonymous II	De musica antiqua et nova	ANO2DEM
3:370–75	Anonymous III	Compendiolum artis veteris ac novae	ANO3COM
3:376–79	Anonymous IV	Compendium artis mensurabilis tam veteris quam novae	ANO4COM
3:379–98	Anonymous V	Ars cantus mensurabilis	ANO5ARS
3:398–403	Anonymous VI	De musica mensurabili	ANO6DEM
3:404–8	Anonymous VII	De diversis maneriebus in musica mensurabili	ANO7DED

---

[3] As an Italian treatise, this text is not included in the TML; it does, however, appear in the *saggi musicali italiani* database for Italian Music Theory and Aesthetics (http://www.music.indiana.edu/smi).

3:409–11	Anonymous VIII	Regulae de contrapuncto	ANO8REG
3:413–15	Anonymous X	De minimis notulis	ANO10DEM
3:416–75	Anonymous XI	Tractatus de musica plana et mensurabili	ANO11TRA
3:475–95	Anonymous XII	Tractatus de musica	ANO12TRA
4:1–16	Tinctoris, Johannes	Expositio manus	TINEXP
4:16–41	Tinctoris, Johannes	Liber de natura et proprietate tonorum	TINNAT
4:41–46	Tinctoris, Johannes	Tractatus de notis et pausis	TINTRAN
4:46–53	Tinctoris, Johannes	Tractatus de regulari valore notarum	TINTRAR
4:54–66	Tinctoris, Johannes	Liber imperfectionum notarum musicalium	TINLIB
4:66–70	Tinctoris, Johannes	Tractatus alterationum	TINTRALT
4:70–76	Tinctoris, Johannes	Tractatus super punctis musicalibus	TINTRAP
4:76–119	Tinctoris, Johannes	Liber de arte contrapuncti, Liber primus	TINCON1
4:119–47	Tinctoris, Johannes	Liber de arte contrapuncti, Liber secundus	TINCON2
4:147–53	Tinctoris, Johannes	Liber de arte contrapuncti, Liber tertius	TINCON3
4:153–77	Tinctoris, Johannes	Proportionale musices	TINPRO
4:177–91	Tinctoris, Johannes	Diffinitorium musicae	TINDIF
4:191–95	Tinctoris, Johannes	Complexus effectuum musices	TINCOM1
4:195–200	Tinctoris, Johannes	Complexus viginti effectuum nobilis artis musices	TINCOM2
4:200–206	Anonymous	Quatuor Principalia I	QUAPRIB1
4:206–19	Anonymous	Quatuor Principalia II	QUAPRIB2
4:219–54	Anonymous	Quatuor Principalia III	QUAPRIB3

4:254–98	Anonymous	Quatuor Principalia IV	QUAPRIB4
4:298–313	Johannes Gallicus dictus Carthusiensis seu de Mantua	Ritus canendi vetustissimus et novus, liber primus	GALRIT1
4:313–28	Johannes Gallicus dictus Carthusiensis seu de Mantua	Ritus canendi vetustissimus et novus, liber secundus	GALRIT2
4:328–45	Johannes Gallicus dictus Carthusiensis seu de Mantua	Ritus canendi vetustissimus et novus, liber tertius	GALRIT3
4:345–72	Johannes Gallicus dictus Carthusiensis seu de Mantua	Vera quamque facilis ad cantandum atque brevis introductio	GALRITS1
4:372–83	Johannes Gallicus dictus Carthusiensis seu de Mantua	Incipit liber secundus de sex, ut, re, mi, fa, sol, la, sillabis	GALRITS2
4:383–96	Johannes Gallicus dictus Carthusiensis seu de Mantua	Incipit liber tertius de contrapuncto praefationcula	GALRITS3
4:396–409	Johannes Gallicus dictus Carthusiensis seu de Mantua	Incipit praefationcula in tam admirabilem quam tacitam et quietissimam novorum concinentiam	GALTRA

4:409–21	Johannes Gallicus dictus Carthusiensis seu de Mantua	Tacita nunc inchoatur stupendaque numerorum musica	GALLIB
4:421–33	Antonius de Luca	Ars cantus figurati	LUCARS
4:434–69	Anonymous	Tractatus de musica figurata et de contrapuncto ab anonymo auctore	TRADEM

Corpus scriptorum de musica, ed. Gilbert Reaney, 41 vols.
(n.p.: American Institute of Musicology; Neuhausen-Stuttgart:
Hänssler Verlag, 1950–   )

Page	Author	Title	Filename[4]
1:43–200	Johannes Afflige-mensis	De musica cum tonario	JOHDEM
2:1–72	Aribo	De musica	ARIDEM
3/1:3–142	Jacobus Leodiensis	Speculum musicae, Liber primus	JACSP1A
3/1:142–229	Jacobus Leodiensis	Speculum musicae, Liber primus	JACSP1B
3/2:1–128	Jacobus Leodiensis	Speculum musicae, Liber secundus	JACSP2A
3/2:128–231	Jacobus Leodiensis	Speculum musicae, Liber secundus	JACSP2B
3/2:232–309	Jacobus Leodiensis	Speculum musicae, Liber secundus	JACSP2C
3/3:1–89	Jacobus Leodiensis	Speculum musicae, Liber tertius	JACSP3A
3/3:89–163	Jacobus Leodiensis	Speculum musicae, Liber tertius	JACSP3B
3/4:1–126	Jacobus Leodiensis	Speculum musicae, Liber quartus	JACSP4
3/5:1–90	Jacobus Leodiensis	Speculum musicae, Liber quintus	JACSP5A
3/5:90–184	Jacobus Leodiensis	Speculum musicae, Liber quintus	JACSP5B

---

[4]The filetype is TEXT throughout. In cases where no filename is supplied, the text has not yet appeared in the TML.

3/6:1–161	Jacobus Leodiensis	Speculum musicae, Liber sextus	JACSP6A
3/6:161–317	Jacobus Leodiensis	Speculum musicae, Liber sextus	JACSP6B
3/7:1–98	Jacobus Leodiensis	Speculum musicae, Liber septimus	JACSP7
4:79–234	Guido d'Arezzo	Micrologus	GUIMICR
6:31–210	Marchetus de Padua	Pomerium	MARPOME
7/1:13–121	Ugolino Urbevetanis	Declaratio musicae disciplinae, liber primus	UGODEC1A
7/1:121–230	Ugolino Urbevetanis	Declaratio musicae disciplinae, liber primus	UGODEC1B
7/2:1–53	Ugolino Urbevetanis	Declaratio musicae disciplinae, liber secundus	UGODEC2
7/2:54–167	Ugolino Urbevetanis	Declaratio musicae disciplinae, liber tertius	UGODEC3A
7/2:167–266	Ugolino Urbevetanis	Declaratio musicae disciplinae, liber tertius	UGODEC3B
7/3:1–84	Ugolino Urbevetanis	Declaratio musicae disciplinae, liber quartus	UGODEC4
7/3:85–226	Ugolino Urbevetanis	Declaratio musicae disciplinae, liber quintus	UGODEC5
7/3:227–53	Ugolino Urbevetanis	Tractatus monochordi	UGOTRAM
8:13–31	Philippe de Vitry	Ars nova	VITARNO
8:55–69	Anonymous	Ars mensurandi motetos	ANOARS
8:72–78	Anonymous	Regula de monocordo	REGDEM
8:80–81	Anonymous	Sub brevissimo compendio Philippus de Vitriaco in musica incipit	ANOOMD
8:84–93	Anonymous	De arte musicae	ANOART
9:21–48	Anonymous	Jesus. Libellus musicae adiscendae valde utilis et est dialogus. Discipulus et magister sunt locutores	ANOLIB
10:17–57	Hothby, Johannes	Excitatio quaedam musicae artis per refutationem	HOTEXC
10:61–76	Hothby, Johannes	Dialogus in arte musica	HOTDIA

11:15–59	Guilielmus monachus	De preceptis artis musice et pratice compendiosus libellus	MONPREC
12:15–31	Willelmus	Breviarium regulare musicae	WILBRE
12:40–51	Anonymous	Tractatus de figuris sive de notis	TRADEF
12:58–61	Torkesey, Johannes	Trianguli et scuti declaratio de proportionibus musicae mensurabilis	TORTRI
13:29–56	Anonymous	De musica mensurabili	ANODEM
13:65–79	Anonymous	De semibrevibus caudatis	ANOSEM
14:42–146	Odington, Walter	Summa de speculatione musice	ODISUM
15:16–24	Petrus Picardus	Ars motettorum compilata breviter	PETARS
15:38–54	Anonymous	Ars musicae mensurabilis secundum Franconem	ANOFIG
15:66–72	Anonymous	Compendium musicae mensurabilis artis antiquae	ANOCOM
16:11–37	Anonymous	Tractatulus de cantu mensurali seu figurativo musice artis	ANOTRA
17:47–107	Johannes de Muris	Notitia artis musicae	MURNOT
17:119–45	Johannes de Muris	Compendium musicae practicae	MURCOM
17:147–59	Petrus de Sancto Dionysio	Tractatus de Musica	PSDTRA
17:160–66	Anonymous	De figuris	ANODEF
18:23–82	Franco	Ars cantus mensurabilis	FRAACM
19:15–46	Boen, Johannes	Ars (musicae)	BOENMU
20:30–122	Aegidius Zamorensis, Iohannes	Liber artis musicae	ZAMLIB
21:53–135	Aurelianus Reomensis	Musica disciplina	AURMD
21:136–53	Aurelianus Reomensis	Musica disciplina, cap. VIII-XVI	AURMDAP
22/1:65–104	Tinctoris, Johannes	Liber de natura et proprietate tonorum	TINLDN
22/1:109–20	Tinctoris, Johannes	Tractatus de notis et pausis	TINTDN

22/1:125 –38	Tinctoris, Johannes	Tractatus de regulari valore notarum	TINTDR
22/1:143 –67	Tinctoris, Johannes	Liber imperfectionum notarum musicalium	TINLIMP
22/1:173 –79	Tinctoris, Johannes	Tractatus alterationum	TINTRAL
22/1:185 –98	Tinctoris, Johannes	Tractatus de punctis	TINTDP
22/2:11– 89	Tinctoris, Johannes	Liber de arte contrapuncti, Liber primus	TINCPT1
22/2:31– 57	Tinctoris, Johannes	Expositio manus	TINEM
22/2:90– 145	Tinctoris, Johannes	Liber de arte contrapuncti, Liber secundus	TINCPT2
22/2:146 –57	Tinctoris, Johannes	Liber de arte contrapuncti, Liber tertius	TINCPT3
22/2:165 –77	Tinctoris, Johannes	Complexus effectuum musices	TINCOM
22/2a:9– 60	Tinctoris, Johannes	Proportionale musices	TINPROM
23:11–75	Willehelmus Hirsaugensis	Musica	WILMUS
24:21–41	Anonymous	Epistola Sancti Bernardi De revisione cantus Cisterciensis, et Tractatus cantum quem Cisterciensis Ordinis ecclesiae cantare	BEREPI
25:19– 112	Amerus	Practica artis musice	AMEPRA
26:43–44	Hothby, Johannes	[De arte contrapuncti]	HOTDAC
26:63–69	Hothby, Johannes	Regulae contrapuncti	HOTRC
26:101–3	Hothby, Johannes	Regulae supra contrapunctum	HOTRSC
27:26–97	Johannes Verulus de Anagnia	Liber de musica	VERLDM
28:43– 206	Wylde, Johannes	Musica manualis cum tonale	WYLMUS
29:vi– xxv	Petrus de Cruce Ambianensis	Tractatus de tonis	PETTRAC

30:13–28	Anonymous	De valore notularum tam veteris quam novae artis	ANO2DEV
30:33–41	Anonymous	Compendium musicae mensurabilis tam veteris quam novae artis	ANO4CMM
30:51–62	Anonymous	De diversis manieribus in musica mensurabili	ANO7DDM
31:19–24	Hothby, Johannes	Sequuntur regulae cantus mensurati eiusdem Ottobi	HOTRCM1
31:27–31	Hothby, Johannes	De cantu figurato secundum eundem fratrem Johannem Hothbi Carmelitam	HOTDCF1
31:39–44	Hothby, Johannes	Regulae Magistri Johannis Hoctobi anglici cantus figurati	HOTDCF2
31:51–59	Hothby, Johannes	Regulae cantus mensurati secundum Johannem Otteby	HOTRCM2
31:74–98	Walsingham, Thomas	Regulae Magistri Thomae Walsingham de figuris compositis et non compositis, et de cantu perfecto et imperfecto, et de modis incipiunt	WALREG
33:36–57	Anonymous	Compendium musices	ANOCMU
34:13–21	Johannes dictus Balloce	Abreviatio Magistri Franconis	BALABM
34:27–36	Anonymous	Compendium musicae mensurabilis artis antiquae	ANOCMM
34:49–58	Anonymous	Compendium musicae mensurabilis artis antiquae	ANOCOMM
34:69–73	Anonymous	Tractatus artis antiquae cum explicatione mensurae binariae	ANOTAA
35:41–93	Anonymous	Tractatus cantus figurati	ANO12TCF
36:	Anonymous	De musica libellus	
36:	Anonymous	Tractatus de discantu	
36:	Pseudo-Franco de Colonia	Compendium discantus	
38:	Antonius de Luca	Ars cantus figurati	
38:	Anonymous	Capitulum de quattuor mensuris	
38:	Anonymous	Tractatulus mensurationum	
38:	Anonymous	Compendium breve de proportionibus	
38:	Anonymous	Tractatulus prolationum cum tabulis	

1

39:	Hothby, Johannes	Regulae super proportiones	
39:	Hothby, Johannes	De proportionibus	
39:	Anonymous	Tractatus de contrapunto	
40:	Anonymous	Tractatus de contrapuncto et de musica mensurabili	
41:	Anonymous	Ars et practica cantus figurativi	
41:	Anonymous	[Regulae cantandi contrapunctum]	
41:	Anonymous	De contrapuncto	
41:	Anonymous	De vera et compendiosa seu regulari constructione contrapuncti	
41:	Anonymous	De contrapuncto plano	
41:	Anonymous	[Regulae de contrapuncto]	
41:	Anonymous	De consonantia et dissonantia	
41:	Anonymous	De formatione contrapuncti tales dantur regulae	
41:	Anonymous	[Excerpta de consonantiis et de contrapuncto]	
41:	Anonymous	[Regulae contrapuncti]	
41:	Anonymous	Iuxta artem conficiendi [compositiones] quam alii compositionis artem dicunt vel vocitant	

Divitiae Musicae Artis, ed. Joseph Smits van Waesberghe, Series A, 10 vols. (nine published)
(Buren: Knuf; Laaber: Laaber-Verlag, 1975–1988)

Page	Author	Title	Filename[5]
A/I:24–93	Anonymous	Commentum super tonos	ANOCST
A/II:12–29	Adelboldus	Epistola cum tractatu de musica instrumentali humanaque ac mundana	ADETRA
A/III:58–81	Guido d'Arezzo	Prologus in antiphonarium	GUIPRO
A/IV:92–133	Guido d'Arezzo	Regulae rhythmicae	GUIREG

---

[5]The filetype is TEXT throughout.

A/VIa:27, 42–55, 59, 61, 65, 67, 71, 73, 75, 77, 84-85, 91-92, 95, 103-4,111-14, and 116-19	Berno Augiensis	De mensurando monochordo	BERNDEM
A/VIb:31–37	Berno Augiensis	Interpolationen	BERNINT
A/VII:35–53	Heinricus Augustensis	Musica	HEIMUS
A/VIIIa:39–101	Anonymous	Summula	ANOSUM
A/IXa:21	Jacobus Leodiensis	Tractatus de consonantiis musicalibus	JACDCM
A/IXa:47–87	Jacobus Leodiensis	Tractatus de intonatione tonorum	JACDIT
A/IXa:88–122	Jacobus Leodiensis	Compendium de musica	JACCDM
A/Xa:14–38	Osbernus Cantuariensis (?)	De vocum consonantiis	OSBMUS
A/Xb:33–41	Anonymous	Tractatuli	ANOTRA17

Critical Texts, ed. Albert Seay, 14 vols. (Colorado Springs: Colorado College Music Press, 1977–1981)[6]

Page	Author	Title	Filename[7]
2:1–13[8]	Anonymous	Quaestiones et solutiones advidendum tam mensurabilis cantus quam immensurabilis musica	ANOQS
4:1–22	Tallanderius, Petrus	Lectura	TALLEC
5:1–25	Villa Dei, Alexander de	Carmen de musica cum glossis	VILCAR
6:1–71	Johannes de Olomons	Palma choralis	JOHPAL

[6]Volumes 1, 3, and 9–10 do not contain Latin treatises.
[7]The filetype is TEXT throughout.
[8]The balance of the treatise is in Italian.

7:1–5	Carlerius, Egidius	Tractatus de duplici ritu cantus ecclesiastici in divinis officiis et primo de simplici	CARLTRA
7:5–13	Carlerius, Egidius	De cantu iubiliationis armonicae et utilitate eius	CARLCAN
8:1–8	Guillermus de Podio	Ars musicorum liber VI	GUIARS6
8:9–34	Guillermus de Podio	Ars musicorum liber VIII	GUIARS8
11:1–93	Bonaventura da Brescia	Brevis collectio artis musicae	BONBRE
12:1–60	Rossetti, Biagio	Libellus de rudimentis musices: Compendium musicae	ROSLIB1
12:62–94	Rossetti, Biagio	Libellus de rudimentis musices: De choro et organo compendium	ROSLIB2
13:1–78	Johannes Gallicus	Ritus canendi [Pars prima]	GALRC1
14:1–89	Johannes Gallicus	Ritus canendi [Pars secunda]	GALRC2

Texts/Translations, ed. Albert Seay, 3 vols. (Colorado Springs: Colorado College Music Press, 1978–1980)

Page	Author	Title	Filename[9]
1:2–62	Anonymous II	Tractatus de discantu	ANOTDD
2:2–48	Vanneo, Stephano	Recanetum de musica aurea, liber II, capituli XX-XXXVII	VANREC
3:2–34	Kromer, Marcin	De musica figurata	KRODEM

Greek and Latin Music Theory, ed. Thomas J. Mathiesen, 10 vols. (Lincoln: University of Nebraska Press, 1984–   )[10]

Page	Author	Title	Filename[11]
1:26–94	Prosdocimo de' Beldo-mandi	Contrapunctus	PROCON
2:30–246	Anonymous	Berkeley Manuscript	BERMAN

---

[9]The filetype is TEXT throughout.

[10]Volumes 3 and 8 in this series do not contain Latin treatises.

[11]The filetype is TEXT throughout.

4:46–62	Prosdocimo de' Beldomandi	Brevis summula proportionum quantum ad musicam pertinet	PROBRE1
4:64–118	Prosdocimo de' Beldomandi	Parvus tractatulus de modo monacordum dividendi	PROPAR
5:100–254	Stoquerus, Gaspar	De musica verbali libri duo	STODEM
6:66–102	Anonymous	Tractatus figurarum	TRAFIG
7:80–178	Robertus de Handlo	Regule	HANREG
7:180–344	Hanboys, Johannes	Summa	HANSUM
9:42–232	Ciconia, Johannes	Nova musica, liber primus de consonantiis	CICNM1
9:234–336	Ciconia, Johannes	Nova musica, liber secundus de speciebus	CICNM2
9:338–60	Ciconia, Johannes	Nova musica, liber tertius de proportionibus	CICNM3
9:362–410	Ciconia, Johannes	Nova musica, liber quartus de accidentibus	CICNM4
9:412–46	Ciconia, Johannes	De proportionibus	CICPROP
10:124–258	Anonymous	Ars cantus mensurabilis mensurata per modos iuris	ANO5ACM

Thesaurus Musicarum Latinarum
Canon of Data Files

Author: Aaron, Petrus

Treatise: Libri tres de institutione harmonica, liber primus

Incipit: Magnum est Flamini quod heri sum pollicitus nec me quidem poenitet aut sententiam

File name: **AARIH1**   Data input by: Jessica Burr

File type: **TEXT**   Data checked by: Elisabeth Honn & Andreas Giger

  MS: Print: **X**   Data approved by: Thomas J. Mathiesen

Filelist: 16th   File size: 71K   Annotations:

Source of data:

Libri tres de institutione harmonica (Bononiae, In aedibus Benedicti Hectoris Bibliopolae Bononiensis, 1516; reprint ed., New York: Broude Bros., 1978), ff. Air-Cviv.

The incipit is preceded by dedicatory epistles, beginning: "Scio, te non ignorare Clarissime Eques Hieronyme Sancte Petre ... " and "Fuit mihi tecum Petre Aaron vetus, et constans benivolentia ...." An additional fascicle of corrigenda was published later, perhaps in response to criticisms from Gaffurio; it is included in the Broude Bros. reprint but not in the 1970 reprint published in Bologna by Forni. The corrigenda are not simple corrections of typographical errors but rather clarifications, elaborations, and retractions. The text of the corrigenda is accordingly included in the TML as a separate file: AARIHCOR TEXT. See also AARIH2 TEXT and AARIH3 TEXT.

Author: Aaron, Petrus

Treatise: Libri tres de institutione harmonica, liber secundus

Incipit: Copiose ac luculenter mi Aaron quae ad cantum planum pertinere uidebantur

File name: **AARIH2**   Data input by: Jessica Burr

File type: **TEXT**   Data checked by: Elisabeth Honn & Andreas Giger

  MS: Print: **X**   Data approved by: Thomas J. Mathiesen

Filelist: 16th   File size: 79K   Annotations:

Source of data:

Libri tres de institutione harmonica (Bononiae, In aedibus Benedicti Hectoris Bibliopolae Bononiensis, 1516; reprint ed., New York: Broude Bros., 1978), ff. Cviv-Eviiir.

An additional fascicle of corrigenda was published later, perhaps in response to criticisms from Gaffurio; it is included in the Broude Bros. reprint but not in the 1970 reprint published in Bologna by Forni. The corrigenda are not simple corrections of typographical errors but rather clarifications, elaborations, and retractions. The text of the corrigenda is accordingly included in the TML as a separate file: AARIHCOR TEXT. See also AARIH1 TEXT and AARIH3 TEXT.

1

Author: Aaron, Petrus
Treatise: Libri tres de institutione harmonica, liber tertius
Incipit: Flaminius. Non possem mi Aaron verbis assequi, quanta te de hisce rebus

File name: **AARIH3**   Data input by: Jessica Burr
File type: **TEXT**   Data checked by: Elisabeth Honn & Andreas Giger
  MS: Print: **X**   Data approved by: Thomas J. Mathiesen
Filelist: 16th   File size: 111K   Annotations:

Source of data:
  Libri tres de institutione harmonica
  (Bononiae, In aedibus Benedicti Hectoris
  Bibliopolae Bononiensis, 1516; reprint
  ed., New York: Broude Bros., 1978), ff.
  Eviiiv-Hxr.

An additional fascicle of corrigenda was published later, perhaps in response to criticisms from Gaffurio; it is included in the Broude Bros. reprint but not in the 1970 reprint published in Bologna by Forni. The corrigenda are not simple corrections of typographical errors but rather clarifications, elaborations, and retractions. The text of the corrigenda is accordingly included in the TML as a separate file: AARIHCOR TEXT. See also AARIH1 TEXT and AARIH2 TEXT.

Author: Aaron, Petrus
Treatise: Libri tres de institutione harmonica; Petrus Aaron Florentinus ad Lectorem
Incipit: Quaedam lector humanissime in nostris institutionibus obscuriora quibusdam

File name: **AARIHCOR**   Data input by: Andreas Giger
File type: **TEXT**   Data checked by: Michael W. Lundell
  MS: Print: **X**   Data approved by: Thomas J. Mathiesen
Filelist: 16th   File size: 8K   Annotations:

Source of data:
  Libri tres de institutione harmonica
  (Bononiae, In aedibus Benedicti Hectoris
  Bibliopolae Bononiensis, [1516?]; reprint
  ed., New York: Broude Bros., 1978), ff.
  Iir-Iiiv.

This fascicle of corrigenda was published separately, perhaps in response to criticisms from Gaffurio; it is included in the Broude Bros. reprint but not in the 1970 reprint published in Bologna by Forni. The corrigenda are not simple corrections of typographical errors but rather clarifications, elaborations, and retractions. Cf. AARIH1 TEXT, AARIH2 TEXT, and AARIH3 TEXT.

Author: Abbot Guido
Treatise: Regulae de arte musica
Incipit: Cantum, a beato papa Gregorio editum, quelibet se habere fatentur ecclesie.

File name: **ABGURAM**   Data input by: Stephen E. Hayes
File type: **TEXT**   Data checked by: Peter Lefferts & Angela Mariani
  MS: Print: **X**   Data approved by: Thomas J. Mathiesen
Filelist: 12th   File size: 123K   Annotations:

Source of data:
  Scriptorum de musica medii aevi nova
  series a Gerbertina altera, 4 vols., ed.
  Edmond de Coussemaker (Paris: Durand,
  1864-76; reprint ed., Hildesheim: Olms,
  1963), 2:150-92.

The graphics files for this treatise are ABGURAM 01GF-ABGURAM 12GF. The final part of this text includes the treatise otherwise ascribed to Gui de Chalis (see GUICHA TEXT).

Author: Abbot Guido

Treatise: Regulae organi

Incipit: Si cantus ascendit duas voces, et organum incipit in dupplici voce

File name: **ABGUREG**   Data input by: Stephen E. Hayes

File type: **TEXT**   Data checked by: Peter Lefferts & Elisabeth Honn

  MS: Print: **X**   Data approved by: Thomas J. Mathiesen

Filelist: 12th   File size: 6K   Annotations:

Source of data:

Cecily Sweeney, "The Regulae organi Guidonis Abbatis and 12th Century Organum/Discant Treatises," Musica disciplina 43 (1989): 27-30. Used by permission of the American Institute of Musicology (Tempo Music Publications, 3773 West 95th Street, Leawood, KS 66206).

The incipit is preceded by a four-line verse, beginning: "Ars probat artificem, quae scribitur arte Guidonis ...." Cf. GUICHA TEXT.

Author: Adamus de Fulda

Treatise: Musica, pars prima

Incipit: Partem primam agressurus cogitavi mecum, perficiendum fore, nisi divini auxilii

File name: **FULMUS1**   Data input by: Sergei Lebedev

File type: **TEXT**   Data checked by: Angela Mariani

  MS: Print: **X**   Data approved by: Thomas J. Mathiesen

Filelist: 15th   File size: 33K   Annotations:

Source of data:

Scriptores ecclesiastici de musica sacra potissimum, 3 vols., ed. Martin Gerbert (St. Blaise: Typis San-Blasianis, 1784; reprint ed., Hildesheim: Olms, 1963), 3:329-41.

A long dedicatory preface precedes the treatise, beginning: "Clarissimo iurisconsulto Ioachim Luntaler advocato consistoriali, amico, fautorique singularissimo Adam de Fulda ...."

Author: Adamus de Fulda

Treatise: Musica, pars secunda

Incipit: Sunt autem imprimis septem consideranda, per quae tamquam per magis principalia

File name: **FULMUS2**   Data input by: Sergei Lebedev

File type: **TEXT**   Data checked by: Angela Mariani

  MS: Print: **X**   Data approved by: Thomas J. Mathiesen

Filelist: 15th   File size: 45K   Annotations:

Source of data:

Scriptores ecclesiastici de musica sacra potissimum, 3 vols., ed. Martin Gerbert (St. Blaise: Typis San-Blasianis, 1784; reprint ed., Hildesheim: Olms, 1963), 3:341-58.

A long prologue precedes the treatise, beginning: "Credimus diversa fore hominum studia, quibus aliis sua scripta insinuant,..." The graphics files for this treatise are FULMUS2 01GF-FULMUS2 06GF.

Author: Adamus de Fulda

Treatise: Musica, pars tertia

Incipit: Mensuralis musicae haec est descriptio, cuius figurae in signis positivis possunt

File name: **FULMUS3**   Data input by: Sergei Lebedev

File type: **TEXT**   Data checked by: Angela Mariani & Bradley Tucker

MS: Print: **X**   Data approved by: Thomas J. Mathiesen

Filelist: 15th   File size: 22K   Annotations:

Source of data:

Scriptores ecclesiastici de musica sacra potissimum, 3 vols., ed. Martin Gerbert (St. Blaise: Typis San-Blasianis, 1784; reprint ed., Hildesheim: Olms, 1963), 3:359-66.

A long prologue precedes the treatise, beginning: "Amphionem Dircaeum, Antiopae Lyci coniugis Nictaei Thebani regis filiae ...." The graphics file for this treatise is FULMUS3 01GF.

Author: Adamus de Fulda

Treatise: Musica, pars quarta

Incipit: Proportio est duorum numerorum inaequalitas, Boetio teste. Ex hac definitione

File name: **FULMUS4**   Data input by: Sergei Lebedev

File type: **TEXT**   Data checked by: Angela Mariani & Bradley Tucker

MS: Print: **X**   Data approved by: Thomas J. Mathiesen

Filelist: 15th   File size: 30K   Annotations:

Source of data:

Scriptores ecclesiastici de musica sacra potissimum, 3 vols., ed. Martin Gerbert (St. Blaise: Typis San-Blasianis, 1784; reprint ed., Hildesheim: Olms, 1963), 3:367-81.

A long prologue precedes the treatise, beginning: "Iubal filium Lamech sonorum proportiones priorem invenisse,..." The graphics files for this treatise are FULMUS4 01GF-FULMUS4 07GF.

Author: Adelboldus

Treatise: Epistola cum tractatu de musica instrumentali humanaque ac mundana

Incipit: Desiderio tuo, fili carissime, gratuito condescenderem, si rationi praeviae preces

File name: **ADETRA**   Data input by: John Gray

File type: **TEXT**   Data checked by: Oliver Ellsworth & Andreas Giger

MS: Print: **X**   Data approved by: Thomas J. Mathiesen

Filelist: 9th-11th   File size: 25K   Annotations:

Source of data:

Adalboldi episcopi Ultraiectensis Epistola cum tractatu de musica instrumentali humanaque ac mundana, ed. Joseph Smits van Waesberghe, Divitiae musicae artis, A/II (Buren: Knuf, 1981), 12-29. Used by kind permission of the Laaber-Verlag.

The treatise itself opens with an Introductio (beginning "Creatrix omnium sapientia creaturas omnes ..."). The edition is based on Rome, Biblioteca Apostolica Vaticana, Barberinus lat. 283, ff. 37-44.

4

Author: Adelboldus

Treatise: Musica

Incipit: Ut vero indubitanter consonantiarum ratio colligatur, tali brevissimo ac simplici effici

File name: **ADEMUS** Data input by: Bradley Jon Tucker

File type: **TEXT** Data checked by: Benito V. Rivera

MS: Print: **X** Data approved by: Thomas J. Mathiesen

Filelist: 9th-11th File size: 30K Annotations:

Source of data:
Scriptores ecclesiastici de musica sacra potissimum, 3 vols., ed. Martin Gerbert (St. Blaise: Typis San-Blasianis, 1784; reprint ed., Hildesheim: Olms, 1963), 1:303-12.

The graphics files for this treatise are ADEMUS 01GF-ADEMUS 04GF. Cf. ADEMUSI TEXT.

Author: Adelboldus

Treatise: Musica

Incipit: Ut vero indubitanter consonantiarum ratio colligatur, tali brevissimo ac simplici effici

File name: **ADEMUSI** Data input by: Jingfa Sun

File type: **TEXT** Data checked by: Andreas Giger

MS: Print: **X** Data approved by: Thomas J. Mathiesen

Filelist: 9th-11th File size: 27K Annotations:

Source of data:
Patrologia cursus completus, series latina, ed. J. P. Migne, 221 vols. (Paris: Garnier, 1844-1904), 140:1109-20.

The graphics file for this treatise is ADEMUSI 01GF. The figures for Schema 2-4 were not included in this edition, but cross-references have been provided in this file to the respective figures in the Gerbert edition (i.e., ADEMUS 02GF-ADEMUS 04GF). Cf. ADEMUS TEXT.

Author: Aegidius de Murino

Treatise: Tractatus cantus mensurabilis

Incipit: Primo accipe tenorem alicujus antiphone vel responsorii

File name: **AEGTRA** Data input by: C. Matthew Balensuela

File type: **TEXT** Data checked by: Oliver B. Ellsworth

MS: Print: **X** Data approved by: Thomas J. Mathiesen

Filelist: 14th File size: 14K Annotations:

Source of data:
Scriptorum de musica medii aevi nova series a Gerbertina altera, 4 vols., ed. Edmond de Coussemaker (Paris: Durand, 1864-76; reprint ed., Hildesheim: Olms, 1963), 3:124-28.

Author: Aegidius Zamorensis, Iohannes

Treatise: Ars musica

Incipit: Musicae artis plures fuisse legimus inventores, secundum varias opiniones

File name: **ZAMLAM**   Data input by: Patricia Starr

File type: **TEXT**   Data checked by: Charles M. Atkinson

  MS: Print: **X**   Data approved by: Thomas J. Mathiesen

Filelist: 14th   File size: 63K   Annotations:

Source of data: The treatise is preceded by a prologue,
  Scriptores ecclesiastici de musica sacra   beginning: "Reverendo et in bono Iesu patri
  potissimum, 3 vols., ed. Martin Gerbert   sibi karissimo domino et amico, domino fratri
  (St. Blaise: Typis San-Blasianis, 1784;   Iohanni, ordinis fratrum Minorum generali
  reprint ed., Hildesheim: Olms, 1963),   ministro: ..."
  2:370-93.

Author: Aegidius Zamorensis, Iohannes

Treatise: Liber artis musicae

Incipit: Musicae artis plures fuisse legimus inuentores, secundum uarias opiniones

File name: **ZAMLIB**   Data input by: Stephen E. Hayes

File type: **TEXT**   Data checked by: Peter M. Lefferts & A. Mariani

  MS: Print: **X**   Data approved by: Thomas J. Mathiesen

Filelist: 14th   File size: 64K   Annotations:

Source of data: The treatise is preceded by a prologue,
  Johannes Aegidius de Zamora, Ars   beginning: "Reuerendo et in bono Iesu patri
  musica, ed. Michel Robert-Tissot, Corpus   sibi carissimo domino et amico, domino fratri
  scriptorum de musica, vol. 20 ([Rome]:   Iohanni Ordinis Fratrum Minorum generali
  American Institute of Musicology, 1974),   ministro, ..."
  30-122 (even). Used by permission.

Author: Agricola, Martinus

Treatise: Rudimenta musices

Incipit: Musica, secundum Augustinum, est bene modulandi scientia.

File name: **AGRRUD**   Data input by: Peter Slemon

File type: **TEXT**   Data checked by: Andreas Giger

  MS: Print: **X**   Data approved by: Thomas J. Mathiesen

Filelist: 16th   File size: 37K   Annotations:

Source of data: The graphics files for this treatise are
  Rvdimenta mvsices, qvibvs canendi   AGRRUD 01GF-AGRRUD 18GF.
  artificivm compendiosissime complexum,
  pueris vna cum monochordi dimensione
  traditur (Vitebergae apud Geor. Rhaw,
  1539; reprint ed., New York: Broude
  Bros., 1966).

Author: Al-Farabi

Treatise: De ortu scientiarum, Dictio de cognoscenda causa unde orta est ars musice

Incipit: Dico quod postquam substancia mota fuit, accidit ei sonus, qui divisus fuit in tres

File name: **FARORT**

File type: **TEXT**

MS: Print: **X**

Filelist: 12th   File size: 6K

Data input by: Stephen E. Hayes

Data checked by: Peter Lefferts & Elisabeth Honn

Data approved by: Thomas J. Mathiesen

Annotations:

Source of data:

Henry George Farmer, ed. and trans., Al-Farabi's Arabic-Latin Writings on Music, Collection of Oriental Writers on Music, vol. 2 (Glasgow: The Civic Press, 1934; reprint ed., London: Hinrichsen Edition Ltd., 1965), 44-48.

De ortu scientiarum as preserved in Oxford, Bodleian Library, e. Museo 125, ff. 186v-187v (De assignanda causa ex qua scite sunt sciencie philosophie et ordo earum, Text B); Paris, Bibliothèque nationale, lat. 6298, ff. 160-61 (Liber Alfarabii de ortu scientiarum, Text P3); and London, British Library, Sloane 2461, ff. 26r-27v (Gundissalinus, Compendium scientiarum [De divisione philosophiae], Text F).

Author: Al-Farabi

Treatise: De scientiis

Incipit: Scientia vero musice comprehendit in summa cognitionem specierum armoniarum

File name: **FARSCI**

File type: **TEXT**

MS: Print: **X**

Filelist: 12th   File size: 4K

Data input by: Andreas Giger

Data checked by: Elisabeth Honn

Data approved by: Thomas J. Mathiesen

Annotations:

Source of data:

Max Haas, "Studien zur mittelalterlichen Musiklehre I: Eine Übersicht über die Musiklehre im Kontext der Philosophie des 13. und frühen 14. Jahrhunderts," in Aktuelle Fragen der musikbezogenen Mittelalterforschung: Texte zu einem Basler Kolloquium des Jahres 1975, Forum Musicologicum: Basler Beiträge zur Musikgeschichte, vol. 3, ed. Hans Oesch and Wulf Arlt (Winterthur: Amadeus Verlag, 1982), 420-21.

Based on Paris, Bibliothèque nationale, lat. 9335, f. 148r-v, Gerard of Cremona's Latin translation of Al-Farabi's definition of musical science from his De scientiis. Cf. FARSCIE TEXT.

Author: Al-Farabi

Treatise: De scientiis

Incipit: Scientia uero musice, comprehendit in summa, cognitionem specierum armoniarum

File name: **FARSCIE**

File type: **TEXT**

MS: Print: **X**

Filelist: 12th   File size: 12K

Data input by: Stephen E. Hayes

Data checked by: Peter Lefferts & Elisabeth Honn

Data approved by: Thomas J. Mathiesen

Annotations:

Source of data:

Henry George Farmer, ed. and trans., Al-Farabi's Arabic-Latin Writings on Music, Collection of Oriental Writers on Music, vol. 2 (Glasgow: The Civic Press, 1934; reprint ed., London: Hinrichsen Edition Ltd., 1965), 21-31.

De scientiis as preserved in Paris, Bibliothèque nationale, lat. 9335, f. 148r-v (Gerard of Cremona's Latin translation of De scientiis, Text A); London, British LIbrary, Cotton Vesp.B.X (John of Seville, De divisione omnium scientiarum, Text B); Vincent of Beauvais, Speculum doctrinale (Venice, 1494), lib. 17, cap. 15sq. (Text D); and London, British Library, Sloane 2461, ff. 26r-27v (Gundissalinus, Compendium scientiarum, Text F). Cf. FARSCI TEXT.

Author: Alcuinus, Flaccus

Treatise: Musica

Incipit: Octo tonos in Musica consistere musicus scire debet, per quos omnis modulatio

File name: **ALCMUS**

File type: **TEXT**

MS: Print: **X**

Filelist: 6th-8th   File size: 3K

Data input by: Stephen E. Hayes

Data checked by: Peter M. Lefferts

Data approved by: Thomas J. Mathiesen

Annotations:

Also ascribed to Albinus.

Source of data:

Scriptores ecclesiastici de musica sacra potissimum, 3 vols., ed. Martin Gerbert (St. Blaise: Typis San-Blasianis, 1784; reprint ed., Hildesheim: Olms, 1963), 1:26-27.

Author: Amerus

Treatise: Practica artis musice

Incipit: Licet michi ipsi in omni sciencia nimis sim insufficiens de ipsius auxilio qui dat

File name: **AMEPRA**

File type: **TEXT**

MS: Print: **X**

Filelist: 13th   File size: 84K

Data input by: Stephen E. Hayes

Data checked by: Peter M. Lefferts & Kirk Ditzler

Data approved by: Thomas J. Mathiesen

Annotations:

The graphics files for this treatise are AMEPRA 01GF-AMEPRA 57GF.

Source of data:

Ameri Practica artis musice (1271), ed. Cesarino Ruini, Corpus scriptorum de musica, vol. 25 (n.p.: American Institute of Musicology, 1977), 19-112. Used by permission.

Author: Ancina Fossaniensis, Juvenal

Treatise: De musica

Incipit: Etsi Musica humanum inventum est, cantus tamen nonnullos usque adeo suaves

File name: **ANCMUS** Data input by: John Csonka

File type: **TEXT** Data checked by: Bradley Jon Tucker

MS: Print: **X** Data approved by: Thomas J. Mathiesen

Filelist: 16th File size: 2K Annotations:

Source of data:

Adrien de la Fage, Essais de dipthérographie musicale (Paris: Legouix, 1864), 344-45.

Based on Rome, Biblioteca Vallicelliana, O.26. This text includes only five short propositions on music drawn from a larger set of propositions on philosophy and medicine, written in 1565.

Author: Anonymous

Treatise: [Ad organum faciendum]

Incipit: Cum multi ueterum ac modernorum de diaphonia satis indiscrete tractassent ego

File name: **ADORFBB** Data input by: Angela Mariani

File type: **TEXT** Data checked by: Peter Slemon

MS: Print: **X** Data approved by: Thomas J. Mathiesen

Filelist: 9th-11th File size: 5K Annotations:

Source of data:

Hans Heinrich Eggebrecht and Frieder Zaminer, eds., Ad organum faciendum. Lehrschriften der Mehrstimmigkeit in nachguidonischer Zeit, Neue Studien zur Musikwissenschaft, vol. 3 (Mainz: B. Schotts Söhne, 1970), 159-60.

Based on Berlin, Staatsbibliothek der Stiftung Preussischer Kulturbesitz, theol. lat. quart. 261, ff. 50v-51v. This represents a fragment of the treatise commonly known as Ad organum faciendum, sometimes also called the Milan organum treatise. Cf. ADORF TEXT.

Author: Anonymous

Treatise: [Ad organum faciendum]

Incipit: Significatum organi aliud naturale aliud remotum a natura. Naturale est illud

File name: **ADORFBR** Data input by: Angela Mariani

File type: **TEXT** Data checked by: Peter Slemon

MS: Print: **X** Data approved by: Thomas J. Mathiesen

Filelist: 9th-11th File size: 3K Annotations:

Source of data:

Hans Heinrich Eggebrecht and Frieder Zaminer, eds., Ad organum faciendum. Lehrschriften der Mehrstimmigkeit in nachguidonischer Zeit, Neue Studien zur Musikwissenschaft, vol. 3 (Mainz: B. Schotts Söhne, 1970), 175.

Based on Bruges, Stadsbibliotheek, 528, ff. 54vb-55ra. This represents a fragment of the treatise commonly known as Ad organum faciendum, sometimes also called the Milan organum treatise. Cf. ADORF TEXT.

Author: Anonymous

Treatise: [Ad organum faciendum]

Incipit: Vocum copulationes dicuntur. omni symphonia et de omni cantu dicatur.

File name: **ADORFBA**   Data input by: Angela Mariani

File type: **TEXT**   Data checked by: Peter Slemon

MS: Print: **X**   Data approved by: Thomas J. Mathiesen

Filelist: 9th-11th File size: 4K   Annotations:

Source of data:

Hans Heinrich Eggebrecht and Frieder Zaminer, eds., Ad organum faciendum. Lehrschriften der Mehrstimmigkeit in nachguidonischer Zeit, Neue Studien zur Musikwissenschaft, vol. 3 (Mainz: B. Schotts Söhne, 1970), 149-50.

Based on Berlin, Staatsbibliothek der Stiftung Preussischer Kulturbesitz, theol. lat. quart. 261, f. 48r-v. This represents a fragment of the treatise commonly known as Ad organum faciendum, sometimes also called the Milan organum treatise. Cf. ADORF TEXT.

Author: Anonymous

Treatise: [Ars musica]

Incipit: Huius artis experientiam quaerere cupientibus, a figura manus inchoandum est

File name: **ANOARSMU**   Data input by: Stephen E. Hayes

File type: **TEXT**   Data checked by: Peter M. Lefferts & Andreas Giger

MS: Print: **X**   Data approved by: Thomas J. Mathiesen

Filelist: 13th   File size: 31K   Annotations:

Source of data:

Marie Louise Göllner, ed., The Manuscript Cod. lat. 5539 of the Bavarian State Library, Musicological Studies and Documents, vol. 43 (Neuhausen-Stuttgart: Hänssler-Verlag, American Institute of Musicology, 1993), 69-94. Used by permission of the American Institute of Musicology (Tempo Music Publications, 3773 West 95th Street, Leawood, KS 66206).

Document IIIa. The treatise is preceded by a dedicatory prologue, beginning: "Reverentissimo domino ac patri H[einrico] ratysponensi episcopo subditorum humillimus ...." The graphics files for this treatise are ANOARSMU 01GF-ANOARSMU 18GF. Cf. METANO3 TEXT.

Author: Anonymous

Treatise: [Capitulum de vocibus applicatis verbis]

Incipit: Postquam in precedenti capitulo dictum est de partibus et consideracione

File name: **ANOCAP**   Data input by: Andreas Giger

File type: **TEXT**   Data checked by: Elisabeth Honn

MS: Print: **X**   Data approved by: Thomas J. Mathiesen

Filelist: 14th   File size: 8K   Annotations:

Source of data:

Santorre Debenedetti, "Un trattatello del secolo XIV sopra la poesia musicale," Studi medievali 2 (1906-7): 79-80.

Based on Venice, Biblioteca Nazionale Marciana, lat. XII/97 (coll. 4125), ff. 19-20. The capitulum is appended to Antonio da Tempo's Summa artis rithmici vulgaris Dictaminis.

Author: Anonymous

Treatise: [De discantu]

Incipit: ... quinta et descendat per unam vocem erit in octaua vel incipiat in tercia

File name: **ANODIS** Data input by: Peter M. Lefferts

File type: **MOBB842** Data checked by: Michael W. Lundell

 MS: **X** Print: Data approved by: Thomas J. Mathiesen

Filelist: 14th File size: 1K   Annotations:

Source of data: =RISM BIII/4:110-15. This fragment of text

 Oxford, Bodleian Library, Bodley 842 has been published in Klaus-Jürgen Sachs,

 (S.C. 2575), f. 76r.   "Zur Tradition der Klangschritt-Lehre: Die

              Texte mit der Formel 'Si cantus ascendit ...'

              und ihre Verwandten," Archiv für

              Musikwissenschaft 28 (1971): 264.

Author: Anonymous

Treatise: [De discantu et contranota]

Incipit: Circa modum discantandi primo attendendum est.

File name: **ANODDC** Data input by: Peter M. Lefferts

File type: **MLBL2145** Data checked by: Michael W. Lundell

 MS: **X** Print: Data approved by: Thomas J. Mathiesen

Filelist: 14th File size: 9K   Annotations:

Source of data: =RISM BIII/4:46-47. The graphics file for this

 London, British Library, Additional treatise is ANODDC 01GF. Cf. ANOCMD

 21455, ff. 9v-11r.   TEXT.

Author: Anonymous

Treatise: [De discantu et contranota]

Incipit: Circa modum discantandi primo attendendum est.

File name: **ANOCMD** Data input by: Peter M. Lefferts

File type: **TEXT** Data checked by: Elisabeth Honn

 MS: Print: **X** Data approved by: Thomas J. Mathiesen

Filelist: 14th File size: 6K   Annotations:

Source of data: Edited from London, British Library,

 Manfred Bukofzer, Geschichte des Additional 21455, f. 9v. The graphics file for

 englischen Diskants und des   this treatise is ANOCMD 01GF. Cf.

 Fauxbourdons nach den theoretischen ANODDC MLBL2145.

 Quellen, Sammlung

 musikwissenschaftlicher Abhandlungen,

 Band 21 (Strassbourg: Heitz, 1936),

 138-40.

Author: Anonymous

Treatise: [De discantu et contranota]

Incipit: Septem sunt concordancie in discantu, videlicet unisonus. tercia, quinta, sexta

File name: **ANODDCS**   Data input by: Peter M. Lefferts

File type: **TEXT**   Data checked by: Elisabeth Honn

MS: Print: **X**   Data approved by: Thomas J. Mathiesen

Filelist: 14th   File size: 2K   Annotations:

Source of data: Edited from London, British Library,
  Manfred Bukofzer, Geschichte des   Additional 21455, f. 11r. Cf. ANODDC
  englischen Diskants und des   MLBL2145 and ANOCMD TEXT.
  Fauxbourdons nach den theoretischen
  Quellen, Sammlung
  musikwissenschaftlicher Abhandlungen,
  Band 21 (Strassbourg: Heitz, 1936), 141.

Author: Anonymous

Treatise: [De harmonia planetarum]

Incipit: Da per armoniam distanciam planetarum

File name: **ANOHARP**   Data input by: Peter M. Lefferts

File type: **MOBB842**   Data checked by: Michael W. Lundell

MS: **X**   Print: Data approved by: Thomas J. Mathiesen

Filelist: 14th   File size: 2K   Annotations:

Source of data: =RISM BIII/4:110-15.
  Oxford, Bodleian Library, Bodley 842
  (S.C. 2575), f. 46v.

Author: Anonymous

Treatise: [De intervallis]

Incipit: Tonus dicitur a tonando quia prima uox est qui naturaliter tonat.

File name: **ANOINT**   Data input by: Peter M. Lefferts

File type: **MLBLH978**   Data checked by: Michael W. Lundell

MS: **X**   Print: Data approved by: Thomas J. Mathiesen

Filelist: 13th   File size: 3K   Annotations:

Source of data: =RISM BIII/4:80-81. The incipit, which
  London, British Library, Harley 978, ff.   appears on f. 15r, is preceded on f. 14r by a
  14r-15r.   diagram of interlocking natural, hard, and soft
      hexachords, and an untexted melody
      demonstrating these mutations. This is
      followed on ff. 14v-15r by a musical
      mnemonic on the text "Est tonus sic ut.re.ut
      aut re.mi.re. uel fa.sol.fa. sol.la.sol. solet hic
      sonare ...." The graphics files for this treatise
      are ANOINT 01GF-ANOINT 03GF. Cf.
      ANOEST MLBLL763.

Author: Anonymous

Treatise: [De intervallis]

Incipit: Tonus est regula quo de omni cantu in fine diiudicat

File name: **ANOIN** Data input by: Peter M. Lefferts

File type: **MOBB842** Data checked by: Michael W. Lundell

MS: **X** Print: Data approved by: Thomas J. Mathiesen

Filelist: 14th File size: 1K Annotations:

Source of data: =RISM BIII/4:110-15. The graphics file for
  Oxford, Bodleian Library, Bodley 842 this treatise is ANOIN 01GF.
  (S.C. 2575), ff. 44v-45r.

Author: Anonymous

Treatise: [De mensurabili musica]

Incipit: Cum de mensurabili musica sit nostra presens intencio

File name: **ANOMM** Data input by: Peter M. Lefferts

File type: **MLBL2145** Data checked by: Michael W. Lundell

MS: **X** Print: Data approved by: Thomas J. Mathiesen

Filelist: 14th File size: 15K Annotations:

Source of data: =RISM BIII/4:46-47. The graphics files for
  London, British Library, Additional this treatise are ANOMM 01GF-ANOMM
  21455, ff. 3r-6r. 02GF. Cf. REGDEM TEXT.

Author: Anonymous

Treatise: [De musica mensurata]

Incipit: Pro facili informatione eorum, qui ad culmen artis musicae scientiae pervenire

File name: **ANOBRI** Data input by: Stephen E. Hayes

File type: **TEXT** Data checked by: Peter M. Lefferts & Andreas Giger

MS: Print: **X** Data approved by: Thomas J. Mathiesen

Filelist: 15th File size: 30K Annotations:

Source of data: Based on Kremsmünster,
  P. Altman Kellner, "Ein Mensuraltraktat Benediktinerstiftsbibliothek 312, ff.
  aus der Zeit um 1400," Anzeiger der 210v-212v. The treatise is commonly known
  Oesterreichischen Akademie der as the "Brieger Anonymous." The graphics file
  Wissenschaften, for this treatise is ANOBRI 01GF.
  philosophisch-historische Klasse 94
  (1957): 73-85. Used by permission.

Author: Anonymous

Treatise: [De origine musice artis]

Incipit: De origine Musice Artis quia rudem lectorem vidimus in primis tacuimus.

File name: **ANODEO**

File type: **MLBLL763**

MS: **X**   Print:

Filelist: 14th   File size: 38K

Source of data:
London, British Library, Lansdowne 763, ff. 69r-87v.

Data input by: Peter M. Lefferts

Data checked by: Michael W. Lundell

Data approved by: Thomas J. Mathiesen

Annotations:
=RISM BIII/4:87-91. The graphics files for this treatise are ANODEO 01GF-33GF (ANODEO 33GF is an "arbor diagram" of the sort that appears in treatises dealing with mensural hierarchies [e.g., Quatuor principalia and the treatise of Johannes Vetulus de Anagnia], but it does not seem to pertain specifically to this treatise). The treatise begins (ff. 69r-71r) with a Guidonian miscellany drawn from the Micrologus (chapters 20, 13, etc.); this is followed by an elaborate tonary (ff. 71r-85r) and then the summary of a tonary (ff. 85r-87r). The principal tonary reflects the Sarum rite (see Michel Huglo, Les tonaires: Inventaire, analyse, comparaison [Paris: Société francaise de musicologie, 1971], 345).

Author: Anonymous

Treatise: [De prolatione]

Incipit: Quatuor sunt signa per que facile cognosci potest omnis cantus

File name: **ANOPROL**

File type: **MOBB842**

MS: **X**   Print:

Filelist: 14th   File size: 1K

Source of data:
Oxford, Bodleian Library, Bodley 842 (S.C. 2575), f. 47v.

Data input by: Peter M. Lefferts

Data checked by: Michael W. Lundell

Data approved by: Thomas J. Mathiesen

Annotations:
=RISM BIII/4:110-15.

Author: Anonymous

Treatise: [De proportione]

Incipit: Primus habet m .ne. sic sextus tercius atque septimus octauus fieri dicit

File name: **ANOPROP**

File type: **MOBB842**

MS: **X**   Print:

Filelist: 14th   File size: 1K

Source of data:
Oxford, Bodleian Library, Bodley 842 (S.C. 2575), f. 46v.

Data input by: Peter M. Lefferts

Data checked by: Michael W. Lundell

Data approved by: Thomas J. Mathiesen

Annotations:
=RISM BIII/4:110-15.

Author: Anonymous

Treatise: [De proportionibus et de intervallis]

Incipit: ... decem et octo. Inter sedecim et octodecim unus numerus intercidit

File name: **ANOPI**   Data input by: Peter M. Lefferts

File type: **MOBB842**   Data checked by: Michael W. Lundell

  MS: **X**   Print: Data approved by: Thomas J. Mathiesen

Filelist: 14th   File size: 7K   Annotations:

Source of data: =RISM BIII/4:110-15. On the first section of
  Oxford, Bodleian Library, Bodley 842   this text, cf. Boethius, De institutione musica
  (S.C. 2575), ff. 74r-75v.   1.16.

Author: Anonymous

Treatise: [Fragmenta]

Incipit: Isidora. Musica est ars modulandi sono cantuque consistens

File name: **ANOFRAG**   Data input by: Peter M. Lefferts

File type: **MOBB842**   Data checked by: Michael W. Lundell

  MS: **X**   Print: Data approved by: Thomas J. Mathiesen

Filelist: 14th   File size: 2K   Annotations:

Source of data: =RISM BIII/4:110-15. The graphics file for
  Oxford, Bodleian Library, Bodley 842   this treatise is ANOFRAG 01GF.
  (S.C. 2575), ff. 77v-78r.

Author: Anonymous

Treatise: [Mensura cymbalorum]

Incipit: [Varia]

File name: **ANOCYM**   Data input by: Andreas Giger

File type: **TEXT**   Data checked by: Elisabeth Honn

  MS: Print: **X**   Data approved by: Thomas J. Mathiesen

Filelist: 14th   File size: 51K   Annotations:

Source of data: This file contains twenty-two different texts
  J. Smits van Waesberghe, ed., Cymbala drawn from manuscripts of various dates
  (Bells in the Middle Ages), Musicological (primarily eleventh through thirteenth
  Studies and Documents, vol. 1 (Rome: century).
  American Institute of Musicology, 1951),
  37-61. Used by permission of the
  American Institute of Musicology
  (Tempo Music Publications, 3773 West
  95th Street, Leawood, KS 66206).

Author: Anonymous

Treatise: [Miscellanea]

Incipit: Diapente et diatesseron Simphonie et intense et remisse pariter consonantia<m>

File name: **ANOSPI**   Data input by: Elisabeth Honn

File type: **TEXT**   Data checked by: Andreas Giger

MS: Print: **X**   Data approved by: Thomas J. Mathiesen

Filelist: 9th-11th File size: 10K   Annotations:

Source of data:

Karl-Werner Gümpel, "Spicilegium Rivipullense," Archiv für Musikwissenschaft 35 (1978): 57-61. Used by permission.

A collection of short texts from Ripoll 42. The incipit given above is the text for the music (ANOSPI 01GF) included at the beginning of the article. The incipit for the first text is: "De Guidonis musica. Omnes autenti quinto loco a se principia ..."; for the second text: "Incipit interrogatio. Discipulus. Diapason quid est? ..."; for the third text: "Qualiter metiatur monocordus. Si uis metiri monocordum, ..."; and for the fourth text: "De Enquiriadis monocordi diuisione. Enquiridiadis (sic!) namque monocordi ...."

Author: Anonymous

Treatise: [Musica disciplina]

Incipit: Musica disciplina est, quae de numeris loquitur, qui ad aliquid sunt his, qui

File name: **ANOMUSD**   Data input by: Michael W. Lundell

File type: **TEXT**   Data checked by: Andreas Giger

MS: Print: **X**   Data approved by: Thomas J. Mathiesen

Filelist: 14th   File size: 12K   Annotations:

Source of data:

Renate Federhofer-Königs, "Ein unvollständiger Musiktraktat des 14. Jahrhunderts in Ms. 1201 der Universitätsbibliothek Graz," Kirchenmusikalisches Jahrbuch 44 (1960): 14-19. Used by permission.

This text is commonly known as the Graz Anonymous.

Author: Anonymous

Treatise: [Opusculum musicum]

Incipit: Ut pateat euidenter monochordi. quot et quibus pleri licet nescienter diuersis

File name: **MUSICAO**   Data input by: Peter M. Lefferts

File type: **MOBB842**   Data checked by: Michael W. Lundell

MS: **X**   Print: Data approved by: Thomas J. Mathiesen

Filelist: 14th   File size: 2K   Annotations:

Source of data:

Oxford, Bodleian Library, Bodley 842 (S.C. 2575), ff. 45v-46r.

=RISM BIII/4:110-15. This file contains the text for a didactic musical example, given in MUSICAO 01GF. The same text appears in St. Paul, Archiv des Benediktinerstiftes, 135/1, ff. 18v-19r. See Lawrence Gushee, "The Tabula Monochordi of Magister Nicolaus de Luduno," in Essays on Medieval Music in Honor of David G. Hughes, ed. Graeme M. Boone, Isham Library Papers, no. 4 (Cambridge: Harvard University Department of Music; Harvard University Press, 1995), 140-41.

Author: Anonymous

Treatise: [Regulae de musica]

Incipit: Omnium humanarum actionum seu studiorum que moderantur ... sicut dicit Hugo

File name: **METANO2**   Data input by: Angela Mariani

File type: **TEXT**   Data checked by: Bradley Jon Tucker

MS: Print: **X**   Data approved by: Thomas J. Mathiesen

Filelist: 13th   File size: 28K   Annotations:

Source of data:

Dominicus Mettenleiter, Musikgeschichte der Stadt Regensburg (Regensburg: J. G. Bössenecker, 1866), 61-70 partim.

The treatise is preceded by a dedicatory prologue, beginning: "Venerantissimis et in Christo plurimum diligendis dominis suis...." Based on Erlangen. Universitätsbibliothek, 193.

Author: Anonymous

Treatise: [Rhythmica]

Incipit: Pes est syllabarum et temporum certa dinumeratio ... pedes disyallabi sunt quattuor

File name: **ANOPES**   Data input by: Andreas Giger

File type: **TEXT**   Data checked by: Elisabeth Honn

MS: Print: **X**   Data approved by: Thomas J. Mathiesen

Filelist: 13th   File size: 4K   Annotations:

Source of data:

Max Haas, "Studien zur mittelalterlichen Musiklehre I: Eine Übersicht über die Musiklehre im Kontext der Philosophie des 13. und frühen 14. Jahrhunderts," in Aktuelle Fragen der musikbezogenen Mittelalterforschung: Texte zu einem Basler Kolloquium des Jahres 1975, Forum Musicologicum: Basler Beiträge zur Musikgeschichte, vol. 3, ed. Hans Oesch and Wulf Arlt (Winterthur: Amadeus Verlag, 1982), 425.

Based on a list appearing in Oxford, Bodleian Library, Bodley 77, f. 139. The graphics file for this treatise is ANOPES 01GF.

Author: Anonymous

Treatise: [Tractatulus de musica]

Incipit: Cantus dicitur autenticus melodia cuius diapente recipit inferius et dyatesseron

File name: **ANOCADI**   Data input by: Stephen E. Hayes

File type: **TEXT**   Data checked by: Peter M. Lefferts & Andreas Giger

MS: Print: **X**   Data approved by: Thomas J. Mathiesen

Filelist: 13th   File size: 4K   Annotations:

Source of data:

Marie Louise Göllner, ed., The Manuscript Cod. lat. 5539 of the Bavarian State Library, Musicological Studies and Documents, vol. 43 (Neuhausen-Stuttgart: Hänssler-Verlag, American Institute of Musicology, 1993), 110-13. Used by permission of the American Institute of Musicology (Tempo Music Publications, 3773 West 95th Street, Leawood, KS 66206).

Document IIIc. The graphics files for this treatise are ANOCADI 01GF-ANOCADI 04GF. Cf. METANO3 TEXT.

Author: Anonymous

Treatise: [Tractatulus de musica]

Incipit: Est musica mundana, humana et instrumentalis. De instrumentali agit Boethius

File name: **ANOTRDM**   Data input by: Ulrike Hascher-Burger

File type: **TEXT**   Data checked by: Michael W. Lundell

  MS: Print: **X**   Data approved by: Thomas J. Mathiesen

Filelist: 13th   File size: 18K   Annotations:

Source of data:
  Unpublished critical text by Ulrike Hascher-Burger (Sonderholm 67, NL-2133 Hoofdorp, The Netherlands), used with the kind permission of the owner.

Based on Munich, Bayerische Staatsbibliothek, Clm 28186, ff. 258r-259v; Florence, Biblioteca Medicea-Laurenziana, 29/9, ff. 143v-145r; and Kraków, Biblioteka Jagiellonska, 754, ff. 43v, 42r-42v, and 44r. Cf. ANOTRDMK MKBJ754 and ANTRDMM MMBS2818.

Author: Anonymous

Treatise: [Tractatulus de musica]

Incipit: Est musica mundana. humana et instrumentalis. De instrumentali agit Boecius

File name: **ANOTRDMK**   Data input by: Michael W. Lundell

File type: **MKBJ754**   Data checked by: Andreas Giger

  MS: **X**   Print: Data approved by: Thomas J. Mathiesen

Filelist: 13th   File size: 18K   Annotations:

Source of data:
  Krakow, Biblioteka Jagiellonska, 754, ff. 43v, 42r-v, and 44r.

Cf. ANOTRDM TEXT and ANTRDMM MMBS2818.

Author: Anonymous

Treatise: [Tractatulus de musica]

Incipit: Est musica humana mundana et instrumentalis De instrumentali agit Boecius

File name: **ANOTRDM**   Data input by: Michael W. Lundell

File type: **MMBS2818**   Data checked by: Andreas Giger

  MS: **X**   Print: Data approved by: Thomas J. Mathiesen

Filelist: 13th   File size: 18K   Annotations:

Source of data:
  Munich, Bayerische Staatsbibliothek, Clm 28186, ff. 258r-259v.

Cf. ANOTRDM TEXT and ANTRDMK MKBJ754.

Author: Anonymous

Treatise: [Tractatus de cantu mensurabili]

Incipit: (De notulis) Sciendum est quod in notulis pro exigentia motellorum, conductorum

File name: **ANOCANT**	Data input by: Stephen E. Hayes	
File type: **TEXT**	Data checked by: Peter Lefferts & Bradley Tucker	
MS: Print: **X**	Data approved by: Thomas J. Mathiesen	
Filelist: 13th File size: 4K	Annotations:	

Source of data:
Michel Huglo, "Le traité de cantus mensurabilis du manuscrit de Bamberg," in Pax et Sapientia: Studies in Text and Music of Liturgical Tropes and Sequences in Memory of Gordon Anderson, ed. Ritva Jacobsson, Acta universitatis stockholmiensis, Studia latina stockholmiensia, vol. 29 (Stockholm: Almqvist & Wiksell, 1986), 94-95. Used by permission.

The graphics file for this treatise is ANOCANT 01GF.

Author: Anonymous

Treatise: [Tractatus de musica]

Incipit: Differentia est inter motetos, ballados, vireletos et rondellos et fugas.

File name: **ANOTDM**	Data input by: Stephen E. Hayes	
File type: **TEXT**	Data checked by: Peter M. Lefferts & Andreas Giger	
MS: Print: **X**	Data approved by: Thomas J. Mathiesen	
Filelist: 15th File size: 3K	Annotations:	

Source of data:
Martin Staehelin, "Beschreibungen und Beispiele musikalischer Formen in einem unbeachteten Traktat des frühen 15. Jahrhunderts" Archiv für Musikwissenschaft 31 (1974): 239. Used by permission.

Based on Philadelphia, University of Pennsylvania, Charles Patterson Van Pelt Library, lat. 36; and Schloss Harburg, Fürstlich Oettingen- Wallerstein'sche Bibliothek und Kunstsammlung, cod. II, 1, 2°, 38.

Author: Anonymous

Treatise: [Tractatus de musica]

Incipit: Musica est motus vocum rationabilium in arsim et a thesim, id est in elevatione

File name: **ANOMIC**	Data input by: Stephen E. Hayes	
File type: **TEXT**	Data checked by: Peter M. Lefferts & Andreas Giger	
MS: Print: **X**	Data approved by: Thomas J. Mathiesen	
Filelist: 14th File size: 21K	Annotations:	

Source of data:
Renate Federhofer-Königs, "Ein anonymer Musiktraktat aus der 2. Hälfte des 14. Jahrhunderts in der Stiftsbibliothek Michaelbeuern/Salzburg," Kirchenmusikalisches Jahrbuch 46 (1962): 44-54. Used by permission.

Based on Michaelbeuern (Salzburg), Bibliothek des Benediktinerstiftes, cod. man. cart. 95, ff. 148r-153r. The treatise is dated 1369. The graphics file for this treatise is ANOMIC 01GF.

THESAURUS MUSICARUM LATINARUM: Canon of Data Files

Author: Anonymous

Treatise: [Tractatus de musica]

Incipit: Musica est motus vocum rationabilium in arsim item thesim, idest inclinationem

File name: **ANOPHIL**   Data input by: Stephen E. Hayes

File type: **TEXT**   Data checked by: Peter M. Lefferts & Andreas Giger

MS: Print: **X**   Data approved by: Thomas J. Mathiesen

Filelist: 15th   File size: 19K   Annotations:

Source of data:

Andres Briner, "Ein anonymer unvollständiger Musiktraktat des 15. Jahrhunderts in Philadelphia, USA," Kirchenmusikalisches Jahrbuch 50 (1966): 27-38. Used by permission.

Based on Philadelphia, University of Pennsylvania, latin 36, ff. 207v-216v. The manuscript as a whole carries the date 1437 (on f. 58r). The graphics files for this treatise are ANOPHIL 01GF-ANOPHIL 05GF.

Author: Anonymous

Treatise: [Tractatus de musica]

Incipit: Pro themate presentis operis assummo Cassiodorum in quadam epistola

File name: **ANOPRO**   Data input by: Peter Slemon

File type: **TEXT**   Data checked by: Kirk Ditzler

MS: Print: **X**   Data approved by: Thomas J. Mathiesen

Filelist: 15th   File size: 18K   Annotations:

Source of data:

Dénes von Bartha, "Studien zum musikalischen Schrifttum des 15. Jahrhunderts," Archiv für Musikforschung 1 (1936): 180-99.

Based on Munich, Bayerische Staatsbibliothek, Clm 1573 (in the hand of U. Fugger).

Author: Anonymous

Treatise: [Tractatus de musica]

Incipit: Quoniam circa artem musicam necessaria quedam ad utilitatem cantantium tractare

File name: **LAMTRAC**   Data input by: Sandra Pinegar

File type: **MSBCLV30**   Data checked by: Michael W. Lundell

MS: **X** Print: Data approved by: Thomas J. Mathiesen

Filelist: 13th   File size: 79K   Annotations:

Source of data:

Siena, Biblioteca comunale, L.V.30, ff. 14r-32r.

=RISM BIII/2:120-23. The incipit is preceded by the heading "SANCTI. SPIRITVS. ADSIT. NOBIS. GRATIA." This treatise is now commonly ascribed to Magister Lambert. The graphics files for this treatise are LAMTRAC 01GF-LAMTRAC 12GF. Cf. ARITRA TEXT and BEDMUS TEXT.

Author: Anonymous

Treatise: [Tractatus de musica]

Incipit: Quoniam inter septem artes liberales primatum optinet musica. testante Boetio.

File name: **ANOTRAC**	Data input by: Charles Burnett & Michael Lundell
File type: **MCBOLT1**	Data checked by: Michael Lundell & Charles Burnett
MS: **X** Print:	Data approved by: Thomas J. Mathiesen
Filelist: 13th File size: 33K	Annotations:

Source of data:
Cashel (Tipperary), G. P. A. Bolton Library (formerly Cathedral Library), no. 1, 59-70.

Major sections of the text parallel ANOMUPO TEXT (the "Louvain Treatise") and ARSORG TEXT (the "Vatican Organum Treatise"). There are additional shorter parallels here and there throughout.

Author: Anonymous

Treatise: [Tractatus de organo]

Incipit: Diaphonia duplex cantus est; cuius talis est diffinitio. Organum est vox sequens

File name: **ANOMON**	Data input by: Bradley Jon Tucker
File type: **TEXT**	Data checked by: Peter Slemon
MS: Print: **X**	Data approved by: Thomas J. Mathiesen
Filelist: 12th File size: 4K	Annotations:

Source of data:
Jacques Handschin, "Der Organum-Traktat von Montpellier," in Studien zur Musikgeschichte. Festschrift für Guido Adler zum 75. Geburtstag (Wien: Universal, 1930), 50-51.

Based on Montpellier, Bibliothèque de l'Université, Section de Médecine, H 384, ff. 122-123. The treatise is sometimes known as the Handschin Anonymous. Cf. ANOMONT TEXT and ANOORG TEXT.

Author: Anonymous

Treatise: [Tractatus de organo]

Incipit: Diaphonia duplex cantus est. cuius talis est diffinitio. Organum est uox sequens

File name: **ANOMONT**	Data input by: Angela Mariani
File type: **TEXT**	Data checked by: Peter Slemon
MS: Print: **X**	Data approved by: Thomas J. Mathiesen
Filelist: 12th File size: 4K	Annotations:

Source of data:
Hans Heinrich Eggebrecht and Frieder Zaminer, eds., Ad organum faciendum. Lehrschriften der Mehrstimmigkeit in nachguidonischer Zeit, Neue Studien zur Musikwissenschaft, vol. 3 (Mainz: B. Schotts Söhne, 1970), 187-88.

Based on Montpellier, Bibliothèque de l'Université, Section de Médecine, H 384, ff. 122-123. The treatise is sometimes known as the Handschin Anonymous. Cf. ANOMON TEXT and ANOORG TEXT.

Author: Anonymous

Treatise: [Tractatus de organo]

Incipit: Diaphonia duplex cantus est; cuius talis est diffinitio. Organum est vox sequens

File name: **ANOORG**   Data input by: Stephen E. Hayes

File type: **TEXT**   Data checked by: Peter M. Lefferts & Andreas Giger

MS: Print: **X**   Data approved by: Thomas J. Mathiesen

Filelist: 12th   File size: 4K   Annotations:

Source of data:

Fred Blum, "Another Look at the Montpellier Organum Treatise," Musica disciplina 13 (1959): 21-24. Used by permission of the American Institute of Musicology (Tempo Music Publications, 3773 West 95th Street, Leawood, KS 66206).

Based on Montpellier, Bibliothèque de l'Université, Section de Médecine, H 384, ff. 122-123. The treatise is sometimes known as the Handschin Anonymous. The graphics file for this treatise is ANOORG 01GF. Cf. ANOMON TEXT and ANOMONT TEXT.

Author: Anonymous

Treatise: [Versus de musica]

Incipit: Dum Domino psalles. psallendo tu tria serves.

File name: **ANOVER**   Data input by: Andreas Giger

File type: **TEXT**   Data checked by: Andreas Giger

MS: Print: **X**   Data approved by: Thomas J. Mathiesen

Filelist: 12th   File size: 2K   Annotations:

Source of data:

S. A. van Dijk, "Saint Bernard and the Instituta Patrum of Saint Gall," Musica disciplina 4 (1950): 109. Used by permission of the American Institute of Musicology (Tempo Music Publications, 3773 West 95th Street, Leawood, KS 66206).

Based on Oxford, Corpus Christi College, D 44, f. 194r: "Rubrica de modo cantandi et psallendi divinum officium."

Author: Anonymous

Treatise: Ad organum faciendum

Incipit: Cum obscuritas diaphonia multis et perplurimum tardis in ingenio difficultatem

File name: **ADORF**   Data input by: Angela Mariani

File type: **TEXT**   Data checked by: Benito V. Rivera

MS: Print: **X**   Data approved by: Thomas J. Mathiesen

Filelist: 9th-11th   File size: 19K   Annotations:

Source of data:

Jay A. Huff, ed. and trans., Ad organum faciendum et Item de organo, Musical Theorists in Translation, vol. 8 (Brooklyn, NY: Institute of Mediaeval Music, Ltd., [1963]), 41-67 (odd). Used by permission.

Commonly known as the Milan organum treatise, which is based on Milan, Biblioteca Ambrosiana M.17.sup. Cf. ADORFA TEXT, ADORFAC TEXT, ADORFBA TEXT, ADORFBB TEXT, and ADORFBR TEXT.

Author: Anonymous

Treatise: Ad organum faciendum

Incipit: Cum obscuritas diaphoniae multis et perplurimum tardis ingenio difficultatem praestet

File name: **ADORFA**

File type: **TEXT**

MS: Print: **X**

Filelist: 9th-11th File size: 12K

Data input by: Stephen E. Hayes

Data checked by: Peter Lefferts & Luminita Aluas

Data approved by: Thomas J. Mathiesen

Source of data:

Edmond de Coussemaker, Histoire de l'harmonie au moyen-age (Paris: V. Didron, 1852), 226-43.

Annotations:

Commonly known as the Milan organum treatise (Document I in the Coussemaker Histoire), which is based on Milan, Biblioteca Ambrosiana M.17.sup. The treatise proper is preceded by musical examples on the texts "Cunctipotens genitor," "Benedicamus domino," and "Hoc sit vobis iter." The graphics files for this treatise are ADORFA 01GF-ADORFA 05GF. Cf. ADORF TEXT, ADORFAC TEXT, ADORFBA TEXT, ADORFBB TEXT, and ADORFBR TEXT.

Author: Anonymous

Treatise: Ad organum faciendum

Incipit: Cum obscuritas diaphonie multis et perplurimum tardis in ingenio difficultatem prestet

File name: **ADORFAC**

File type: **TEXT**

MS: Print: **X**

Filelist: 9th-11th File size: 13K

Data input by: Angela Mariani

Data checked by: Bradley Jon Tucker

Data approved by: Thomas J. Mathiesen

Source of data:

Hans Heinrich Eggebrecht and Frieder Zaminer, eds., Ad organum faciendum. Lehrschriften der Mehrstimmigkeit in nachguidonischer Zeit, Neue Studien zur Musikwissenschaft, vol. 3 (Mainz: B. Schotts Söhne, 1970), 45-49 and 111-15.

Annotations:

Commonly known as the Milan organum treatise, which is based on Milan, Biblioteca Ambrosiana M.17.sup. The treatise proper is preceded by musical examples on the texts "Cunctipotens genitor," "Benedicamus domino," and "Hoc sit vobis iter." The graphics files for this treatise are ADORFAC 01GF-ADORFAC 03GF. Cf. ADORF TEXT, ADORFA TEXT, ADORFBA TEXT, ADORFBB TEXT, and ADORFBR TEXT.

Author: Anonymous

Treatise: Alia musica

Incipit: De harmonica consideratione Boetius ita disseruit quia neque solum in terminis

File name: **ALIMU**

File type: **TEXT**

MS: Print: **X**

Data input by: Jingfa Sun

Data checked by: Andreas Giger

Data approved by: Thomas J. Mathiesen

Filelist: 9th-11th File size: 72K

Source of data:

Patrologia cursus completus, series latina, ed. J. P. Migne, 221 vols. (Paris: Garnier, 1844-1904), 132:929-58.

Annotations:

In this version, the treatise concludes with three additional sections: "De mensuris organicarum fistularum," "De cymbalorum ponderibus," and "De quinque symphoniis." These probably do not form a part of the Alia musica, which is devoted to modal theory. Gerbert (followed in this edition) included all these texts as part of Hucbald's Musica (see HUCHAR TEXT), but they are now commonly considered anonymous. The graphics files for this treatise are ALIMU 01GF-ALIMU 02GF. Cf. ALIMUS TEXT and ALIMUSI TEXT.

Author: Anonymous

Treatise: Alia musica

Incipit: De harmonica consideratione Boetius ita disseruit: quia neque solum in terminis

File name: **ALIMUS**

File type: **TEXT**

MS: Print: **X**

Data input by: Stephen E. Hayes

Data checked by: Peter Lefferts & Bradley Tucker

Data approved by: Thomas J. Mathiesen

Filelist: 9th-11th File size: 73K

Source of data:

Scriptores ecclesiastici de musica sacra potissimum, 3 vols., ed. Martin Gerbert (St. Blaise: Typis San-Blasianis, 1784; reprint ed., Hildesheim: Olms, 1963), 1:125-52.

Annotations:

In this version, the treatise concludes with three additional sections: "De mensuris organicarum fistularum," "De cymbalorum ponderibus," "De modis," and "De quinque symphoniis." These probably do not form a part of the Alia musica, which is devoted to modal theory. Gerbert included all these texts as part of Hucbald's Musica (see HUCHAR TEXT), but they are now commonly considered anonymous. The graphics files for this treatise are ALIMUS 01GF-ALIMUS 03GF. Cf. ALIMU TEXT, ALIMUSI TEXT, and ALIAMU TEXT.

Author: Anonymous

Treatise: Alia musica

Incipit: De harmonica consideratione Boetius ita disseruit: quia neque solum in terminis

File name: **ALIMUSI**

File type: **TEXT**

MS: Print: **X**

Data input by: Nigel Gwee

Data checked by: Kirk Ditzler

Data approved by: Thomas J. Mathiesen

Filelist: 9th-11th File size: 64K

Source of data:

Edmund Brooks Heard, "Alia musica: A Chapter in the History of Music Theory" (Ph.D. dissertation, University of Wisconsin, 1966), 119-229 (odd only).

Annotations:

Cf. ALIMU TEXT, ALIMUS TEXT, and ALIAMU TEXT.

Author: Anonymous

Treatise: Alia musica

Incipit: Tonus primus NONANOEANE, qui graece dicitur autentos protos

File name: **ALIAMU**   Data input by: Steven E. Hayes

File type: **TEXT**   Data checked by: Peter Lefferts & Andreas Giger

MS: Print: **X**   Data approved by: Thomas J. Mathiesen

Filelist: 9th-11th   File size: 69K   Annotations:

Source of data:

Jacques Chailley, ed., Alia musica (Traité de musique du IXe siècle): Edition critique commentée avec une introduction sur l'origine de la nomenclature modale pseudo-grecque au Moyen-Age (Paris: Centre de documentation universitaire et Société d'édition d'enseignement supérieur réunis, 1965), 85-88, 90-97, 99-111, 113-18, 120-30, 133-45, 147-74, 176-81, and 183-212. Used by permission.

This edition presents the treatise in three sections: a "First Quidam," beginning on p. 85 with the incipit shown above; a "Principal Treatise," beginning on p. 95 "De harmonica consideratione Boetius ita disseruit"; and a "Second Quidam (Nova expositio)," beginning on p. 183 "A prima quoque specie diapason quae est mese." The graphics file for this treatise is ALIAMU 01GF. Cf. ALIMU TEXT, ALIMUS TEXT, and ALIMUSI TEXT.

Author: Anonymous

Treatise: Ars cantus mensurabilis mensurata per modos iuris

Incipit: "Cantabo Domino in vita mea." Pro huius, opusculi mei humilis, intentione tria oportet

File name: **ANO5ACM**   Data input by: C. Matthew Balensuela

File type: **TEXT**   Data checked by: Andreas Giger

MS: Print: **X**   Data approved by: Thomas J. Mathiesen

Filelist: 14th   File size: 57K   Annotations:

Source of data:

Ars cantus mensurabilis mensurata per modos iuris, ed. and trans. C. Matthew Balensuela, Greek and Latin Music Theory, vol. 10 (Lincoln: University of Nebraska Press, 1994), 124-258 (even-numbered pages only). Used by permission.

The graphics files for this treatise are ANO5ACM 01GF-ANO5ACM 08GF. Cf. ANO5ARS TEXT.

Author: Anonymous

Treatise: Ars et modus pulsandi organa secundum modum novissimum inventum per

Incipit: Nota quod omnes uoces totius organi tam toni quam semitoni possunt esse

File name: **ANOAMP**   Data input by: John Gray

File type: **TEXT**   Data checked by: Oliver Ellsworth & Andreas Giger

MS: Print: **X**   Data approved by: Thomas J. Mathiesen

Filelist: 14th   File size: 4K   Annotations:

Source of data:

R. Casimiri, "Un trattatello per organisti di anonimo del sec. XIV," Note d'archivio per la storia musicale 19 (1942): 100-101.

The incipit is preceded by a line of notation given as the following series of letters: C.D.E.F.G.Abh.C.+D.+E.F.+ G.+A.bh.C.+D.+E.F.÷G.+A.bh.C.+D.

Author: Anonymous

Treatise: Ars mensurandi motetos

Incipit: Sex sunt species principales sive concordantie discantus: unisonus, semiditonus

File name: **ANOARS**

File type: **TEXT**

MS: Print: **X**

Filelist: 14th File size: 14K

Source of data:
 Philippi de Vitriaco Ars nova, ed. Gilbert Reaney, André Gilles, and Jean Maillard, Corpus scriptorum de musica, vol. 8 ([Rome]: American Institute of Musicology, 1964), 55-69. Used by permission.

Data input by: Stephen E. Hayes

Data checked by: Peter Lefferts & Luminita Aluas

Data approved by: Thomas J. Mathiesen

Annotations:
 The text was first published in Musica disciplina 10 (1956): 38-52 (even only).

Author: Anonymous

Treatise: Ars musica

Incipit: Huius artis (musicae) experienciam querere cupientibus a figuram manus inchoandum

File name: **METANO3**

File type: **TEXT**

MS: Print: **X**

Filelist: 13th File size: 25K

Source of data:
 Dominicus Mettenleiter, Musikgeschichte der Stadt Regensburg (Regensburg: J. G. Bössenecker, 1866), 70-78 partim.

Data input by: Angela Mariani

Data checked by: Bradley Jon Tucker

Data approved by: Thomas J. Mathiesen

Annotations:
 The treatise is preceded by a dedicatory prologue, beginning: "Reverentissimo domino patri.... ratysponensi episcopo subditorum humillimus ...." Based on Munich, Bayerische Staatsbibliothek, Clm 5539. Cf. ANOARSMU TEXT.

Author: Anonymous

Treatise: Ars musica

Incipit: Quatuor ut reges infra sua regna sedentes;

File name: **ANOFRA6**

File type: **TEXT**

MS: Print: **X**

Filelist: 13th File size: 2K

Source of data:
 Adrien de la Fage, Essais de dipthérographie musicale (Paris: Legouix, 1864), 483-84.

Data input by: John Csonka

Data checked by: Jan Herlinger & Angela Mariani

Data approved by: Thomas J. Mathiesen

Annotations:
 Based on Rome, Biblioteca Apostolica Vaticana, lat. 4357.

Author: Anonymous

Treatise: Ars musicae mensurabilis secundum Franconem

Incipit: Figura est repraesentatio vocis in aliquo modorum ordinatae.

File name: **ANOFIG**	Data input by: Stephen E. Hayes
File type: **TEXT**	Data checked by: Peter Lefferts & Bradley Tucker
MS:　　　Print: **X**	Data approved by: Thomas J. Mathiesen

Filelist: 13th　　　File size: 8K

Source of data:

Petrus Picardus, Ars motettorum compilata breviter, ed. F. Alberto Gallo; Anonymus, Ars musicae mensurabilis secundum Franconem (Mss. Paris, Bibl. Nat., lat. 15129; Uppsala, Universiteitsbibl., C 55), ed. Gilbert Reaney and André Gilles; Anonymus, Compendium musicae mensurabilis artis antiquae (Ms. Faenza, Biblioteca Comunale 117), ed. F. Alberto Gallo, Corpus scriptorum de musica, vol. 15 ([Rome]: American Institute of Musicology, 1971), 38-54 (even). Used by permission.

Annotations:

The graphics files for this treatise are ANOFIG 01GF-ANOFIG 04GF. See also ANOQUA (including, however, only pp. 274-83).

Author: Anonymous

Treatise: Ars musicae mensurabilis secundum Franconem

Incipit: Mensurabilis musica est cantus longis brevibusque temporibus mensuratus.

File name: **ANOARSM**	Data input by: Stephen E. Hayes
File type: **TEXT**	Data checked by: Peter Lefferts & Bradley Tucker
MS:　　　Print: **X**	Data approved by: Thomas J. Mathiesen

Filelist: 13th　　　File size: 8K

Source of data:

Petrus Picardus, Ars motettorum compilata breviter, ed. F. Alberto Gallo; Anonymus, Ars musicae mensurabilis secundum Franconem (Mss. Paris, Bibl. Nat., lat. 15129; Uppsala, Universiteitsbibl., C 55), ed. Gilbert Reaney and André Gilles; Anonymus, Compendium musicae mensurabilis artis antiquae (Ms. Faenza, Biblioteca Comunale 117), ed. F. Alberto Gallo, Corpus scriptorum de musica, vol. 15 ([Rome]: American Institute of Musicology, 1971), 39-53 (odd). Used by permission.

Annotations:

Based on Uppsala, Universiteitsbibl., C 55. The graphics file for this treatise is ANOARSM 01GF.

Author: Anonymous

Treatise: Ars musice

Incipit: Musica est vna de septem artibus, quas liberales appelamus

File name: **ANOAM**　　Data input by: Mchael W. Lundell

File type: **TEXT**　　Data checked by: Andreas Giger

　MS:　　　Print: **X**　　Data approved by: Thomas J. Mathiesen

Filelist: 15th　　File size: 5K　　Annotations:

Source of data:　　　　　　　　　　Based on Barcelona, Biblioteca Central de la
Karl-Werner Gümpel, "Zur　　　　　Disputación Provincial, M. 1327, ff. lxxi-lxxii.
Frühgeschichte der vulgärsprachlichen
spanischen und katalanischen
Musiktheorie," in Gesammelte Aufsätze
zur Kulturgeschichte Spaniens, ed.
Johannes Vincke, Spanische Forschungen
der Görresgesellschaft, I/24 (Münster:
Aschendorff, 1968), 326-29.

Author: Anonymous

Treatise: Ars musice

Incipit: Quatuor ecce tropi natura matre creati

File name: **WFANON2**　　Data input by: Bradley Jon Tucker

File type: **TEXT**　　Data checked by: Angela Mariani

　MS:　　　Print: **X**　　Data approved by: Thomas J. Mathiesen

Filelist: 12th　　File size: 4K　　Annotations:

Source of data:　　　　　　　　　　The text is preceded by a circular diagram (see
Johannes Wolf, "Anonymi cujusdam　　WFANON2 01GF) illustrating the ethical
Codex Basiliensis," Vierteljahresschrift　　character of the church modes.
für Musikwissenschaft 9 (1893): 410-12.

Author: Anonymous

Treatise: Ars organi

Incipit: Organum est cantus subsequens precedentem, quia cantor debet precedere

File name: **ARSORG**　　Data input by: Angela Mariani

File type: **TEXT**　　Data checked by: Benito V. Rivera

　MS:　　　Print: **X**　　Data approved by: Thomas J. Mathiesen

Filelist: 12th　　File size: 12K　　Annotations:

Source of data:　　　　　　　　　　The graphics files for this treatise are
Irving Godt and Benito V. Rivera, "The　　ARSORG 01GF-ARSORG 50GF.
Vatican Organum Treatise: A Color
Reproduction, Transcription, and
Translation," in Gordon Athol Anderson
(1929-1981) in memoriam von seinen
Studenten, Freunden und Kollegen, 2
vols. (Henryville, PA: Institute of
Mediaeval Music, Ltd., 1984),
2:293-345/11. Used by permission.

THESAURUS MUSICARUM LATINARUM: Canon of Data Files

Author: Anonymous

Treatise: Berkeley Manuscript

Incipit: Quoniam in antelapsis temporibus quamplures de cantibus

File name: **BERMAN**	Data input by: Oliver B. Ellsworth
File type: **TEXT**	Data checked by: Matthew Balensuela & Alice Clark
MS: Print: **X**	Data approved by: Margaret Bent

Filelist: 14th   File size: 92K   Annotations:

Source of data:

The Berkeley Manuscript, ed. and trans. by Oliver B. Ellsworth, Greek and Latin Music Theory, vol. 2 (Lincoln: University of Nebraska Press, 1984), 30-246. Used by permission.

The graphics files for this treatise are BERMAN 01GF-BERMAN 24GF.

Author: Anonymous

Treatise: Cartula de cantu plano

Incipit: Et dixit <Guido>: Qui nescit palmam, in uanum tendit ad musicam.

File name: **ANOCAR**	Data input by: Andreas Giger
File type: **TEXT**	Data checked by: Elisabeth Honn
MS: Print: **X**	Data approved by: Thomas J. Mathiesen

Filelist: 14th   File size: 5K   Annotations:

Source of data:

Karl-Werner Gümpel, "Gregorianischer Gesang und Musica ficta: Bemerkungen zur spanischen Musiklehre des 15. Jahrhunderts," Archiv für Musikwissenschaft 47 (1990): 144-47. Used by permission.

Based on Barcelona, Biblioteca de Catalunya, M. 883, ff. 70v-71v. The graphics file for this treatise is ANOCAR 01GF.

Author: Anonymous

Treatise: Cologne Organum Treatise

Incipit: Diaphoniam seu organum constat ex diatessaron symphonia naturaliter dirivari.

File name: **COLORG**	Data input by: Bradley Jon Tucker
File type: **TEXT**	Data checked by: Angela Mariani
MS: Print: **X**	Data approved by: Thomas J. Mathiesen

Filelist: 9th-11th   File size: 2K   Annotations:

Source of data:

Hans Müller, ed., Hucbalds echte und unechte Schriften über Musik (Leipzig: B. G. Teubner, 1884), 79-80.

This treatise is sometimes cited as Müller's Anonymous I. Cf. COLORGR TEXT and COLORGS TEXT.

Author: Anonymous

Treatise: Cologne Organum Treatise

Incipit: Diaphoniam seu organum constat ex diatessaron symphonia naturaliter derivari.

File name: **COLORGS** Data input by: Andreas Giger

File type: **TEXT** Data checked by: Elisabeth Honn

MS: Print: **X** Data approved by: Thomas J. Mathiesen

Filelist: 9th-11th File size: 3K Annotations:

Source of data:

Hans Schmid, ed., Musica et scholica enchiriadis una cum aliquibus tractatulis adiunctis, Bayerische Akademie der Wissenschaften, Veröffentlichungen der Musikhistorischen Kommission, Band 3 (München: Bayerische Akademie der Wissenschaften; C. H. Beck, 1981), 222-23. Used by permission.

This treatise is sometimes cited as Müller's Anonymous I. Cf. COLORG TEXT and COLÓRGR TEXT.

Author: Anonymous

Treatise: Cologne Organum Treatise

Incipit: Diaphoniam seu organum constat (!) ex diatessaron symphonia naturaliter derivari.

File name: **COLORGR** Data input by: Bradley Jon Tucker

File type: **TEXT** Data checked by: Angela Mariani

MS: Print: **X** Data approved by: Thomas J. Mathiesen

Filelist: 9th-11th File size: 2K Annotations:

Source of data:

Hugo Riemann, Geschichte der Musiktheorie im IX.-XIX. Jahrhundert (Berlin: Hesse, 1898), 20.

This treatise is sometimes cited as Müller's Anonymous I. The Latin text is also reproduced in Hugo Riemann, History of Music Theory, Books I and II: Polyphonic Theory to the Sixteenth Century, trans., with preface, commentary, and notes by Raymond H. Haggh (Lincoln: University of Nebraska Press, 1966; reprint ed., New York: Da Capo, 1974), 13. Cf. COLORG TEXT and COLORGS TEXT.

Author: Anonymous

Treatise: Commemoratio brevis de tonis et psalmis modulandis

Incipit: Debitum servitutis nostrae, qui ad ministerium laudationis deputamur, non solum

File name: **ANOCOMB** Data input by: Stephen E. Hayes

File type: **TEXT** Data checked by: Peter Lefferts & Bradley Tucker

MS: Print: **X** Data approved by: Thomas J. Mathiesen

Filelist: 9th-11th File size: 22K Annotations:

Source of data:

Scriptores ecclesiastici de musica sacra potissimum, 3 vols., ed. Martin Gerbert (St. Blaise: Typis San-Blasianis, 1784; reprint ed., Hildesheim: Olms, 1963), 1:213-29.

Gerbert ascribed the treatise to Hucbald, but the attribution is no longer generally accepted. The graphics files for this treatise are ANOCOMB 01GF-ANOCOMB 14GF. Cf. ANOCOBR TEXT.

Author: Anonymous

Treatise: Commemoratio brevis de tonis et psalmis modulandis

Incipit: Debitum servitutis nostrae, qui ad ministerium laudationis deputamur, non solum

File name: **ANOCOBR**   Data input by: Stephen E. Hayes

File type: **TEXT**   Data checked by: Peter Slemon & Angela Mariani

MS: Print: **X**   Data approved by: Thomas J. Mathiesen

Filelist: 9th-11th File size: 23K   Annotations:

Source of data:
Patrologia cursus completus, series latina, ed. J. P. Migne, 221 vols. (Paris: Garnier, 1844-1904), 132:1025-42.

The graphics files for this treatise are ANOCOBR 01GF-ANOCOBR 08GF. Cf. ANOCOMB TEXT.

Author: Anonymous

Treatise: Commentarius in Micrologum Guidonis Aretini

Incipit: Micros graece, brevis latine; logos sermo, inde micrologus Guidonis

File name: **GUICOM**   Data input by: Laurel Carter & Luminita Aluas

File type: **TEXT**   Data checked by: Thomas J. Mathiesen

MS: Print: **X**   Data approved by: Oliver B. Ellsworth

Filelist: 12th   File size: 136K   Annotations:

Source of data:
Commentarius anonymus in Micrologum Guidonis Aretini, ed. P. Cölestin Vivell, O.S.B., Kais. Akademie der Wissenschaften in Wien, philosophisch-historische Klasse, Sitzungsberichte, 185/5 (Wien: Hölder, 1917).

Author: Anonymous

Treatise: Commentum super tonos

Incipit: Dilectissimo coepiscopo e., a. divina gratia dispensante episcopus.

File name: **ANOCST**   Data input by: Andreas Giger

File type: **TEXT**   Data checked by: Elisabeth Honn

MS: Print: **X**   Data approved by: Thomas J. Mathiesen

Filelist: 9th-11th File size: 24K   Annotations:

Source of data:
De numero tonorum litterae episcopi A. ad coepiscopum E. missae ac Commentum super tonos episcopi E. (ad 1000), ed. Joseph Smits van Waesberghe, Divitiae musicae artis, A/I (Buren: Knuf, 1975), 24-93 (even pages only). Used by kind permission of the Laaber-Verlag.

Based on Naples, Biblioteca nazionale, VIII D 14, ff. 19r-40v. The graphics files for this treatise are ANOCST 01GF-ANOCST 19GF. See also ANOCSTO.

Author: Anonymous

Treatise: Commentum super tonos

Incipit: Dilectissimo coepiscopo e., a. dispensante divina gratia episcopus.

File name: **ANOCSTO**	Data input by: Andreas Giger
File type: **TEXT**	Data checked by: Elisabeth Honn
MS: Print: **X**	Data approved by: Thomas J. Mathiesen

Filelist: 9th-11th File size: 15K

Source of data:

De numero tonorum litterae episcopi A. ad coepiscopum E. missae ac Commentum super tonos episcopi E. (ad 1000), ed. Joseph Smits van Waesberghe, Divitiae musicae artis, A/I (Buren: Knuf, 1975), 24-93 (odd pages only). Used by kind permission of the Laaber-Verlag.

Annotations:

Based on Berlin, Staatsbibliothek Preussischer Kulturbesitz, lat. 8vo 265, ff. 1v-8r. See also ANOCST.

Author: Anonymous

Treatise: Compendium breve artis musicae

Incipit: Gaudent breuitate moderni. Quandoque punctus quadratus, aut nota quadrata

File name: **ANOCBA**	Data input by: Sandra Pinegar
File type: **MBAV5320**	Data checked by: Michael W. Lundell
MS: **X** Print:	Data approved by: Thomas J. Mathiesen

Filelist: 13th   File size: 8K

Source of data:

Rome, Bibliotheca Apostolica Vaticana, lat. 5320, ff. 80r-83v.

Annotations:

=RISM BIII/2:98. The date 1476 appears at the end of the treatise in this manuscript. Cf. ANOCMM TEXT, ANOCOM TEXT, ANOCOMM TEXT, ANOTDD TEXT, ANO2TRA TEXT, ANO3DEC TEXT, BALABM TEXT, and BALABR TEXT.

Author: Anonymous

Treatise: Compendium musicae mensurabilis artis antiquae

Incipit: Gaudent brevitate moderni. Quandocumque nota quadrata vel punctus quadratus

File name: **ANOCMM**	Data input by: Peter Slemon
File type: **TEXT**	Data checked by: Bradley Jon Tucker
MS: Print: **X**	Data approved by: Thomas J. Mathiesen

Filelist: 13th   File size: 11K

Source of data:

Johannes dictus Balloce, Abreviatio magistri Franconis; Anonymus, Compendium musicae mensurabilis artis antiquae (Ms. Saint-Dié, Bibl. Municipale, 42), ed. Gilbert Reaney; Anonymus, Compendium musicae mensurabilis artis antiquae (Ms. Wien, Nationalbibl., 5003); Anonymus, Tractatus artis antiquae cum explicatione mensurae binariae (Ms. Wien, Nationalbibl., 5003), ed. Heinz Ristory, Corpus scriptorum de musica, vol. 34 (n.p.: American Institute of Musicology, 1987), 27-36. Used by permission.

Annotations:

Based on Saint-Dié, Bibliothèque Municipale, 42. The graphics file for this treatise is ANOCMM 01GF. Cf. ANOCOM TEXT, ANOCOMM TEXT, ANOTDD TEXT, ANO2TRA TEXT, ANO3DEC TEXT, BALABM TEXT, and BALABR TEXT.

Author: Anonymous

Treatise: Compendium musicae mensurabilis artis antiquae

Incipit: Gaudent brevitate moderni. Quandocumque punctus quadratus vel nota quadrata

File name: **ANOCOM**   Data input by: Stephen E. Hayes

File type: **TEXT**   Data checked by: Peter Lefferts & Bradley Tucker

MS: Print: **X**   Data approved by: Thomas J. Mathiesen

Filelist: 13th   File size: 12K   Annotations:

Source of data:

Petrus Picardus, Ars motettorum compilata breviter, ed. F. Alberto Gallo; Anonymus, Ars musicae mensurabilis secundum Franconem (Mss. Paris, Bibl. Nat., lat. 15129; Uppsala, Universiteitsbibl., C 55), ed. Gilbert Reaney and André Gilles; Anonymus, Compendium musicae mensurabilis artis antiquae (Ms. Faenza, Biblioteca Comunale 117), ed. F. Alberto Gallo, Corpus scriptorum de musica, vol. 15 ([Rome]: American Institute of Musicology, 1971), 66-72. Used by permission.

Also known as the Faenza Anonymous. The graphics file for this treatise is ANOCOM 01GF. Cf. ANOCOMM TEXT, ANOCMM TEXT, ANOTDD TEXT, ANO2TRA TEXT, ANO3DEC TEXT, BALABM TEXT, and BALABR TEXT.

Author: Anonymous

Treatise: Compendium musicae mensurabilis artis antiquae

Incipit: Gaudent brevitate moderni. Quandocumque nota quadrata vel punctus quadratus

File name: **ANOCOMM**   Data input by: Peter Slemon

File type: **TEXT**   Data checked by: Andreas Giger

MS: Print: **X**   Data approved by: Thomas J. Mathiesen

Filelist: 13th   File size: 11K   Annotations:

Source of data:

Johannes dictus Balloce, Abreviatio magistri Franconis; Anonymus, Compendium musicae mensurabilis artis antiquae (Ms. Saint-Dié, Bibl. Municipale, 42), ed. Gilbert Reaney; Anonymus, Compendium musicae mensurabilis artis antiquae (Ms. Wien, Nationalbibl., 5003); Anonymus, Tractatus artis antiquae cum explicatione mensurae binariae (Ms. Wien, Nationalbibl., 5003), ed. Heinz Ristory, Corpus scriptorum de musica, vol. 34 (n.p.: American Institute of Musicology, 1987), 49-58. Used by permission.

Based on Vienna, Nationalbibliothek, 5003. The graphics files for this treatise are ANOCOMM 01GF-ANOCOMM 02GF. Cf. ANOCOM TEXT, ANOCMM TEXT, ANOTDD TEXT, ANO2TRA TEXT, ANO3DEC TEXT, BALABM TEXT, and BALABR TEXT.

Author: Anonymous
Treatise: Compendium musicae mensurabilis tam veteris quam novae artis
Incipit: Si quis artem musicae mensurabilis tam veterem quam novam

File name: **ANO4CMM**   Data input by: Peter Slemon
File type: **TEXT**   Data checked by: Andreas Giger
  MS: Print: **X**   Data approved by: Thomas J. Mathiesen
Filelist: 15th   File size: 11K   Annotations:

Source of data:
Anonymus de valore notvlarum tam veteris qvam novae artis (Ms. Paris, Bibl. Nat., lat. 15128); Anonymus compendium mvsicae mensvrabilis tam veteris qvam novae artis (Ms. Paris, Bibl. Nat., lat. 15128); Anonymus de diversis maneriebvs in mvsica mensvrabili (Ms. Saint-Dié, Bibl. Municipale 42), ed. Gilbert Reaney, Corpus scriptorum de musica, vol. 30 (n.p.: American Institute of Musicology, 1982), 33-41. Used by permission.

Based on Paris, Bibliothèque Nationale, lat. 15128. The graphics file for this treatise is ANO4CMM 01GF. Cf. ANO4COM TEXT.

Author: Anonymous
Treatise: Compendium musices
Incipit: Proprietas in musica est derivatio plurium vocum, ab uno eodemque principio.

File name: **ANOCMU**   Data input by: Peter Slemon
File type: **TEXT**   Data checked by: Angela Mariani
  MS: Print: **X**   Data approved by: Thomas J. Mathiesen
Filelist: 16th   File size: 31K   Annotations:

Source of data:
Anonymus, Compendium musices, Venetiis, 1499-1597, ed. David Crawford, Corpus scriptorum de musica, vol. 33 (n.p.: American Institute of Musicology, 1985), 36-57. Used by permission.

Based on the 1513 edition published in Venice by Lucantonio Giunta. The graphics files for this treatise are ANOCMU 01GF-ANOCMU 12GF.

Author: Anonymous
Treatise: Compendium totius artis motetorum
Incipit: Primo punctus quadratus vel nota quadrata est duplex, vel est caudatus vel non.

File name: **WFANON3**   Data input by: Stephen E. Hayes
File type: **TEXT**   Data checked by: Peter Lefferts & Luminita Aluas
  MS: Print: **X**   Data approved by: Thomas J. Mathiesen
Filelist: 14th   File size: 12K   Annotations:

Source of data:
Johannes Wolf, "Ein anonymer Musiktraktat aus der ersten Zeit der 'Ars Nova,'" Kirchenmusikalisches Jahrbuch 21 (1908): 34-38.

Commonly known as Wolf's Anonymous 3; based on Erfurt, Wissenschaftliche Allgemeinbibliothek octavo 94. The graphics file for this treatise is WFANON3 01GF.

Author: Anonymous

Treatise: Constitutiones capellae pontificiae

Incipit: Pauli III. Pontificis maximi anno undecimo 1545. Cantorum pontificii systematis

File name: **ANOCON**
File type: **TEXT**
MS:　　　　Print: **X**
Filelist: 16th　　　File size: 43K

Data input by: Bradley Jon Tucker
Data checked by: Benito V. Rivera
Data approved by: Thomas J. Mathiesen

Source of data:
Scriptores ecclesiastici de musica sacra potissimum, 3 vols., ed. Martin Gerbert (St. Blaise: Typis San-Blasianis, 1784; reprint ed., Hildesheim: Olms, 1963), 3:382-96.

Annotations:
"Communicavit mecum qui hodie Capellae pontificiae praeest Iosephus Santarelli."

Author: Anonymous

Treatise: Contrapunctus

Incipit: Quoniam homine senescente senescunt et ea, que hominis sunt, et deteriorantur

File name: **ANOVIC**
File type: **TEXT**
MS:　　　　Print: **X**
Filelist: 15th　　　File size: 9K

Data input by: Elisabeth Honn
Data checked by: Andreas Giger
Data approved by: Thomas J. Mathiesen

Source of data:
Karl-Werner Gümpel and Klaus-Jürgen Sachs, "Der anonyme Contrapunctus-Traktat aus Ms. Vich 208," Archiv für Musikwissenschaft 31 (1974): 93-97. Used by permission.

Annotations:
Based on Vich (Catalonia), Museo Episcopal, 208 (Inv. Nr. 7977), ff. 3r-8r.

Author: Anonymous

Treatise: De arte discantandi

Incipit: Quando duae notae sunt in unisono et tertia ascendit, prima debet esse in quinto

File name: **ARTDIS**
File type: **TEXT**
MS:　　　　Print: **X**
Filelist: 13th　　　File size: 11K

Data input by: Stephen E. Hayes
Data checked by: Peter M. Lefferts
Data approved by: Thomas J. Mathiesen

Source of data:
Edmond de Coussemaker, Histoire de l'harmonie au moyen-age (Paris: V. Didron, 1852), 262-73.

Annotations:
Document V in the Coussemaker Histoire; based on Paris, Bibliothèque Nationale, lat. 15139. The graphics file for this treatise is ARTDIS 01GF.

Author: Anonymous

Treatise: De arte musicae

Incipit: Quoniam per ignorantiam artis musicae multi, et maxime temporibus modernis

File name: **ANOART**

File type: **TEXT**

MS: Print: **X**

Filelist: 14th   File size: 14K

Data input by: Stephen E. Hayes

Data checked by: Peter Lefferts & Luminita Aluas

Data approved by: Thomas J. Mathiesen

Annotations:

Source of data:
Philippi de Vitriaco Ars nova, ed. Gilbert Reaney, André Gilles, and Jean Maillard, Corpus scriptorum de musica, vol. 8 ([Rome]: American Institute of Musicology, 1964), 84-93. Used by permission.

The graphics file for this treatise is ANOART 01GF. The text was first published in Musica disciplina 15 (1961): 29-38. Cf. ANO3COM TEXT.

Author: Anonymous

Treatise: De cantibus quae supra modum intenduntur vel remittuntur

Incipit: In defectionibus hujusmodi solet necessario synemenon in superibus aliquando

File name: **ANOCAN**

File type: **TEXT**

MS: Print: **X**

Filelist: 9th-11th File size: 4K

Data input by: John Csonka

Data checked by: Bradley Jon Tucker

Data approved by: Thomas J. Mathiesen

Annotations:

Source of data:
Adrien de la Fage, Essais de dipthérographie musicale (Paris: Legouix, 1864), 87-89.

Based on Rome, Biblioteca Vallicelliana, B.81. The anonymous fragment is followed by a brief excerpt beginning: "Primus tonus; primus hemitonius; ultimus."

Author: Anonymous

Treatise: De cantu organico

Incipit: Ad evidentiam cantus organici est sciendum, quod cantus organicus dividitur

File name: **AGANOCO**

File type: **TEXT**

MS: Print: **X**

Filelist: 14th   File size: 14K

Data input by: Stephen E. Hayes

Data checked by: Peter Lefferts & Luminita Aluas

Data approved by: Thomas J. Mathiesen

Annotations:

Source of data:
H. Angles, "De cantu organico: tratado de un autor catalán del siglo XIV," Anuario musical 13 (1958): 18-24.

Sometimes known as Angles Anonymous 1958; based on Barcelona, Catedral, cuaderno de papel in octavo. The graphics files for this treatise are AGANOCO 01GF-AGANOCO 02GF.

Author: Anonymous

Treatise: De diversis manieribus in musica mensurabili

Incipit: ... ascendo vel descendo, ut hic supra. Sic formantur breves plicatae

File name: **ANO7DDM**   Data input by: Peter Slemon

File type: **TEXT**   Data checked by: Andreas Giger

  MS: Print: **X**   Data approved by: Thomas J. Mathiesen

Filelist: 14th   File size: 11K   Annotations:

Source of data:

Anonymus de valore notvlarum tam veteris qvam novae artis (Ms. Paris, Bibl. Nat., lat. 15128); Anonymus compendium mvsicae mensvrabilis tam veteris qvam novae artis (Ms. Paris, Bibl. Nat., lat. 15128); Anonymus de diversis maneriebvs in mvsica mensvrabili (Ms. Saint-Dié, Bibl. Municipale 42), ed. Gilbert Reaney, Corpus scriptorum de musica, vol. 30 (n.p.: American Institute of Musicology, 1982), 51-62. Used by permission.

Based on Saint-Dié, Bibliothèque Municipale, 42. The graphics file for this treatise is ANO7DDM 01GF. Cf. ANO7DED TEXT.

Author: Anonymous

Treatise: De divisione monacordi

Incipit: Dicendum est de prolacione proporcionis per divisionem monacordi

File name: **ANODIV**   Data input by: Peter M. Lefferts

File type: **MOBB842**   Data checked by: Michael W. Lundell

  MS: **X**   Print: Data approved by: Thomas J. Mathiesen

Filelist: 14th   File size: 3K   Annotations:

Source of data:

Oxford, Bodleian Library, Bodley 842 (S.C. 2575), f. 47r-v.

=RISM BIII/4:110-15. The graphics file for this treatise is ANODIV 01GF.

Author: Anonymous

Treatise: De expositione musice

Incipit: Quoniam prosam artis musice mensurabilis ab excellentibus in arte musicis

File name: **ANO1279**   Data input by: Jingfa Sun

File type: **TEXT**   Data checked by: Angela Mariani

  MS: Print: **X**   Data approved by: Thomas J. Mathiesen

Filelist: 13th   File size: 265K   Annotations:

Source of data:

Heinrich Sowa, ed., Ein anonymer glossierter Mensuraltraktat 1279, Königsberger Studien zur Musikwissenschaft, vol. 9 (Kassel: Bärenreiter, 1930), 1-132.

Based on Munich, Bayerische Staatsbibliothek, Clm 14523. The graphics files for this treatise are ANO1279 01GF-ANO1279 07GF. Cf. ANODMM TEXT.

Author: Anonymous

Treatise: De figuris

Incipit: Duplex est notula, ligata scilicet et non ligata. Notularum non ligatarum

File name: **ANODEF**

File type: **TEXT**

MS: Print: **X**

Filelist: 14th   File size: 9K

Data input by: Stephen E. Hayes

Data checked by: Peter Lefferts & Luminita Aluas

Data approved by: Thomas J. Mathiesen

Annotations:

Source of data:

Johannis de Muris Notitia artis musicae et Compendium musicae practicae; Petrus de Sancto Dionysio Tractatus de musica, ed. Ulrich Michels, Corpus scriptorum de musica, vol. 17 ([Rome]: American Institute of Musicology, 1972), 160-66. Used by permission.

The graphics file for this treatise is ANODEF 01GF. This text replaces part of the treatise by Petrus de Sancto Dionysio in several manuscripts (see p. 160).

Author: Anonymous

Treatise: De mensura fistularum in organis

Incipit: Fac tibi fistulam secundum aestimationem, utpote unius ulnae et dimidiae langam

File name: **ANOFIS**

File type: **TEXT**

MS: Print: **X**

Filelist: 12th   File size: 12K

Data input by: Stephen E. Hayes

Data checked by: Peter Lefferts & Angela Mariani

Data approved by: Thomas J. Mathiesen

Annotations:

Source of data:

Scriptores ecclesiastici de musica sacra potissimum, 3 vols., ed. Martin Gerbert (St. Blaise: Typis San-Blasianis, 1784; reprint ed., Hildesheim: Olms, 1963), 2:283-87.

Author: Anonymous

Treatise: De modis musicis

Incipit: Autenticus autoralis et auctoritate plenus: unde et libros antiquissimos siue firmitate

File name: **ANODM**

File type: **TEXT**

MS: Print: **X**

Filelist: 9th-11th File size: 3K

Data input by: Elisabeth Honn

Data checked by: Andreas Giger

Data approved by: Thomas J. Mathiesen

Annotations:

Source of data:

Terence Bailey, "De modis musicis: A New Edition and Explanation," Kirchenmusikalisches Jahrbuch 61-62 (1977-78): 50-54. Used by permission.

Cf. p. 149 in Gerbert's edition of the Alia musica (ALIMUS TEXT).

Author: Anonymous
Treatise: De musica
Incipit: De quantitate discreta mobili est musica: est enim de sono vel est contractus
File name: **ANOQM**   Data input by: Andreas Giger
File type: **TEXT**   Data checked by: Elisabeth Honn
  MS: Print: **X**   Data approved by: Thomas J. Mathiesen
Filelist: 13th   File size: 8K   Annotations:
Source of data: Based on Barcelona, Archivo de la Corona de
  Max Haas, "Studien zur mittelalterlichen   Arágon, Ripoll 109, f. 139r-v.
  Musiklehre I: Eine Übersicht über die
  Musiklehre im Kontext der Philosophie
  des 13. und frühen 14. Jahrhunderts," in
  Aktuelle Fragen der musikbezogenen
  Mittelalterforschung: Texte zu einem
  Basler Kolloquium des Jahres 1975,
  Forum Musicologicum: Basler Beiträge
  zur Musikgeschichte, vol. 3, ed. Hans
  Oesch and Wulf Arlt (Winterthur:
  Amadeus Verlag, 1982), 354-55 and
  358-59.

Author: Anonymous
Treatise: De musica
Incipit: Notandum est quod regula subscripta debet doceri per magistros omnibus illis qui
File name: **ANOMUS2**   Data input by: John Csonka
File type: **TEXT**   Data checked by: Jan Herlinger & Angela Mariani
  MS: Print: **X**   Data approved by: Thomas J. Mathiesen
Filelist: 15th   File size: 10K   Annotations:
Source of data: Based on Rome, Biblioteca Vallicelliana,
  Adrien de la Fage, Essais de   C.105. Known as La Fage Anonymous II.
  dipthérographie musicale (Paris: Legouix,
  1864), 423-28.

Author: Anonymous
Treatise: De musica
Incipit: Semidictonus est inaequalium notarum consonantia, tonum perfectum cum semitonio
File name: **ANOFRA4**   Data input by: John Csonka
File type: **TEXT**   Data checked by: Jan Herlinger & Angela Mariani
  MS: Print: **X**   Data approved by: Thomas J. Mathiesen
Filelist: 15th   File size: 10K   Annotations:
Source of data: Based on Florence, Biblioteca
  Adrien de la Fage, Essais de   Medicea-Laurenziana, 29.16. The treatise is
  dipthérographie musicale (Paris: Legouix,   fragmentary, beginning with chapter 73.
  1864), 346-50.

Author: Anonymous

Treatise: De musica et de transformatione specialiter

Incipit: Grecam litteram ideo moderni maluerunt ponere quam latinam, ut Greci per hoc

File name: **ANODMT** Data input by: Michael Lundell & Elisabeth Honn

File type: **TEXT** Data checked by: Andreas Giger

MS: Print: **X** Data approved by: Thomas J. Mathiesen

Filelist: 9th-11th File size: 18K Annotations:

Source of data:
Heinrich Sowa, Quellen zur
Transformation der Antiphonen: Tonar-
und Rhythmusstudien (Kassel:
Bärenreiter, 1935), 154-60.

Based on Leipzig, Universitätsbibliothek,
1492.

Author: Anonymous

Treatise: De musica et tonis tractatus

Incipit: Ex omni innumera varietate numerorum pauci et numerabiles inventi sunt

File name: **METANO1** Data input by: Angela Mariani

File type: **TEXT** Data checked by: Bradley Jon Tucker

MS: Print: **X** Data approved by: Thomas J. Mathiesen

Filelist: 12th File size: 14K Annotations:

Source of data:
Dominicus Mettenleiter, Musikgeschichte
der Stadt Regensburg (Regensburg:
Bössenecker, 1866), 13-21.

Also known as the Murrscher Anonymous.
Based on Munich, Bayerische
Staatsbibliothek, Clm 14865b.

Author: Anonymous

Treatise: De musica mensurabili

Incipit: Omnis ars sive doctrina honorabiliorem habet rationem

File name: **ANODEM** Data input by: Stephen E. Hayes

File type: **TEXT** Data checked by: Peter Lefferts & Bradley Tucker

MS: Print: **X** Data approved by: Thomas J. Mathiesen

Filelist: 14th File size: 48K Annotations:

Source of data:
Anonymus, De musica mensurabili, ed.
Cecily Sweeney; Anonymus, De
semibrevibus caudatis, ed. André Gilles
and Cecily Sweeney, Corpus scriptorum
de musica, vol. 13 ([Rome]: American
Institute of Musicology, 1971), 29-56.
Used by permission.

The graphics file for this treatise is ANODEM
01GF. See also CAMDEM.

Author: Anonymous

Treatise: De musica mensurata

Incipit: Quoniam prosam artis musicae mensurabilis ab excellentibus in arte musicis

File name: **ANODMM**

File type: **TEXT**

MS: Print: **X**

Filelist: 13th   File size: 291K

Data input by: Jeremy Yudkin

Data checked by: Bradley Jon Tucker

Data approved by: Thomas J. Mathiesen

Annotations:

Source of data:

De musica mensurata: The Anonymous of St. Emmeram, ed. and trans. Jeremy Yudkin, Music: Scholarship and Performance (Bloomington: Indiana University Press, 1990), 64-288 (even), 338-48. Used by permission.

This text makes use of superscript numbers to key the various glosses to specific words or phrases. In this file, superscript numbers are indicated by their placement within brackets immediately following the word (i.e., without an intervening space) to which they pertain. The graphics files for this treatise are ANODMM 01GF-ANODMM 05GF. Cf. ANO1279 TEXT.

Author: Anonymous

Treatise: De octo tonis vbi nascuntur et oriuntur aut efficiuntur

Incipit: Septem orbes septem planetarum cum dulcissima armonia voluuntur

File name: **ANOOCT**

File type: **MLBLL763**

MS: **X**   Print:

Filelist: 14th   File size: 3K

Data input by: Peter M. Lefferts

Data checked by: Michael W. Lundell

Data approved by: Thomas J. Mathiesen

Annotations:

Source of data:

London, British Library, Lansdowne 763, f. 52r-v.

=RISM BIII/4:87-91.

Author: Anonymous

Treatise: De origine et effectu musicae

Incipit: Musica est scientia recte canendi, sive scientia de numero relato ad sonum.

File name: **ANOOREF**

File type: **TEXT**

MS: Print: **X**

Filelist: 15th   File size: 16K

Data input by: Stephen E. Hayes

Data checked by: Peter M. Lefferts & Andreas Giger

Data approved by: Thomas J. Mathiesen

Annotations:

Source of data:

Gilbert Reaney, "The Anonymous Treatise De origine et effectu musicae, an Early 15th Century Commonplace Book of Music Theory," Musica disciplina 37 (1983): 109-19. Text copyright 1985. Used by permission of the American Institute of Musicology (Tempo Music Publications, 3773 West 95th Street, Leawood, KS 66206).

Cf. ANOORI MLBLL763.

Author: Anonymous

Treatise: De origine et effectu musice

Incipit: MVsica. est sciencia recte canendi. siue sciencia de numero relato ad sonum.

File name: **ANOORI**	Data input by: Peter M. Lefferts
File type: **MLBLL763**	Data checked by: Julie Langford-Johnson
MS: **X** Print:	Data approved by: Thomas J. Mathiesen
Filelist: 15th File size: 14K	Annotations:

Source of data:
London, British Library, Lansdowne 763, ff. 55v-59r.

=RISM BIII/4:87-91. This text is edited in Gilbert Reaney, "The Wylde Anonymous," Musica disciplina 37 (1983): 109-19 (ANOOREF TEXT).

Author: Anonymous

Treatise: De plana musica breve compendium

Incipit: Quoniam de plana musica sive de compositione gammatis breviter

File name: **ANODMP**	Data input by: Stephen E. Hayes
File type: **TEXT**	Data checked by: Peter M. Lefferts & Andreas Giger
MS: Print: **X**	Data approved by: Thomas J. Mathiesen
Filelist: 13th File size: 18K	Annotations:

Source of data:
André Gilles, "De musica plana breve compendium (Un témoignage de l'enseignement de Lambertus)," Musica disciplina 43 (1989): 39-51. Used by permission of the American Institute of Musicology (Tempo Music Publications, 3773 West 95th Street, Leawood, KS 66206).

The incipit is preceded by a list of chapter headings. The graphics files for this treatise are ANODMP 01GF-ANODMP 02GF.

Author: Anonymous

Treatise: De semibrevibus caudatis

Incipit: Primo nota quod omnes notulae sunt aequivocae: sic tempus ac semibrevis

File name: **ANOSEM**	Data input by: Stephen E. Hayes
File type: **TEXT**	Data checked by: Peter Lefferts & Bradley Tucker
MS: Print: **X**	Data approved by: Thomas J. Mathiesen
Filelist: 14th File size: 21K	Annotations:

Source of data:
Anonymus, De musica mensurabili, ed. Cecily Sweeney; Anonymus, De semibrevibus caudatis, ed. André Gilles and Cecily Sweeney, Corpus scriptorum de musica, vol. 13 ([Rome]: American Institute of Musicology, 1971), 65-79. Used by permission.

Based on Paris, Bibliothèque Ste. Geneviève, 1257.

Author: Anonymous

Treatise: De sinemenis

Incipit: Sequitur de sinemenis sic: b c, cujus medium erit [sqb] parvum.

File name: **ANODES**   Data input by: Luminita Aluas

File type: **TEXT**   Data checked by: Margaret Bent

MS: Print: **X**   Data approved by: Albert C. Rotola, S.J.

Filelist: 13th   File size: 6K   Annotations:

Source of data:
Scriptorum de musica medii aevi nova series a Gerbertina altera, 4 vols., ed. Edmond de Coussemaker (Paris: Durand, 1864-76; reprint ed., Hildesheim: Olms, 1963), 1:364-65.

Author: Anonymous

Treatise: De tonorum agnicionibus

Incipit: De tonorum agnicionibus singulorum et differenciarum secundum varias incepciones

File name: **ANOTON**   Data input by: Peter M. Lefferts

File type: **MLBLR12**   Data checked by: Andreas Giger

MS: **X**   Print: Data approved by: Thomas J. Mathiesen

Filelist: 14th   File size: 3K   Annotations:

Source of data:
London, British Library, Royal 12.C.VI, ff. 52r-53v.

=RISM BIII/4:93-94. The graphics files for this treatise are ANOTON 01GF-ANOTON 03GF.

Author: Anonymous

Treatise: De tractatu tonorum

Incipit: Primum tractatum huius voluminis de symphonia id est vocum motione prosecuti

File name: **SCHANO**   Data input by: Jingfa Sun

File type: **TEXT**   Data checked by: Bradley Jon Tucker

MS: Print: **X**   Data approved by: Thomas J. Mathiesen

Filelist: 12th   File size: 35K   Annotations:

Source of data:
Marius Schneider, Geschichte der Mehrstimmigkeit: Historische und phänomenologische Studien (Berlin: Gebrüder Bornträger, 1934; reprint ed., Tutzing: Hans Schneider, 1969), 106-18.

The graphics files for this treatise are SCHANO 01GF-SCHANO 02GF.

Author: Anonymous

Treatise: De valore notularum tam veteris quam novae artis

Incipit: Ad evidentiam valoris notularum, sciendum quod, quotienscumque nota

File name: **ANO2DEV**   Data input by: Peter Slemon

File type: **TEXT**   Data checked by: Kirk Ditzler

MS: Print: **X**   Data approved by: Thomas J. Mathiesen

Filelist: 14th   File size: 17K   Annotations:

Source of data:

Anonymus de valore notvlarum tam veteris qvam novae artis (Ms. Paris, Bibl. Nat., lat. 15128); Anonymus compendium mvsicae mensvrabilis tam veteris qvam novae artis (Ms. Paris, Bibl. Nat., lat. 15128); Anonymus de diversis maneriebvs in mvsica mensvrabili (Ms. Saint-Dié, Bibl. Municipale 42), ed. Gilbert Reaney, Corpus scriptorum de musica, vol. 30 (n.p.: American Institute of Musicology, 1982), 13-28. Used by permission.

Based on Paris, Bibliothèque Nationale, lat. 15128. The graphics file for this treatise is ANO2DEV 01GF. Cf. ANO2DEM TEXT.

Author: Anonymous

Treatise: Discantus positio vulgaris

Incipit: Uiso igitur quid sit discantus: quedam precogniciones sunt uidende.

File name: **DISPOSI**   Data input by: Sandra Pinegar

File type: **MPBN1666**   Data checked by: M. Lundell & J. Langford-Johnson

MS: **X**   Print: Data approved by: Thomas J. Mathiesen

Filelist: 13th   File size: 10K   Annotations:

Source of data:

Paris, Bibliothèque nationale, lat. 16663, ff. 64v-66v.

=RISM BIII/1:124. Cf. DISPOS TEXT, DISPOVU TEXT, and DISVUL TEXT.

Author: Anonymous

Treatise: Discantus positio vulgaris

Incipit: Viso igitur quid sit discantus, quedam precognitiones sunt vidende.

File name: **DISPOS**   Data input by: Bradley Jon Tucker

File type: **TEXT**   Data checked by: Jan Herlinger

MS: Print: **X**   Data approved by: Thomas J. Mathiesen

Filelist: 13th   File size: 9K   Annotations:

Source of data:

Scriptorum de musica medii aevi nova series a Gerbertina altera, 4 vols., ed. Edmond de Coussemaker (Paris: Durand, 1864-76; reprint ed., Hildesheim: Olms, 1963), 1:94-97.

Cf. DISPOVU TEXT, DISVUL TEXT, and DISPOSI MPBN1666.

Author: Anonymous

Treatise: Discantus positio vulgaris

Incipit: Viso igitur, quid sit discantus, quaedam precognitiones sunt videndae.

File name: **DISPOVU** Data input by: Stephen E. Hayes

File type: **TEXT** Data checked by: Peter M. Lefferts & Kirk Ditzler

MS: Print: **X** Data approved by: Thomas J. Mathiesen

Filelist: 13th File size: 9K Annotations:

Source of data: Cf. DISPOS TEXT, DISVUL TEXT, and
Hieronymus de Moravia, Tractatus de DISPOSI MPBN1666.
musica, ed. S. M. Cserba, Freiburger
Studien zur Musikwissenschaft, vol. 2
(Regensburg: Pustet, 1935), 189-94.

Author: Anonymous

Treatise: Discantus vulgaris positio

Incipit: Nunc vero de cantu ecclesiastico, secundum scilicet quod discantus subjicitur

File name: **DISVUL** Data input by: Stephen E. Hayes

File type: **TEXT** Data checked by: Peter Lefferts & Luminita Aluas

MS: Print: **X** Data approved by: Thomas J. Mathiesen

Filelist: 13th File size: 7K Annotations:

Source of data: Document III in the Coussemaker Histoire;
Edmond de Coussemaker, Histoire de based on Paris, Bibliothèque Nationale, lat.
l'harmonie au moyen-age (Paris: V. 16663. Cf. DISPOS TEXT, DISPOVU TEXT,
Didron, 1852), 247-53. and DISPOSI MPBN1666.

Author: Anonymous

Treatise: Distinccio inter colores musicales, et armorum heroum

Incipit: Numerus sexdecim. est numerus perfectissimus. quia semper potest diuidi in duas

File name: **ANODIST** Data input by: Peter M. Lefferts

File type: **MLBLL763** Data checked by: Michael W. Lundell

MS: **X** Print: Data approved by: Thomas J. Mathiesen

Filelist: 14th File size: 3K Annotations:

Source of data: =RISM BIII/4:87-91. The graphics file for this
London, British Library, Lansdowne 763, treatise is ANODIST 01GF.
ff. 88v-89r.

Author: Anonymous

Treatise: Diverse conclusiones

Incipit: Prima conclusio quod longa possit inperfecta per breuem probatur

File name: **ANODC** Data input by: Peter M. Lefferts

File type: **MOBB842** Data checked by: Michael W. Lundell

MS: **X** Print: Data approved by: Thomas J. Mathiesen

Filelist: 14th File size: 6K Annotations:

Source of data: =RISM BIII/4:110-15. This text is derived
Oxford, Bodleian Library, Bodley 842 from Johannes de Muris's Notitia artis
(S.C. 2575), ff. 76r-77v. musicae.

Author: Anonymous
Treatise: Dulce ingenium (Versio Parisiensis et Brugensis)
Incipit: Dulce ingenium musicae, quamvis instrumentis plurimis vigeat

File name: **ANODUL**   Data input by: Andreas Giger
File type: **TEXT**   Data checked by: Elisabeth Honn
 MS: Print: **X**   Data approved by: Thomas J. Mathiesen
Filelist: 9th-11th File size: 18K   Annotations:

Source of data:
Anonymi saeculi decimi vel undecimi tractatus de musica "Dulce ingenium musicae," ed. Michael Bernhard, Bayerische Akademie der Wissenschaften, Veröffentlichungen der musikhistorischen Kommission, Band 6 (München: Bayerische Akademie der Wissenschaften; C. H. Beck, 1987), 14-26. Used by permission.

Based on Paris, Bibliothèque nationale, lat. 8663, ff. 50r-51r; and Bruges, Stadsbibliotheek, 532, ff. 1r-4r. The graphics files for this treatise are ANODUL 01GF-ANODUL 02GF. Cf. ANODUL2 TEXT.

Author: Anonymous
Treatise: Dulce ingenium (Versio Pragensis)
Incipit: Dulce ingenium artis musicae, quamvis plurimis instrumentis vigeat

File name: **ANODUL2**   Data input by: Andreas Giger
File type: **TEXT**   Data checked by: Elisabeth Honn
 MS: Print: **X**   Data approved by: Thomas J. Mathiesen
Filelist: 9th-11th File size: 28K   Annotations:

Source of data:
Anonymi saeculi decimi vel undecimi tractatus de musica "Dulce ingenium musicae," ed. Michael Bernhard, Bayerische Akademie der Wissenschaften, Veröffentlichungen der musikhistorischen Kommission, Band 6 (München: Bayerische Akademie der Wissenschaften; C. H. Beck, 1987), 27-43. Used by permission.

Based on Praha, Statni Knihovna XIX C 26, ff. 12v-18v. Cf. ANODUL TEXT.

Author: Anonymous
Treatise: Epistola Sancti Bernardi De revisione cantus Cisterciensis, et Tractatus cantum
Incipit: Cantum quem Cisterciensis ordinis ecclesiae cantare consueverant, licet gravis

File name: **BEREPI**   Data input by: Stephen E. Hayes
File type: **TEXT**   Data checked by: Peter Lefferts & Angela Mariani
 MS: Print: **X**   Data approved by: Thomas J. Mathiesen
Filelist: 12th   File size: 31K   Annotations:

Source of data:
Epistola S. Bernardi De revisione cantus Cisterciensis, et Tractatus Cantum quem Cisterciensis Ordinis ecclesiae cantare, ed. F. J. Guentner, Corpus scriptorum de musica, vol. 24 ([Rome]: American Institute of Musicology, 1974), 21-41. Used by permission.

A long prologue precedes the treatise, beginning: "Bernardus humilis Abbas Claraevallis omnibus transcripturis hoc Antiphonarium sive cantaturis in illo: Inter cetera quae optime aemulati sunt patres nostri, Cisterciensis videlicet ordinis inchoatores, ..."

Author: Anonymous
Treatise: Est tonus sic
Incipit: Est tonus sic Vt Re Vt. vel Re My Re. vel Fa Sol Fa. vel Sol. La Sol.

File name: **ANOEST**	Data input by: Peter M. Lefferts
File type: **MLBLL763**	Data checked by: Michael W. Lundell
MS: **X** Print:	Data approved by: Thomas J. Mathiesen
Filelist: 14th File size: 2K	Annotations:

Source of data:
London, British Library, Lansdowne 763, ff. 54r-55r.

=RISM BIII/4:87-91. The incipit is contained in the first graphic. The graphics files for this treatise are ANOEST 01GF-ANOEST 03GF. Cf. ANOINT MLBLH978.

Author: Anonymous
Treatise: Et octo tonorum incipit tractatus metricus
Incipit: Primus est tonus Re La. Re Fa. quoque secundus.

File name: **ANOOCTT**	Data input by: Peter M. Lefferts
File type: **MLBLL763**	Data checked by: Michael W. Lundell
MS: **X** Print:	Data approved by: Thomas J. Mathiesen
Filelist: 14th File size: 2K	Annotations:

Source of data:
London, British Library, Lansdowne 763, f. 68v.

=RISM BIII/4:87-91.

Author: Anonymous
Treatise: Fragmenta musica
Incipit: Proportio est divisarum rerum ad se invicem comparabilis collatio.

File name: **ANOFRA**	Data input by: John Csonka
File type: **TEXT**	Data checked by: Bradley Jon Tucker
MS: Print: **X**	Data approved by: Thomas J. Mathiesen
Filelist: 13th File size: 15K	Annotations:

Source of data:
Adrien de la Fage, Essais de dipthérographie musicale (Paris: Legouix, 1864), 67-78.

Based on Paris, Bibliothèque Nationale, supp. lat. 990. The incipit is preceded by various liturgical verses.

Author: Anonymous
Treatise: Fragmenta musica
Incipit: Incipit dialogus de musica:--Interrogatio. Musica a quo inventa?

File name: **ANOFRA2**	Data input by: John Csonka
File type: **TEXT**	Data checked by: Jan Herlinger & Angela Mariani
MS: Print: **X**	Data approved by: Thomas J. Mathiesen
Filelist: 12th File size: 15K	Annotations:

Source of data:
Adrien de la Fage, Essais de dipthérographie musicale (Paris: Legouix, 1864), 185-94.

Based on Paris, Bibliothèque Nationale, Colbertinus lat. 7211. The graphics file for this treatise is ANOFRA2 01GF.

Author: Anonymous
Treatise: Fragmenta musica
Incipit: Aurea personet lyra clara modulamina;

File name: **ANOFRA3**   Data input by: John Csonka
File type: **TEXT**   Data checked by: Bradley Jon Tucker
MS: Print: **X**   Data approved by: Thomas J. Mathiesen
Filelist: 12th   File size: 13K   Annotations:

Source of data:
Adrien de la Fage, Essais de
dipthérographie musicale (Paris: Legouix,
1864), 275-79, 281-84, 286-88.

Based on Florence, Biblioteca nazionale
centrale, Magliabechiana 565. This section of
La Fage begins with the Cantus Philomelae
and continues with a Guidonian commentary,
Notker's "Prologus sequentiarum," and a series
of verses on music. The graphics files for this
treatise are ANOFRA3 01GF-ANOFRA3
05GF.

Author: Anonymous
Treatise: Fragmentum
Incipit: His litteris et hac supputatione plena calculatio est cognita.

File name: **ANOFRA7**   Data input by: John Csonka
File type: **TEXT**   Data checked by: Jan Herlinger & Angela Mariani
MS: Print: **X**   Data approved by: Thomas J. Mathiesen
Filelist: 15th   File size: 3K   Annotations:

Source of data:
Adrien de la Fage, Essais de
dipthérographie musicale (Paris: Legouix,
1864), 496.

Based on Paris, Bibliothèque Nationale,
Colbertinus lat. 7461.

Author: Anonymous
Treatise: Instituta patrum de modo psallendi sive cantandi
Incipit: Sancti Patres nostri antiqui docuerunt et instituerunt subditos suos, praecipientes

File name: **PATPSAL**   Data input by: Stephen E. Hayes
File type: **TEXT**   Data checked by: Peter Lefferts & Angela Mariani
MS: Print: **X**   Data approved by: Thomas J. Mathiesen
Filelist: 13th   File size: 10K   Annotations:

Source of data:
Scriptores ecclesiastici de musica sacra
potissimum, 3 vols., ed. Martin Gerbert
(St. Blaise: Typis San-Blasianis, 1784;
reprint ed., Hildesheim: Olms, 1963),
1:5-8.

Gerbert ascribed this treatise to the time of the
Church Fathers, but it is now thought to have
been written after 1220.

Author: Anonymous

Treatise: Introductorium musicae

Incipit: (M)usica est recte modulandi scientia. Et deducitur a musa vocabulo greco quod

File name: **ANOLEIP**   Data input by: Peter Slemon

File type: **TEXT**   Data checked by: Bradley Jon Tucker

MS: Print: **X**   Data approved by: Thomas J. Mathiesen

Filelist: 16th   File size: 55K   Annotations:

Source of data:
Hugo Riemann, "Anonymi Introductorium musicae (c. 1500)," Monatshefte für Musikgeschichte 29 (1897): 149-54, 157-64; 30 (1898): 1-8, 11-19.

The incipit is preceded first by a hexachord diagram and then by the heading "De definitione musice ejusque diuisione." The graphics files for this treatise are ANOLEIP 01GF-ANOLEIP16GF.

Author: Anonymous

Treatise: Jesus. Libellus musicae adiscendae valde utilis et est dialogus. Discipulus et

Incipit: Discipulus: Modo quaeritur quid est musica? Magister: Est veraciter canendi

File name: **ANOLIB**   Data input by: Stephen E. Hayes

File type: **TEXT**   Data checked by: Peter Lefferts & Bradley Tucker

MS: Print: **X**   Data approved by: Thomas J. Mathiesen

Filelist: 15th   File size: 33K   Annotations:

Source of data:
Anonymus. Ex codice Vaticano lat. 5129, ed. Albert Seay, Corpus scriptorum de musica, vol. 9 ([Rome]: American Institute of Musicology, 1964), 21-48. Used by permission.

Based on Rome, Biblioteca Apostolica Vaticana, lat. 5129. The graphics files for this treatise are ANOLIB 01GF-ANOLIB 05GF.

Author: Anonymous

Treatise: Liber musicae

Incipit: Decem sunt modi quorum tantum tres dicuntur consonantiae, scilicet diatesseron

File name: **ANOLIBM**   Data input by: John Gray

File type: **TEXT**   Data checked by: Oliver Ellsworth & Andreas Giger

MS: Print: **X**   Data approved by: Thomas J. Mathiesen

Filelist: 14th   File size: 44K   Annotations:

Source of data:
G. Pannain, "Liber musicae. Un teorico anonimo del XIV secolo." Rivista musicale Italiana 27 (1920): 409-39.

The incipit is preceded by the heading "Unde constet diatesseron." The graphics files for this treatise are ANOLIBM 01GF-ANOLIBM 03GF.

Author: Anonymous
Treatise: Mensura monocordi
Incipit: In monocordo, quod dicitur Fortunatiani, illa mensura tenenda est
File name: **ANOMMON**   Data input by: Andreas Giger
File type: **TEXT**   Data checked by: Elisabeth Honn
  MS: Print: **X**   Data approved by: Thomas J. Mathiesen
Filelist: 9th-11th   File size: 3K   Annotations:
Source of data:
  Hans Schmid, ed., Musica et scholica
  enchiriadis una cum aliquibus tractatulis
  adiunctis, Bayerische Akademie der
  Wissenschaften, Veröffentlichungen der
  Musikhistorischen Kommission, Band 3
  (München: Bayerische Akademie der
  Wissenschaften; C. H. Beck, 1981), 238.
  Used by permission.

Author: Anonymous
Treatise: Mensura monochordi Boetii
Incipit: Totum monochordum partire inprimis in quatuor, et in initio monochordi pone F.
File name: **ANOMEN**   Data input by: Stephen E. Hayes
File type: **TEXT**   Data checked by: Peter Lefferts & Angela Mariani
  MS: Print: **X**   Data approved by: Thomas J. Mathiesen
Filelist: 12th   File size: 12K   Annotations:
Source of data: Cf. ANOMMB TEXT.
  Scriptores ecclesiastici de musica sacra
  potissimum, 3 vols., ed. Martin Gerbert
  (St. Blaise: Typis San-Blasianis, 1784;
  reprint ed., Hildesheim: Olms, 1963),
  1:344-48.

Author: Anonymous
Treatise: Mensura monochordi Boetii
Incipit: Totum monochordum partire in primis in quatuor, et in initio monochordi pone F.
File name: **ANOMMB**   Data input by: John Gray
File type: **TEXT**   Data checked by: Oliver Ellsworth & Andreas Giger
  MS: Print: **X**   Data approved by: Thomas J. Mathiesen
Filelist: 12th   File size: 12K   Annotations:
Source of data: Cf. ANOMEN TEXT.
  Patrologia cursus completus, series latina,
  ed. J. P. Migne, 221 vols. (Paris: Garnier,
  1844-1904), 151:687-92.

Author: Anonymous
Treatise: Metrologus liber
Incipit: In nomine sancte et indiuidue Trinitatis incipit. de plana musica id est breuis sermo.
File name: **ANOMET**   Data input by: Peter M. Lefferts
File type: **MLBLL763**   Data checked by: Julie Langford-Johnson
  MS: **X**   Print: Data approved by: Thomas J. Mathiesen
Filelist: 14th   File size: 29K   Annotations:
Source of data: =RISM BIII/4:87-91. The graphics file for this
  London, British Library, Lansdowne 763,   treatise is ANOMET 01GF.
  ff. 61r-68v.

Author: Anonymous

Treatise: Modus cantandi in mensuralibus

Incipit: Iam sequitur de valoribus notarum et hoc iam dictatur.

File name: **ANOMOD**   Data input by: Stephen E. Hayes

File type: **TEXT**   Data checked by: Peter M. Lefferts & Andreas Giger

MS: Print: **X**   Data approved by: Thomas J. Mathiesen

Filelist: 15th   File size: 16K   Annotations:

Source of data:
Lorenz Welker, "Ein anonymer
Mensuraltraktat in der Sterzinger
Miszellaneen-Handschrift," Archiv für
Musikwissenschaft 48 (1991): 255-81.
Used by permission.

Based on Sterzing/Vipiteno [Südtirol],
Stadtarchiv/Rathaus (no signature). The
graphics files for this treatise are ANOMOD
01GF-ANOMOD 02GF.

Author: Anonymous

Treatise: Monacho qua mente sit psallendum

Incipit: Iunior quidam monachus, D. Antonii Abbatis discipulus, missus est aliquando

File name: **MONPSAL**   Data input by: Stephen E. Hayes

File type: **TEXT**   Data checked by: Peter Lefferts & Angela Mariani

MS: Print: **X**   Data approved by: Thomas J. Mathiesen

Filelist: 6th-8th   File size: 4K   Annotations:

Source of data:
Scriptores ecclesiastici de musica sacra
potissimum, 3 vols., ed. Martin Gerbert
(St. Blaise: Typis San-Blasianis, 1784;
reprint ed., Hildesheim: Olms, 1963),
1:4-5.

Author: Anonymous

Treatise: Monachus quidam de Sherbourn talem musicam profert de Sancta Maria Magdalene

Incipit: Ex altera parte secuntur versus mistici huic gamme pertinente

File name: **ANODESA**   Data input by: Peter M. Lefferts

File type: **MLBLL763**   Data checked by: Michael W. Lundell

MS: **X**   Print: Data approved by: Thomas J. Mathiesen

Filelist: 14th   File size: 3K   Annotations:

Source of data:
London, British Library, Lansdowne 763,
ff. 52v-53v.

=RISM BIII/4:87-91. The incipit is preceded
by a solmisation figure. The graphics file for
this treatise is ANODESA 01GF.

Author: Anonymous

Treatise: Monochordum Encheriadis

Incipit: Monochordum Encheriadis constat in X et VIII cordis, ex quatuor videlicet gravibus

File name: **ANOMONEN**   Data input by: John Gray

File type: **TEXT**   Data checked by: Oliver Ellsworth & Andreas Giger

MS: Print: **X**   Data approved by: Thomas J. Mathiesen

Filelist: 12th   File size: 3K   Annotations:

Source of data:
Patrologia cursus completus, series latina,
ed. J. P. Migne, 221 vols. (Paris: Garnier,
1844-1904), 151:693-94.

Author: Anonymous

Treatise: Musica enchiriadis

Incipit: Sicut vocis articulatae elementariae atque individuae partes sunt litterae

File name: **MUSENC** Data input by: Stephen E. Hayes

File type: **TEXT** Data checked by: Peter Lefferts & Bradley Tucker

MS: Print: **X** Data approved by: Thomas J. Mathiesen

Filelist: 9th-11th File size: 38K Annotations:

Source of data:

Scriptores ecclesiastici de musica sacra potissimum, 3 vols., ed. Martin Gerbert (St. Blaise: Typis San-Blasianis, 1784; reprint ed., Hildesheim: Olms, 1963), 1:152-73.

The text is assigned to Hucbald in Gerbert's edition, but this attribution is no longer accepted. The graphics files for this treatise are MUSENC 01GF-MUSENC14GF. Cf. MUSENCH TEXT.

Author: Anonymous

Treatise: Musica enchiriadis

Incipit: Sicut vocis articulatae elementariae atque individuae partes sunt litterae

File name: **MUSENCH** Data input by: Jingfa Sun

File type: **TEXT** Data checked by: Andreas Giger

MS: Print: **X** Data approved by: Thomas J. Mathiesen

Filelist: 9th-11th File size: 39K Annotations:

Source of data:

Patrologia cursus completus, series latina, ed. J. P. Migne, 221 vols. (Paris: Garnier, 1844-1904), 132:957-82.

The text is assigned to Hucbald in this edition (following Gerbert), but this attribution is no longer accepted. The graphics files for this treatise are MUSENCH 01GF-MUSENCH 08GF. Cf. MUSENC TEXT.

Author: Anonymous

Treatise: Musicae liber

Incipit: Quemodmodum, ut ait ille venerabilis doctor Ambrosius, in quodam sermone

File name: **ANOMUS** Data input by: John Csonka

File type: **TEXT** Data checked by: Jan Herlinger & Angela Mariani

MS: Print: **X** Data approved by: Thomas J. Mathiesen

Filelist: 14th File size: 14K Annotations:

Source of data:

Adrien de la Fage, Essais de dipthérographie musicale (Paris: Legouix, 1864), 241-48.

Based on Rome, Biblioteca Vallicelliana, B.83. Known as La Fage Anonymous III. The graphics file for this treatise is ANOMUS 01GF.

Author: Anonymous

Treatise: Practica musicae artis mensurabilis

Incipit: Gaudent brevitate moderni. Quandocunque punctus quadratus seu nota quadrata

File name: **ANOPRA**   Data input by: Stephen E. Hayes

File type: **TEXT**   Data checked by: Peter M. Lefferts & Andreas Giger

MS: Print: **X**   Data approved by: Thomas J. Mathiesen

Filelist: 13th   File size: 9K   Annotations:

Source of data:

Marie Louise Göllner, ed., The Manuscript Cod. lat. 5539 of the Bavarian State Library, Musicological Studies and Documents, vol. 43 (Neuhausen-Stuttgart: Hänssler-Verlag, American Institute of Musicology, 1993), 101-8. Used by permission of the American Institute of Musicology (Tempo Music Publications, 3773 West 95th Street, Leawood, KS 66206).

Document IIIb. The graphics file for this treatise is ANOPRA 01GF.

Author: Anonymous

Treatise: Proportio est duarum rerum

Incipit: Proporcio. est duarum rerum equalium vel inequalium adinuicem habitudo

File name: **ANODUA**   Data input by: Peter M. Lefferts

File type: **MLBLL763**   Data checked by: Michael W. Lundell

MS: **X**   Print: Data approved by: Thomas J. Mathiesen

Filelist: 14th   File size: 5K   Annotations:

Source of data:

London, British Library, Lansdowne 763, ff. 123r-124r.

=RISM BIII/4:87-91. The graphics files for this treatise are ANODUA 01GF-ANODUA 02GF.

Author: Anonymous

Treatise: Quaedam de arte discantandi

Incipit: Figura est repraesentatio vocis in aliquo modorum ordinatae.

File name: **ANOQUA**   Data input by: Stephen E. Hayes

File type: **TEXT**   Data checked by: Peter Lefferts & Luminita Aluas

MS: Print: **X**   Data approved by: Thomas J. Mathiesen

Filelist: 13th   File size: 15K   Annotations:

Source of data:

Edmond de Coussemaker, Histoire de l'harmonie au moyen-age (Paris: V. Didron, 1852), 274-94.

Document VI in the Coussemaker Histoire; based on Paris, Bibliothèque Nationale, lat. 15129. The graphics files for this treatise are ANOQUA 01GF-ANOQUA 04GF. Cf. ANOFIG TEXT (Corpus scriptorum de musica, vol. 15).

Author: Anonymous

Treatise: Quaestiones et solutiones advidendum tam mensurabilis cantus quam

Incipit: Primo videndum est quid sit introductio et unde dicatur. Secundo quot modis dividitur.

File name: **ANOQS** Data input by: Nigel Gwee

File type: **TEXT** Data checked by: Peter Slemon

MS: Print: **X** Data approved by: Thomas J. Mathiesen

Filelist: 15th File size: 26K Annotations:

Source of data:

Anonymous (15th Century), Quaestiones et solutiones, ed. Albert Seay, Critical Texts, no. 2 (Colorado Springs: Colorado College Music Press, 1977). Used by permission.

The graphics file for this treatise is ANOQS 01GF. Only the Latin text (pp. 1-12) has been included here; the balance of the treatise (pp. 13-34) is in Italian.

Author: Anonymous

Treatise: Qualiter debeant fieri organa

Incipit: Si quis concordiam organorum scire uoluerit ita inchoare studeat.

File name: **ANOQUAL** Data input by: Peter Slemon

File type: **MPBN7400** Data checked by: Bradley Jon Tucker

MS: **X** Print: Data approved by: Thomas J. Mathiesen

Filelist: 13th File size: 4K Annotations:

Source of data:

Paris, Bibliothèque Nationale, lat. 7400 A, ff. 24v-25v

=RISM BIII/1:108. The graphics files for this treatise are ANOQUAL 01GF-ANOQUAL 02GF.

Author: Anonymous

Treatise: Quatuor Principalia I

Incipit: Pro aliquali notitia de Musica habenda. Primo, videndum est quid sit Musica

File name: **QUAPRIA1** Data input by: Stephen E. Hayes

File type: **MLBL4909** Data checked by: Bradley Jon Tucker

MS: **X** Print: Data approved by: Peter M. Lefferts

Filelist: 14th File size: 11K Annotations:

Source of data:

London, British Library, Additional 4909, ff. 17v-20r.

=RISM BIII/4:25-27. The graphics file for this treatise is QUAPRIA1 01GF. Version A of the Quatuor Principalia (also partially preserved in British Library, Cotton Tiberius B.IX; see also QUAPRIB). The treatise is ascribed to Simon Tunstede in Coussemaker, but this attribution is not generally accepted. See also QUAPRIA2 through QUAPRIA4.

Author: Anonymous

Treatise: Quatuor Principalia II

Incipit: Secundo. Principaliter videndum est, primo, de Arte Musicae

File name: **QUAPRIA2**   Data input by: Stephen E. Hayes

File type: **MLBL4909**   Data checked by: Bradley Jon Tucker

MS: **X**   Print: Data approved by: Peter M. Lefferts

Filelist: 14th   File size: 26K   Annotations:

Source of data:
London, British Library, Additional 4909,
ff. 20v-26v.

=RISM BIII/4:25-27. The graphics file for this treatise is QUAPRIA2 01GF-QUAPRIA2 02GF. Version A of the Quatuor Principalia (also partially preserved in British Library, Cotton Tiberius B.IX; see also QUAPRIB). The treatise is ascribed to Simon Tunstede in Coussemaker, but this attribution is not generally accepted. See also QUAPRIA1 and QUAPRIA3 through QUAPRIA4.

Author: Anonymous

Treatise: Quatuor Principalia III

Incipit: In superioribus particulis dictum est de divisione Musicae

File name: **QUAPRIA3**   Data input by: Stephen E. Hayes

File type: **MLBL4909**   Data checked by: Bradley Jon Tucker

MS: **X**   Print: Data approved by: Peter M. Lefferts

Filelist: 14th   File size: 19K   Annotations:

Source of data:
London, British Library, Additional 4909,
ff. 26v-31v.

=RISM BIII/4:25-27. The graphics files for this treatise are QUAPRIA3 01GF-QUAPRIA3 03GF. Version A of the Quatuor Principalia (also partially preserved in British Library, Cotton Tiberius B.IX; see also QUAPRIB). The treatise is ascribed to Simon Tunstede in Coussemaker, but this attribution is not generally accepted. See also QUAPRIA1 through QUAPRIA2 and QUAPRIA4.

Author: Anonymous

Treatise: Quatuor Principalia IV

Incipit: Dictis aliquibus circa planum Cantum, restat aliud dicendum de cantu

File name: **QUAPRIA4**   Data input by: Stephen E. Hayes

File type: **MLBL4909**   Data checked by: Bradley Jon Tucker

MS: **X**   Print: Data approved by: Peter M. Lefferts

Filelist: 14th   File size: 79K   Annotations:

Source of data:
London, British Library, Additional 4909,
ff. 31v-56r.

=RISM BIII/4:25-27. The graphics files for this treatise are QUAPRIA4 01GF-QUAPRIA4 08GF. Version A of the Quatuor Principalia (also partially preserved in British Library, Cotton Tiberius B.IX; see also ANO1DEM and QUAPRIB). The treatise is ascribed to Simon Tunstede in Coussemaker, but this attribution is not generally accepted. See also QUAPRIA1 through QUAPRIA3.

Author: Anonymous
Treatise: Quatuor Principalia I
Incipit: Quemadmodum inter triticum et zizania quamdiu herba est
File name: **QUAPRIB1**   Data input by: Stephen E. Hayes
File type: **TEXT**   Data checked by: Peter M. Lefferts
  MS: Print: **X**   Data approved by: Thomas J. Mathiesen
Filelist: 14th   File size: 20K   Annotations:
Source of data: Version B of the Quatuor Principalia (version
  Scriptorum de musica medii aevi nova   A is partially preserved in British Library,
  series a Gerbertina altera, 4 vols., ed.   Cotton Tiberius B.IX; and fully preserved in
  Edmond de Coussemaker (Paris: Durand,   British Library, Additional 4909, ff. 17v-56;
  1864-76; reprint ed., Hildesheim: Olms,   see QUAPRIA and ANO1DEM). The treatise
  1963), 4:200-206.   is ascribed to Simon Tunstede in
    Coussemaker, but this attribution is not
    generally accepted. See also QUAPRIB2
    through QUAPRIB4.

Author: Anonymous
Treatise: Quatuor Principalia II
Incipit: Ante inventionem hujus artis, homines naturaliter cantibus utebantur
File name: **QUAPRIB2**   Data input by: Stephen E. Hayes
File type: **TEXT**   Data checked by: Peter M. Lefferts
  MS: Print: **X**   Data approved by: Thomas J. Mathiesen
Filelist: 14th   File size: 36K   Annotations:
Source of data: The graphics files for this treatise are
  Scriptorum de musica medii aevi nova   QUAPRIB2 01GF-QUAPRIB2 04GF. Version
  series a Gerbertina altera, 4 vols., ed.   B of the Quatuor Principalia (version A is
  Edmond de Coussemaker (Paris: Durand,   partially preserved in British Library, Cotton
  1864-76; reprint ed., Hildesheim: Olms,   Tiberius B.IX; and fully preserved in British
  1963), 4:206-19.   Library, Additional 4909, ff. 17v-56; see
    QUAPRIA and ANO1DEM). The treatise is
    ascribed to Simon Tunstede in Coussemaker,
    but this attribution is not generally accepted.
    See also QUAPRIB1 and QUAPRIB3 through
    QUAPRIB4.

Author: Anonymous
Treatise: Quatuor Principalia III
Incipit: In superioribus particulis dictum est de divisione musicae
File name: **QUAPRIB3**   Data input by: Stephen E. Hayes
File type: **TEXT**   Data checked by: Peter M. Lefferts
  MS: Print: **X**   Data approved by: Thomas J. Mathiesen
Filelist: 14th   File size: 82K   Annotations:
Source of data: The graphics files for this treatise are
  Scriptorum de musica medii aevi nova   QUAPRIB3 01GF-QUAPRIB3 19GF. Version
  series a Gerbertina altera, 4 vols., ed.   B of the Quatuor Principalia (version A is
  Edmond de Coussemaker (Paris: Durand,   partially preserved in British Library, Cotton
  1864-76; reprint ed., Hildesheim: Olms,   Tiberius B.IX; and fully preserved in British
  1963), 4:219-54.   Library, Additional 4909, ff. 17v-56; see
    QUAPRIA and ANO1DEM). The treatise is
    ascribed to Simon Tunstede in Coussemaker,
    but this attribution is not generally accepted.
    See also QUAPRIB1 through QUAPRIB2 and
    QUAPRIB4.

Author: Anonymous

Treatise: Quatuor Principalia IV

Incipit: Cum omnis quantitas aut est continua aut discreta

File name: **QUAPRIB4**   Data input by: Stephen E. Hayes

File type: **TEXT**   Data checked by: Peter M. Lefferts

  MS: Print: **X**   Data approved by: Thomas J. Mathiesen

Filelist: 14th   File size: 118K   Annotations:

Source of data:

Scriptorum de musica medii aevi nova series a Gerbertina altera, 4 vols., ed. Edmond de Coussemaker (Paris: Durand, 1864-76; reprint ed., Hildesheim: Olms, 1963), 4:254-98.

The graphics files for this treatise are QUAPRIB4 01GF-QUAPRIB4 16GF. Version B of the Quatuor Principalia (version A is partially preserved in British Library, Cotton Tiberius B.IX; and fully preserved in British Library, Additional 4909, ff. 17v-56; see QUAPRIA and ANO1DEM). The treatise is ascribed to Simon Tunstede in Coussemaker, but this attribution is not generally accepted. See also QUAPRIB1 through QUAPRIB3.

Author: Anonymous

Treatise: Quid est cantus?

Incipit: Quid est cantus? peritia musicae, artis, inflexio vocis et modulatio.

File name: **ANOQUID**   Data input by: Andreas Giger

File type: **TEXT**   Data checked by: Michael W. Lundell

  MS: Print: **X**   Data approved by: Thomas J. Mathiesen

Filelist: 9th-11th File size: 5K   Annotations:

Source of data:

Peter Wagner, "Un piccolo trattato sul canto ecclesiastico," Rassegna gregoriana 3 (1904): 482-84.

Based on Rome, Biblioteca Apostolica Vaticana, Palatinus lat. 235, ff. 38v-39r. The treatise is sometimes known as the Vatican Anonymous.

Author: Anonymous

Treatise: Quomodo de arithmetica procedit musica

Incipit: Quinque sunt in Arithmetica inaequalitatis genera. Ex quibus tria postrema respuens

File name: **ANOQUO**   Data input by: Bradley Jon Tucker

File type: **TEXT**   Data checked by: Angela Mariani

  MS: Print: **X**   Data approved by: Thomas J. Mathiesen

Filelist: 9th-11th File size: 17K   Annotations:

Source of data:

Scriptores ecclesiastici de musica sacra potissimum, 3 vols., ed. Martin Gerbert (St. Blaise: Typis San-Blasianis, 1784; reprint ed., Hildesheim: Olms, 1963), 2:55-61.

The graphics file for this treatise is ANOQUO 01GF. Cf. ANOQUOM TEXT.

Author: Anonymous

Treatise: Quomodo de arithmetica procedit musica

Incipit: Quinque sunt in Arithmetica inaequalitatis genera. Ex quibus tria postrema respuens

File name: **ANOQUOM** Data input by: Jingfa Sun

File type: **TEXT** Data checked by: Angela Mariani

MS: Print: **X** Data approved by: Thomas J. Mathiesen

Filelist: 9th-11th File size: 17K Annotations:

Source of data: The graphics file for this treatise is
Patrologia cursus completus, series latina, ANOQUOM 01GF. Cf. ANOQUO TEXT.
ed. J. P. Migne, 221 vols. (Paris: Garnier,
1844-1904), 141:435-44.

Author: Anonymous

Treatise: Regula de monocordo

Incipit: [Gamma], A, B, C, D, E, F, G, a, b, h [sqb], c, d, e, f, g, aa, bb, hh [sqb][sqb], cc, dd.

File name: **REGDEM** Data input by: Stephen E. Hayes

File type: **TEXT** Data checked by: Peter Lefferts & Bradley Tucker

MS: Print: **X** Data approved by: Thomas J. Mathiesen

Filelist: 14th File size: 17K Annotations:

Source of data: The text is edited from London, British
"A London Source for the Ars Nova of Library, Additional 21455, ff. 8v, 3r-5v, and
Philippe de Vitry," in Philippi de Vitriaco 6r. The text was first published in Musica
Ars nova, ed. Gilbert Reaney, André disciplina 12 (1958): 60-66. The graphics files
Gilles, and Jean Maillard, Corpus for this treatise are REGDEM
scriptorum de musica, vol. 8 ([Rome]: 01GF-REGDEM 02GF. Cf. ANOMM TEXT.
American Institute of Musicology, 1964),
72-78. Used by permission.

Author: Anonymous

Treatise: Regula de monocordo

Incipit: In primis. [Gamma], a, b, c, d, e, f, g, a, b, [sqb], c, d, e, f, g, a, b, [sqb], c, d.

File name: **REGDEML** Data input by: Peter M. Lefferts

File type: **MLBL2145** Data checked by: Michael W. Lundell

MS: **X** Print: Data approved by: Thomas J. Mathiesen

Filelist: 14th File size: 3K Annotations:

Source of data: =RISM BIII/4:46-47. Cf. ANOMM TEXT and
London, British Library, Additional REGDEM TEXT.
21455, f. 8v.

Author: Anonymous

Treatise: Regula discantus

Incipit: Primus gradus incipit in diapason hoc est in octaua nota.

File name: **ANORD** Data input by: Peter M. Lefferts

File type: **MLBL2145** Data checked by: Michael W. Lundell

MS: **X** Print: Data approved by: Thomas J. Mathiesen

Filelist: 14th File size: 12K Annotations:

Source of data: =RISM BIII/4:46-47. The graphics files for
London, British Library, Additional this treatise are ANORD 01GF-ANORD
21455, ff. 6r-7r. 02GF.

Author: Anonymous
Treatise: Regule Magistri Johannis de Muris incipiunt
Incipit: INtendentes sciencie musicalis exquirere cognicionem ad sonum applicatum

File name: **MURREG** Data input by: Peter M. Lefferts
File type: **MLBLL763** Data checked by: Michael W. Lundell
 MS: **X** Print: Data approved by: Thomas J. Mathiesen
Filelist: 14th File size: 14K Annotations:

Source of data:
 London, British Library, Lansdowne 763, ff. 95r-98r.

=RISM BIII/4:87-91. Th graphics file for this treatise is MURREG 01GF. The manuscript attribution to Johannes de Muris is not accepted by modern authorities.

Author: Anonymous
Treatise: Scholia enchiriadis de arte musica
Incipit: Discipulus. Musica quid est? Magister. Bene modulandi scientia. D. Bene modulari

File name: **SCHENC** Data input by: Stephen E. Hayes
File type: **TEXT** Data checked by: Peter Lefferts & Bradley Tucker
 MS: Print: **X** Data approved by: Thomas J. Mathiesen
Filelist: 9th-11th File size: 91K Annotations:

Source of data:
 Scriptores ecclesiastici de musica sacra potissimum, 3 vols., ed. Martin Gerbert (St. Blaise: Typis San-Blasianis, 1784; reprint ed., Hildesheim: Olms, 1963), 1:173-212.

The graphics files for this treatise are SCHENC 01GF-SCHENC 12GF. Cf. SCHEN TEXT.

Author: Anonymous
Treatise: Scholia enchiriadis de arte musica
Incipit: Discipulus. Musica quid est? Magister. Bene modulandi scientia. D. Bene modulari

File name: **SCHEN** Data input by: Stephen E. Hayes
File type: **TEXT** Data checked by: Bradley Jon Tucker & Peter Slemon
 MS: Print: **X** Data approved by: Thomas J. Mathiesen
Filelist: 9th-11th File size: 92K Annotations:

Source of data:
 Patrologia cursus completus, series latina, ed. J. P. Migne, 221 vols. (Paris: Garnier, 1844-1904), 132:981-1026.

The graphics files for this treatise are SCHEN 01GF-SCHEN 17GF. Cf. SCHENC TEXT.

Author: Anonymous
Treatise: Species plani cantus sunt terdecim
Incipit: Vnisonus. Semitonus. Tonus. Semiditonus. Ditonus. Diateseron. Tritonus. Diapente.

File name: **ANOSPE** Data input by: Andreas Giger
File type: **TEXT** Data checked by: Michael W. Lundell
 MS: Print: **X** Data approved by: Thomas J. Mathiesen
Filelist: 15th File size: 8K Annotations:

Source of data:
 Karl-Werner Gümpel and Klaus-Jürgen Sachs, "Das Manuskript Girona 91 und sein Contrapunctus-Traktat," Archiv für Musikwissenschaft 45 (1988): 193-96. Used by permission.

Based on Girona (Catalonia), Arxiu Capitular, 91, ff. 118r-119v.

Author: Anonymous
Treatise: Speculum cantancium. siue psallencium
Incipit: Quia omnes septem sciencie liberales .a. septiformi gracia spiritus sancti procedentes

File name: **ANOSPEC**   Data input by: Peter M. Lefferts
File type: **MLBLL763**   Data checked by: Michael W. Lundell
  MS: **X**   Print: Data approved by: Thomas J. Mathiesen
Filelist: 14th   File size: 6K   Annotations:
Source of data: =RISM BIII/4:87-91. The "title" of the treatise
  London, British Library, Lansdowne 763,   is preceded by a short introduction: "Et de
  ff. 59r-60v.   affectu Musice Moralis secundum tradiciones
    antiquorum et sanctorum patrum ex alia parte
    tractatus compendiosus sequitur. qui et
    speculum psallencium nuncupatur."

Author: Anonymous
Treatise: Sub breuissimo compendio Philippo de Vitriaco in musica incipit
Incipit: Omni desideranti notitiam artis musice mensurabilis tam noue quam ueteris obtinere

File name: **ANOOMDE**   Data input by: John Gray
File type: **MSBCLV30**   Data checked by: Andreas Giger
  MS: **X**   Print: Data approved by: Thomas J. Mathiesen
Filelist: 14th   File size: 3K   Annotations:
Source of data: =RISM BIII/2:120-23. The graphics file for
  Siena, Biblioteca comunale, L.V.30, f.   this treatise is ANOOMDE 01GF. Cf.
  129r-v.   ANOOMD TEXT.

Author: Anonymous
Treatise: Sub brevissimo compendio Philippus de Vitriaco in musica incipit
Incipit: Omni desideranti notitiam artis musicae mensurabilis tam novae quam veteris obtinere

File name: **ANOOMD**   Data input by: Stephen E. Hayes
File type: **TEXT**   Data checked by: Peter Lefferts & Luminita Aluas
  MS: Print: **X**   Data approved by: Thomas J. Mathiesen
Filelist: 14th   File size: 4K   Annotations:
Source of data: The text was first published in Musica
  Philippi de Vitriaco Ars nova, ed. Gilbert   disciplina 14 (1960): 30-31. Cf. ANOOMDE
  Reaney, André Gilles, and Jean Maillard,   MSBCLV30.
  Corpus scriptorum de musica, vol. 8
  ([Rome]: American Institute of
  Musicology, 1964), 80-81. Used by
  permission.

Author: Anonymous

Treatise: Summula

Incipit: Dat de psallendi metis pariterque canendi

File name: **ANOSUM**   Data input by: Andreas Giger

File type: **TEXT**   Data checked by: Elisabeth Honn

MS: Print: **X**   Data approved by: Thomas J. Mathiesen

Filelist: 15th   File size: 71K   Annotations:

Source of data:

Summula tractatus metricus de musica glossis commentarioque instructus, ed. Eddie Vetter, Divitiae musicae artis, A/VIIIa (Buren: Knuf, 1988), 39-101. Used by kind permission of the Laaber-Verlag.

Based on Mainz, Stadtbibliothek II 375, ff. 25r-38v; Paris, Bibliothèque Nationale, lat. 16664 (olim Sorb. 1479), ff. 39v-43v; and Rome, Biblioteca Apostolica Vaticana, Pal. lat. 957, ff. 85r-92r. The verses of the Summula are followed by a commentary, beginning: "De regulis, numero, proprietatibus et clavibus finalibus tonorum primum capitulum. Cum ars musica, quae inter philosophiae ...." An Appendix contains some additional verses by Johannes de Velle. The graphics files for this treatise are ANOSUM 01GF-ANOSUM 10GF.

Author: Anonymous

Treatise: Tonale Sancti Bernardi

Incipit: Discipulus. Quid est tonus? Magister. Regula, naturam et formam cantuum regularium

File name: **BERTON**   Data input by: Stephen E. Hayes

File type: **TEXT**   Data checked by: Peter Lefferts & Angela Mariani

MS: Print: **X**   Data approved by: Thomas J. Mathiesen

Filelist: 12th   File size: 19K   Annotations:

Source of data:

Scriptores ecclesiastici de musica sacra potissimum, 3 vols., ed. Martin Gerbert (St. Blaise: Typis San-Blasianis, 1784; reprint ed., Hildesheim: Olms, 1963), 2:265-77.

The graphics files for this treatise are BERTON 01GF-BERTON 08GF.

Author: Anonymous

Treatise: Tractatuli

Incipit: [varia]

File name: **ANOTRA17**   Data input by: Andreas Giger

File type: **TEXT**   Data checked by: Elisabeth Honn

MS: Print: **X**   Data approved by: Thomas J. Mathiesen

Filelist: 12th   File size: 12K   Annotations:

Source of data:

Codex Oxoniensis Bibl. Bodl. Rawl. C 270: Pars B, XVII Tractatuli a quodam studioso peregrino ad annum MC collecti, ed. Joseph Smits van Waesberghe, Divitiae musicae artis, A/Xb (Buren: Knuf, 1980), 33-41. Used by kind permission of the Laaber-Verlag.

Based on Oxford, Bodleian Library, Rawl. C 270, ff. 9v-22v. The incipits for the treatises included in this file are: "Quisquis velis camenarum," "Proportio est duarum rerum ad se invicem," "Proportio est rerum diversarum apta comparatio," "Partes quidem diapason sunt diapente et diatessaron," and "Est autem in musicis diapason."

Author: Anonymous

Treatise: Tractatulus de cantu mensurali seu figurativo musice artis

Incipit: Quoniam cantum mensuralem seu figuratum musice artis multi ignorantes solent

File name: **ANOTRA**   Data input by: Stephen E. Hayes

File type: **TEXT**   Data checked by: Bradley Jon Tucker

MS: Print: **X**   Data approved by: Thomas J. Mathiesen

Filelist: 14th   File size: 45K   Annotations:

Source of data:

Anonymus, Tractatulus de cantu
mensurali seu figurativo musice artis
(MS. Melk, Stiftsbibliothek 950), ed. F.
Alberto Gallo, Corpus scriptorum de
musica, vol. 16 ([Rome]: American
Institute of Musicology, 1971), 11-37.
Used by permission.

The so-called Melk Anonymous. The graphics
file for this treatise is ANOTRA 01GF.

Author: Anonymous

Treatise: Tractatus

Incipit: Diatessaron alia constat ex tono et semitonio et tono, ut ab A in D; alia ex semitonio

File name: **BECANO**   Data input by: Firoozeh Khazrai

File type: **TEXT**   Data checked by: Bradley Jon Tucker

MS: Print: **X**   Data approved by: Thomas J. Mathiesen

Filelist: 9th-11t   File size: 10K   Annotations:

Source of data:

Adolf Becker, "Ein Erfurter Traktat über
gregorianische Musik," Archiv für
Musikwissenschaft 1 (1918-19): 151-61.

The graphics files for this treatise are
BECANO 01GF-BECANO 09GF.

Author: Anonymous

Treatise: Tractatus artis antiquae cum explicatione mensurae binariae

Incipit: Notandum quod, muteto vel conducto qui mensurabiliter cantantur

File name: **ANOTAA**   Data input by: Peter Slemon

File type: **TEXT**   Data checked by: Michael W. Lundell

MS: Print: **X**   Data approved by: Thomas J. Mathiesen

Filelist: 13th   File size: 6K   Annotations:

Source of data:

Johannes dictus Balloce, Abreviatio
magistri Franconis; Anonymus,
Compendium musicae mensurabilis artis
antiquae (Ms. Saint-Dié, Bibl.
Municipale, 42), ed. Gilbert Reaney;
Anonymus, Compendium musicae
mensurabilis artis antiquae (Ms. Wien,
Nationalbibl., 5003); Anonymus,
Tractatus artis antiquae cum explicatione
mensurae binariae (Ms. Wien,
Nationalbibl., 5003), ed. Heinz Ristory,
Corpus scriptorum de musica, vol. 34
(n.p.: American Institute of Musicology,
1987), 69-73. Used by permission.

Based on Vienna, Nationalbibliothek, 5003, ff.
202v-204r. The graphics file for this treatise is
ANOTAA 01GF.

Author: Anonymous

Treatise: Tractatus cantandi graduale. Graduali Cisterciensi prologi instar praemissus

Incipit: Sicut notatores Antiphonarium praemunivimus, ita et eos qui gradualia notaturi sunt

File name: **ANOCIST**　　Data input by: Andreas Giger

File type: **TEXT**　　　Data checked by: Elisabeth Honn

　MS:　　　Print: **X**　　Data approved by: Thomas J. Mathiesen

Filelist: 12th　　File size: 6K　　　　Annotations:

Source of data:

　Patrologia cursus completus, series latina,
　ed. J. P. Migne, 221 vols. (Paris: Garnier,
　1844-1904), 182:1151-54.

Author: Anonymous

Treatise: Tractatus cantus figurati

Incipit: Quoniam per magis noti notitiam ad ignoti facilius devenitur notitiam

File name: **ANO12TCF**　　Data input by: Peter Slemon

File type: **TEXT**　　　Data checked by: Angela Mariani

　MS:　　　Print: **X**　　Data approved by: Thomas J. Mathiesen

Filelist: 15th　　File size: 59K　　　Annotations:

Source of data:　　　　　　　　The graphics files for this treatise are
　Anonymus, Tractatus et compendium　　ANO12TCF 01GF-ANO12TCF 08GF. A
　cantus figurati (Mss. London, British　　revision of Jill Palmer, "Coussemaker's
　Libr., Add. 34200; Regensburg,　　Anonymous XII: A Text, Translation, and
　Proskesche Musikbibl., 98 th. 4o), ed. Jill　Commentary (M.A. thesis, Brigham Young
　M. Palmer, Corpus scriptorum de musica,　University, 1975). Cf. ANO12TRA TEXT and
　vol. 35 (n.p.: American Institute of　　ANOCOMP TEXT.
　Musicology; Hänssler Verlag, 1990),
　41-93. Used by permission.

Author: Anonymous

Treatise: Tractatus cuiusdam monachi de musica

Incipit: Quindecim chordae habentur in monochordo secundum Boetium.

File name: **WFANON1**　　Data input by: Firoozeh Khazrai

File type: **TEXT**　　　Data checked by: Bradley Jon Tucker

　MS:　　　Print: **X**　　Data approved by: Thomas J. Mathiesen

Filelist: 12th　　File size: 34K　　　Annotations:

Source of data:　　　　　　　　The graphics files for this treatise are
　Johannes Wolf, "Ein anonymer　　WFANON1 01GF-WFANON1 02GF. The
　Musiktraktat des elften bis zwölften　　text is edited from Darmstadt 1988, ff.
　Jahrhunderts," Vierteljahresschrift für　　182r-189v.
　Musikwissenschaft 9 (1893): 194-226.

Author: Anonymous

Treatise: Tractatus de figuris sive de notis

Incipit: Cum in isto tractatu de figuris sive de notis, quae sunt et de earum proprietatibus

File name: **TRADEF**

File type: **TEXT**

MS:　　　Print: **X**

Filelist: 14th　　File size: 25K

Data input by: Stephen E. Hayes

Data checked by: Peter Lefferts & Bradley Tucker

Data approved by: Thomas J. Mathiesen

Annotations:

Source of data:

Ms. Oxford, Bodley 842 (Willelmus), Breviarium regulare musicae; Ms. British Museum, Royal 12. C. VI., Tractatus de figuris sive de notis; Johannes Torkesey, Declaratio trianguli et scuti, Corpus scriptorum de musica, vol. 12 ([Rome]: American Institute of Musicology, 1966), 40-51. Used by permission.

The graphics files for this treatise are TRADEF 01GF-TRADEF 02GF. The text is edited from London, British Library, Royal 12.C.VI., ff. 54-58. Cf. ANO6TRA TEXT.

Author: Anonymous

Treatise: Tractatus de musica

Incipit: Viso de gravibus ordine ad acutas, notatoque quomodo ex speciebus diatessaron

File name: **ANOFRA5**

File type: **TEXT**

MS:　　　Print: **X**

Filelist: 12th　　File size: 14K

Data input by: John Csonka

Data checked by: Jan Herlinger & Angela Mariani

Data approved by: Thomas J. Mathiesen

Annotations:

Source of data:

Adrien de la Fage, Essais de dipthérographie musicale (Paris: Legouix, 1864), 355-62.

Based on Florence, Biblioteca nazionale centrale, Magliabechiana XIX.D.19. The treatise is sometimes known as La Fage Anonymous I (=St. Martial Anonymous). The treatise is followed by a few lines of a "documentum tonorum." The graphics file for this treatise is ANOFRA5 01GF.

Author: Anonymous

Treatise: Tractatus de musica

Incipit: Omni desideranti notitiam artis mensurabilis tam noue quam ueteris obtinere

File name: **AGANONT**

File type: **TEXT**

MS:　　　Print: **X**

Filelist: 15th　　File size: 11K

Data input by: Stephen E. Hayes

Data checked by: Peter Lefferts & Luminita Aluas

Data approved by: Thomas J. Mathiesen

Annotations:

Source of data:

Higini Angles, "Dos tractats medievals de musica figurada," in Musikwissenschaftliche Beiträge: Festschrift für Johannes Wolf zu seinem sechzigsten Geburtstag, ed. W. Lott, H. Osthoff, and W. Wolffheim (Berlin: Breslauer, 1929), 6-10.

Sometimes known as Angles Anonymous 1929; based on Sevilla, Biblioteca Capitular y Colombina 5.II.25 [in Catedral metropolitana].

Author: Anonymous

Treatise: Tractatus de musica compendium cantus figurati

Incipit: Praesens compendium secundum famosiores musicos in quindecim capitula

File name: **ANOCOMP**   Data input by: Stephen E. Hayes

File type: **TEXT**   Data checked by: Peter M. Lefferts & Andreas Giger

MS: Print: **X**   Data approved by: Thomas J. Mathiesen

Filelist: 15th   File size: 23K   Annotations:

Source of data:

Jill Palmer, "A Late Fifteenth-Century Anonymous Mensuration Treatise (Ssp) Salzburg, Erzabtei St. Peter, a VI 44, 1490; cod. pap.; 206 x 149 mm. 75ff.," Musica disciplina 39 (1985): 89-103. Text copyright 1986. Used by permission of the American Institute of Musicology (Tempo Music Publications, 3773 West 95th Street, Leawood, KS 66206).

The graphics files for this treatise are ANOCOMP 01GF-ANOCOMP 02GF. Cf. ANO12TCF TEXT and ANO12TRA TEXT.

Author: Anonymous

Treatise: Tractatus de musica figurata et de contrapuncto ab anonymo auctore

Incipit: Item notandum quod septem sunt reformationes in manu videlicet:

File name: **TRADEM**   Data input by: Stephen E. Hayes

File type: **TEXT**   Data checked by: Peter Lefferts & Bradley Tucker

MS: Print: **X**   Data approved by: Thomas J. Mathiesen

Filelist: 15th   File size: 28K   Annotations:

Source of data:

Scriptorum de musica medii aevi nova series a Gerbertina altera, 4 vols., ed. Edmond de Coussemaker (Paris: Durand, 1864-76; reprint ed., Hildesheim: Olms, 1963), 4:434-69.

Text edited from Paris, Bibliothèque Nationale, lat. 16664, ff. 62v-85v. The graphics files for this treatise are TRADEM 01GF-TRADEM 36GF.

Author: Anonymous

Treatise: Tractatus de musica mensurabili

Incipit: Quoniam circa artem musicalis sciencie hodiernis temporibus cantando delyrant

File name: **WFANON4**   Data input by: Stephen E. Hayes

File type: **TEXT**   Data checked by: Peter Lefferts & Luminita Aluas

MS: Print: **X**   Data approved by: Thomas J. Mathiesen

Filelist: 15th   File size: 42K   Annotations:

Source of data:

Johannes Wolf, "Ein Breslauer Mensuraltraktat des 15. Jahrhunderts," Archiv für Musikwissenschaft 1 (1918-19): 331-45.

Commonly known as Wolf's Anonymous 4 or the Breslau Anonymous; based on Breslau, Biblioteka Uniwersytecka cart.IV.Qu.16. The graphics files for this treatise are WFANON4 01GF-WFANON4 03GF. Cf. ARITRA TEXT, BEDMUS TEXT, and LAMTRAC MSBCLV30.

Author: Anonymous

Treatise: Tractatus de musica plana et organica

Incipit: Musica est ars recte canendi sono cantuque consistens.

File name: **ANOMUPO**   Data input by: Stephen E. Hayes

File type: **TEXT**   Data checked by: Peter Lefferts & Angela Mariani

MS: Print: **X**   Data approved by: Thomas J. Mathiesen

Filelist: 13th   File size: 34K   Annotations:

Source of data:

Scriptorum de musica medii aevi nova series a Gerbertina altera, 4 vols., ed. Edmond de Coussemaker (Paris: Durand, 1864-76; reprint ed., Hildesheim: Olms, 1963), 2:484-98.

The so-called "Louvain Treatise." The graphics files for this treatise are ANOMUPO 01GF-ANOMUPO 06GF.

Author: Anonymous

Treatise: Tractatus figurarum

Incipit: Incipit tractatus figurarum per quas diversimode discantatur

File name: **TRAFIG**   Data input by: Philip E. Schreur

File type: **TEXT**   Data checked by: C. Matthew Balensuela

MS: Print: **X**   Data approved by: Thomas J. Mathiesen

Filelist: 14th   File size: 14K   Annotations:

Source of data:

Tractatus figurarum, ed. and trans. by Philip E. Schreur, Greek and Latin Music Theory, vol. 6 (Lincoln: University of Nebraska Press, 1989), 66-102. Used by permission.

The treatise is ascribed to Philippus de Caserta in CS III. The graphics file for this treatise is TRAFIG 01GF.

Author: Anonymous

Treatise: Vita Sancti Remigii

Incipit: Isti versus sunt scripti in scrinio corporis sancti Remigii in linea superiori

File name: **REMVIT**   Data input by: John Csonka

File type: **TEXT**   Data checked by: Jan Herlinger & Bradley Tucker

MS: Print: **X**   Data approved by: Thomas J. Mathiesen

Filelist: 9th-11th   File size: 3K   Annotations:

Source of data:

Adrien de la Fage, Essais de dipthérographie musicale (Paris: Legouix, 1864), 474-75.

Based on Monte Cassino, Arch. 494. The graphics file for this treatise is REMVIT 01GF.

Author: Anonymous 1

Treatise: Tractatus de consonantiis musicalibus

Incipit: Tredecim consonantie sunt quibus omnis cantus ecclesiaticus contexitur.

File name: **ANO1TRA**   Data input by: Bradley Jon Tucker

File type: **TEXT**   Data checked by: Thomas J. Mathiesen

MS: Print: **X**   Data approved by: Oliver B. Ellsworth

Filelist: 13th   File size: 15K   Annotations:

Source of data:

Scriptorum de musica medii aevi nova series a Gerbertina altera, 4 vols., ed. Edmond de Coussemaker (Paris: Durand, 1864-76; reprint ed., Hildesheim: Olms, 1963), 1:296-302.

The graphics files for this treatise are ANO1TRA 01GF-ANO1TRA 02GF.

Author: Anonymous 2

Treatise: Tractatus de discantu

Incipit: Gaudent brevitate moderni. Quandocunque punctus quadratus, vel nota quadrata

File name: **ANO2TRA**   Data input by: Bradley Jon Tucker

File type: **TEXT**   Data checked by: Peter M. Lefferts

  MS: Print: **X**   Data approved by: Thomas J. Mathiesen

Filelist: 13th   File size: 24K   Annotations:

Source of data:

Scriptorum de musica medii aevi nova series a Gerbertina altera, 4 vols., ed. Edmond de Coussemaker (Paris: Durand, 1864-76; reprint ed., Hildesheim: Olms, 1963), 1:303-19.

The graphics files for this treatise are ANO2TRA 01GF-ANO2TRA 08GF. Cf. ANOCOM TEXT, ANOCOMM TEXT, ANOCMM TEXT, ANOTDD TEXT, and ANO3DEC TEXT.

Author: Anonymous 3

Treatise: De cantu mensurabili

Incipit: Gaudent brevitate moderni. Quandocunque nota quadrata, vel punctus quadratus

File name: **ANO3DEC**   Data input by: Luminita Aluas

File type: **TEXT**   Data checked by: Margaret Bent

  MS: Print: **X**   Data approved by: Albert C. Rotola, S.J.

Filelist: 13th   File size: 15K   Annotations:

Source of data:

Scriptorum de musica medii aevi nova series a Gerbertina altera, 4 vols., ed. Edmond de Coussemaker (Paris: Durand, 1864-76; reprint ed., Hildesheim: Olms, 1963), 1:319-27.

The graphics files for this treatise are ANO3DEC 01GF-ANO3DEC 03GF. Cf. ANOCOM TEXT, ANOCOMM TEXT, ANOCMM TEXT, ANOTDD TEXT, and ANO2TRA TEXT.

Author: Anonymous 4

Treatise: [Musica]

Incipit: Cognita modulatione melorum secundum viam octo troporum et secundum usum

File name: **ANO4MUS**   Data input by: Angela Mariani

File type: **TEXT**   Data checked by: Bradley Jon Tucker

  MS: Print: **X**   Data approved by: Thomas J. Mathiesen

Filelist: 13th   File size: 135K   Annotations:

Source of data: Cf. ANO4DEM TEXT.

Fritz Reckow, Der Musiktraktat des Anonymus 4, 2 vols., Beihefte zum Archiv für Musikwissenschaft, vols. 4-5 (Wiesbaden: Steiner, 1967), 1:22-89. Used by permission.

Author: Anonymous 4

Treatise: De mensuris et discantu

Incipit: Cognita modulatione melorum, secundum viam octo troporum, et secundum usum

File name: **ANO4DEM**   Data input by: Luminita Aluas

File type: **TEXT**   Data checked by: Sandra Pinegar

MS: Print: **X**   Data approved by: Thomas J. Mathiesen

Filelist: 13th   File size: 132K   Annotations:

Source of data:

Scriptorum de musica medii aevi nova series a Gerbertina altera, 4 vols., ed. Edmond de Coussemaker (Paris: Durand, 1864-76; reprint ed., Hildesheim: Olms, 1963), 1:327-64.

Cf. ANO4MUS TEXT.

Author: Anonymous 5

Treatise: De discantu

Incipit: Est autem unisonus quando due voces manent in uno et eodem loco

File name: **ANO5DED**   Data input by: Luminita Aluas

File type: **TEXT**   Data checked by: Margaret Bent

MS: Print: **X**   Data approved by: Albert C. Rotola, S.J.

Filelist: 14th   File size: 9K   Annotations:

Source of data:

Scriptorum de musica medii aevi nova series a Gerbertina altera, 4 vols., ed. Edmond de Coussemaker (Paris: Durand, 1864-76; reprint ed., Hildesheim: Olms, 1963), 1:366-68.

The graphics file for this treatise is ANO5DED 01GF.

Author: Anonymous 6

Treatise: Tractatus de figuris sive de notis

Incipit: Cum in isto tractatu de figuris sive de notis, que sunt, et de earum proprietatibus

File name: **ANO6TRA**   Data input by: Luminita Aluas

File type: **TEXT**   Data checked by: Margaret Bent

MS: Print: **X**   Data approved by: Albert C. Rotola, S.J.

Filelist: 14th   File size: 25K   Annotations:

Source of data:

Scriptorum de musica medii aevi nova series a Gerbertina altera, 4 vols., ed. Edmond de Coussemaker (Paris: Durand, 1864-76; reprint ed., Hildesheim: Olms, 1963), 1:369-77.

The graphics files for this treatise are ANO6TRA 01GF-ANO6TRA 02GF. Cf. TRADEF TEXT.

Author: Anonymous 7

Treatise: De musica libellus

Incipit: Modus in musica est debita mensuratio temporis, scilicet per longas et breves

File name: **ANO7DEM**   Data input by: Luminita Aluas

File type: **TEXT**   Data checked by: Charles M. Atkinson

MS: Print: **X**   Data approved by: Thomas J. Mathiesen

Filelist: 13th   File size: 15K   Annotations:

Source of data: The graphics file for this treatise is

Scriptorum de musica medii aevi nova   ANO7DEM 01GF.
series a Gerbertina altera, 4 vols., ed.
Edmond de Coussemaker (Paris: Durand,
1864-76; reprint ed., Hildesheim: Olms,
1963), 1:378-83.

Author: Anonymous I

Treatise: De musica antiqua et nova

Incipit: Dictis aliquibus circa planum cantum, restat aliud dicendum de cantu

File name: **ANO1DEM**   Data input by: Peter M. Lefferts

File type: **TEXT**   Data checked by: Stephen E. Hayes

MS: Print: **X**   Data approved by: Thomas J. Mathiesen

Filelist: 14th   File size: 80K   Annotations:

Source of data: Equivalent to the Quartum Principale of the

Scriptorum de musica medii aevi nova   Quatuor Principale, Version A (partially
series a Gerbertina altera, 4 vols., ed.   preserved in British Library, Cotton Tiberius
Edmond de Coussemaker (Paris: Durand,   B.IX; and fully preserved in British Library,
1864-76; reprint ed., Hildesheim: Olms,   Additional 4909, ff. 17v-56). The graphics
1963), 3:334-64.   files for this treatise are ANO1DEM
    01GF-ANO1DEM 08GF. Cf. QUAPRIA
    MLBL4909 and QUAPRIB TEXT.

Author: Anonymous I

Treatise: Musica

Incipit: Duo semisphaeria, quas magadas vocant, concavo instrumento hinc et hinc

File name: **ANO1MUS**   Data input by: Stephen E. Hayes

File type: **TEXT**   Data checked by: Peter Lefferts & Angela Mariani

MS: Print: **X**   Data approved by: Thomas J. Mathiesen

Filelist: 9th-11th File size: 19K   Annotations:

Source of data: The incipit is preceded the following list of

Scriptores ecclesiastici de musica sacra   contents: "Argumentum. 1. Triplicis generis
potissimum, 3 vols., ed. Martin Gerbert   divisio in monochordo. 2. Diatonicum genus.
(St. Blaise: Typis San-Blasianis, 1784;   3. Chromaticum et enharmonicum. 4.
reprint ed., Hildesheim: Olms, 1963),   Chordarum nomina. 5. Quinque tetrachorda. 6.
1:330-38.   Consonantiae; 7. Earumque species. 8. Octo
    cantionum modi." The graphics file for this
    treatise is ANO1MUS 01GF. Cf. ANO1MU
    TEXT and BERNDEM TEXT.

Author: Anonymous I

Treatise: Musica

Incipit: Duo semisphaeria, quas magadas vocant, concavo instrumento hinc et hinc

File name: **ANO1MU**   Data input by: John Gray

File type: **TEXT**   Data checked by: Oliver Ellsworth & Andreas Giger

MS: Print: **X**   Data approved by: Thomas J. Mathiesen

Filelist: 9th-11th File size: 19K   Annotations:

Source of data:

Patrologia cursus completus, series latina, ed. J. P. Migne, 221 vols. (Paris: Garnier, 1844-1904), 151:673-82.

The incipit is preceded the following list of contents: "Argumentum.--1. Triplicis generis divisio in monochordo. 2. Diatonicum genus. 3. Chromaticum et enharmonicum. 4. Chordarum nomina. 5. Quinque tetrachorda. 6. Consonantiae; 7. Earumque species. 8. Octo cantionum modi." The graphics file for this treatise is ANO1MU 01GF. Cf. ANO1MUS TEXT and BERNDEM TEXT.

Author: Anonymous II

Treatise: De musica antiqua et nova

Incipit: Ad evidentiam valoris notularum, sciendum quod quotienscumque nota

File name: **ANO2DEM**   Data input by: Luminita Aluas

File type: **TEXT**   Data checked by: Thomas J. Mathiesen

MS: Print: **X**   Data approved by: Benito V. Rivera

Filelist: 14th   File size: 18K   Annotations:

Source of data:

Scriptorum de musica medii aevi nova series a Gerbertina altera, 4 vols., ed. Edmond de Coussemaker (Paris: Durand, 1864-76; reprint ed., Hildesheim: Olms, 1963), 3:364-70.

The graphics file for this treatise is ANO2DEM 01GF. Cf. ANO2DEV TEXT.

Author: Anonymous II

Treatise: Tractatus de discantu

Incipit: Gaudent brevitate moderni. Quandocumque punctus quadratus vel nota quadrata

File name: **ANOTDD**   Data input by: Peter Slemon

File type: **TEXT**   Data checked by: Bradley Jon Tucker

MS: Print: **X**   Data approved by: Thomas J. Mathiesen

Filelist: 13th   File size: 26K   Annotations:

Source of data:

Anonymous II, Tractatus de discantu, ed. Albert Seay, Texts/Translations, no. 1 (Colorado Springs: Colorado College Music Press, 1978), 2-62. Used by permission.

The graphics files for this treatise are ANOTDD 01GF-ANOTDD 19GF. Cf. ANOCOM TEXT, ANOCOMM TEXT, ANOCMM TEXT, ANO2TRA TEXT, and ANO3DEC TEXT.

Author: Anonymous II
Treatise: Tractatus de musica
Incipit: Quinque sunt consonantiae musicae, diatessaron, quae et sesquitertia dicitur

File name: **ANO2TDM**   Data input by: Stephen E. Hayes
File type: **TEXT**   Data checked by: Peter Lefferts & Angela Mariani
  MS: Print: **X**   Data approved by: Thomas J. Mathiesen
Filelist: 12th   File size: 14K   Annotations:
Source of data: Cf. ANO2TRDM TEXT.
  Scriptores ecclesiastici de musica sacra
  potissimum, 3 vols., ed. Martin Gerbert
  (St. Blaise: Typis San-Blasianis, 1784;
  reprint ed., Hildesheim: Olms, 1963),
  1:338-42.

Author: Anonymous II
Treatise: Tractatus de musica
Incipit: Quinque sunt consonantiae musicae, Diatessaron, quae et sesquitertia dicitur

File name: **ANO2TRDM**   Data input by: John Gray
File type: **TEXT**   Data checked by: Oliver Ellsworth & Andreas Giger
  MS: Print: **X**   Data approved by: Thomas J. Mathiesen
Filelist: 12th   File size: 14K   Annotations:
Source of data: Cf. ANO2TDM TEXT.
  Patrologia cursus completus, series latina,
  ed. J. P. Migne, 221 vols. (Paris: Garnier,
  1844-1904), 151:681-86.

Author: Anonymous III
Treatise: Compendiolum artis veteris ac novae
Incipit: Quoniam per ignorantiam artis musice multi, et maxime temporibus moderni,

File name: **ANO3COM**   Data input by: Luminita Aluas
File type: **TEXT**   Data checked by: Thomas J. Mathiesen
  MS: Print: **X**   Data approved by: Benito V. Rivera
Filelist: 14th   File size: 14K   Annotations:
Source of data: The graphics file for this treatise is
  Scriptorum de musica medii aevi nova   ANO3COM 01GF.
  series a Gerbertina altera, 4 vols., ed.
  Edmond de Coussemaker (Paris: Durand,
  1864-76; reprint ed., Hildesheim: Olms,
  1963), 3:370-75.

Author: Anonymous III
Treatise: Fragmentum musices
Incipit: Ab omni superparticulari si continuam ei superparticularem quis auferat proportionem

File name: **ANO3FRA**   Data input by: Stephen E. Hayes
File type: **TEXT**   Data checked by: Peter Lefferts & Angela Mariani
  MS: Print: **X**   Data approved by: Thomas J. Mathiesen
Filelist: 12th   File size: 6K   Annotations:
Source of data: Cf. ANO3FRAM TEXT.
  Scriptores ecclesiastici de musica sacra
  potissimum, 3 vols., ed. Martin Gerbert
  (St. Blaise: Typis San-Blasianis, 1784;
  reprint ed., Hildesheim: Olms, 1963),
  1:343-44.

Author: Anonymous III
Treatise: Fragmentum musices
Incipit: Ab omni superparticulari si continuam ei superparticularem quis auferat proportionem

File name: **ANO3FRAM**
File type: **TEXT**
MS: Print: **X**
Filelist: 12th   File size: 6K
Source of data:
  Patrologia cursus completus, series latina,
  ed. J. P. Migne, 221 vols. (Paris: Garnier,
  1844-1904), 151:685-88.

Data input by: John Gray
Data checked by: Oliver Ellsworth & Andreas Giger
Data approved by: Thomas J. Mathiesen
Annotations:
  Cf. ANO3FRA TEXT.

Author: Anonymous IV
Treatise: Compendium artis mensurabilis tam veteris quam novae
Incipit: Si quis artem musice mensurabilis tam veterem quam novam

File name: **ANO4COM**
File type: **TEXT**
MS: Print: **X**
Filelist: 15th   File size: 10K
Source of data:
  Scriptorum de musica medii aevi nova
  series a Gerbertina altera, 4 vols., ed.
  Edmond de Coussemaker (Paris: Durand,
  1864-76; reprint ed., Hildesheim: Olms,
  1963), 3:376-79.

Data input by: Luminita Aluas
Data checked by: Anne Stone
Data approved by: Thomas J. Mathiesen
Annotations:
  Cf. ANO4CMM TEXT.

Author: Anonymous OP
Treatise: Tractatus de musica
Incipit: Quod punctus per sui additionem possit facere brevem alterari.

File name: **ANOPTRA**
File type: **TEXT**
MS: Print: **X**
Filelist: 14th   File size: 12K
Source of data:
  Ulrich Michels, "Der Musiktraktat des
  Anonymus OP: Ein frühes
  Theoretiker-Zeugnis der Ars nova,"
  Archiv für Musikwissenschaft 26 (1969):
  56-62. Used by permission.

Data input by: Stephen E. Hayes
Data checked by: Peter M. Lefferts
Data approved by: Thomas J. Mathiesen
Annotations:
  Based on Oxford, Bodleian Library, Bodley
  77; and Paris, Bibliothèque Nationale, lat.
  14741.

Author: Anonymous V
Treatise: Ars cantus mensurabilis
Incipit: Ad honorem et gloriam Sanctissime Trinitatis

File name: **ANO5ARS**
File type: **TEXT**
MS: Print: **X**
Filelist: 15th   File size: 49K
Source of data:
  Scriptorum de musica medii aevi nova
  series a Gerbertina altera, 4 vols., ed.
  Edmond de Coussemaker (Paris: Durand,
  1864-76; reprint ed., Hildesheim: Olms,
  1963), 3:379-98.

Data input by: C. Matthew Balensuela
Data checked by: Sandra Pinegar
Data approved by: Thomas J. Mathiesen
Annotations:
  The graphics files for this treatise are
  ANO5ARS 01GF-ANO5ARS 03GF. Cf.
  ANO5ACM TEXT.

Author: Anonymous VI

Treatise: De musica mensurabili

Incipit: Quum dictum sit musicam in numero ternario sumere perfectionem

File name: **ANO6DEM**   Data input by: Luminita Aluas

File type: **TEXT**   Data checked by: Anne Stone

MS: Print: **X**   Data approved by: Thomas J. Mathiesen

Filelist: 14th   File size: 15K   Annotations:

Source of data: The graphics files for this treatise are
  Scriptorum de musica medii aevi nova   ANO6DEM 01GF-ANO6DEM 02GF.
  series a Gerbertina altera, 4 vols., ed.
  Edmond de Coussemaker (Paris: Durand,
  1864-76; reprint ed., Hildesheim: Olms,
  1963), 3:398-403.

Author: Anonymous VII

Treatise: De diversis maneriebus in musica mensurabili

Incipit: Sic formantur breves plicate:

File name: **ANO7DED**   Data input by: Luminita Aluas

File type: **TEXT**   Data checked by: Bradley Jon Tucker

MS: Print: **X**   Data approved by: Jan Herlinger

Filelist: 14th   File size: 11K   Annotations:

Source of data: Cf. ANO7DDM TEXT.
  Scriptorum de musica medii aevi nova
  series a Gerbertina altera, 4 vols., ed.
  Edmond de Coussemaker (Paris: Durand,
  1864-76; reprint ed., Hildesheim: Olms,
  1963), 3:404-8.

Author: Anonymous VIII

Treatise: Regulae de contrapuncto

Incipit: Consonantie contrapuncti demonstrativi ad oculum sunt sex

File name: **ANO8REG**   Data input by: Luminita Aluas

File type: **TEXT**   Data checked by: Bradley Jon Tucker

MS: Print: **X**   Data approved by: Thomas J. Mathiesen

Filelist: 15th   File size: 8K   Annotations:

Source of data:
  Scriptorum de musica medii aevi nova
  series a Gerbertina altera, 4 vols., ed.
  Edmond de Coussemaker (Paris: Durand,
  1864-76; reprint ed., Hildesheim: Olms,
  1963), 3:409-11.

Author: Anonymous X

Treatise: De minimis notulis

Incipit: Item notandum quod notularum species quantum plures

File name: **ANO10DEM**   Data input by: Luminita Aluas

File type: **TEXT**   Data checked by: Bradley Jon Tucker

MS: Print: **X**   Data approved by: Thomas J. Mathiesen

Filelist: 15th   File size: 8K   Annotations:

Source of data:

Scriptorum de musica medii aevi nova
series a Gerbertina altera, 4 vols., ed.
Edmond de Coussemaker (Paris: Durand,
1864-76; reprint ed., Hildesheim: Olms,
1963), 3:413-15.

The graphics file for this treatise is
ANO10DEM 01GF.

Author: Anonymous XI

Treatise: [Tractatus de musica plana et mensurabili]

Incipit: Item diceres, quare musica studetur? Respondetur quod illo modo: quod cultus divinus

File name: **ANO11TDM**   Data input by: Hannah Jo Smith & Brian Palmer

File type: **TEXT**   Data checked by: Peter M. Lefferts & Andreas Giger

MS: Print: **X**   Data approved by: Thomas J. Mathiesen

Filelist: 15th   File size: 145K   Annotations:

Source of data:

Richard J. Wingell, "Anonymous XI (CS
III): An Edition, Translation, and
Commentary," 3 vols. (Ph.D. dissertation,
University of Southern California, 1973),
1:1-173. Used by permission.

Based on London, British Library, Additional
34200, ff. 1-41r. The graphics files for this
treatise are ANO11TDM 01GF-ANO11TDM
39GF. Cf. ANO11TRA TEXT.

Author: Anonymous XI

Treatise: Tractatus de musica plana et mensurabili

Incipit: Quare musica studetur? Respondetur quod illo modo: quod cultus divinus

File name: **ANO11TRA**   Data input by: Luminita Aluas

File type: **TEXT**   Data checked by: Bradley Jon Tucker

MS: Print: **X**   Data approved by: Thomas J. Mathiesen

Filelist: 15th   File size: 142K   Annotations:

Source of data:

Scriptorum de musica medii aevi nova
series a Gerbertina altera, 4 vols., ed.
Edmond de Coussemaker (Paris: Durand,
1864-76; reprint ed., Hildesheim: Olms,
1963), 3:416-75.

The graphics files for this treatise are
ANO11TRA 01GF-ANO11TRA 29GF. Cf.
ANO11TDM TEXT.

Author: Anonymous XII
Treatise: Tractatus de musica
Incipit: Quoniam per magis noti notitiam ad ignoti facilius devenitur notitiam

File name: **ANO12TRA**   Data input by: Bradley Jon Tucker
File type: **TEXT**   Data checked by: Thomas J. Mathiesen
MS: Print: **X**   Data approved by: Oliver B. Ellsworth
Filelist: 15th   File size: 57K   Annotations:

Source of data:
Scriptorum de musica medii aevi nova
series a Gerbertina altera, 4 vols., ed.
Edmond de Coussemaker (Paris: Durand,
1864-76; reprint ed., Hildesheim: Olms,
1963), 3:475-95.

The graphics files for this treatise are
ANO12TRA 01GF-ANO12TRA 05GF. Cf.
ANO12TCF TEXT and ANOCOMP TEXT.

Author: Antonius de Luca
Treatise: Ars cantus figurati
Incipit: Qualiter in arte practica mensurabilis cantus erudiri mediocriter affectans

File name: **LUCARS**   Data input by: Stephen E. Hayes
File type: **TEXT**   Data checked by: Peter Lefferts & Bradley Tucker
MS: Print: **X**   Data approved by: Thomas J. Mathiesen
Filelist: 15th   File size: 20K   Annotations:

Source of data:
Scriptorum de musica medii aevi nova
series a Gerbertina altera, 4 vols., ed.
Edmond de Coussemaker (Paris: Durand,
1864-76; reprint ed., Hildesheim: Olms,
1963), 4:421-33.

The graphics files for this treatise are
LUCARS 01GF-LUCARS 08GF.

Author: Aribo
Treatise: De musica
Incipit: Domno suo Ellenhardo praesulum dignissimo, in universa morum honestate praeclaro

File name: **ARIDEM**   Data input by: John Gray
File type: **TEXT**   Data checked by: Oliver Ellsworth & Luminita Aluas
MS: Print: **X**   Data approved by: Thomas J. Mathiesen
Filelist: 9th-11th   File size: 96K   Annotations:

Source of data:
Aribo, De musica, ed. J. Smits van
Waesberghe, Corpus scriptorum de
musica, vol. 2 ([Rome]: American
Institute of Musicology, 1951), 1-72.
Used by permission.

The graphics files for this treatise are
ARIDEM 01GF-ARIDEM 05GF. Cf.
ARIMUS TEXT and ARIMU TEXT.

Author: Aribo

Treatise: Musica

Incipit: Domno suo Ellenhardo praesulum dignissimo in universa morum honestate praeclaro

File name: **ARIMUS**   Data input by: Sean Ferguson

File type: **TEXT**   Data checked by: Charles Atkinson

MS: Print: **X**   Data approved by: Thomas J. Mathiesen

Filelist: 9th-11th   File size: 94K   Annotations:

Source of data:

  Scriptores ecclesiastici de musica sacra
potissimum, 3 vols., ed. Martin Gerbert
(St. Blaise: Typis San-Blasianis, 1784;
reprint ed., Hildesheim: Olms, 1963),
2:197-230.

The graphics files for this treatise are
ARIMUS 01GF-ARIMUS 05GF. Cf.
ARIDEM TEXT and ARIMU TEXT.

Author: Aribo

Treatise: Musica

Incipit: Domno suo Ellenhardo praesulum dignissimo in universa morum honestate praeclaro

File name: **ARIMU**   Data input by: Jingfa Sun

File type: **TEXT**   Data checked by: C. Atkinson, B.Tucker, P. Slemon

MS: Print: **X**   Data approved by: Thomas J. Mathiesen

Filelist: 9th-11th   File size: 93K   Annotations:

Source of data:

  Patrologia cursus completus, series latina,
ed. J. P. Migne, 221 vols. (Paris: Garnier,
1844-1904), 150:1307-46.

The graphics files for this treatise are ARIMU
01GF-ARIMU 03GF. Cf. ARIDEM TEXT
and ARIMUS TEXT.

Author: Aristotle

Treatise: Tractatus de musica

Incipit: Quoniam circa artem musicam necessaria quedam ad utilitatem constantium

File name: **ARITRA**   Data input by: Bradley Jon Tucker

File type: **TEXT**   Data checked by: Thomas J. Mathiesen

MS: Print: **X**   Data approved by: Oliver B. Ellsworth

Filelist: 13th   File size: 78K   Annotations:

Source of data:

  Scriptorum de musica medii aevi nova
series a Gerbertina altera, 4 vols., ed.
Edmond de Coussemaker (Paris: Durand,
1864-76; reprint ed., Hildesheim: Olms,
1963), 1:251-81.

This treatise is now commonly ascribed to
Magister Lambert. The graphics files for this
treatise are ARITRA 01GF-ARITRA 12GF.
Cf. BEDMUS TEXT and LAMTRAC
MSBCLV30.

Author: Arnulphus de Sancto Gilleno

Treatise: Tractatulus de differentiis et generibus cantorum

Incipit: Existimo, quod nunc temporis quatuor principales sunt differentiae cantorum.

File name: **ARNTRA**   Data input by: Bradley Jon Tucker

File type: **TEXT**   Data checked by: Angela Mariani

MS: Print: **X**   Data approved by: Thomas J. Mathiesen

Filelist: 14th   File size: 9K   Annotations:

Source of data:

  Scriptores ecclesiastici de musica sacra
potissimum, 3 vols., ed. Martin Gerbert
(St. Blaise: Typis San-Blasianis, 1784;
reprint ed., Hildesheim: Olms, 1963),
3:316-18.

Author: Augustinus, Aurelius

Treatise: De musica, liber primus

Incipit: Magister: Modus, qui pes est? Discipulus: Pyrrhichius. M. Quot temporum est?

File name: **AUGDEM1**   Data input by: Angela Mariani

File type: **TEXT**   Data checked by: Bradley Jon Tucker

  MS: Print: **X**   Data approved by: Thomas J. Mathiesen

Filelist: 4th-5th   File size: 49K   Annotations:

Source of data: See also AUGDEM2-6.

  Patrologia cursus completus, series latina,
  ed. J. P. Migne, 221 vols. (Paris: Garnier,
  1844-1904), 32:1081-1100.

Author: Augustinus, Aurelius

Treatise: De musica, liber secundus

Incipit: M. Attende igitur diligenter, et nunc demum accipe quasi alterum nostrae disputationis

File name: **AUGDEM2**   Data input by: Angela Mariani

File type: **TEXT**   Data checked by: Bradley Jon Tucker

  MS: Print: **X**   Data approved by: Thomas J. Mathiesen

Filelist: 4th-5th   File size: 45K   Annotations:

Source of data: See also AUGDEM1 and AUGDEM3-6.

  Patrologia cursus completus, series latina,
  ed. J. P. Migne, 221 vols. (Paris: Garnier,
  1844-1904), 32:1099-1116.

Author: Augustinus, Aurelius

Treatise: De musica, liber tertius

Incipit: M. Tertius hic sermo postulat, ut quoniam de pedum amicitia quadam concordiaque

File name: **AUGDEM3**   Data input by: Angela Mariani

File type: **TEXT**   Data checked by: Bradley Jon Tucker

  MS: Print: **X**   Data approved by: Thomas J. Mathiesen

Filelist: 4th-5th   File size: 85K   Annotations:

Source of data: See also AUGDEM1-2 and AUGDEM4-6.

  Patrologia cursus completus, series latina,
  ed. J. P. Migne, 221 vols. (Paris: Garnier,
  1844-1904), 32:1115-28.

Author: Augustinus, Aurelius

Treatise: De musica, liber quartus

Incipit: M. Redeamus ergo ad metri considerationem, propter cujus progressum ac

File name: **AUGDEM4**   Data input by: Bradley Jon Tucker

File type: **TEXT**   Data checked by: Angela Mariani

  MS: Print: **X**   Data approved by: Thomas J. Mathiesen

Filelist: 4th-5th   File size: 55K   Annotations:

Source of data: See also AUGDEM1-3 and AUGDEM5-6.

  Patrologia cursus completus, series latina,
  ed. J. P. Migne, 221 vols. (Paris: Garnier,
  1844-1904), 32:1127-48.

Author: Augustinus, Aurelius
Treatise: De musica, liber quintus
Incipit: M. Quid sit versus, inter doctos veteres non parva luctatione quaesitum est
File name: **AUGDEM5**   Data input by: Bradley Jon Tucker
File type: **TEXT**   Data checked by: Angela Mariani
  MS: Print: **X**   Data approved by: Thomas J. Mathiesen
Filelist: 4th-5th   File size: 43K   Annotations:
Source of data: See also AUGDEM1-4 and AUGDEM6.
  Patrologia cursus completus, series latina,
  ed. J. P. Migne, 221 vols. (Paris: Garnier,
  1844-1904), 32:1147-62.

Author: Augustinus, Aurelius
Treatise: De musica, liber sextus
Incipit: M. Satis diu pene atque adeo plane pueriliter per quinque libros in vestigiis
File name: **AUGDEM6**   Data input by: Bradley Jon Tucker
File type: **TEXT**   Data checked by: Angela Mariani
  MS: Print: **X**   Data approved by: Thomas J. Mathiesen
Filelist: 4th-5th   File size: 90K   Annotations:
Source of data: See also AUGDEM1-5.
  Patrologia cursus completus, series latina,
  ed. J. P. Migne, 221 vols. (Paris: Garnier,
  1844-1904), 32:1161-94.

Author: Aurelianus Reomensis
Treatise: Musica disciplina
Incipit: Musicam disciplinam non esse contemnendam, multa et antiquorum, gentilium
File name: **AURMUS**   Data input by: Stephen E. Hayes
File type: **TEXT**   Data checked by: Peter Lefferts & Angela Mariani
  MS: Print: **X**   Data approved by: Thomas J. Mathiesen
Filelist: 9th-11th File size: 100K   Annotations:
Source of data: The graphics file for this treatise is AURMUS
  Scriptores ecclesiastici de musica sacra   01GF. The preface to the treatise begins:
  potissimum, 3 vols., ed. Martin Gerbert   "Christianorum nobilissimo, nobilium,
  (St. Blaise: Typis San-Blasianis, 1784;   virorumque praestantissimo, atque honoris
  reprint ed., Hildesheim: Olms, 1963),   culmine Apostolici nobilissime sublimato ..."
  1:27-63.   Cf. AURMD TEXT and AURMUSD TEXT.

Author: Aurelianus Reomensis
Treatise: Musica disciplina
Incipit: Musicam disciplinam non esse contempnendam, multa et antiquorum gentilium
File name: **AURMUSD**   Data input by: Bradley Jon Tucker
File type: **TEXT**   Data checked by: Kirk Ditzler
  MS: Print: **X**   Data approved by: Thomas J. Mathiesen
Filelist: 9th-11th File size: 100K   Annotations:
Source of data: The preface to the treatise begins:
  Joseph Perry Ponte III, "Aureliani   "Cristianorum nobilissimo, nobilium,
  Reomensis Musica disciplina: A Revised   virorumque praestantissimo, atque honoris
  Text, Translation, and Commentary," 3   culmine apostolici nobilissime sublimato ..."
  vols. (Ph.D. dissertation, Brandeis   The graphics files for this treatise are
  University, 1961), 2:1-199 (odd only).   AURMUSD 01GF-AURMUSD 03GF. Cf.
  Used by permission.   AURMD TEXT and AURMUS TEXT.

Author: Aurelianus Reomensis

Treatise: Musica disciplina

Incipit: Musicam disciplinam non esse contempnendam, multa et antiquorum gentilium

File name: **AURMD**   Data input by: Stephen E. Hayes

File type: **TEXT**   Data checked by: Peter Lefferts & Angela Mariani

MS: Print: **X**   Data approved by: Thomas J. Mathiesen

Filelist: 9th-11th   File size: 100K   Annotations:

Source of data: The graphics files for this treatise are
Aureliani Reomensis Musica disciplina,   AURMD 01GF-AURMD 02GF. The preface
ed. Lawrence Gushee, Corpus scriptorum   to the treatise is preceded by a colophon verse,
de musica, vol. 21 ([Rome]: American   beginning: "Quisquis hoc legerit, magno cum
Institute of Musicology, 1975), 53-135.   iure patratu ...." The preface itself begins:
Used by permission.   "Cristianorum nobilissimo nobilium,
virorumque praestantissimo, atque honoris
culmine apostolici nobilissime sublimato ..."
Cf. AURMUS TEXT and AURMUSD TEXT.

Author: Aurelianus Reomensis

Treatise: Musica disciplina, cap. VIII-XVI

Incipit: Propitia divinitatis gratia nutuque favente divino, tonorum sive ut nonnulli tenorum

File name: **AURMDAP**   Data input by: Stephen E. Hayes

File type: **TEXT**   Data checked by: Peter Lefferts & Angela Mariani

MS: Print: **X**   Data approved by: Thomas J. Mathiesen

Filelist: 9th-11th   File size: 39K   Annotations:

Source of data: This appendix represents an alternate version
Aureliani Reomensis Musica disciplina,   of chapters 8-16 found in Oxford, Bodleian
ed. Lawrence Gushee, Corpus scriptorum   Library, Canonici misc. 212, ff. 40r-48v.
de musica, vol. 21 ([Rome]: American   8.38-10.29 and 16.9-19.89 have been omitted
Institute of Musicology, 1975), 136-53.   because they differ only slightly from the text
Used by permission.   preserved in AURMD.

Author: Aurelianus Reomensis

Treatise: Musica disciplina

Incipit: Quisquis hoc legerit magno cum jure patratum

File name: **AUREPI**   Data input by: John Csonka

File type: **TEXT**   Data checked by: Bradley Jon Tucker

MS: Print: **X**   Data approved by: Thomas J. Mathiesen

Filelist: 9th-11th   File size: 1K   Annotations:

Source of data: This is simply the seven-line Aurelian
Adrien de la Fage, Essais de   epigram, based on Rome, Biblioteca
dipthérographie musicale (Paris: Legouix,   Casanatense, G.III.6.
1864), 343.

Author: Beda [Ps.]

Treatise: Musica quadrata seu mensurata

Incipit: Quoniam circa artem musicam necessaria quaedam ad utilitatem cantantium tractare

File name: **BEDMUS**   Data input by: John Gray

File type: **TEXT**   Data checked by: Oliver Ellsworth & Andreas Giger

  MS: Print: **X**   Data approved by: Thomas J. Mathiesen

Filelist: 13th   File size: 43K   Annotations:

Source of data: Although attributed to the Venerable Bede in

Patrologia cursus completus, series latina, the Patrologia latina, the text is now
ed. J. P. Migne, 221 vols. (Paris: Garnier, commonly ascribed to Magister Lambert. The
1844-1904), 90:919-38. graphics files for this treatise are BEDMUS
01GF-BEDMUS 02GF. Cf. ARITRA TEXT
and LAMTRAC MSBCLV30.

Author: Beda [Ps.]

Treatise: Musica theorica

Incipit: Notandum est quod omnis ars in ratione continetur. Musica quoque in ratione

File name: **BEDMUST**   Data input by: John Gray

File type: **TEXT**   Data checked by: Oliver Ellsworth & Andreas Giger

  MS: Print: **X**   Data approved by: Thomas J. Mathiesen

Filelist: 6th-8th   File size: 31K   Annotations:

Source of data: Although attributed to the Venerable Bede in

Patrologia cursus completus, series latina, the Patrologia latina, the text is commonly
ed. J. P. Migne, 221 vols. (Paris: Garnier, assumed to be of a later date.
1844-1904), 90:909-20.

Author: Bernelinus

Treatise: Cita et vera divisio monochordi in diatonico genere

Incipit: Dimidium proslambanomenos est Mese, huius autem dimidium est nete hyperboleon

File name: **BERNDIV**   Data input by: Stephen E. Hayes

File type: **TEXT**   Data checked by: Peter M. Lefferts

  MS: Print: **X**   Data approved by: Thomas J. Mathiesen

Filelist: 9th-11th File size: 36K   Annotations:

Source of data: The graphics files for this treatise are

Scriptores ecclesiastici de musica sacra BERNDIV 01GF-BERNDIV 08GF. Cf.
potissimum, 3 vols., ed. Martin Gerbert BERNDIVM TEXT.
(St. Blaise: Typis San-Blasianis, 1784;
reprint ed., Hildesheim: Olms, 1963),
1:312-30.

Author: Bernelinus

Treatise: Cita et vera divisio monochordi in diatonico genere

Incipit: Dimidium proslambanomenos est Mese, hujus autem dimidium est nete hyperboleon

File name: **BERNDIVM**   Data input by: John Gray

File type: **TEXT**   Data checked by: Oliver Ellsworth & Andreas Giger

  MS: Print: **X**   Data approved by: Thomas J. Mathiesen

Filelist: 9th-11th File size: 36K   Annotations:

Source of data: The graphics files for this treatise are

Patrologia cursus completus, series latina, BERNDIVM 01GF-BERNDIVM 06GF. Cf.
ed. J. P. Migne, 221 vols. (Paris: Garnier, BERNDIV TEXT.
1844-1904), 151:653-74.

Author: Berno Augiensis

Treatise: De consona tonorum diversitate

Incipit: Igitur octo tonis manifestum est musicam consistere, per quos musicae modulationis

File name: **BERNDEC**   Data input by: Patricia Starr

File type: **TEXT**   Data checked by: Charles M. Atkinson

MS: Print: **X**   Data approved by: Thomas J. Mathiesen

Filelist: 9th-11th File size: 28K   Annotations:

Source of data:

Scriptores ecclesiastici de musica sacra potissimum, 3 vols., ed. Martin Gerbert (St. Blaise: Typis San-Blasianis, 1784; reprint ed., Hildesheim: Olms, 1963), 2:114-24.

The treatise is preceded by a short prooemium, beginning: "Berno gratia Dei, etsi non merito, tamen officio Abba. Dilectissimis in Christo filiis Purchardo et Kerungo, unacum caeteris in dominicarum scholarum gymnasio Augiae vacantibus, de virtute in virtutem diatim proficere, ut Deum deorum in Sion valeant conspicere." Cf. BERNDCT TEXT.

Author: Berno Augiensis

Treatise: De consona tonorum diversitate

Incipit: Igitur octo tonis manifestum est musicam consistere, per quos musicae modulationis

File name: **BERNDCT**   Data input by: Patricia Starr

File type: **TEXT**   Data checked by: Peter Slemon

MS: Print: **X**   Data approved by: Thomas J. Mathiesen

Filelist: 9th-11th File size: 9K   Annotations:

Source of data:

Patrologia cursus completus, series latina, ed. J. P. Migne, 221 vols. (Paris: Garnier, 1844-1904), 142:1155-58.

The treatise is preceded by a short prooemium, beginning: "Berno gratia Dei, et si non merito, tamen officio abba, dilectissimis in Christo filiis Purchardo et Kerungo, una cum caeteris in dominicarum scholarum gymnasio Augiae vacantibus, de virtute in virtutem diatim proficere, ut Deum deorum in Sion valeant conspicere." Cf. BERNDEC TEXT.

Author: Berno Augiensis

Treatise: De mensurando monochordo

Incipit: Quicumque aliquod sibi artificium inchoat: semper ad eventum festinat

File name: **BERNDEM**   Data input by: Andreas Giger

File type: **TEXT**   Data checked by: Elisabeth Honn

MS: Print: **X**   Data approved by: Thomas J. Mathiesen

Filelist: 9th-11th File size: 27K   Annotations:

Source of data:

Bernonis Augiensis Abbatis De arte musica disputationes traditae: De mensurando monochordo, ed. Joseph Smits van Waesberghe, Divitiae musicae artis, A/VIa (Buren: Knuf, 1978), 27, 42-55, 59, 61, 65, 67, 71, 73, 75, 77, 84-85, 91-92, 95, 103-4,111-14, and 116-19. Used by kind permission of the Laaber-Verlag.

Based on Vienna, Österreichische Nationalbibliothek, cpv 51, ff. 52r-55r. The manuscript as a whole has been dated to the 12th century. The graphics file for this treatise is BERNDEM 01GF. Cf. ANO1MU TEXT and ANO1MUS TEXT.

Author: Berno Augiensis

Treatise: De varia psalmorum atque cantuum modulatione

Incipit: Ut enim maiorum firmat auctoritas, omnis veteris testamenti scriptura inprimis

File name: **BERNVAR**   Data input by: Patricia Starr

File type: **TEXT**   Data checked by: Charles Atkinson & Angela Mariani

 MS: Print: **X**   Data approved by: Thomas J. Mathiesen

Filelist: 9th-11th   File size: 69K   Annotations:

Source of data:
  Scriptores ecclesiastici de musica sacra potissimum, 3 vols., ed. Martin Gerbert (St. Blaise: Typis San-Blasianis, 1784; reprint ed., Hildesheim: Olms, 1963), 2:91-114.

The treatise is preceded by a short prooemium, beginning: "Berno qui quod vult deus, Meginfrido, Eipennoni, dilectis in Christo Fratribus, perenne immarcescibilis gloriae decus." Cf. BERNVARP TEXT.

Author: Berno Augiensis

Treatise: De varia psalmorum atque cantuum modulatione

Incipit: Ut enim majorum firmat auctoritas, omnis Veteris Testamenti Scriptura inprimis

File name: **BERNVARP**   Data input by: Jingfa Sun

File type: **TEXT**   Data checked by: Charles Atkinson & Andreas Giger

 MS: Print: **X**   Data approved by: Thomas J. Mathiesen

Filelist: 9th-11th   File size: 69K   Annotations:

Source of data:
  Patrologia cursus completus, series latina, ed. J. P. Migne, 221 vols. (Paris: Garnier, 1844-1904), 142:1131-54.

The treatise is preceded by a short prooemium, beginning: "Berno qui quod vult deus, Meginfrido, Eipennoni, dilectis in Christo fratribus, perenne immarcescibilis gloriae decus." Cf. BERNVAR TEXT.

Author: Berno Augiensis

Treatise: Interpolationen

Incipit: [varia]

File name: **BERNINT**   Data input by: Andreas Giger

File type: **TEXT**   Data checked by: Elisabeth Honn

 MS: Print: **X**   Data approved by: Thomas J. Mathiesen

Filelist: 9th-11th   File size: 18K   Annotations:

Source of data:
  Bernonis Augiensis Abbatis De arte musica disputationes traditae: Quae ratio est inter tria opera de arte musica Bernonis Augiensis, ed. Joseph Smits van Waesberghe, Divitiae musicae artis, A/VIb (Buren: Knuf, 1979), 31-37. Used by kind permission of the Laaber-Verlag.

Author: Berno Augiensis

Treatise: Musica seu Prologus in Tonarium

Incipit: Omnis igitur regularis monochordi constitutio secundum praeclaram disertissimi viri

File name: **BERNPRO**   Data input by: Patricia Starr

File type: **TEXT**   Data checked by: Charles Atkinson & Bradley Tucker

MS: Print: **X**   Data approved by: Thomas J. Mathiesen

Filelist: 9th-11th   File size: 49K   Annotations:

Source of data:

Scriptores ecclesiastici de musica sacra potissimum, 3 vols., ed. Martin Gerbert (St. Blaise: Typis San-Blasianis, 1784; reprint ed., Hildesheim: Olms, 1963), 2:62-79.

The treatise is preceded by a short preface, beginning: "Domino Deoque dilecto Piligrino, vero mundi huius advenae et peregrino, Berno licet ...." Cf. BERNMUS TEXT.

Author: Berno Augiensis

Treatise: Musica seu Prologus in Tonarium

Incipit: Omnis igitur regularis monochordi constitutio, secundum praeclaram disertissimi viri

File name: **BERNMUS**   Data input by: Jingfa Sun

File type: **TEXT**   Data checked by: Andreas Giger

MS: Print: **X**   Data approved by: Thomas J. Mathiesen

Filelist: 9th-11th   File size: 49K   Annotations:

Source of data:

Patrologia cursus completus, series latina, ed. J. P. Migne, 221 vols. (Paris: Garnier, 1844-1904), 142:1097-1116.

The treatise is preceded by a short preface, beginning: "Domino Deoque dilecto Piligrino, vero mundi huius advenae et peregrino, Berno licet ...." Cf. BERNPRO TEXT.

Author: Berno Augiensis

Treatise: Tonabius [sic]

Incipit: Authenticus protus constat ex prima specie diapente, et ex prima specie diatessaron

File name: **BERNTO**   Data input by: Angela Mariani

File type: **TEXT**   Data checked by: Peter Slemon

MS: Print: **X**   Data approved by: Thomas J. Mathiesen

Filelist: 9th-11th   File size: 30K   Annotations:

Source of data: Cf. BERNTON TEXT.

Patrologia cursus completus, series latina, ed. J. P. Migne, 221 vols. (Paris: Garnier, 1844-1904), 142:1115-30.

Author: Berno Augiensis

Treatise: Tonarius

Incipit: Authenticus protus constat ex prima specie diapente, et ex prima specie diatessaron

File name: **BERNTON**   Data input by: Patricia Starr

File type: **TEXT**   Data checked by: Charles Atkinson & Angela Mariani

MS: Print: **X**   Data approved by: Thomas J. Mathiesen

Filelist: 9th-11th   File size: 29K   Annotations:

Source of data: Cf. BERNTO TEXT.

Scriptores ecclesiastici de musica sacra potissimum, 3 vols., ed. Martin Gerbert (St. Blaise: Typis San-Blasianis, 1784; reprint ed., Hildesheim: Olms, 1963), 2:79-91.

Author: Bertrandus Prudentius

Treatise: De arte musica

Incipit: Utilis in multis ars musica rebus habetur;

File name: **BERTARM**   Data input by: John Csonka

File type: **TEXT**   Data checked by: Jan Herlinger & Bradley Tucker

MS: Print: **X**   Data approved by: Thomas J. Mathiesen

Filelist: 9th-11th   File size: 11K   Annotations:

Source of data:

Adrien de la Fage, Essais de dipthérographie musicale (Paris: Legouix, 1864), 293-94, 297-303.

Based on Paris, Bibliothèque Nationale, Colbertinus lat. 2627. The treatise of Bertrandus is preceded by a set of verses on the first nine numbers, beginning "Ordine primigeno nomen jam possidet igin," and three lines in honor of St. Vivianus.

Author: Beurhusius, Fredericus

Treatise: Erotematum musicae liber primus

Incipit: Quid est musica. Musica est ars bene canendi. Unde dicta est musica. Musica a Musis

File name: **BEUERO1**   Data input by: Yury Popov

File type: **TEXT**   Data checked by: Sergei Lebedev & Andreas Giger

MS: Print: **X**   Data approved by: Thomas J. Mathiesen

Filelist: 16th   File size: 56K   Annotations:

Source of data:

Erotematum musicae libri duo, ex optimis huius artis scriptoribus vera perspicuaque methodo descripti (Noribergae, In officina typographica Catharinae Gerlachin, et Haeredum Ioannis Montani, 1580; reprint ed., Cologne: Arno Volk, 1969), 1-68.

The pagination in this file follows the modern pagination added in the reprint. The treatise is preceded by various dedicatory verses and prefaces, beginning: "Musica quas habeat merito celeberrima laudes," "Ingenii humani praeclarum inventum est ars Musica," "Cum omnes res utiles et salutares," and "Musica grata deo, cujus Deus extitit"; and a figure headed "Typus musicae." The graphics for this treatise are BEUERO1 01GF-BEUERO1 10GF. Continues in BEUERO2.

Author: Beurhusius, Fredericus

Treatise: Erotematum musicae liber secundus

Incipit: Quae pars harmonica? Harmonica pars est de sonorum inflexione ad bene canendum

File name: **BEUERO2**   Data input by: Yury Popov

File type: **TEXT**   Data checked by: Sergei Lebedev & Andreas Giger

MS: Print: **X**   Data approved by: Thomas J. Mathiesen

Filelist: 16th   File size: 36K   Annotations:

Source of data:

Erotematum musicae libri duo, ex optimis huius artis scriptoribus vera perspicuaque methodo descripti (Noribergae, In officina typographica Catharinae Gerlachin, et Haeredum Ioannis Montani, 1580; reprint ed., Cologne: Arno Volk, 1969), 68-125.

The pagination in this file follows the modern pagination added in the reprint. The graphics for this treatise are BEUERO2 01GF-BEUERO2 11GF. Continued from BEUERO1.

Author: Beurhusius, Fredericus

Treatise: Musicae rudimenta e pleniore eius descriptione itemque exempla quaedam facilia ad

Incipit: Quid est musica? Musica est ars bene canendi. Quot sunt partes musicae?

File name: **BEUMUS1**   Data input by: Jingfa Sun

File type: **TEXT**   Data checked by: Charles Atkinson & Elisabeth Honn

MS: Print: **X**   Data approved by: Thomas J. Mathiesen

Filelist: 16th   File size: 16K   Annotations:

Source of data:

Musicae Rudimenta e pleniore eius
descriptione itemque exempla quaedam
facilia ad puerilem exercitationem e bonis
auctoribus (Tremoniae, excudebat
Albertus Sartorius, 1581; transcribed in
Beiträge zur rheinischen
Musikgeschichte, vol. 38, Köln: Arno
Volk, 1960), 1-17.

The treatise is preceded by various dedicatory
verses and prefaces, beginning: "Suavis ab
excelso manavit musica Olympo," "Quam
nobile Dei donum et maxime homine dignum
sit musica." The graphics files for this treatise
are BEUMUS1 01GF-BEUMUS1 04GF.
Continues in BEUMUS2.

Author: Beurhusius, Fredericus

Treatise: Musicae rudimenta e pleniore eius descriptione itemque exempla quaedam facilia ad

Incipit: Quae pars harmonica? Harmonica pars est de sonorum inflexione ad bene canendum

File name: **BEUMUS2**   Data input by: Jingfa Sun

File type: **TEXT**   Data checked by: Charles Atkinson & Elisabeth Honn

MS: Print: **X**   Data approved by: Thomas J. Mathiesen

Filelist: 16th   File size: 12K   Annotations:

Source of data:

Musicae Rudimenta e pleniore eius
descriptione itemque exempla quaedam
facilia ad puerilem exercitationem e bonis
auctoribus (Tremoniae, excudebat
Albertus Sartorius, 1581; transcribed in
Beiträge zur rheinischen
Musikgeschichte, vol. 38, Köln: Arno
Volk, 1960), 18-51.

Continued from BEUMUS1. The graphics
files for this treatise are BEUMUS2
01GF-BEUMUS2 28GF.

Author: Boen, Johannes

Treatise: Ars (musicae)

Incipit: [L,B,S,M] Hec sunt quatuor note, quibus omnis mensurabilis contexitur cantelena.

File name: **BOENMU**   Data input by: Stephen E. Hayes

File type: **TEXT**   Data checked by: Peter Lefferts & Bradley Tucker

MS: Print: **X**   Data approved by: Thomas J. Mathiesen

Filelist: 14th   File size: 53K   Annotations:

Source of data:

Johannis Boen, Ars (musicae), ed. F.
Alberto Gallo, Corpus scriptorum de
musica, vol. 19 ([Rome]: American
Institute of Musicology, 1972), 15-46.
Used by permission.

The graphics file for this treatise is BOENMU
01GF. Cf. BOENMUS TEXT.

Author: Boen, Johannes
Treatise: Musica
Incipit: Musicalis scientia, que sonorum respicit intervalla et de proportionibus gravis
File name: **BOENMUS**   Data input by: Stephen E. Hayes
File type: **TEXT**   Data checked by: Peter Lefferts & Elisabeth Honn
MS: Print: **X**   Data approved by: Thomas J. Mathiesen
Filelist: 14th   File size: 89K   Annotations:
Source of data: The graphics files for this treatise are
Wolf Frobenius, Johannes Boens Musica   BOENMUS 01GF-BOENMUS 04GF. Cf.
und seine Konsonanzenlehre (Stuttgart: BOENMU TEXT.
Musikwissenschaftliche
Verlags-Gesellschaft, 1971), 32-78. Used
by permission.

Author: Boethius, Anicius Manlius Severinus
Treatise: De institutione musica, liber primus
Incipit: Omnium quidem perceptio sensuum ita sponte ac naturaliter quibusdam uiuentibus
File name: **BOEMUS1C**   Data input by: Michael W. Lundell
File type: **MCTC944**   Data checked by: Oliver B. Ellsworth
MS: **X**   Print: Data approved by: Thomas J. Mathiesen
Filelist: 6th-8th   File size: 73K   Annotations:
Source of data: =RISM BIII/4:15-20. The graphics files for
Cambridge, Trinity College, R.15.22   this treatise are BOEMUS1C
(944), ff. 5r-27r.   01GF-BOEMUS1C 13GF. Cf. BOEMUS1
      TEXT and BOEDIM1 TEXT.

Author: Boethius, Anicius Manlius Severinus
Treatise: De institutione musica, liber secundus
Incipit: Superius volumen cuncta digessit. quae nunc diligentius demonstranda esse
File name: **BOEMUS2C**   Data input by: Michael W. Lundell
File type: **MCTC944**   Data checked by: Oliver B. Ellsworth
MS: **X**   Print: Data approved by: Thomas J. Mathiesen
Filelist: 6th-8th   File size: 70K   Annotations:
Source of data: =RISM BIII/4:15-20. The graphics files for
Cambridge, Trinity College, R.15.22   this treatise are BOEMUS2C
(944), ff. 27v-48v.   01GF-BOEMUS2C 08GF. Cf. BOEMUS2
      TEXT and BOEDIM2 TEXT.

Author: Boethius, Anicius Manlius Severinus
Treatise: De institutione musica, liber tertius
Incipit: Superiore volumine demonstratum est diatessaron consonantiam ex duobus tonis
File name: **BOEMUS3C**   Data input by: Michael W. Lundell
File type: **MCTC944**   Data checked by: Julie Langford-Johnson
MS: **X**   Print: Data approved by: Thomas J. Mathiesen
Filelist: 6th-8th   File size: 52K   Annotations:
Source of data: =RISM BIII/4:15-20. The incipit is preceded
Cambridge, Trinity College, R.15.22   by a list of the sixteen chapter headings and
(944), ff. 48v-65v.   the heading for the first chapter, beginning:
      "Adversus Aristoxenum demonstratio
      superparticularem proportionem ...." The
      graphics files for this treatise are BOEMUS3C
      01GF-BOEMUS3C 24GF. Cf. BOEMUS3
      TEXT and BOEDIM3 TEXT.

Author: Boethius, Anicius Manlius Severinus
Treatise: De institutione musica, liber quartus
Incipit: Etsi omnia quae demonstranda erant superioris libri tractatione digessimus

File name: **BOEMUS4C**   Data input by: Michael W. Lundell
File type: **MCTC944**   Data checked by: Julie Langford-Johnson
MS: **X**   Print: Data approved by: Thomas J. Mathiesen
Filelist: 6th-8th   File size: 82K   Annotations:
Source of data: =RISM BIII/4:15-20. The incipit is preceded
Cambridge, Trinity College, R.15.22   by a list of the seventeen chapter headings and
(944), ff. 65v-91r.   the heading for the first chapter, beginning:
"Vocum differentias in quantitate consistere."
The graphics files for this treatise are
BOEMUS4C 01GF-BOEMUS4C 21GF. Cf.
BOEMUS4 TEXT and BOEDIM4 TEXT.

Author: Boethius, Anicius Manlius Severinus
Treatise: De institutione musica, liber primus
Incipit: Omnium quidem perceptio sensuum ita sponte ac naturaliter quibusdam viventibus

File name: **BOEMUS1**   Data input by: Calvin M. Bower
File type: **TEXT**   Data checked by: Luminita Aluas & P. Mathiesen
MS: Print: **X**   Data approved by: Thomas J. Mathiesen
Filelist: 6th-8th   File size: 66K   Annotations:
Source of data: The incipit is preceded by a list of the
Boethii De institutione musica libri   thirty-four chapter headings and the heading
quinque, ed. Godofredus Friedlein   for the first chapter (or, Proemium):
(Leipzig: B. G. Teubner, 1867), 177-225.   "Proemium. Musicam naturaliter nobis esse
coniunctam et mores vel honestare vel
evertere." The graphics files for this treatise
are BOEMUS1 01GF-BOEMUS1 03GF. Cf.
BOEDIM1 TEXT.

Author: Boethius, Anicius Manlius Severinus
Treatise: De institutione musica, liber secundus
Incipit: Proemium. Superius volumen cuncta digessit, quae nunc diligentius demonstranda

File name: **BOEMUS2**   Data input by: Calvin M. Bower
File type: **TEXT**   Data checked by: Bradley Jon Tucker
MS: Print: **X**   Data approved by: Thomas J. Mathiesen
Filelist: 6th-8th   File size: 65K   Annotations:
Source of data: The incipit is preceded by a list of the
Boethii De institutione musica libri   thirty-one chapter headings. The graphics file
quinque, ed. Godofredus Friedlein   for this treatise is BOEMUS2 01GF. Cf.
(Leipzig: B. G. Teubner, 1867), 225-67.   BOEDIM2 TEXT.

Author: Boethius, Anicius Manlius Severinus
Treatise: De institutione musica, liber tertius
Incipit: Superiore volumine demonstratum est diatessaron consonantiam ex duobus tonis

File name: **BOEMUS3**	Data input by: Calvin M. Bower
File type: **TEXT**	Data checked by: Andreas Giger
MS:　　　Print: **X**	Data approved by: Thomas J. Mathiesen

Filelist: 6th-8th　File size: 47K

Source of data:　　　　　　　　　　　Annotations:
Boethii De institutione musica libri
quinque, ed. Godofredus Friedlein
(Leipzig: B. G. Teubner, 1867), 268-300.

The incipit is preceded by a list of the sixteen chapter headings and the heading for the first chapter, beginning: "Adversum Aristoxenum demonstratio superparticularem proportionem ...." The graphics files for this treatise are BOEMUS3 01GF-BOEMUS3 06GF. Cf. BOEDIM3 TEXT.

Author: Boethius, Anicius Manlius Severinus
Treatise: De institutione musica, liber quartus
Incipit: Etsi omnia, quae demonstranda est superioris libri tractatione digressimus

File name: **BOEMUS4**	Data input by: Claudia Di Luca
File type: **TEXT**	Data checked by: Andreas Giger
MS:　　　Print: **X**	Data approved by: Thomas J. Mathiesen

Filelist: 6th-8th　File size: 78K

Source of data:　　　　　　　　　　　Annotations:
Boethii De institutione musica libri
quinque, ed. Godofredus Friedlein
(Leipzig: B. G. Teubner, 1867), 300-349.

The incipit is preceded by a list of the eighteen chapter headings and the heading for the first chapter, beginning: "Vocum differentias in quantitate consistere." The graphics files for this treatise are BOEMUS4 01GF-BOEMUS4 09GF. Cf. BOEDIM4 TEXT.

Author: Boethius, Anicius Manlius Severinus
Treatise: De institutione musica, liber quintus
Incipit: Proemium. Post monochordi regularis divisionem adicienda esse arbitror ea

File name: **BOEMUS5**	Data input by: Claudia Di Luca
File type: **TEXT**	Data checked by: Andreas Giger
MS:　　　Print: **X**	Data approved by: Thomas J. Mathiesen

Filelist: 6th-8th　File size: 33K

Source of data:　　　　　　　　　　　Annotations:
Boethii De institutione musica libri
quinque, ed. Godofredus Friedlein
(Leipzig: B. G. Teubner, 1867), 349-71.

The incipit is preceded by a list of the thirty chapter headings. The graphics file for this treatise is BOEMUS5 01GF. Cf. BOEDIM5 TEXT.

Author: Boethius, Anicius Manlius Severinus
Treatise: De institutione musica, liber primus
Incipit: Omnium quidem perceptio sensuum, ita sponte ac naturaliter quibusdam viventibus

File name: **BOEDIM1**   Data input by: Stephen E. Hayes
File type: **TEXT**   Data checked by: Peter Lefferts & Bradley Tucker
  MS: Print: **X**   Data approved by: Thomas J. Mathiesen
Filelist: 6th-8th   File size: 67K   Annotations:

Source of data:

Patrologia cursus completus, series latina, ed. J. P. Migne, 221 vols. (Paris: Garnier, 1844-1904), 63:1167-96.

The incipit is preceded by the heading for the first chapter: "Caput primum. Musica naturaliter nobis esse conjunctam, et mores vel honestare vel evertere." The graphics files for this treatise are BOEDIM1 01GF-BOEDIM1 06GF. Please note that the graphics in this edition are hopelessly garbled; in accord with the policy of the TML, the data in this text and the accompanying graphics reflect the state of the edition. Cf. BOEMUS1 TEXT.

Author: Boethius, Anicius Manlius Severinus
Treatise: De institutione musica, liber secundus
Incipit: Prooemium. Superius volumen cunctas digessit, quae nunc diligentius explicanda esse

File name: **BOEDIM2**   Data input by: Stephen E. Hayes
File type: **TEXT**   Data checked by: Peter Lefferts & Bradley Tucker
  MS: Print: **X**   Data approved by: Thomas J. Mathiesen
Filelist: 6th-8th   File size: 64K   Annotations:

Source of data:

Patrologia cursus completus, series latina, ed. J. P. Migne, 221 vols. (Paris: Garnier, 1844-1904), 63:1195-1224.

The graphics files for this treatise are BOEDIM2 01GF-BOEDIM2 09GF. Please note that the graphics in this edition are hopelessly garbled; in accord with the policy of the TML, the data in this text and the accompanying graphics reflect the state of the edition. Cf. BOEMUS2 TEXT.

Author: Boethius, Anicius Manlius Severinus
Treatise: De institutione musica, liber tertius
Incipit: Superiore volumine demonstratum est diatessaron consonantiam ex duobus tonis

File name: **BOEDIM3**   Data input by: Stephen E. Hayes
File type: **TEXT**   Data checked by: Peter Lefferts & Bradley Tucker
  MS: Print: **X**   Data approved by: Thomas J. Mathiesen
Filelist: 6th-8th   File size: 43K   Annotations:

Source of data:

Patrologia cursus completus, series latina, ed. J. P. Migne, 221 vols. (Paris: Garnier, 1844-1904), 63:1223-46.

The incipit is preceded by the chapter heading, beginning: "Adversus Aristoxenum demonstratio ...." The graphics files for this treatise are BOEDIM3 01GF-BOEDIM3 13GF. Please note that the graphics in this edition are hopelessly garbled; in accord with the policy of the TML, the data in this text and the accompanying graphics reflect the state of the edition. Cf. BOEMUS3 TEXT.

Author: Boethius, Anicius Manlius Severinus
Treatise: De institutione musica, liber quartus
Incipit: Etsi omnia quae demonstranda erant superioris libri tractatione digessimus

File name: **BOEDIM4**   Data input by: Stephen E. Hayes
File type: **TEXT**   Data checked by: Peter Lefferts & Bradley Tucker
MS: Print: **X**   Data approved by: Thomas J. Mathiesen
Filelist: 6th-8th   File size: 74K   Annotations:

Source of data:
Patrologia cursus completus, series latina, ed. J. P. Migne, 221 vols. (Paris: Garnier, 1844-1904), 63:1245-86.

The incipit is preceded by the chapter heading: "Vocum differentias in quantitate consistere." The graphics files for this treatise are BOEDIM4 01GF-BOEDIM4 19GF. Please note that the graphics in this edition are hopelessly garbled; in accord with the policy of the TML, the data in this text and the accompanying graphics reflect the state of the edition. Cf. BOEMUS4 TEXT.

Author: Boethius, Anicius Manlius Severinus
Treatise: De institutione musica, liber quintus
Incipit: Post monochordi regularis divisionem adjicienda arbitror esse ea in quibus veteres

File name: **BOEDIM5**   Data input by: Stephen E. Hayes
File type: **TEXT**   Data checked by: Peter Lefferts & Bradley Tucker
MS: Print: **X**   Data approved by: Thomas J. Mathiesen
Filelist: 6th-8th   File size: 34K   Annotations:

Source of data:
Patrologia cursus completus, series latina, ed. J. P. Migne, 221 vols. (Paris: Garnier, 1844-1904), 63:1285-1300.

The graphics files for this treatise are BOEDIM5 01GF-BOEDIM5 05GF. Please note that the graphics in this edition are garbled; in accord with the policy of the TML, the data in this text and the accompanying graphics reflect the state of the edition. Cf. BOEMUS5 TEXT.

Author: Bonaventura da Brescia
Treatise: Brevis collectio artis musicae
Incipit: Incipit brevis collectio artis musicae, tam ex determinationibus antiquorum

File name: **BONBRE**   Data input by: Nigel Gwee
File type: **TEXT**   Data checked by: Peter Slemon
MS: Print: **X**   Data approved by: Thomas J. Mathiesen
Filelist: 15th   File size: 140K   Annotations:

Source of data:
Bonaventura da Brescia, Brevis collectio artis musicae, ed. Albert Seay, Critical Texts, no. 11 (Colorado Springs: Colorado College Music Press, 1980). Used by permission.

The graphics files for this treatise are BONBRE 01GF-BONBRE 27GF.

Author: Burtius, Nicolaus

Treatise: Musices opusculum, tractatus primus

Incipit: Quoniam vt inquit Cicero: in libello qui de vniuersitate nuncupatur: circa finem.

File name: **BURMUS1**   Data input by: Firoozeh Khazrai

File type: **TEXT**   Data checked by: Peter Slemon

MS: Print: **X**   Data approved by: Thomas J. Mathiesen

Filelist: 15th   File size: 95K   Annotations:

Source of data:

Nicolai Burtij parmensis: musices professoris: ac iuris pontificij studiosissimi: musices opusculum incipit: cum defensione Guidonis aretini: aduersus quendam hyspanum veritatis preuaricatorem (Bologna: Ugo Ruggeri, 1487; reprint ed., Bologna: Forni, 1969).

The incipit is preceded by a long preface, beginning: "Cum multi velut vmbra declinauere anni quibus ab adolescentia ...." See also BURMUS2 and BURMUS3. The graphics files for this treatise are BURMUS1 01GF-BURMUS1 03GF.

Author: Burtius, Nicolaus

Treatise: Musices opusculum, tractatus secundus

Incipit: Cogitanti mihi viri disertissimi quod nullus est suauior animi cibus teste Lactantio.

File name: **BURMUS2**   Data input by: Firoozeh Khazrai

File type: **TEXT**   Data checked by: Peter Slemon

MS: Print: **X**   Data approved by: Thomas J. Mathiesen

Filelist: 15th   File size: 18K   Annotations:

Source of data:

Nicolai Burtij parmensis: musices professoris: ac iuris pontificij studiosissimi: musices opusculum incipit: cum defensione Guidonis aretini: aduersus quendam hyspanum veritatis preuaricatorem (Bologna: Ugo Ruggeri, 1487; reprint ed., Bologna: Forni, 1969).

See also BURMUS1 and BURMUS3. The graphics files for this treatise are BURMUS2 01GF-BURMUS2 02GF.

Author: Burtius, Nicolaus

Treatise: Musices opusculum, tractatus secundus, capitulum VI

Incipit: Quem enim a teneris unguiculis, ut aiunt greci, contrapunctum didicerim vobis

File name: **BURMUSX**   Data input by: Peter M. Lefferts

File type: **TEXT**   Data checked by: Elisabeth Honn

MS: Print: **X**   Data approved by: Thomas J. Mathiesen

Filelist: 15th   File size: 4K   Annotations:

Source of data: Cf. BURMUS2 TEXT.

Manfred Bukofzer, Geschichte des englischen Diskants und des Fauxbourdons nach den theoretischen Quellen, Sammlung musikwissenschaftlicher Abhandlungen, Band 21 (Strassbourg: Heitz, 1936), 156-58.

Author: Burtius, Nicolaus

Treatise: Musices opusculum, tractatus tertius

Incipit: Bene res se habet: iacta sunt fundamenta vt inquit eximius orator.

File name: **BURMUS3**   Data input by: Firoozeh Khazrai

File type: **TEXT**   Data checked by: Peter Slemon

MS: Print: **X**   Data approved by: Thomas J. Mathiesen

Filelist: 15th   File size: 89K   Annotations:

Source of data: See also BURMUS1 and BURMUS2. The
Nicolai Burtij parmensis: musices   graphics file for this treatise is BURMUS3
professoris: ac iuris pontificij   01GF.
studiosissimi: musices opusculum incipit:
cum defensione Guidonis aretini:
aduersus quendam hyspanum veritatis
preuaricatorem (Bologna: Ugo Ruggeri,
1487; reprint ed., Bologna: Forni, 1969).

Author: Capuanus, Nicolaus

Treatise: Compendium musicale

Incipit: Cum igitur humana natura scire desiderat, ideo divina clementia philosophis peritiam

File name: **NICCOM**   Data input by: John Csonka

File type: **TEXT**   Data checked by: Angela Mariani

MS: Print: **X**   Data approved by: Thomas J. Mathiesen

Filelist: 15th   File size: 52K   Annotations:

Source of data: Based on Rome, Biblioteca Casanatense,
Adrien de la Fage, Essais de   C.VI,2; fonds Baini. The graphics files for this
dipthérographie musicale (Paris: Legouix,   treatise are NICCOM 01GF-NICCOM 15GF.
1864), 308-38.

Author: Carlerius, Egidius

Treatise: De cantu iubiliationis armonicae et utilitate eius

Incipit: Musicam triphariam doctores quidam esse dixerunt, scilicet, armonicam, organicam

File name: **CARLCAN**   Data input by: Peter Slemon

File type: **TEXT**   Data checked by: Angela Mariani

MS: Print: **X**   Data approved by: Thomas J. Mathiesen

Filelist: 15th   File size: 14K   Annotations:

Source of data:

Egidius Carlerius, Duo tractatuli de
musica, ed. Albert Seay, Critical Texts,
no.7 (Colorado Springs: Colorado
College Music Press, 1977), 5-13. Used
by permission.

Author: Carlerius, Egidius

Treatise: Tractatus de duplici ritu cantus ecclesiastici in divinis officiis et primo de simplici

Incipit: Quaesivit quidam devotus, quid est quod in multis ecclesiis tam cathedralibus

File name: **CARLTRA**   Data input by: Peter Slemon

File type: **TEXT**   Data checked by: Angela Mariani

MS: Print: **X**   Data approved by: Thomas J. Mathiesen

Filelist: 15th   File size: 9K   Annotations:

Source of data:

Egidius Carlerius, Duo tractatuli de
musica, ed. Albert Seay, Critical Texts,
no.7 (Colorado Springs: Colorado
College Music Press, 1977), 1-5. Used by
permission.

Author: Cassiodorus, Aurelius

Treatise: Institutiones musicae, seu excerpta ex eiusdem libro, de artibus ac disciplinis

Incipit: Gaudentius quidam de Musica scribens, Pythagoram dicit huius rei invenisse

File name: **CASINS**   Data input by: Stephen E. Hayes

File type: **TEXT**   Data checked by: Peter M. Lefferts

MS: Print: **X**   Data approved by: Thomas J. Mathiesen

Filelist: 6th-8th   File size: 12K   Annotations:

Source of data: Book 2.5. Cf. CASIM TEXT and CASINST

Scriptores ecclesiastici de musica sacra   TEXT.
potissimum, 3 vols., ed. Martin Gerbert
(St. Blaise: Typis San-Blasianis, 1784;
reprint ed., Hildesheim: Olms, 1963),
1:15-19.

Author: Cassiodorus, Aurelius

Treatise: Institutiones musicae, seu excerpta ex eiusdem libro, de artibus ac disciplinis

Incipit: Gaudentius quidam, de musica scribens, Pythagoram dicit hujus rei invenisse

File name: **CASIM**   Data input by: Stephen E. Hayes

File type: **TEXT**   Data checked by: Peter Lefferts & Bradley Tucker

MS: Print: **X**   Data approved by: Thomas J. Mathiesen

Filelist: 6th-8th   File size: 12K   Annotations:

Source of data: Book 2.5. Cf. CASINS TEXT and CASINST

Patrologia cursus completus, series latina,   TEXT.
ed. J. P. Migne, 221 vols. (Paris: Garnier,
1844-1904), 70:1208-12.

Author: Cassiodorus, Aurelius

Treatise: Institutionum liber secundus saecularium litterarum

Incipit: Gaudentius quidam, de musica scribens, Pythagoram dicit huius rei invenisse

File name: **CASINST**   Data input by: Stephen E. Hayes

File type: **TEXT**   Data checked by: Peter Lefferts & Angela Mariani

MS: Print: **X**   Data approved by: Thomas J. Mathiesen

Filelist: 6th-8th   File size: 12K   Annotations:

Source of data: Book 2.5. Cf. CASINS TEXT and CASIM

Cassiodori senatoris Institutiones, ed. R.   TEXT.
A. B. Mynors (Oxford: Clarendon, 1937),
142-50.

Author: Ciconia, Johannes

Treatise: De proportionibus

Incipit: Omnem sapientiam omnemque naturam philosophiam credimus procedere

File name: **CICPROP**   Data input by: Oliver B. Ellsworth

File type: **TEXT**   Data checked by: Andreas Giger

MS: Print: **X**   Data approved by: Thomas J. Mathiesen

Filelist: 15th   File size: 27K   Annotations:

Source of data:

Johannes Ciconia, Nova musica and De proportionibus, ed. and trans. by Oliver B. Ellsworth, Greek and Latin Music Theory, vol. 9 (Lincoln: University of Nebraska Press, 1993), 412-46 (even-numbered pages only). Used by permission.

The incipit is preceded by a complete listing of the twenty-five chapter headings and a dedicatory preface, beginning: "Venerabili viro et egregio domino presbytero Johanni Gasparo ...." De proportionibus is an adaptation of Book III of the Nova musica (CICNM3 TEXT). In Faenza, Biblioteca Comunale, 117, De proportionibus is followed by a long gloss in a later hand (see Ellsworth, 3-5 and 24-25).

Author: Ciconia, Johannes

Treatise: Nova musica

Incipit: Dulcis celebs, Urania, annue auspicio;

File name: **CICNM**   Data input by: John Csonka

File type: **TEXT**   Data checked by: Angela Mariani

MS: Print: **X**   Data approved by: Thomas J. Mathiesen

Filelist: 15th   File size: 14K   Annotations:

Source of data:

Adrien de la Fage, Essais de dipthérographie musicale (Paris: Legouix, 1864), 375-83.

The graphics file for this treatise is CICNM 01GF. Based on Florence, Biblioteca Riccardiana, 734. The text is preceded by a complete transcription of the rubrics for Books I-V. On pp. 381-83, La Fage includes two excerpts from an anonymous Tractatus, beginning "Consonantiae sunt quinque: scilicet unisonus, ..."

Author: Ciconia, Johannes

Treatise: Nova musica, liber primus de consonantiis

Incipit: In prephatione Nove Musice nobis placuit de eius magnitudine intimare

File name: **CICNM1**   Data input by: Oliver B. Ellsworth

File type: **TEXT**   Data checked by: Andreas Giger

MS: Print: **X**   Data approved by: Thomas J. Mathiesen

Filelist: 15th   File size: 101K   Annotations:

Source of data:

Johannes Ciconia, Nova musica and De proportionibus, ed. and trans. by Oliver B. Ellsworth, Greek and Latin Music Theory, vol. 9 (Lincoln: University of Nebraska Press, 1993), 42-232 (even-numbered pages only). Used by permission.

The graphics files for this treatise are CICNM1 01GF-CICNM1 25GF. Following the preface (the incipit of which is given above), a complete listing of the seventy-four chapter headings appears, which is in turn followed by the "Prologus," beginning: "Musicam antiquam antiquorum voto editam, ..." Continues in CICNM2-4.

Author: Ciconia, Johannes
Treatise: Nova musica, liber secundus de speciebus
Incipit: Cum enim omnis musica de consonantiis tractet, ut Musica sillabarum refert

File name: **CICNM2**   Data input by: Oliver B. Ellsworth
File type: **TEXT**   Data checked by: Andreas Giger
  MS: Print: **X**   Data approved by: Thomas J. Mathiesen
Filelist: 15th   File size: 57K   Annotations:

Source of data:
Johannes Ciconia, Nova musica and De proportionibus, ed. and trans. by Oliver B. Ellsworth, Greek and Latin Music Theory, vol. 9 (Lincoln: University of Nebraska Press, 1993), 234-336 (even-numbered pages only). Used by permission.

The graphics files for this treatise are CICNM2 01GF-CICNM2 14GF. Following the prologue (the incipit of which is given above), a complete listing of the fifty-nine chapter headings appears, which is in turn followed by the first chapter, beginning: "Species vero in musica secundum Boetium est quaedam positio ...." Continued from CICNM1; continues in CICNM3-4.

Author: Ciconia, Johannes
Treatise: Nova musica, liber tertius de proportionibus
Incipit: Musica ars a nobis sub arboris figura visa est. Nam arbor musice magnitudo eius est.

File name: **CICNM3**   Data input by: Oliver B. Ellsworth
File type: **TEXT**   Data checked by: Andreas Giger
  MS: Print: **X**   Data approved by: Thomas J. Mathiesen
Filelist: 15th   File size: 17K   Annotations:

Source of data:
Johannes Ciconia, Nova musica and De proportionibus, ed. and trans. by Oliver B. Ellsworth, Greek and Latin Music Theory, vol. 9 (Lincoln: University of Nebraska Press, 1993), 338-60 (even-numbered pages only). Used by permission.

Following the prologue (the incipit of which is given above), a complete listing of the twenty-one chapter headings appears, which is in turn followed by the first chapter, beginning: "Omnem sapientiam omnemque veram philosophiam ...." Continued from CICNM2; continues in CICNM4.

Author: Ciconia, Johannes

Treatise: Nova musica, liber quartus de accidentibus

Incipit: Musica est ars spectabilis et suavis, ut in primo libro rettulimus

File name: **CICNM4**   Data input by: Oliver B. Ellsworth

File type: **TEXT**   Data checked by: Andreas Giger

MS: Print: **X**   Data approved by: Thomas J. Mathiesen

Filelist: 15th   File size: 37K   Annotations:

Source of data:

Johannes Ciconia, Nova musica and De proportionibus, ed. and trans. by Oliver B. Ellsworth, Greek and Latin Music Theory, vol. 9 (Lincoln: University of Nebraska Press, 1993), 362-410 (even-numbered pages only). Used by permission.

The graphics files for this treatise are CICNM4 01GF-CICNM4 03GF. Following the prologue (the incipit of which is given above), a complete listing of the fourteen chapter headings appears, which is in turn followed by the first chapter, beginning: "Consuetudo antiquorum philosophorum fuit de omnibus ...." Following the explicit (p. 390), a new section appears, titled "De tribus generibus melorum," beginning: "Boetius: His igitur expeditis, dicendum est de generibus melorum...." The individual titles of the eight chapters precede the incipit in Rome, Biblioteca Apostolica Vaticana, lat. 5320. Ellsworth (pp. 23-24) provides a review of the various assessments of this section by previous scholars. Continued from CICNM3.

Author: Cochlaeus, Johannes

Treatise: Tetrachordum musices, tractatus primus

Incipit: Quid est musica? Est bene modulandi scientia. Augustinus. Vel est facultas

File name: **COCTET1**   Data input by: Svetlana Khlybova

File type: **TEXT**   Data checked by: Sergei Lebedev & Andreas Giger

MS: Print: **X**   Data approved by: Thomas J. Mathiesen

Filelist: 16th   File size: 29K   Annotations:

Source of data:

Tetrachordum musices Ioannis Coclei Norici artium magistri Nurnbergae aeditum pro iuuentute Laurentiana in primis dein pro ceteris quoque Musarum Tyrunculis (Nurnbergae, impressi in officina excusoria Friderici Peypus, 1514), ff. Air-Bir.

The incipit is preceded by two verses; a dedicatory preface addressed to Antonius Kress, beginning: "Cum tua beneficentia Praestabilissime domine Praeposite ..."; and the chapter heading "De diffinitione musice." The graphics files for this treatise are COCTET1 01GF-COCTET1 04GF. Continues in COCTET2-4.

Author: Cochlaeus, Johannes

Treatise: Tetrachordum musices, tractatus secundus

Incipit: Quid est musica plana? Quae in suis notis aequam seruat mensuram absque

File name: **COCTET2**　　Data input by: Svetlana Khlybova

File type: **TEXT**　　　Data checked by: Sergei Lebedev & Andreas Giger

　MS:　　　Print: **X**　　Data approved by: Thomas J. Mathiesen

Filelist: 16th　　File size: 19K　　　Annotations:

Source of data:

Tetrachordum musices Ioannis Coclei Norici artium magistri Nurnbergae aeditum pro iuuentute Laurentiana in primis dein pro ceteris quoque Musarum Tyrunculis (Nurnbergae, impressi in officina excusoria Friderici Peypus, 1514), ff. Bir-Civ.

The incipit is preceded by the chapter heading "De musica plana in genere. Caput primum." The graphics files for this treatise are COCTET2 01GF-COCTET2 07GF. Continues from COCTET1 and in COCTET3-4.

Author: Cochlaeus, Johannes

Treatise: Tetrachordum musices, tractatus tertius

Incipit: Quid est tonus? Est regula per ascensum et descensum quemuis cantum in fine

File name: **COCTET3**　　Data input by: Svetlana Khlybova

File type: **TEXT**　　　Data checked by: Sergei Lebedev & Andreas Giger

　MS:　　　Print: **X**　　Data approved by: Thomas J. Mathiesen

Filelist: 16th　　File size: 20K　　　Annotations:

Source of data:

Tetrachordum musices Ioannis Coclei Norici artium magistri Nurnbergae aeditum pro iuuentute Laurentiana in primis dein pro ceteris quoque Musarum Tyrunculis (Nurnbergae, impressi in officina excusoria Friderici Peypus, 1514), ff. Civ-Diiiir.

The incipit is preceded by the chapter heading "De toni diffinitione ad divisione. Caput I." The graphics files for this treatise are COCTET3 01GF-COCTET3 08GF. Continues from COCTET1-2 and in COCTET4.

Author: Cochlaeus, Johannes

Treatise: Tetrachordum musices, tractatus quartus

Incipit: Quid est Musica mensuralis? Quae in suis notis secundum signorum ac figurarum

File name: **COCTET4**　　Data input by: Svetlana Khlybova

File type: **TEXT**　　　Data checked by: Sergei Lebedev & Andreas Giger

　MS:　　　Print: **X**　　Data approved by: Thomas J. Mathiesen

Filelist: 16th　　File size: 39K　　　Annotations:

Source of data:

Tetrachordum musices Ioannis Coclei Norici artium magistri Nurnbergae aeditum pro iuuentute Laurentiana in primis dein pro ceteris quoque Musarum Tyrunculis (Nurnbergae, impressi in officina excusoria Friderici Peypus, 1514), ff. Diiiiv-Fiiiir.

The incipit is preceded by the chapter heading "De Musica mensurali. Caput primum." The graphics files for this treatise are COCTET4 01GF-COCTET4 10GF. Continues from COCTET1-3.

Author: Critopulus, hieromonachus, Metrophanes
Treatise: Epistola de vocibus in musica liturgica Graecorum usitatis
Incipit: Dubitare multae eruditionis documentum est. Etenim indubiae cognitionis initium

File name: **CRIEPI**

File type: **TEXT**

MS: Print: **X**

Filelist: 17th   File size: 6K

Data input by: Bradley Jon Tucker

Data checked by: Benito V. Rivera

Data approved by: Thomas J. Mathiesen

Annotations:

Source of data:
Scriptores ecclesiastici de musica sacra potissimum, 3 vols., ed. Martin Gerbert (St. Blaise: Typis San-Blasianis, 1784; reprint ed., Hildesheim: Olms, 1963), 3:398-402.

The incipit is preceded by the salutation: "Honoratissimo et clarissimo Domino Ioanni Henrico Kirchbergero, Medicinae Doctori spectatissimo, gratiam et misericordiam a triuno et consubstantiali Deo."

Author: Dietricus
Treatise: Regulae super discantum et ad discernendum ipsas notas discantus
Incipit: Ad discendam artem discantandi notandum est, quod omnis discantus uno sex

File name: **DIEREG**

File type: **TEXT**

MS: Print: **X**

Filelist: 13th   File size: 5K

Data input by: Stephen E. Hayes

Data checked by: Peter Lefferts & Luminita Aluas

Data approved by: Thomas J. Mathiesen

Annotations:

Source of data:
Hans Müller, Eine Abhandlung über Mensuralmusik in der Karlsruher Handschrift St. Peter pergamen. 29a, Mittheilungen aus der Grossherzoglich Badischen Hof- und Landesbibliothek und Münzsammlung, Band 4 (Leipzig: B. G. Teubner, 1886), 5-7.

Commonly known as the Karlsruhe Anonymous.

Author: Dionysius Lewis de Ryckel
Treatise: De arte musicali, prima pars: Musica speculativa
Incipit: Utilitas huius scientie musicalis magna est et mirabilis atque virtuosa ualde.

File name: **GENTSPE**

File type: **MGRU70**

MS: **X**   Print:

Filelist: 15th   File size: 145K

Data input by: P. Slemon & J. Langford-Johnson

Data checked by: Michael W. Lundell

Data approved by: Thomas J. Mathiesen

Annotations:

Source of data:
Gent, Rijksuniversiteit, 70 (71), ff. 78r-106r.

=RISM BIII/1:65-69. The graphics files for this treatise are GENTSPE 01GF-GENTSPE 10GF. See also GENTPRA.

Author: Dionysius Lewis de Ryckel
Treatise: De arte musicali, secunda pars: Musica practica
Incipit: Ibi incipere debet musice practica: ubi desinit eius theorica.

File name: **GENTPRA**

File type: **MGRU70**

MS: **X**   Print:

Filelist: 15th   File size: 77K

Data input by: Peter Slemon

Data checked by: Michael W. Lundell

Data approved by: Thomas J. Mathiesen

Annotations:

Source of data:
Gent, Rijksuniversiteit, 70 (71), ff. 106v-123v.

=RISM BIII/1:65-69. The graphics files for this treatise are GENTPRA 01GF-GENTPRA 12GF. See also GENTSPE.

Author: Dresseler, Gallus
Treatise: Praecepta musicae poeticae
Incipit: Musica omnibus temporibus apud bonos et doctos in magno precio fuit.

File name: **DREPRA** Data input by: Peter Slemon
File type: **TEXT** Data checked by: Andreas Giger
MS: Print: **X** Data approved by: Thomas J. Mathiesen
Filelist: 16th File size: 55K Annotations:
Source of data: Text edited from Berlin, Deutsche
Bernhard Engelke, "Praecepta mvsicae Staatsbibliothek, theor. quarto 84. The
poeticae a D: Gallo Dresselero," graphics files for this treatise are DREPRA
Geschichtsblätter für Stadt und Land 01GF-DREPRA 12GF.
Magdeburg 49-50 (1914-15): 213-50.

Author: Eberhardus Frisingensis
Treatise: Tractatus de mensura fistularum
Incipit: Mensuram fistularum dicturi pauca praemittere volumus

File name: **EBETRA** Data input by: Stephen E. Hayes
File type: **TEXT** Data checked by: Peter Lefferts & Angela Mariani
MS: Print: **X** Data approved by: Thomas J. Mathiesen
Filelist: 12th File size: 10K Annotations:
Source of data: The graphics file for this treatise is EBETRA
Scriptores ecclesiastici de musica sacra 01GF.
potissimum, 3 vols., ed. Martin Gerbert
(St. Blaise: Typis San-Blasianis, 1784;
reprint ed., Hildesheim: Olms, 1963),
2:279-82.

Author: Engelbertus Admontensis
Treatise: De musica, tractatus primus
Incipit: Propter amicorum et familiarium dilectionem et complacentiam, quibus totum volo

File name: **ENGDEM1** Data input by: Patricia Starr & Sean Ferguson
File type: **TEXT** Data checked by: Charles Atkinson & Bradley Tucker
MS: Print: **X** Data approved by: Thomas J. Mathiesen
Filelist: 14th File size: 32K Annotations:
Source of data: See also ENGDEM2-4.
Scriptores ecclesiastici de musica sacra
potissimum, 3 vols., ed. Martin Gerbert
(St. Blaise: Typis San-Blasianis, 1784;
reprint ed., Hildesheim: Olms, 1963),
2:287-98.

Author: Engelbertus Admontensis

Treatise: De musica, tractatus secundus

Incipit: Postquam in prima parte huius tractatus circa voces et sonos musicos pro

File name: **ENGDEM2**   Data input by: Patricia Starr & Sean Ferguson

File type: **TEXT**   Data checked by: Charles Atkinson

  MS: Print: **X**   Data approved by: Thomas J. Mathiesen

Filelist: 14th   File size: 66K   Annotations:

Source of data: See also ENGDEM1 and 3-4.
  Scriptores ecclesiastici de musica sacra
  potissimum, 3 vols., ed. Martin Gerbert
  (St. Blaise: Typis San-Blasianis, 1784;
  reprint ed., Hildesheim: Olms, 1963),
  2:298-320.

Author: Engelbertus Admontensis

Treatise: De musica, tractatus tertius

Incipit: Modo iam in duabus partibus huius tractatus praehabitis et praedeclaratis aliquibus

File name: **ENGDEM3**   Data input by: Patricia Starr & Sean Ferguson

File type: **TEXT**   Data checked by: Charles Atkinson & Bradley Tucker

  MS: Print: **X**   Data approved by: Thomas J. Mathiesen

Filelist: 14th   File size: 47K   Annotations:

Source of data: See also ENGDEM1-2 and 4. The graphics
  Scriptores ecclesiastici de musica sacra   files for this treatise are ENGDEM3
  potissimum, 3 vols., ed. Martin Gerbert   01GF-ENGDEM3 03GF.
  (St. Blaise: Typis San-Blasianis, 1784;
  reprint ed., Hildesheim: Olms, 1963),
  2:320-38.

Author: Engelbertus Admontensis

Treatise: De musica, tractatus quartus

Incipit: Finitis tribus partibus huius tractatus nostri de Musica, ad quartam partem

File name: **ENGDEM4**   Data input by: Patricia Starr & Sean Ferguson

File type: **TEXT**   Data checked by: Charles Atkinson

  MS: Print: **X**   Data approved by: Thomas J. Mathiesen

Filelist: 14th   File size: 89K   Annotations:

Source of data: See also ENGDEM1-3. The graphics files for
  Scriptores ecclesiastici de musica sacra   this treatise are ENGDEM4 01GF-ENGDEM4
  potissimum, 3 vols., ed. Martin Gerbert   04GF.
  (St. Blaise: Typis San-Blasianis, 1784;
  reprint ed., Hildesheim: Olms, 1963),
  2:338-69.

Author: Faber Stapulensis, Jacobus

Treatise: Elementa musicalia

Incipit: Interuallum est soni grauis, acutique spaciorum habitudo. Spacium vocamus neruum

File name: **STAPMUS**	Data input by: Elisabeth Honn
File type: **TEXT**	Data checked by: Andreas Giger
MS: Print: **X**	Data approved by: Thomas J. Mathiesen
Filelist: 15th File size: 200K	Annotations:

Source of data:

In hoc opere contenta. | Arithmetica decem libris demonstrata | Musica libris demonstrata quattuor | Epitome in libros arithmeticos diui Seuerini Boetij | Rithmimachie ludus qui et pugna numerorum appellatur (Paris: Joannes Higmanus et Volgangus Hopilius, 1496), ff. f1r-h6v.

The incipit is preceded by a dedicatory preface to Nicolaus de Haqueville, beginning "Decreueram clarissime vir nulli meas elementorum musicalium ..."; a second preface addressed to Jacobus Labinius and Jacobus Turbelinus, beginning " Quod inter oratorem atque rhetora ..."; a list of ancient and medieval writers on the subject of music; and the heading "Argumentum quottuor librorum musices." The graphics for this treatise are STAPMUS 01GF-STAPMUS 14GF.

Author: Finck, Hermann

Treatise: Practica musica

Incipit: Inter caeteras praeclaras artes quae uere dei dona sunt, non infimum locum

File name: **FINPRA**	Data input by: Claudia Di Luca
File type: **TEXT**	Data checked by: Andreas Giger & Elisabeth Honn
MS: Print: **X**	Data approved by: Thomas J. Mathiesen
Filelist: 16th File size: 164K	Annotations:

Source of data:

Practica musica Hermanni Finckii, exempla variorum signorum, proportionum et canonum, iudicium de tonis, ac quaedam de arte suaviter et artificiose cantandi continens (Vitebergae, excusa typis haeredum Georgii Rhaw, 1556).

The treatise is preceded by a dedicatory epistle, beginning: "Totum opificium hominis plenum est ingentium miraculorum" and an engraving of "Musica." The graphics files for this treatise are FINPRA 01GF-FINPRA 84GF.

Author: Folianus, Ludovicus

Treatise: Musica theorica, sectio prima

Incipit: Mvsicae facvltatis svbiectvm: Quod: Numerus sonorus: appellatur: nihil aliud est:

File name: **FOLMUS1**	Data input by: Nigel Gwee
File type: **TEXT**	Data checked by: Sandra Pinegar
MS: Print: **X**	Data approved by: Thomas J. Mathiesen
Filelist: 16th File size: 46K	Annotations:

Source of data:

Ludovici Foliani Mutinensis de musica theorica (Venice: Io. Antonius et Fratres de Sabio, 1529; reprint ed., Bologna: Forni, 1970).

The incipit is preceded by a reader's preface, beginning: "Qvisquis es: qui nostram accedis ad Musicam ..."; a table of contents; and the chapter heading: "Quid subiectum Musices: et cur illa dicatur scientia media: et subalternata: et quis operis huius ordo." The graphics files for this treatise are FOLMUS1 01GF-FOLMUS1 11GF. See also FOLMUS2 and FOLMUS3.

Author: Folianus, Ludovicus

Treatise: Musica theorica, sectio secunda

Incipit: Dvo tantum genera proportionum ueteres et praesertim Pythagorici: ad musicas

File name: **FOLMUS2**   Data input by: Nigel Gwee

File type: **TEXT**   Data checked by: Sandra Pinegar

MS: Print: **X**   Data approved by: Thomas J. Mathiesen

Filelist: 16th   File size: 72K   Annotations:

Source of data:
Ludovici Foliani Mutinensis de musica theorica (Venice: Io. Antonius et Fratres de Sabio, 1529; reprint ed., Bologna: Forni, 1970).

The incipit is preceded by the chapter heading "Quomodo unaquaeque consonantia suae aptetur proportioni." The graphics files for this treatise are FOLMUS2 01GF-FOLMUS2 28GF. See also FOLMUS1 and FOLMUS3.

Author: Folianus, Ludovicus

Treatise: Musica theorica, sectio tertia

Incipit: Nvnctis iam quae mihi ante monochordi diuisionem: expedienda uidebantur:

File name: **FOLMUS3**   Data input by: Nigel Gwee

File type: **TEXT**   Data checked by: Sandra Pinegar

MS: Print: **X**   Data approved by: Thomas J. Mathiesen

Filelist: 16th   File size: 54K   Annotations:

Source of data:
Ludovici Foliani Mutinensis de musica theorica (Venice: Io. Antonius et Fratres de Sabio, 1529; reprint ed., Bologna: Forni, 1970).

The incipit is preceded by the chapter heading "De monochordi diuisione." The graphics files for this treatise are FOLMUS3 01GF-FOLMUS3 05GF. See also FOLMUS1 and FOLMUS2.

Author: Franco

Treatise: Ars cantus mensurabilis

Incipit: Cum inquiunt de plana musica quidam philosophi sufficienter tractauerint

File name: **FRAACME**   Data input by: Sandra Pinegar

File type: **MPBN1666**   Data checked by: J. Langford-Johnson & M. Lundell

MS: **X**   Print: Data approved by: Thomas J. Mathiesen

Filelist: 13th   File size: 37K   Annotations:

Source of data:
Paris, Bibliothèque nationale, lat. 16663, ff. 76v-83r.

=RISM BIII/1:124. Cf. FRAACM TEXT, FRAACMO MOBB842, FRAARS TEXT, FRAARSC TEXT, and FRAARSCM TEXT. The graphics files for this treatise are FRAACME 01GF-FRAACME 06GF.

Author: Franco

Treatise: Ars cantus mensurabilis

Incipit: Cum, inquiunt, de plana musica quidam philosophi sufficienter tractaverint

File name: **FRAARS**   Data input by: Bradley Jon Tucker

File type: **TEXT**   Data checked by: Charles M. Atkinson

MS: Print: **X**   Data approved by: Thomas J. Mathiesen

Filelist: 13th   File size: 37K   Annotations:

Source of data:
Scriptorum de musica medii aevi nova series a Gerbertina altera, 4 vols., ed. Edmond de Coussemaker (Paris: Durand, 1864-76; reprint ed., Hildesheim: Olms, 1963), 1:117-36.

The graphics files for this treatise are FRAARS 01GF-FRAARS 05GF. See also FRAACM, FRAACME MPBN1666, FRAACMO, FRAARSCM, and FRAARSC.

THESAURUS MUSICARUM LATINARUM: Canon of Data Files

Author: Franco
Treatise: Ars cantus mensurabilis
Incipit: Cum, inquiunt, de plana musica quidam philosophi sufficienter tractaverint

File name: **FRAARSCM**	Data input by: Bradley Jon Tucker
File type: **TEXT**	Data checked by: Peter M. Lefferts & Kirk Ditzler
MS: Print: **X**	Data approved by: Thomas J. Mathiesen
Filelist: 13th File size: 35K	Annotations:

Source of data:
Hieronymus de Moravia, Tractatus de musica, ed. S. M. Cserba, Freiburger Studien zur Musikwissenschaft, vol. 2 (Regensburg: Pustet, 1935), 230-59.

The graphics files for this treatise are FRAARSCM 01GF-FRAARSCM 06GF. See also FRAACM, FRAACME MPBN1666, FRAACMO MOBB842, FRAARS, and FRAARSC.

Author: Franco
Treatise: Ars cantus mensurabilis
Incipit: Cum de plana musica quidam philosophi sufficienter tractauerint

File name: **FRAACMO**	Data input by: Peter M. Lefferts
File type: **MOBB842**	Data checked by: Michael W. Lundell
MS: **X** Print:	Data approved by: Thomas J. Mathiesen
Filelist: 13th File size: 35K	Annotations:

Source of data:
Oxford, Bodleian Library, Bodley 842 (S.C. 2575), ff. 49r-59v.

=RISM BIII/4:110-15. The incipit is preceded by a listing of the chapter headings. The graphics files for this treatise are FRAACMO 01GF-FRAACMO 10GF. See also FRAACM, FRAACME MPBN1666, FRAARS, FRAARSCM, and FRAARSC.

Author: Franco
Treatise: Ars cantus mensurabilis
Incipit: Cum de plana musica quidam philosophi sufficienter tractaverint

File name: **FRAARSC**	Data input by: Laurel Carter
File type: **TEXT**	Data checked by: Luminita Aluas
MS: Print: **X**	Data approved by: Albert C. Rotola, S.J.
Filelist: 13th File size: 33K	Annotations:

Source of data:
Scriptores ecclesiastici de musica sacra potissimum, 3 vols., ed. Martin Gerbert (St. Blaise: Typis San-Blasianis, 1784; reprint ed., Hildesheim: Olms, 1963), 3:1-16.

The graphics files for this treatise are FRAARSC 01GF-FRAARSC 03GF. See also FRAACM, FRAACME MPBN1666, FRAACMO MOBB842, FRAARSCM, and FRAARS.

Author: Franco

Treatise: Ars cantus mensurabilis

Incipit: Cum de plana musica quidam philosophi sufficienter tractaverint

File name: **FRAACM**

File type: **TEXT**

MS: Print: **X**

Filelist: 13th   File size: 35K

Data input by: Stephen E. Hayes

Data checked by: Peter Lefferts & Bradley Tucker

Data approved by: Thomas J. Mathiesen

Annotations:

Source of data:

Franconis de Colonia, Ars cantus mensurabilis, ed. Gilbert Reaney and André Gilles, Corpus scriptorum de musica, vol. 18 ([Rome]: American Institute of Musicology, 1974), 23-82. Used by permission.

The graphics files for this treatise are FRAACM 01GF-FRAACM 05GF. See also FRAACME MPBN1666, FRAACMO MOBB842, FRAARS, FRAARSCM, and FRAARSC.

Author: Franco

Treatise: Compendium discantus

Incipit: Primo enim notandum tredecim esse species consonanciarum et dissonanciarum

File name: **FRACOMO**

File type: **MOBB842**

MS: **X**   Print:

Filelist: 13th   File size: 6K

Data input by: Peter M. Lefferts

Data checked by: Michael W. Lundell

Data approved by: Thomas J. Mathiesen

Annotations:

Source of data:

Oxford, Bodleian Library, Bodley 842 (S.C. 2575), ff. 60r-62v.

=RISM BIII/4:110-15. The incipit is preceded by a listing of the chapter headings. The graphics file for this treatise is FRACOMO 01GF. See also FRACOM.

Author: Franco

Treatise: Compendium discantus

Incipit: Primo vero notandum tredecim esse species consonantiarum et dissonantiarum

File name: **FRACOM**

File type: **TEXT**

MS: Print: **X**

Filelist: 13th   File size: 6K

Data input by: Bradley Jon Tucker

Data checked by: Thomas J. Mathiesen

Data approved by: Albert C. Rotola, S.J.

Annotations:

Source of data:

Scriptorum de musica medii aevi nova series a Gerbertina altera, 4 vols., ed. Edmond de Coussemaker (Paris: Durand, 1864-76; reprint ed., Hildesheim: Olms, 1963), 1:154-56.

The incipit is preceded by the heading for the first chapter: "Premissis consonantiis et dissonantiis, continet quinque regulas ascendendi in discantu. Ego Franco de Colonia utililati juvenam cupiens deservire, compendiosum tractatum de discantu, ut subsequeretur, composui." See also FRACOMO.

Author: Frosch, Johannes

Treatise: Rerum musicarum opusculum rarum ac insigne

Incipit: Iam vero telam nobis (ut aiunt) exordientibus, non suppetet facultas

File name: **FRORER**   Data input by: Claudia Di Luca

File type: **TEXT**   Data checked by: Andreas Giger

MS: Print: **X**   Data approved by: Thomas J. Mathiesen

Filelist: 16th   File size: 162K   Annotations:

Source of data:

Rerum musicarum opusculum rarum ac insigne, totius eius negotii rationem mira industria et brevitate complectens, iam recens publicatum (Argentorati, apud Petrum Schoeffer et Mathiam Apiarium, 1535).

The treatise is preceded by a table of contents, three verses (beginning "Si tibi sunt Musae," "Huc propera," and "Vade age parve liber"), a dedicatory epistle (beginning "Miraberis forsan illustris pariter atque Clarissime Comes"), an index, and a preface (beginning "Etsi cuiquam (Lector amice) ad hoc"). The graphics files for this treatise are FRORER 01GF-FRORER 18GF.

Author: Gaffurio, Franchino

Treatise: Apologia adversus Ioannem Spatarium et complices musicos Bononienses

Incipit: Occasionem dicendi de te prebes Ioannes Spatarie qui in alios dicere solitus es.

File name: **GAFAPO**   Data input by: Jessica Burr

File type: **TEXT**   Data checked by: Bradley Jon Tucker

MS: Print: **X**   Data approved by: Thomas J. Mathiesen

Filelist: 16th   File size: 42K   Annotations:

Source of data:

Apologia Franchini Gafurii Musici adversus Ioannem Spatarium et complices musicos Bononienses (Turin: Augustinus de Vicomercato, 1520; reprint ed., New York: Broude Bros., 1979).

The graphics files for this treatise are GAFAPO 01GF-GAFAPO 06GF.

Author: Gaffurio, Franchino

Treatise: De harmonia musicorum instrumentorum opus, liber primus

Incipit: Mos fuit apud Antiquos uir Amplissime: quem posteriores per manus traditum

File name: **GAFHAR1**   Data input by: Nigel Gwee & John Csonka

File type: **TEXT**   Data checked by: Peter Slemon

MS: Print: **X**   Data approved by: Thomas J. Mathiesen

Filelist: 16th   File size: 127K   Annotations:

Source of data:

Franchini Gafurii Laudensis Regii Musici publice profitentis: Delubrique Mediolanensis Phonasci: de Harmonia Musicorum Instrumentorum Opus (Milan: Gotardus Pontanus, 1518; reprint eds., New York: Broude Bros., [1979]; Bologna: Forni, 1972).

The first book is preceded dedicatory poems and a list of contents. The graphics files for this treatise are GAFHAR1 01GF-GAFHAR1 11GF. See also GAFHAR2, GAFHAR3, and GAFHAR4.

Author: Gaffurio, Franchino

Treatise: De harmonia musicorum instrumentorum opus, liber secundus

Incipit: Chromatici Generis chordae ita per tetrachorda disponuntur: ut tertia tantum chorda

File name: **GAFHAR2**   Data input by: Nigel Gwee & John Csonka

File type: **TEXT**   Data checked by: Peter Slemon

　MS:　　Print: **X**   Data approved by: Thomas J. Mathiesen

Filelist: 16th　　File size: 154K   Annotations:

Source of data:

Franchini Gafurii Laudensis Regii Musici publice profitentis: Delubrique Mediolanensis Phonasci: de Harmonia Musicorum Instrumentorum Opus (Milan: Gotardus Pontanus, 1518; reprint eds., New York: Broude Bros., [1979]; Bologna: Forni, 1972).

The book begins with the chapter heading "De Genere Chromatico Caput Primum." The graphics files for this treatise are GAFHAR2 01GF-GAFHAR2 37GF. See also GAFHAR1, GAFHAR3, and GAFHAR4.

Author: Gaffurio, Franchino

Treatise: De harmonia musicorum instrumentorum opus, liber tertius

Incipit: Rationem extremorum sonorum in harmonia inuicem consonantium harmonica

File name: **GAFHAR3**   Data input by: Nigel Gwee

File type: **TEXT**   Data checked by: Peter Slemon

　MS:　　Print: **X**   Data approved by: Thomas J. Mathiesen

Filelist: 16th　　File size: 59K   Annotations:

Source of data:

Franchini Gafurii Laudensis Regii Musici publice profitentis: Delubrique Mediolanensis Phonasci: de Harmonia Musicorum Instrumentorum Opus (Milan: Gotardus Pontanus, 1518; reprint eds., New York: Broude Bros., [1979]; Bologna: Forni, 1972).

The book begins with the chapter heading "De Continua proportionalitate Arythmetica et eius proprietatibus Caput Primum." The graphics files for this treatise are GAFHAR3 01GF-GAFHAR3 04GF. See also GAFHAR1, GAFHAR2, and GAFHAR4.

Author: Gaffurio, Franchino

Treatise: De harmonia musicorum instrumentorum opus, liber quartus et ultimus

Incipit: Modos apud ueteres de mente Aristotelis trigesimi luciditate Problematis Petrus

File name: **GAFHAR4**   Data input by: Nigel Gwee

File type: **TEXT**   Data checked by: Peter Slemon

　MS:　　Print: **X**   Data approved by: Thomas J. Mathiesen

Filelist: 16th　　File size: 83K   Annotations:

Source of data:

Franchini Gafurii Laudensis Regii Musici publice profitentis: Delubrique Mediolanensis Phonasci: de Harmonia Musicorum Instrumentorum Opus (Milan: Gotardus Pontanus, 1518; reprint eds., New York: Broude Bros., [1979]; Bologna: Forni, 1972).

The book begins with the chapter heading "Qui priores Modi apud Antiquos fuerint in usu Caput Primum." The graphics files for this treatise are GAFHAR4 01GF-GAFHAR4 04GF. See also GAFHAR1, GAFHAR2, and GAFHAR3.

Author: Gaffurio, Franchino
Treatise: Practica musice
Incipit: Et si harmonicam scientiam plerique cessante usu
File name: **GAFPM1**   Data input by: C. Matthew Balensuela
File type: **TEXT**   Data checked by: Charles M. Atkinson
  MS: Print: **X**   Data approved by: Thomas J. Mathiesen
Filelist: 15th   File size: 82K   Annotations:
Source of data: The graphics files for this treatise are
  Practica musice Franchini Gafori   GAFPM1 01GF-GAFPM1 17GF. See also
  Laudensis (Milan: Ioannes Petrus de GAFPM2, GAFPM3, and GAFPM4
  Lomatio, 1496; reprint ed., New York:
  Broude Bros., 1979).

Author: Gaffurio, Franchino
Treatise: Practica musice
Incipit: Musicam vocis actionem quam superiori volumine
File name: **GAFPM2**   Data input by: C. Matthew Balensuela
File type: **TEXT**   Data checked by: Jan Herlinger
  MS: Print: **X**   Data approved by: Thomas J. Mathiesen
Filelist: 15th   File size: 86K   Annotations:
Source of data: The graphics files for this treatise are
  Practica musice Franchini Gafori   GAFPM2 01GF-GAFPM2 13GF. See also
  Laudensis (Milan: Ioannes Petrus de GAFPM1, GAFPM3, and GAFPM4
  Lomatio, 1496; reprint ed., New York:
  Broude Bros., 1979).

Author: Gaffurio, Franchino
Treatise: Practica musice
Incipit: Harmonici modulaminis Genus auctore Baccheo est
File name: **GAFPM3**   Data input by: C. Matthew Balensuela
File type: **TEXT**   Data checked by: Oliver B. Ellsworth
  MS: Print: **X**   Data approved by: Thomas J. Mathiesen
Filelist: 15th   File size: 62K   Annotations:
Source of data: The graphics files for this treatise are
  Practica musice Franchini Gafori   GAFPM3 01GF-GAFPM3 07GF. See also
  Laudensis (Milan: Ioannes Petrus de GAFPM1, GAFPM2, and GAFPM4
  Lomatio, 1496; reprint ed., New York:
  Broude Bros., 1979).

Author: Gaffurio, Franchino
Treatise: Practica musice
Incipit: Proportio apud Euclidem est duarum quamcaecumque
File name: **GAFPM4**   Data input by: C. Matthew Balensuela
File type: **TEXT**   Data checked by: Oliver B. Ellsworth
  MS: Print: **X**   Data approved by: Thomas J. Mathiesen
Filelist: 15th   File size: 112K   Annotations:
Source of data: The graphics files for this treatise are
  Practica musice Franchini Gafori   GAFPM4 01GF-GAFPM4 50GF. See also
  Laudensis (Milan: Ioannes Petrus de GAFPM1, GAFPM2, and GAFPM3.
  Lomatio, 1496; reprint ed., New York:
  Broude Bros., 1979).

THESAURUS MUSICARUM LATINARUM: Canon of Data Files

Author: Gaffurio, Franchino
Treatise: Theorica musice, liber primus
Incipit: Diuturni studii lectione depraehendi musices disciplinam antiquis temporibus

File name: **GAFTM1**   Data input by: Peter Slemon & Matthew Balensuela
File type: **TEXT**   Data checked by: Bradley Jon Tucker
  MS: Print: **X**   Data approved by: Thomas J. Mathiesen
Filelist: 15th   File size: 84K   Annotations:

Source of data:
  Theorica musice Franchini Gafuri
  Laudensis (Milan: Ioannes Petrus de
  Lomatio, 1492; reprint ed., New York:
  Broude Bros., 1967).

The incipit is preceded by a list of contents for the entire treatise and a dedicatory letter, beginning: "Quorum magis sententiae accedere debeam ...." The graphics files for this treatise are GAFTM1 01GF-GAFTM1 02GF. See also GAFTM2, GAFTM3, GAFTM4, and GAFTM5.

Author: Gaffurio, Franchino
Treatise: Theorica musice, liber secundus
Incipit: Cum omnis institutio cuiuscunque rei a ratione suscepte de beata diffinitione

File name: **GAFTM2**   Data input by: Peter Slemon
File type: **TEXT**   Data checked by: Bradley Jon Tucker
  MS: Print: **X**   Data approved by: Thomas J. Mathiesen
Filelist: 15th   File size: 53K   Annotations:

Source of data:
  Theorica musice Franchini Gafuri
  Laudensis (Milan: Ioannes Petrus de
  Lomatio, 1492; reprint ed., New York:
  Broude Bros., 1967).

The incipit is preceded by the chapter heading "De diffinitione musices et accidentibus sonorum." See also GAFTM1, GAFTM3, GAFTM4, and GAFTM5.

Author: Gaffurio, Franchino
Treatise: Theorica musice, liber tertius
Incipit: Quantitatem duplicem esse Mathematici asserunt Continuam scilicet et discretam

File name: **GAFTM3**   Data input by: Peter Slemon
File type: **TEXT**   Data checked by: Andreas Giger
  MS: Print: **X**   Data approved by: Thomas J. Mathiesen
Filelist: 15th   File size: 67K   Annotations:

Source of data:
  Theorica musice Franchini Gafuri
  Laudensis (Milan: Ioannes Petrus de
  Lomatio, 1492; reprint ed., New York:
  Broude Bros., 1967).

The incipit is preceded by the chapter heading "De Discreta et continua quantitate." The graphics file for this treatise is GAFTM3 01GF. See also GAFTM1, GAFTM2, GAFTM4, and GAFTM5.

THESAURUS MUSICARUM LATINARUM: Canon of Data Files

Author: Gaffurio, Franchino

Treatise: Theorica musice, liber quartus

Incipit: Quoniam omnium uarietate numerorum Macrobius: ac Boetius coeterique Musici

File name: **GAFTM4**	Data input by: Peter Slemon
File type: **TEXT**	Data checked by: Michael W. Lundell
MS: Print: **X**	Data approved by: Thomas J. Mathiesen
Filelist: 15th File size: 46K	Annotations:

Source of data:
Theorica musice Franchini Gafuri Laudensis (Milan: Ioannes Petrus de Lomatio, 1492; reprint ed., New York: Broude Bros., 1967).

Annotations:
The incipit is preceded by the chapter heading "De Consonantiis ex Proportionibus Eductis." The graphics files for this treatise are GAFTM4 01GF-GAFTM4 03GF. See also GAFTM1, GAFTM2, GAFTM3, and GAFTM5.

Author: Gaffurio, Franchino

Treatise: Theorica musice, liber quintus

Incipit: Refert Nicomachus canendi disciplinam primitus adeo simplicem fuisse

File name: **GAFTM5**	Data input by: Peter Slemon
File type: **TEXT**	Data checked by: Michael W. Lundell
MS: Print: **X**	Data approved by: Thomas J. Mathiesen
Filelist: 15th File size: 83K	Annotations:

Source of data:
Theorica musice Franchini Gafuri Laudensis (Milan: Ioannes Petrus de Lomatio, 1492; reprint ed., New York: Broude Bros., 1967).

Annotations:
The incipit is preceded by the chapter heading "De inuentione et dispositione sonorum." The graphics files for this treatise are GAFTM5 01GF-GAFTM5 09GF. See also GAFTM1, GAFTM2, GAFTM3. and GAFTM4.

Author: Gerlandus

Treatise: Fragmenta de musica

Incipit: Item de fistulis Gerlandus. Si fistulae aequalis grossitudinis fuerint, et maior minorem

File name: **GERFRA**	Data input by: Stephen E. Hayes
File type: **TEXT**	Data checked by: Peter M. Lefferts
MS: Print: **X**	Data approved by: Thomas J. Mathiesen
Filelist: 12th File size: 5K	Annotations:

Source of data:
Scriptores ecclesiastici de musica sacra potissimum, 3 vols., ed. Martin Gerbert (St. Blaise: Typis San-Blasianis, 1784; reprint ed., Hildesheim: Olms, 1963), 2:277-78.

Author: Glareanus, Henricus

Treatise: Dodecachordum, Liber primus

Incipit: Musica duplex est, Theorice ac pratice. Theorice circa rerum musicarum

File name: **GLADOD1**   Data input by: Sean Ferguson

File type: **TEXT**   Data checked by: Charles Atkinson & Bradley Tucker

MS: Print: **X**   Data approved by: Thomas J. Mathiesen

Filelist: 16th   File size: 172K   Annotations:

Source of data:
[Dodekachordon] (Basle: Henrichus Petri, 1547; reprint ed., New York: Broude Bros., 1967), 1-64.

The treatise itself is preceded by a long dedicatory preface, beginning: "Timotheum Milesium, artis Musices authorem celeberrimum, Reuerendissime Pater ..."; a list of authors cited in the treatise; a list of chapters in each of the three books; an index of "cantiones mensurales"; and a detailed index of terms and subjects. The graphics files for this treatise are GLADOD1 01GF-GLADOD1 20GF. See also GLADOD2 and GLADOD3.

Author: Glareanus, Henricus

Treatise: Dodecachordum, Liber secundus

Incipit: Hactenus omnia, quae uisa sunt necessaria, huius scientiae principia

File name: **GLADOD2**   Data input by: Bradley Jon Tucker

File type: **TEXT**   Data checked by: Michael W. Lundell

MS: Print: **X**   Data approved by: Thomas J. Mathiesen

Filelist: 16th   File size: 226K   Annotations:

Source of data:
[Dodekachordon] (Basle: Henrichus Petri, 1547; reprint ed., New York: Broude Bros., 1967), 65-194.

The graphics files for this treatise are GLADOD2 01GF-GLADOD2 67GF. See also GLADOD1 and GLADOD3.

Author: Glareanus, Henricus

Treatise: Dodecachordum, Liber tertius

Incipit: Hactenus omnia, quae uisa sunt necessaria, huius scientiae principia

File name: **GLADOD3**   Data input by: Nigel Gwee

File type: **TEXT**   Data checked by: Bradley Jon Tucker

MS: Print: **X**   Data approved by: Thomas J. Mathiesen

Filelist: 16th   File size: 172K   Annotations:

Source of data:
[Dodekachordon] (Basle: Henrichus Petri, 1547; reprint ed., New York: Broude Bros., 1967), 195-470.

The graphics files for this treatise are GLADOD3 001GF-GLADOD3 225GF. See also GLADOD1 and GLADOD2.

Author: Gresemund, Dietrich

Treatise: Lucubratiunculae bonarum septem artium liberalium, capitulum quintum, De musica

Incipit: Aristobolus. Age nunc, si tibi quicquam nervorum est, musicam tueare

File name: **GRELUC** Data input by: Peter Slemon

File type: **TEXT** Data checked by: Sandra Pinegar

MS: Print: **X** Data approved by: Thomas J. Mathiesen

Filelist: 15th File size: 10K Annotations:

Source of data:

Peter Wagner, "Aus der Musikgeschichte des deutschen Humanismus," Zeitschrift für Musikwissenschaft 3 (1920-21): 22-27.

The chapter was originally published in Theodorici Gresemundi junioris moguntini lucubraciuncle bonarum septem artium liberalium apologiam ejusdemque cum philosophia dialogum et orationem ad rerum publicarum rectores in se complectentes (Mainz: Peter Fridberg, 1494).

Author: Guerson, Guillaume

Treatise: Utillissime musicales regule

Incipit: Quoniam inter cetera mortalium nichil dignius esse constat scientiarum liberalium

File name: **GUEUT** Data input by: Peter Slemon

File type: **TEXT** Data checked by: Andreas Giger

MS: Print: **X** Data approved by: Thomas J. Mathiesen

Filelist: 15th File size: 83K Annotations:

Source of data:

Utillissime musicales Regule cunctis summopere necessarie plani cantus simplisis contrapuncti rerum factarum tonorum et artis accentuandi tam exemplariter quam practice per magistrum Guillermi Guersoni de Villalonga nouitter conpilate (Paris: Michel Thouloze, [c. 1495]).

This is the first edition. Text entered from the exemplar in the British Library, which is missing ff. eiir-eiiiv. The graphics for this treatise are GUEUT 01GF-GUEUT 32GF.

Author: Gui de Chalis

Treatise: Musica

Incipit: Si cantus ascendit duas voces et organum incipit in duplici voce

File name: **GUICHA** Data input by: Stephen E. Hayes

File type: **TEXT** Data checked by: Peter Lefferts & Luminita Aluas

MS: Print: **X** Data approved by: Thomas J. Mathiesen

Filelist: 13th File size: 5K Annotations:

Source of data:

Edmond de Coussemaker, Histoire de l'harmonie au moyen-age (Paris: V. Didron, 1852), 255-58.

Document IV in the Coussemaker Histoire; based on Paris, Bibliothèque Ste. Geneviève, 2284 (olim 1611), ff. 109v-110v. The incipit is preceded by a short verse beginning: "Ars probat artificem quae scribitur arte Guidonis...." The graphics file for this treatise is GUICHA 01GF. The text is also incorporated at the end of Abbott Guido, Regulae de arte musica (ABGURAM TEXT). Cf. ABGUREG TEXT.

Author: Guido d'Arezzo
Treatise: De modorum formulis et cantuum qualitatibus
Incipit: Vox est aer ictus auditu sensibilis quantum in ipso est. Omnis autem vox aut est
File name: **GUIMOD**   Data input by: Firoozeh Khazrai
File type: **TEXT**   Data checked by: Angela Mariani
  MS: Print: **X**   Data approved by: Thomas J. Mathiesen
Filelist: 9th-11th   File size: 64K   Annotations:
Source of data:
  Scriptorum de musica medii aevi nova
  series a Gerbertina altera, 4 vols., ed.
  Edmond de Coussemaker (Paris: Durand,
  1864-76; reprint ed., Hildesheim: Olms,
  1963), 2:78-115.

The treatise is preceded by a Prooemium, beginning: "Vocum modus, veterum editus voto, disgregatus a vero et recto ...." The graphics files for this treatise are GUIMOD 01GF-GUIMOD 10GF.

Author: Guido d'Arezzo
Treatise: De sex motibus vocum ad se invicem et dimensione earum
Incipit: Omnibus ecce modis descripta relatio vocis. Est tonus, in numeris superantur
File name: **GUISEX**   Data input by: Firoozeh Khazrai
File type: **TEXT**   Data checked by: Angela Mariani
  MS: Print: **X**   Data approved by: Thomas J. Mathiesen
Filelist: 9th-11th File size: 3K   Annotations:
Source of data:
  Scriptorum de musica medii aevi nova
  series a Gerbertina altera, 4 vols., ed.
  Edmond de Coussemaker (Paris: Durand,
  1864-76; reprint ed., Hildesheim: Olms,
  1963), 2:115-16.

Author: Guido d'Arezzo
Treatise: Epistola Guidonis Michaeli monacho de ignoto cantu directa
Incipit: Beatissimo atque dulcissimo Fratri Michaeli Guido, per anfractus multos deiectus
File name: **GUIEPI**   Data input by: Sergei Lebedev
File type: **TEXT**   Data checked by: Luminita Aluas
  MS: Print: **X**   Data approved by: Thomas J. Mathiesen
Filelist: 9th-11th File size: 21K   Annotations:
Source of data:
  Scriptores ecclesiastici de musica sacra
  potissimum, 3 vols., ed. Martin Gerbert
  (St. Blaise: Typis San-Blasianis, 1784;
  reprint ed., Hildesheim: Olms, 1963),
  2:43-50.

The graphics file for this treatise is GUIEPI 01GF. Cf. GUIEP TEXT.

Author: Guido d'Arezzo
Treatise: Epistola Guidonis Michaeli monacho de ignoto cantu
Incipit: Beatissimo atque dulcissimo fratri Michaeli Guido, per anfractus multos dejectus
File name: **GUIEP**   Data input by: Jingfa Sun
File type: **TEXT**   Data checked by: Charles Atkinson & Angela Mariani
  MS: Print: **X**   Data approved by: Thomas J. Mathiesen
Filelist: 9th-11th File size: 22K   Annotations:
Source of data:
  Patrologia cursus completus, series latina,
  ed. J. P. Migne, 221 vols. (Paris: Garnier,
  1844-1904), 141:423-32.

The graphics file for this treatise is GUIEP 01GF. Cf. GUIEPI TEXT.

Author: Guido d'Arezzo

Treatise: Micrologus

Incipit: Gymnasio musas placuit reuocare solutas.

File name: **GUIMICB**   Data input by: Julie Langford-Johnson

File type: **MBBR2784**   Data checked by: Michael W. Lundell

MS: **X**   Print: Data approved by: Thomas J. Mathiesen

Filelist: 9th-11th File size: 50K   Annotations:

Source of data: =RISM BIII/1:63. The graphics files for this
Brussels, Bibliothèque Royale, II 784, ff.   treatise are GUIMICB 01GF-GUIMICB
1r-20v.   06GF. Cf. GUIMIC TEXT, GUIMICR TEXT,
    and GUIMICRO TEXT.

Author: Guido d'Arezzo

Treatise: Micrologus

Incipit: Gymnasio musas placuit revocare solutas,

File name: **GUIMIC**   Data input by: Laurel Carter

File type: **TEXT**   Data checked by: Luminita Aluas

MS: Print: **X**   Data approved by: Thomas J. Mathiesen

Filelist: 9th-11th File size: 55K   Annotations:

Source of data: The graphics files for this treatise are GUIMIC
Scriptores ecclesiastici de musica sacra   01GF-GUIMIC 10GF. Cf. GUIMICB
potissimum, 3 vols., ed. Martin Gerbert   MBBR2784, GUIMICR TEXT, and
(St. Blaise: Typis San-Blasianis, 1784;   GUIMICRO TEXT.
reprint ed., Hildesheim: Olms, 1963),
2:2-24.

Author: Guido d'Arezzo

Treatise: Micrologus

Incipit: Gymnasio musas placuit revocare solutas.

File name: **GUIMICRO**   Data input by: Laurel Carter

File type: **TEXT**   Data checked by: Bradley Jon Tucker

MS: Print: **X**   Data approved by: Thomas J. Mathiesen

Filelist: 9th-11th File size: 55K   Annotations:

Source of data: The graphics files for this treatise are
Patrologia cursus completus, series latina,   GUIMICRO 01GF-GUIMICRO 09GF. Cf.
ed. J. P. Migne, 221 vols. (Paris: Garnier,   GUIMICB MBBR2784, GUIMIC TEXT, and
1844-1904), 141:379-406.   GUIMICR TEXT.

Author: Guido d'Arezzo

Treatise: Micrologus

Incipit: Gymnasio musas placuit revocare solutas,

File name: **GUIMICR**   Data input by: Sergei Lebedev

File type: **TEXT**   Data checked by: Luminita Aluas

MS: Print: **X**   Data approved by: Thomas J. Mathiesen

Filelist: 9th-11th File size: 50K   Annotations:

Source of data: The graphics files for this treatise are
Guidonis Aretini Micrologus, ed. Jos.   GUIMICR 01GF-GUIMICR 04GF. Cf.
Smits van Waesberghe, Corpus   GUIMICB MBBR2784, GUIMIC TEXT, and
scriptorum de musica, vol. 4 ([Rome]:   GUIMICRO TEXT.
American Institute of Musicology, 1955),
79-234. Used by permission.

Author: Guido d'Arezzo

Treatise: Prologus in antiphonarium

Incipit: Temporibus nostris super omnes homines fatui sunt cantores

File name: **GUIPRAN**   Data input by: Dolores Pesce

File type: **TEXT**   Data checked by: Angela Mariani & Bradley Tucker

  MS: Print: **X**   Data approved by: Thomas J. Mathiesen

Filelist: 9th-11th   File size: 18K   Annotations:

Source of data: The graphics file for this treatise is GUIPRAN
  Scriptores ecclesiastici de musica sacra   01GF-GUIPRAN 02GF. Cf. GUIPRO TEXT
  potissimum, 3 vols., ed. Martin Gerbert   and GUIPROL TEXT.
  (St. Blaise: Typis San-Blasianis, 1784;
  reprint ed., Hildesheim: Olms, 1963),
  2:34-42.

Author: Guido d'Arezzo

Treatise: Prologus in antiphonarium

Incipit: Temporibus nostris super omnes homines fatui sunt cantores

File name: **GUIPROL**   Data input by: Jingfa Sun

File type: **TEXT**   Data checked by: Angela Mariani

  MS: Print: **X**   Data approved by: Thomas J. Mathiesen

Filelist: 9th-11th   File size: 19K   Annotations:

Source of data: The graphics files for this treatise are
  Patrologia cursus completus, series latina,   GUIPROL 01GF-GUIPROL 02GF. Cf.
  ed. J. P. Migne, 221 vols. (Paris: Garnier,   GUIPRO TEXT and GUIPRAN TEXT.
  1844-1904), 141:413-22.

Author: Guido d'Arezzo

Treatise: Prologus in antiphonarium

Incipit: Temporibus nostris . super omnes homines (:) fatui sunt cantores!

File name: **GUIPRO**   Data input by: Sergei Lebedev

File type: **TEXT**   Data checked by: Elisabeth Honn

  MS: Print: **X**   Data approved by: Thomas J. Mathiesen

Filelist: 9th-11th   File size: 8K   Annotations:

Source of data: The graphics file for this treatise is GUIPRO
  Tres tractatuli Guidonis Aretini: Guidonis   01GF. Cf. GUIPROL TEXT and GUIPRAN
  "Prologus in Antiphonarium," ed. Joseph   TEXT.
  Smits van Waesberghe, Divitiae musicae
  artis, A/III (Buren: Knuf, 1975), 58-81.
  Used by kind permission of the
  Laaber-Verlag.

Author: Guido d'Arezzo

Treatise: Regulae rhythmicae in antiphonarii sui prologum prolatae

Incipit: Musicorum et cantorum magna est distantia, Isti dicunt, illi sciunt, quae componit

File name: **GUIRR**

File type: **TEXT**

MS: Print: **X**

Filelist: 9th-11th File size: 16K

Data input by: Dolores Pesce

Data checked by: Angela Mariani & Bradley Tucker

Data approved by: Thomas J. Mathiesen

Annotations:

Source of data:

Scriptores ecclesiastici de musica sacra potissimum, 3 vols., ed. Martin Gerbert (St. Blaise: Typis San-Blasianis, 1784; reprint ed., Hildesheim: Olms, 1963), 2:25-34.

The treatise is preceded by the short acrostic "Guidonis versus de musicae explanatione, suique nominis ordine" beginning: "Gliscunt corda meis hominum mollita Camenis, Una mihi virtus numeratos contulit ictus, ..." The graphics files for this treatise are GUIRR 01GF-GUIRR 02GF. Cf. GUIRRH TEXT and GUIREG TEXT.

Author: Guido d'Arezzo

Treatise: Regulae rhythmicae in antiphonarii sui prologum prolatae

Incipit: Musicorum et cantorum magna est distantia. Isti dicunt, illi sciunt, quae componit

File name: **GUIRRH**

File type: **TEXT**

MS: Print: **X**

Filelist: 9th-11th File size: 17K

Data input by: Jingfa Sun

Data checked by: Angela Mariani

Data approved by: Thomas J. Mathiesen

Annotations:

Source of data:

Patrologia cursus completus, series latina, ed. J. P. Migne, 221 vols. (Paris: Garnier, 1844-1904), 141:405-14.

The treatise is preceded by the short acrostic "Guidonis versus de musicae explanatione, suique nominis ordine" beginning: "Gliscunt corda meis hominum mollita Camenis, Una mihi virtus numeratos contulit ictus, ..." The graphics files for this treatise are GUIRRH 01GF-GUIRRH 02GF. Cf. GUIRR TEXT and GUIREG TEXT.

Author: Guido d'Arezzo

Treatise: Regulae rhythmicae

Incipit: Musicorum et cantorum magna est distantia. Isti dicunt, illi sciunt, quae componit

File name: **GUIREG**

File type: **TEXT**

MS: Print: **X**

Filelist: 9th-11th File size: 16K

Data input by: Sergei Lebedev

Data checked by: Elisabeth Honn

Data approved by: Thomas J. Mathiesen

Annotations:

Source of data:

Guidonis Aretini "Regulae rhythmicae," ed. Joseph Smits van Waesberghe and Eduard Vetter, Divitiae musicae artis, A/IV (Buren: Knuf, 1985), 92-133. Used by kind permission of the Laaber-Verlag.

The treatise is preceded by the short acrostic beginning: "Gliscunt corda meis hominum mollita camenis, Una mihi virtus numeratos contulit ictus, ..." The graphics files for this treatise are GUIREG 01GF-GUIREG 02GF. Cf. GUIRR TEXT and GUIRRH TEXT.

Author: Guido d'Arezzo [Ps.]

Treatise: Tractatus Guidonis correctorius multorum errorum, qui fiunt in cantu gregoriano in

Incipit: Multorum considerans errorem coactus sum Gregorii cantum, quem multis in locis

File name: **ANOTRA2**   Data input by: Bradley Jon Tucker

File type: **TEXT**   Data checked by: Benito V. Rivera

MS: Print: **X**   Data approved by: Thomas J. Mathiesen

Filelist: 15th   File size: 14K   Annotations:

Source of data:

Scriptores ecclesiastici de musica sacra potissimum, 3 vols., ed. Martin Gerbert (St. Blaise: Typis San-Blasianis, 1784; reprint ed., Hildesheim: Olms, 1963), 2:50-55.

Doubtfully attributed to Guido in Gerbert's edition, the treatise probably dates from the fifteenth century. Cf. ANOTRAC2 TEXT.

Author: Guido d'Arezzo [Ps.]

Treatise: Tractatus Guidonis correctorius multorum errorum, qui fiunt in cantu gregoriano in

Incipit: Multorum considerans errorem coactus sum Gregorii cantum, quem multis in locis

File name: **ANOTRAC2**   Data input by: Jingfa Sun

File type: **TEXT**   Data checked by: Angela Mariani

MS: Print: **X**   Data approved by: Thomas J. Mathiesen

Filelist: 15th   File size: 14K   Annotations:

Source of data:

Patrologia cursus completus, series latina, ed. J. P. Migne, 221 vols. (Paris: Garnier, 1844-1904), 141:431-36.

Doubtfully attributed to Guido in Gerbert's edition, the treatise probably dates from the fifteenth century. Cf. ANOTRA2 TEXT.

Author: Guilielmus monachus

Treatise: De preceptis artis musice et pratice compendiosus libellus

Incipit: Nota quod duplex est prolatio, scilicet major et minor.

File name: **MONPRE**   Data input by: C. Matthew Balensuela

File type: **TEXT**   Data checked by: Luminita Aluas

MS: Print: **X**   Data approved by: Oliver B. Ellsworth

Filelist: 15th   File size: 64K   Annotations:

Source of data:

Scriptorum de musica medii aevi nova series a Gerbertina altera, 4 vols., ed. Edmond de Coussemaker (Paris: Durand, 1864-76; reprint ed., Hildesheim: Olms, 1963), 3:273-307.

The graphics files for this treatise are MONPRE 01GF-MONPRE 19GF. See also MONPREC.

Author: Guilielmus monachus

Treatise: De preceptis artis musice et pratice compendiosus libellus

Incipit: Nota quod duplex est prolatio, scilicet, maior et minor.

File name: **MONPREC**   Data input by: Stephen E. Hayes

File type: **TEXT**   Data checked by: Peter Lefferts & Bradley Tucker

MS: Print: **X**   Data approved by: Thomas J. Mathiesen

Filelist: 15th   File size: 80K   Annotations:

Source of data:

Guilielmi monachi De preceptis artis musicae, ed. Albert Seay, Corpus scriptorum de musica, vol. 11 ([Rome]: American Institute of Musicology, 1965), 15-59. Used by permission.

The graphics files for this treatise are MONPREC 01GF-MONPREC 18GF. See also MONPRE.

Author: Guillermus de Podio

Treatise: Ars musicorum liber VI

Incipit: Contrapunctus secundam tenens musicae cantandi differentiam est duorum vel

File name: **GUIARS6**   Data input by: Peter Slemon

File type: **TEXT**   Data checked by: Angela Mariani

MS: Print: **X**   Data approved by: Thomas J. Mathiesen

Filelist: 15th   File size: 16K   Annotations:

Source of data: See also GUIARS8.

Guillermus de Podio, Ars musicorum libri VI et VIII, ed. Albert Seay, Critical Texts, no. 8 (Colorado Springs: Colorado College Music Press, 1978), 1-8. Used by permission.

Author: Guillermus de Podio

Treatise: Ars musicorum liber VIII

Incipit: De proportionibus cantandi hoc in ultimo volumi dicturi; animadvertendum in primis

File name: **GUIARS8**   Data input by: Peter Slemon

File type: **TEXT**   Data checked by: Angela Mariani

MS: Print: **X**   Data approved by: Thomas J. Mathiesen

Filelist: 15th   File size: 34K   Annotations:

Source of data: See also GUIARS6. The graphics files for this treatise are GUIARS8 01GF-GUIARS8 11GF.

Guillermus de Podio, Ars musicorum libri VI et VIII, ed. Albert Seay, Critical Texts, no. 8 (Colorado Springs: Colorado College Music Press, 1978), 9-34. Used by permission.

Author: Gundissalinus, Dominicus

Treatise: De divisione philosophiae, Liber decimus, "De musica"

Incipit: Circa artem quoque musicam hec eadam inquirenda sunt scilicet: quid sit ipsa

File name: **GUNDDIV**   Data input by: C. Matthew Balensuela

File type: **TEXT**   Data checked by: Andreas Giger

MS: Print: **X**   Data approved by: Thomas J. Mathiesen

Filelist: 12th   File size: 10K   Annotations:

Source of data: Gundissalinus, Archdeacon of Toledo, was also known as Gundisalvus or Gundisalvi.

Dominicus Gundissalinus, De divisione philosophiae, ed. Ludwig Baur, Beiträge zur Geschichte der Philosophie des Mittelalters, IV/2-3 (Münster: Aschendorff, 1903), 96-102.

Author: Hanboys, Johannes

Treatise: Summa

Incipit: Hic incipit musica magistri Franconis cum additionibus et opinionibus diversorum.

File name: **HANSUMA**　　Data input by: Peter M. Lefferts

File type: **TEXT**　　　　Data checked by: Bradley Jon Tucker

　MS:　　Print: **X**　　Data approved by: Thomas J. Mathiesen

Filelist: 14th　　File size: 107K　　Annotations:

Source of data:

Scriptorum de musica medii aevi nova series a Gerbertina altera, 4 vols., ed. Edmond de Coussemaker (Paris: Durand, 1864-76; reprint ed., Hildesheim: Olms, 1963), 1:403-48.

The graphics files for this treatise are HANSUMA 01GF-HANSUMA 02GF. Cf. HANSUM TEXT.

Author: Hanboys, Johannes

Treatise: Summa

Incipit: Hic incipit musica magistri Franconis cum additionibus et opinionibus diversorum.

File name: **HANSUM**　　Data input by: Peter M. Lefferts

File type: **TEXT**　　　Data checked by: Luminita Aluas

　MS:　　Print: **X**　　Data approved by: Thomas J. Mathiesen

Filelist: 14th　　File size: 111K　　Annotations:

Source of data:

Robertus de Handlo, Regule, and Johannes Hanboys, Summa, ed. and trans. by Peter M. Lefferts, Greek and Latin Music Theory, vol. 7 (Lincoln: University of Nebraska Press, 1991), 180-344. Used by permission.

The graphics file for this treatise is HANSUM 01GF. Cf. HANSUMA TEXT.

Author: Heinricus Augustensis

Treatise: Musica

Incipit: Discipulus: Estne musica genus an species? Magister: Species est et subalternum

File name: **HEIMUS**　　Data input by: Andreas Giger

File type: **TEXT**　　　Data checked by: Elisabeth Honn

　MS:　　Print: **X**　　Data approved by: Thomas J. Mathiesen

Filelist: 9th-11th　File size: 22K　　Annotations:

Source of data:

Musica Domni Heinrici Augustensis magistri, ed. Joseph Smits van Waesberghe, Divitiae musicae artis, A/VII (Buren: Knuf, 1977), 35-53. Used by kind permission of the Laaber-Verlag.

Based on Vienna, Österreichische Nationalbibliothek, cpv 51, ff. 90r-91r.

Author: Henricus de Zelandia

Treatise: Tractatus de cantu perfecto et imperfecto

Incipit: Gaudent musicorum discipuli, quod Henricus de Zeelandia

File name: **ZELTRA**   Data input by: C. Matthew Balensuela

File type: **TEXT**   Data checked by: Luminita Aluas

MS: Print: **X**   Data approved by: Albert C. Rotola, S.J.

Filelist: 14th   File size: 10K   Annotations:

Source of data:

Scriptorum de musica medii aevi nova
series a Gerbertina altera, 4 vols., ed.
Edmond de Coussemaker (Paris: Durand,
1864-76; reprint ed., Hildesheim: Olms,
1963), 3:113-15.

Author: Hermannus Contractus

Treatise: Musica

Incipit: In consideranda monochordi positione ea prima speculatio occurrit

File name: **HERMUS**   Data input by: John Snyder

File type: **MRSL1496**   Data checked by: Peter Slemon

MS: **X**   Print: Data approved by: Thomas J. Mathiesen

Filelist: 9th-11th File size: 65K   Annotations:

Source of data: =RISM BIII/4:180-83. In the manuscript,
Rochester, New York, Eastman School of   capitals, small capitals, and a lower-case a
Music, Sibley Library, 92 1100   were used to designate pitches in the various
(Wolffheim 1) (acc. 149,667), 91-130.   octaves. In this file, the capitals have been
retained, the small capitals have been entered
as lower-case letters, and the lower-case a
(when designating an octave) has been entered
as aa. The graphics files for this treatise are
HERMUS 01GF-HERMUS 04GF. Cf.
HERMUSB TEXT, HERMUSE TEXT,
HERMUSG TEXT, and HERMUSP TEXT.

Author: Hermannus Contractus

Treatise: Musica

Incipit: In consideranda monochordi positione ea prima speculatio occurrit

File name: **HERMUSB**   Data input by: John Snyder

File type: **TEXT**   Data checked by: Angela Mariani

MS: Print: **X**   Data approved by: Thomas J. Mathiesen

Filelist: 9th-11th File size: 63K   Annotations:

Source of data: The graphics files for this treatise are
Hermanni Contracti Musica, ed. W.   HERMUSB 01GF-HERMUSB 03GF. Cf.
Brambach (Leipzig: B. G. Teubner,   HERMUS MRSL1496, HERMUSE TEXT,
1884).   HERMUSG TEXT, and HERMUSP TEXT.

Author: Hermannus Contractus

Treatise: Musica

Incipit: In consideranda monochordi positione ea prima speculatio occurrit

File name: **HERMUSE**   Data input by: John Snyder

File type: **TEXT**   Data checked by: Angela Mariani

MS: Print: **X**   Data approved by: Thomas J. Mathiesen

Filelist: 9th-11th File size: 64K   Annotations:

Source of data: The graphics files for this treatise are
Musica Hermanni Contracti, ed. and   HERMUSE 01GF-HERMUSE 05GF. Cf.
trans. Leonard Ellinwood, Eastman   HERMUS MRSL1496, HERMUSB TEXT,
School of Music Studies, no. 2   HERMUSG TEXT, and HERMUSP TEXT.
(Rochester, New York: Eastman School
of Music, 1936).

Author: Hermannus Contractus

Treatise: Musica

Incipit: In consideranda monochordi positione ea prima speculatio occurrit

File name: **HERMUSG**   Data input by: John Snyder

File type: **TEXT**   Data checked by: Bradley Jon Tucker

MS: Print: **X**   Data approved by: Thomas J. Mathiesen

Filelist: 9th-11th File size: 64K   Annotations:

Source of data: The graphics files for this treatise are
Scriptores ecclesiastici de musica sacra   HERMUSG 01GF-HERMUSG 04GF. Cf.
potissimum, 3 vols., ed. Martin Gerbert   HERMUS MRSL1496, HERMUSB TEXT,
(St. Blaise: Typis San-Blasianis, 1784;   HERMUSE TEXT, and HERMUSP TEXT.
reprint ed., Hildesheim: Olms, 1963),
2:125-49.

Author: Hermannus Contractus

Treatise: Musica

Incipit: In consideranda monochordi positione ea prima speculatio occurrit

File name: **HERMUSP**   Data input by: Angela Mariani

File type: **TEXT**   Data checked by: Andreas Giger

MS: Print: **X**   Data approved by: Thomas J. Mathiesen

Filelist: 9th-11th File size: 64K   Annotations:

Source of data: The graphics files for this treatise are
Patrologia cursus completus, series latina,   HERMUSP 01GF-HERMUSP 04GF. Cf.
ed. J. P. Migne, 221 vols. (Paris: Garnier,   HERMUS MRSL1496, HERMUSB TEXT,
1844-1904), 143:413-39.   HERMUSE TEXT, and HERMUSG TEXT.

Author: Hermannus Contractus

Treatise: Versus ad discernendum cantum

Incipit: Versus atque notas Herimannus protulit istas,

File name: **HERVER**   Data input by: Bradley Jon Tucker

File type: **TEXT**   Data checked by: Angela Mariani

MS: Print: **X**   Data approved by: Thomas J. Mathiesen

Filelist: 9th-11th File size: 4K   Annotations:

Source of data: The versus is preceded by an "Explicatio
Scriptores ecclesiastici de musica sacra   litterarum et signorum, quae in sequentibus
potissimum, 3 vols., ed. Martin Gerbert   versibus ocurrunt," beginning "E (e) voces
(St. Blaise: Typis San-Blasianis, 1784;   unisonas ...." The graphics files for this treatise
reprint ed., Hildesheim: Olms, 1963),   are HERVER 01GF-HERVER 06GF.
2:149-53.

Author: Hermannus Contractus

Treatise: Versus ad discernendum cantum

Incipit: Versus atque notas Herimannus protulit istas,

File name: **HERVERP**   Data input by: Andreas Giger

File type: **TEXT**   Data checked by: Michael W. Lundell

MS: Print: **X**   Data approved by: Thomas J. Mathiesen

Filelist: 9th-11th File size: 5K   Annotations:

Source of data:

Patrologia cursus completus, series latina, ed. J. P. Migne, 221 vols. (Paris: Garnier, 1844-1904), 143:439-44.

The versus is preceded by an "Explicatio litterarum et signorum quoe in sequentibus occurrunt," beginning "E., (e) voces unisonas ...." The graphics files for this treatise are HERVERP 01GF-HERVERP 02GF.

Author: Heyden, Sebaldus

Treatise: De arte canendi, ac vero signorum in cantibus usu, liber primus

Incipit: Usu comperimus, longe alium institutionis modum requiri, si quis pueros adhuc

File name: **HEYDAC1**   Data input by: John Gray

File type: **TEXT**   Data checked by: Oliver Ellsworth & Andreas Giger

MS: Print: **X**   Data approved by: Thomas J. Mathiesen

Filelist: 16th   File size: 71K   Annotations:

Source of data:

De arte canendi, ac vero signorum in cantibus usu, libri duo, autore Sebaldo Heyden (Norimbergae apud Ioh. Petreium, 1540).

The incipit is preceded by a dedicatory letter beginning: "Quod ueteri prouerbio posteriores cogitationes plaerunque prudentiores esse dicuntur, uir ornatis ...." The graphics files for this treatise are HEYDAC1 01GF-HEYDAC1 28GF.

Author: Heyden, Sebaldus

Treatise: De arte canendi, ac vero signorum in cantibus usu, liber secundus

Incipit: Hactenus idem fere facere studui, quod probat pictores erga discipulos suos solent

File name: **HEYDAC2**   Data input by: John Gray

File type: **TEXT**   Data checked by: Oliver Ellsworth & Andreas Giger

MS: Print: **X**   Data approved by: Thomas J. Mathiesen

Filelist: 16th   File size: 67K   Annotations:

Source of data:

De arte canendi, ac vero signorum in cantibus usu, libri duo, autore Sebaldo Heyden (Norimbergae apud Ioh. Petreium, 1540).

The graphics files for this treatise are HEYDAC2 01GF-HEYDAC2 82GF. See also HEYDAC1.

Author: Hothby, Johannes

Treatise: [De arte contrapuncti]

Incipit: In primo dico quod contrapunctum requirit habere quatuor res

File name: **HOTDAC**   Data input by: Stephen E. Hayes

File type: **TEXT**   Data checked by: Peter M. Lefferts & Kirk Ditzler

MS: Print: **X**   Data approved by: Thomas J. Mathiesen

Filelist: 15th   File size: 4K   Annotations:

Source of data:

Johannes Hothby, De arte contrapuncti, ed. Gilbert Reaney, Corpus scriptorum de musica, vol. 26 (n.p.: American Institute of Musicology, 1977), 43-44. Used by permission.

Author: Hothby, Johannes

Treatise: De cantu figurato

Incipit: Octo sunt figure mensurabilis cantus, videlicet maxima, longa, brevis, semibrevis

File name: **HOTDEC**	Data input by: Luminita Aluas
File type: **TEXT**	Data checked by: Thomas J. Mathiesen
MS:　　　Print: **X**	Data approved by: Benito V. Rivera

Filelist: 15th　　　File size: 7K　　　　　Annotations:

Source of data:

Scriptorum de musica medii aevi nova series a Gerbertina altera, 4 vols., ed. Edmond de Coussemaker (Paris: Durand, 1864-76; reprint ed., Hildesheim: Olms, 1963), 3:330-32.

The graphics file for this treatise is HOTDEC 01GF.

Author: Hothby, Johannes

Treatise: De cantu figurato secundum eundem fratrem Johannem Hothbi Carmelitam

Incipit: Octo sunt figure mensurabilis cantus, videlicet maxima, longa, brevis, semibrevis

File name: **HOTDCF1**	Data input by: Peter Slemon
File type: **TEXT**	Data checked by: Bradley Jon Tucker
MS:　　　Print: **X**	Data approved by: Thomas J. Mathiesen

Filelist: 15th　　　File size: 7K　　　　　Annotations:

Source of data:

Johannes Hothby, Opera omnia de musica mensurabili; Thomas Walsingham, Regulae de musica mensurabili, ed. Gilbert Reaney, Corpus scriptorum de musica, vol. 31 (Neuhausen-Stuttgart: Haenssler Verlag for the American Institute of Musicology, 1983), 27-31. Used by permission.

Based on Faenza, Biblioteca comunale, 117. The graphics file for this treatise is HOTDCF1 01GF.

Author: Hothby, Johannes

Treatise: Dialogus in arte musica

Incipit: Nos te nostrum carmen facile intellexisse fatemur cum picturae

File name: **HOTDIA**	Data input by: Stephen E. Hayes
File type: **TEXT**	Data checked by: Peter Lefferts & Bradley Tucker
MS:　　　Print: **X**	Data approved by: Thomas J. Mathiesen

Filelist: 15th　　　File size: 22K　　　　　Annotations:

Source of data:

Johannis Octobi Tres tractatuli contra Bartholomeum Ramum, ed. Albert Seay, Corpus scriptorum de musica, vol. 10 ([Rome]: American Institute of Musicology, 1964), 61-76. Used by permission.

Author: Hothby, Johannes

Treatise: Excitatio quaedam musicae artis per refutationem

Incipit: In manus meas incidit liber quidam tuus quem de arte musica conscriptsisti

File name: **HOTEXC**   Data input by: Stephen E. Hayes

File type: **TEXT**   Data checked by: Peter Lefferts & Angela Mariani

  MS: Print: **X**   Data approved by: Thomas J. Mathiesen

Filelist: 15th   File size: 67K   Annotations:

Source of data: The graphics file for this treatise is HOTEXC
  Johannis Octobi Tres tractatuli contra   01GF.
  Bartholomeum Ramum, ed. Albert Seay,
  Corpus scriptorum de musica, vol. 10
  ([Rome]: American Institute of
  Musicology, 1964), 17-57. Used by
  permission.

Author: Hothby, Johannes

Treatise: Regulae cantus mensurati secundum Johannem Otteby

Incipit: Figurae enim cantus choralis sunt 8, sed proprie 5 dumtaxat

File name: **HOTRCM2**   Data input by: Peter Slemon

File type: **TEXT**   Data checked by: Bradley Jon Tucker

  MS: Print: **X**   Data approved by: Thomas J. Mathiesen

Filelist: 15th   File size: 11K   Annotations:

Source of data: Based on London, British Library, Additional
  Johannes Hothby, Opera omnia de musica   10336; and London, Lambeth Palace, 466. The
  mensurabili; Thomas Walsingham,   graphics files for this treatise are HOTRCM2
  Regulae de musica mensurabili, ed.   01GF-HOTRCM2 03GF.
  Gilbert Reaney, Corpus scriptorum de
  musica, vol. 31 (Neuhausen-Stuttgart:
  Haenssler Verlag for the American
  Institute of Musicology, 1983), 51-59.
  Used by permission.

Author: Hothby, Johannes

Treatise: Regulae contrapuncti

Incipit: Nota quod contrapunctus semper debet incipi et finiri per consonantias

File name: **HOTRC**   Data input by: Stephen E. Hayes

File type: **TEXT**   Data checked by: Peter M. Lefferts & Kirk Ditzler

  MS: Print: **X**   Data approved by: Thomas J. Mathiesen

Filelist: 15th   File size: 8K   Annotations:

Source of data: The graphics files for this treatise are HOTRC
  Johannes Hothby, De arte contrapuncti,   01GF-HOTRC 04GF.
  ed. Gilbert Reaney, Corpus scriptorum de
  musica, vol. 26 (n.p.: American Institute
  of Musicology, 1977), 63-69. Used by
  permission.

Author: Hothby, Johannes

Treatise: Regulae Magistri Johannis Hoctobi anglici cantus figurati

Incipit: Figurae cantus figurati sunt octo, videlicet maxima, longa, brevis, semibrevis

File name: **HOTDCF2**   Data input by: Peter Slemon

File type: **TEXT**   Data checked by: Bradley Jon Tucker

 MS: Print: **X**   Data approved by: Thomas J. Mathiesen

Filelist: 15th   File size: 7K   Annotations:

Source of data:

Johannes Hothby, Opera omnia de musica mensurabili; Thomas Walsingham, Regulae de musica mensurabili, ed. Gilbert Reaney, Corpus scriptorum de musica, vol. 31 (Neuhausen-Stuttgart: Haenssler Verlag for the American Institute of Musicology, 1983), 39-44. Used by permission.

Based on Venice, Biblioteca Marciana, lat. VIII/82 (coll. 3047). The graphics file for this treatise is HOTDCF2 01GF.

Author: Hothby, Johannes

Treatise: Regulae super proportionem

Incipit: Omnis numerus habet tot partes quot sub se sunt unitates

File name: **HOTREGP**   Data input by: Luminita Aluas

File type: **TEXT**   Data checked by: Thomas J. Mathiesen

 MS: Print: **X**   Data approved by: Benito V. Rivera

Filelist: 15th   File size: 6K   Annotations:

Source of data:

Scriptorum de musica medii aevi nova series a Gerbertina altera, 4 vols., ed. Edmond de Coussemaker (Paris: Durand, 1864-76; reprint ed., Hildesheim: Olms, 1963), 3:328-30.

Author: Hothby, Johannes

Treatise: Regulae supra contrapunctum

Incipit: Quamvis species sive consonantie discantus infinite sint

File name: **HOTREGC**   Data input by: Luminita Aluas

File type: **TEXT**   Data checked by: Thomas J. Mathiesen

 MS: Print: **X**   Data approved by: Benito V. Rivera

Filelist: 15th   File size: 6K   Annotations:

Source of data: Cf. HOTRSC TEXT.

Scriptorum de musica medii aevi nova series a Gerbertina altera, 4 vols., ed. Edmond de Coussemaker (Paris: Durand, 1864-76; reprint ed., Hildesheim: Olms, 1963), 3:333-34.

Author: Hothby, Johannes

Treatise: Regulae supra contrapunctum

Incipit: Quamvis species sive consonantiae discantus infinitae sint

File name: **HOTRSC**   Data input by: Stephen E. Hayes

File type: **TEXT**   Data checked by: Peter M. Lefferts & Kirk Ditzler

MS: Print: **X**   Data approved by: Thomas J. Mathiesen

Filelist: 15th   File size: 5K   Annotations:

Source of data: Cf. HOTREGC TEXT.
Johannes Hothby, De arte contrapuncti, ed. Gilbert Reaney, Corpus scriptorum de musica, vol. 26 (n.p.: American Institute of Musicology, 1977), 101-3. Used by permission.

Author: Hothby, Johannes

Treatise: Sequuntur regulae cantus mensurati eiusdem Ottobi

Incipit: Octo sunt partes prolationis sive figurae cantus simpliciter mensurabilis sive cantus

File name: **HOTRCM1**   Data input by: Peter Slemon

File type: **TEXT**   Data checked by: Bradley Jon Tucker

MS: Print: **X**   Data approved by: Thomas J. Mathiesen

Filelist: 15th   File size: 8K   Annotations:

Source of data: Based on Florence, Biblioteca Laurenziana,
Johannes Hothby, Opera omnia de musica   plut. XXIX.48. The graphics file for this
mensurabili; Thomas Walsingham,   treatise is HOTRCM1 01GF.
Regulae de musica mensurabili, ed.
Gilbert Reaney, Corpus scriptorum de
musica, vol. 31 (Neuhausen-Stuttgart:
Haenssler Verlag for the American
Institute of Musicology, 1983), 19-24.
Used by permission.

Author: Hucbald

Treatise: De harmonica institutione

Incipit: Ad musicae initiamenta quemlibet ingredientem, qui aliquam scilicet interim

File name: **HUCHAR**   Data input by: Stephen E. Hayes

File type: **TEXT**   Data checked by: Peter M. Lefferts

MS: Print: **X**   Data approved by: Thomas J. Mathiesen

Filelist: 9th-11th File size: 52K   Annotations:

Source of data: The graphics files for this treatise are
Scriptores ecclesiastici de musica sacra   HUCHAR 01GF-HUCHAR 07GF. Cf.
potissimum, 3 vols., ed. Martin Gerbert   ALIMU TEXT, ALIMUS TEXT, and
(St. Blaise: Typis San-Blasianis, 1784;   HUCHARM TEXT.
reprint ed., Hildesheim: Olms, 1963),
1:103-25.

Author: Hucbald

Treatise: De harmonica institutione

Incipit: Ad musicae initiamenta quemlibet ingredientem, qui aliquam scilicet interim

File name: **HUCHARM**   Data input by: Jingfa Sun

File type: **TEXT**   Data checked by: Andreas Giger

MS: Print: **X**   Data approved by: Thomas J. Mathiesen

Filelist: 9th-11th   File size: 52K   Annotations:

Source of data:
Patrologia cursus completus, series latina, ed. J. P. Migne, 221 vols. (Paris: Garnier, 1844-1904), 132:905-29.

The graphics files for this treatise are HUCHARM 01GF-HUCHARM 05GF. Cf. ALIMU TEXT, ALIMUS TEXT, and HUCHAR TEXT.

Author: Hucbald

Treatise: De organo

Incipit: Dictis autem, prout potuimus, his quibus ostendendum erat, qualiter unusquisque

File name: **HUCORG**   Data input by: Firoozeh Khazrai

File type: **TEXT**   Data checked by: Angela Mariani

MS: Print: **X**   Data approved by: Thomas J. Mathiesen

Filelist: 9th-11th   File size: 11K   Annotations:

Source of data:
Scriptorum de musica medii aevi nova series a Gerbertina altera, 4 vols., ed. Edmond de Coussemaker (Paris: Durand, 1864-76; reprint ed., Hildesheim: Olms, 1963), 2:74-78.

This text is no longer generally attributed to Hucbald. The graphics files for this treatise are HUCORG 01GF-HUCORG 02GF.

Author: Ieronimus de Moravia

Treatise: Tractatus de musica

Incipit: Quoniam, ut dicit Boetius in prohemio super musicam

File name: **IERTRA1**   Data input by: C. Matthew Balensuela

File type: **TEXT**   Data checked by: Oliver B. Ellsworth

MS: Print: **X**   Data approved by: Thomas J. Mathiesen

Filelist: 13th   File size: 286K   Annotations:

Source of data:
Scriptorum de musica medii aevi nova series a Gerbertina altera, 4 vols., ed. Edmond de Coussemaker (Paris: Durand, 1864-76; reprint ed., Hildesheim: Olms, 1963), 1:1-89.

The graphics files for this treatise are IERTRA1 01GF-IERTRA 12GF. Tractatus de musica continues in IERTRA2. Cf. IERTDM1 TEXT and IERTDM2 TEXT.

Author: Ieronimus de Moravia
Treatise: Tractatus de musica
Incipit: Quoniam autem sic cantus, ut jam diximus, firmus sive planus, precipue ecclesiasticus

File name: **IERTRA2**
File type: **TEXT**
MS: Print: **X**
Filelist: 13th   File size: 64K

Data input by: C. Matthew Balensuela
Data checked by: Oliver B. Ellsworth
Data approved by: Thomas J. Mathiesen
Annotations:

Source of data:
Scriptorum de musica medii aevi nova series a Gerbertina altera, 4 vols., ed. Edmond de Coussemaker (Paris: Durand, 1864-76; reprint ed., Hildesheim: Olms, 1963), 1:89-94 and 139-54.

The incipit is preceded by the heading "Caput XXV: De modo faciendi novos ecclesiaticos et omnes alios firmos sive planos cantus." The second section of this file, beginning on p. 139, resumes with "CAPUT XXVII. De quibusdam grecorum vocabulorum litterarumque ...." The graphics files for this treatise are IERTRA2 01GF-IERTRA2 02GF. This section of the Tractatus de musica is preceded by IERTRA1. Cf. IERTDM1 TEXT and IERTDM2 TEXT.

Author: Ieronimus de Moravia
Treatise: Tractatus de musica
Incipit: Quoniam, ut dicit Boetius in prohemio super musicam, sicut in visu non sufficit

File name: **IERTDM1**
File type: **TEXT**
MS: Print: **X**
Filelist: 13th   File size: 294K

Data input by: Stephen E. Hayes
Data checked by: Peter M. Lefferts & Andreas Giger
Data approved by: Thomas J. Mathiesen
Annotations:

Source of data:
Hieronymus de Moravia, Tractatus de musica, ed. S. M. Cserba, Freiburger Studien zur Musikwissenschaft, vol. 2 (Regensburg: Pustet, 1935), 3-179.

The edition is based on Paris, Bibliothèque Nationale, lat. 16663. The text continues in IERTDM2. The graphics files for this treatise are IERTDM1 01GF-IERTDM1 14GF. Cf. IERTRA1 TEXT and IERTRA2 TEXT.

Author: Ieronimus de Moravia
Treatise: Tractatus de musica
Incipit: Quoniam, ut dicit Boetius in prohemio super musicam, sicut in visu non sufficit

File name: **IERTDM2**
File type: **TEXT**
MS: Print: **X**
Filelist: 13th   File size: 66K

Data input by: Stephen E. Hayes
Data checked by: Peter M. Lefferts & Andreas Giger
Data approved by: Thomas J. Mathiesen
Annotations:

Source of data:
Hieronymus de Moravia, Tractatus de musica, ed. S. M. Cserba, Freiburger Studien zur Musikwissenschaft, vol. 2 (Regensburg: Pustet, 1935), 179-89, 263-91.

Continued from IERTDM1. The edition is based on Paris, Bibliothèque Nationale, lat. 16663. The graphics file for this treatise is IERTDM2 01GF. Cf. IERTRA1 TEXT and IERTRA2 TEXT.

Author: Isidorus Hispalensis

Treatise: De musica

Incipit: Musica est peritia modulationis sono cantuque consistens; et dicta musica

File name: **ISIDEM**	Data input by: Stephen E. Hayes
File type: **TEXT**	Data checked by: Peter Lefferts & Bradley Tucker
MS: Print: **X**	Data approved by: Thomas J. Mathiesen
Filelist: 6th-8th File size: 14K	Annotations:

Source of data: Cf. ISISEN TEXT and ISIDEMU TEXT.

Patrologia cursus completus, series latina, ed. J. P. Migne, 221 vols. (Paris: Garnier, 1844-1904), 82:163-69.

Author: Isidorus Hispalensis

Treatise: De musica

Incipit: Musica est peritia modulationis sono cantuque consistens. Et dicta musica

File name: **ISIDEMU**	Data input by: Stephen E. Hayes
File type: **TEXT**	Data checked by: Peter Lefferts & Bradley Tucker
MS: Print: **X**	Data approved by: Thomas J. Mathiesen
Filelist: 6th-8th File size: 13K	Annotations:

Source of data: Cf. ISISEN TEXT and ISIDEM TEXT.

Isidori Hispalensis episcopi Etymologiarum sive originum libri XX, 2 vols., ed. W. M. Lindsay (Oxford: Clarendon, 1911), 1:ff. K6r-L2r.

Author: Isidorus Hispalensis

Treatise: Sententiae de musica

Incipit: Musica est peritia modulationis sono cantuque consistens, et dicta Musica

File name: **ISISEN**	Data input by: Stephen E. Hayes
File type: **TEXT**	Data checked by: Peter M. Lefferts
MS: Print: **X**	Data approved by: Thomas J. Mathiesen
Filelist: 6th-8th File size: 16K	Annotations:

Source of data: Cf. ISIDEM TEXT and ISIDEMU TEXT.

Scriptores ecclesiastici de musica sacra potissimum, 3 vols., ed. Martin Gerbert (St. Blaise: Typis San-Blasianis, 1784; reprint ed., Hildesheim: Olms, 1963), 1:20-25.

Author: Jacobus Leodiensis

Treatise: Compendium de musica

Incipit: Dispendiosa sub compendio tradere, facile quoniam non est, manifestum est.

File name: **JACCDM**   Data input by: Andreas Giger

File type: **TEXT**   Data checked by: Elisabeth Honn

　MS:　　　Print: **X**   Data approved by: Thomas J. Mathiesen

Filelist: 14th   File size: 49K   Annotations:

Source of data: Based on Brussels, Bibliothèque Royale
　Jacobi Leodiensis Tractatus de   Albert Ier, 10162/66, ff. 48r-54v. The graphics
　consonantiis musicalibus, Tractatus de   files for this treatise are JACCDM
　intonatione tonorum, Compendium de   01GF-JACCDM 03GF.
　musica, ed. Joseph Smits van
　Waesberghe, Eddie Vetter, and Erik
　Visser, Divitiae musicae artis, A/IXa
　(Buren: Knuf, 1988), 88-122. Used by
　kind permission of the Laaber-Verlag.

Author: Jacobus Leodiensis

Treatise: Speculum musicae, Liber primus

Incipit: Libro tertio de Philosophica Consolatione, Boethius, volens reddere causam

File name: **JACSP1A**   Data input by: John Gray

File type: **TEXT**   Data checked by: Oliver Ellsworth & Luminita Aluas

　MS:　　　Print: **X**   Data approved by: Thomas J. Mathiesen

Filelist: 14th   File size: 258K   Annotations:

Source of data: The graphics files for this treatise are
　Jacobi Leodiensis Speculum musicae, ed.   JACSP1A 01GF-JACSP1A 04GF. Continues
　Roger Bragard, Corpus scriptorum de   in JACSP1B. See also JACSP2A-C,
　musica, vol. 3/1 ([Rome]: American   JACSP3A-B, JACSP4. JACSP5A-B,
　Institute of Musicology, 1955), 3-142.   JACSP6A-B, and JACSP7.
　Used by permission.

Author: Jacobus Leodiensis

Treatise: Speculum musicae, Liber primus

Incipit: Capitulum L. Unitatis ad binarium collatio et numeri imparis ad parem.

File name: **JACSP1B**   Data input by: John Gray

File type: **TEXT**   Data checked by: Oliver Ellsworth & Luminita Aluas

　MS:　　　Print: **X**   Data approved by: Thomas J. Mathiesen

Filelist: 14th   File size: 153K   Annotations:

Source of data: The graphics files for this treatise are
　Jacobi Leodiensis Speculum musicae, ed.   JACSP1B 01GF-JACSP1B 13GF. This
　Roger Bragard, Corpus scriptorum de   section of Book I is preceded by JACSP1A.
　musica, vol. 3/1 ([Rome]: American   See also JACSP2A-C, JACSP3A-B, JACSP4,
　Institute of Musicology, 1955), 142-229.   JACSP5A-B, JACSP6A-B, and JACSP7.
　Used by permission.

Author: Jacobus Leodiensis
Treatise: Speculum musicae, Liber secundus
Incipit: Actus activorum in patiente sunt et disposito si quidem dispositio ad aliquam formam

File name: **JACSP2A**   Data input by: John Gray
File type: **TEXT**   Data checked by: Oliver Ellsworth & Bradley Tucker
MS: Print: **X**   Data approved by: Thomas J. Mathiesen
Filelist: 14th   File size: 264K   Annotations:

Source of data: Jacobi Leodiensis Speculum musicae, ed. Roger Bragard, Corpus scriptorum de musica, vol. 3/2 ([Rome]: American Institute of Musicology, 1961), 1-128. Used by permission.	This section of Book II is followed by JACSP2B-C. See also JACSP1A-B, JACSP3A-B, JACSP4, JACSP5A-B, JACSP6A-B, and JACSP7.

Author: Jacobus Leodiensis
Treatise: Speculum musicae, Liber secundus
Incipit: Capitulum LIII. De commatis simplicitate. Comma consonantia simplex dici potest

File name: **JACSP2B**   Data input by: John Gray
File type: **TEXT**   Data checked by: Oliver Ellsworth & Bradley Tucker
MS: Print: **X**   Data approved by: Thomas J. Mathiesen
Filelist: 14th   File size: 213K   Annotations:

Source of data: Jacobi Leodiensis Speculum musicae, ed. Roger Bragard, Corpus scriptorum de musica, vol. 3/2 ([Rome]: American Institute of Musicology, 1961), 128-231. Used by permission.	This section of Book II is preceded by JACSP2A and followed by JACSP2C. See also JACSP1A-B, JACSP3A-B, JACSP4, JACSP5A-B, JACSP6A-B, and JACSP7.

Author: Jacobus Leodiensis
Treatise: Speculum musicae, Liber secundus
Incipit: Capitulum C. Instantiae contra dicta et ad illas responsio. Forsitan instabitur

File name: **JACSP2C**   Data input by: John Gray
File type: **TEXT**   Data checked by: Oliver Ellsworth & Bradley Tucker
MS: Print: **X**   Data approved by: Thomas J. Mathiesen
Filelist: 14th   File size: 155K   Annotations:

Source of data: Jacobi Leodiensis Speculum musicae, ed. Roger Bragard, Corpus scriptorum de musica, vol. 3/2 ([Rome]: American Institute of Musicology, 1961), 232-309. Used by permission.	This section of Book II is preceded by JACSP2A-B. See also JACSP1A-B, JACSP3A-B, JACSP4, JACSP5A-B, JACSP6A-B, and JACSP7.

Author: Jacobus Leodiensis
Treatise: Speculum musicae, Liber tertius
Incipit: Cum, in superiore libro, de consonantiis quaedam narrata sint, quaedam probata sint

File name: **JACSP3A**   Data input by: John Gray
File type: **TEXT**   Data checked by: Oliver Ellsworth & Bradley Tucker
  MS: Print: **X**   Data approved by: Thomas J. Mathiesen
Filelist: 14th   File size: 155K   Annotations:

Source of data:
Jacobi Leodiensis Speculum musicae, ed.
Roger Bragard, Corpus scriptorum de
musica, vol. 3/3 ([Rome]: American
Institute of Musicology, 1963), 1-89.
Used by permission.

The graphics files for this treatise are
JACSP3A 01GF-JACSP3A 19GF. This
section of Book III is followed by JACSP3B.
See also JACSP1A-B, JACSP2A-C, JACSP4,
JACSP5A-B, JACSP6A-B, and JACSP7.

Author: Jacobus Leodiensis
Treatise: Speculum musicae, Liber tertius
Incipit: Capitulum XXVII. Quod ex numeris contra se primis numeri nascuntur contra se

File name: **JACSP3B**   Data input by: John Gray
File type: **TEXT**   Data checked by: Oliver Ellsworth & Bradley Tucker
  MS: Print: **X**   Data approved by: Thomas J. Mathiesen
Filelist: 14th   File size: 146K   Annotations:

Source of data:
Jacobi Leodiensis Speculum musicae, ed.
Roger Bragard, Corpus scriptorum de
musica, vol. 3/3 ([Rome]: American
Institute of Musicology, 1963), 89-163.
Used by permission.

The graphics files for this treatise are
JACSP3B 01GF-JACSP3B 05GF. This
section of Book III is preceded by JACSP3A.
See also JACSP1A-B, JACSP2A-C, JACSP4,
JACSP5A-B, JACSP6A-B, and JACSP7.

Author: Jacobus Leodiensis
Treatise: Speculum musicae, Liber quartus
Incipit: Ordo poscit naturalis ut absoluta rei cognitio collativam antecedat.

File name: **JACSP4**   Data input by: John Gray
File type: **TEXT**   Data checked by: Oliver Ellsworth & Peter Slemon
  MS: Print: **X**   Data approved by: Thomas J. Mathiesen
Filelist: 14th   File size: 252K   Annotations:

Source of data:
Jacobi Leodiensis Speculum musicae, ed.
Roger Bragard, Corpus scriptorum de
musica, vol. 3/4 ([Rome]: American
Institute of Musicology, 1965), 1-126.
Used by permission.

The graphics files for this treatise are JACSP4
01GF-JACSP4 05GF. See also JACSP1A-B,
JACSP2A-C, JACSP3A-B, JACSP5A-B,
JACSP6A-B, and JACSP7.

Author: Jacobus Leodiensis

Treatise: Speculum musicae, Liber quintus

Incipit: Boethius, musicae doctor eximius, non ignorans quod scientia unius generis subiecti

File name: **JACSP5A**   Data input by: John Gray

File type: **TEXT**   Data checked by: Oliver Ellsworth & Peter Slemon

MS: Print: **X**   Data approved by: Thomas J. Mathiesen

Filelist: 14th   File size: 168K   Annotations:

Source of data:

Jacobi Leodiensis Speculum musicae, ed. Roger Bragard, Corpus scriptorum de musica, vol. 3/5 ([Rome]: American Institute of Musicology, 1968), 1-90. Used by permission.

The graphics files for this treatise are JACSP5A 01GF-JACSP5A 14GF. This section of Book V is followed by JACSP5B. See also JACSP1A-B, JACSP2A-C, JACSP3A-B, JACSP4, JACSP6A-B, and JACSP7.

Author: Jacobus Leodiensis

Treatise: Speculum musicae, Liber quintus

Incipit: Capitulum XXXI. Ratio superius positae descriptionis. Tria tetrachorda tali nobis

File name: **JACSP5B**   Data input by: John Gray

File type: **TEXT**   Data checked by: Oliver Ellsworth & Peter Slemon

MS: Print: **X**   Data approved by: Thomas J. Mathiesen

Filelist: 14th   File size: 184K   Annotations:

Source of data:

Jacobi Leodiensis Speculum musicae, ed. Roger Bragard, Corpus scriptorum de musica, vol. 3/5 ([Rome]: American Institute of Musicology, 1968), 90-184. Used by permission.

The graphics files for this treatise are JACSP5B 01GF-JACSP5B 20GF. This section of Book V is preceded by JACSP5A. See also JACSP1A-B, JACSP2A-C, JACSP3A-B, JACSP4, JACSP6A-B, and JACSP7.

Author: Jacobus Leodiensis

Treatise: Speculum musicae, Liber sextus

Incipit: Unumquodque opus tanto laudabilius est necnon utilius, quanto per illud ad bonum

File name: **JACSP6A**   Data input by: John Gray

File type: **TEXT**   Data checked by: Oliver Ellsworth & Peter Slemon

MS: Print: **X**   Data approved by: Thomas J. Mathiesen

Filelist: 14th   File size: 277K   Annotations:

Source of data:

Jacobi Leodiensis Speculum musicae, ed. Roger Bragard, Corpus scriptorum de musica, vol. 3/6 ([Rome]: American Institute of Musicology, 1973), 1-161. Used by permission.

This section of Book VI is followed by JACSP6B. The graphics files for this treatise are JACSP6A 01GF-JACSP6A 27GF. See also JACSP1A-B, JACSP2A-C, JACSP3A-B, JACSP4, JACSP5A-B, and JACSP7. Cf. JACSM6A-B TEXT.

Author: Jacobus Leodiensis

Treatise: Speculum musicae, Liber sextus

Incipit: <Capitulum LXI. De litteris vel signis monocordi.> Dicunt musice doctores

File name: **JACSP6B**

File type: **TEXT**

MS: Print: **X**

Data input by: John Gray

Data checked by: Oliver Ellsworth & Peter Slemon

Data approved by: Thomas J. Mathiesen

Filelist: 14th   File size: 246K

Annotations:

Source of data:
Jacobi Leodiensis Speculum musicae, ed. Roger Bragard, Corpus scriptorum de musica, vol. 3/6 ([Rome]: American Institute of Musicology, 1973), 161-317. Used by permission.

This section of Book VI is preceded by JACSP6A. The graphics files for this treatise are JACSP1A-B, JACSP2A-C, JACSP3A-B, JACSP4, JACSP5A-B, and JACSP7. Cf. JACSM6A-B TEXT.

Author: Jacobus Leodiensis

Treatise: Speculum musicae, Liber septimus

Incipit: Simplicius, in <commentario> suo super Aristotelis predicamenta, in

File name: **JACSP7**

File type: **TEXT**

MS: Print: **X**

Data input by: John Gray

Data checked by: Oliver Ellsworth & Bradley Tucker

Data approved by: Thomas J. Mathiesen

Filelist: 14th   File size: 180K

Annotations:

Source of data:
Jacobi Leodiensis Speculum musicae, ed. Roger Bragard, Corpus scriptorum de musica, vol. 3/7 ([Rome]: American Institute of Musicology, 1973), 1-98. Used by permission.

The graphics files for this treatise are JACSP7 01GF-JACSP7 05GF. See also JACSP1A-B, JACSP2A-C, JACSP3A-B, JACSP4, JACSP5A-B, and JACSP6A-B. Cf. JACSM7 TEXT.

Author: Jacobus Leodiensis

Treatise: Speculum musicae, Liber sextus

Incipit: Unumquodque opus tanto laudabilius est necnon utilius, quanto per illud ad bonum

File name: **JACSM6A**

File type: **TEXT**

MS: Print: **X**

Data input by: Stephen E. Hayes

Data checked by: Peter M. Lefferts

Data approved by: Oliver B. Ellsworth

Filelist: 14th   File size: 262K

Annotations:

Source of data:
Scriptorum de musica medii aevi nova series a Gerbertina altera, 4 vols., ed. Edmond de Coussemaker (Paris: Durand, 1864-76; reprint ed., Hildesheim: Olms, 1963), 2:193-279.

This section of Book VI is followed by JACSM6B. Coussemaker attributed the text to Johannes de Muris. The graphics files for this treatise are JACSM6A 01GF-JACSM6A 26GF. Cf. JACSP6A-B TEXT.

Author: Jacobus Leodiensis

Treatise: Speculum musicae, Liber sextus

Incipit: Capitulum LXI. [De litteris vel signis monocordi.] Dicunt musice doctores monocordi

File name: **JACSM6B**   Data input by: Stephen E. Hayes

File type: **TEXT**   Data checked by: Peter M. Lefferts

MS: Print: **X**   Data approved by: Oliver B. Ellsworth

Filelist: 14th   File size: 236K   Annotations:

Source of data: Continued from JACSM6A. The graphics files
Scriptorum de musica medii aevi nova   for this treatise are JACSM6B
series a Gerbertina altera, 4 vols., ed.   001GF-JACSM6B 122GF. Cf. JACSP6A-B
Edmond de Coussemaker (Paris: Durand,   TEXT.
1864-76; reprint ed., Hildesheim: Olms,
1963), 2:279-383.

Author: Jacobus Leodiensis

Treatise: Speculum musicae, Liber septimus

Incipit: Simplicius in commento suo super Aristotelis pedicamenta in commendationem

File name: **JACSM7**   Data input by: Stephen E. Hayes

File type: **TEXT**   Data checked by: Oliver Ellsworth & Bradley Tucker

MS: Print: **X**   Data approved by: Thomas J. Mathiesen

Filelist: 14th   File size: 175K   Annotations:

Source of data: Coussemaker attributed the text to Johannes de
Scriptorum de musica medii aevi nova   Muris. The incipit is preceded by a list of
series a Gerbertina altera, 4 vols., ed.   chapter headings. The graphics files for this
Edmond de Coussemaker (Paris: Durand,   treatise are JACSM7 01GF-JACSM7 04GF.
1864-76; reprint ed., Hildesheim: Olms,   Cf. JACSP7 TEXT.
1963), 2:383-433.

Author: Jacobus Leodiensis

Treatise: Tractatus de consonantiis musicalibus

Incipit: Tredecim consonantiae sunt quibus omnis ecclesiasticus cantus contexitur

File name: **JACDCM**   Data input by: Andreas Giger

File type: **TEXT**   Data checked by: Elisabeth Honn

MS: Print: **X**   Data approved by: Thomas J. Mathiesen

Filelist: 14th   File size: 16K   Annotations:

Source of data: Based on Brussels, Bibliothèque Royale
Jacobi Leodiensis Tractatus de   Albert Ier, 10162/66, ff. 13r-15v. The graphics
consonantiis musicalibus, Tractatus de   files for this treatise are JACDCM
intonatione tonorum, Compendium de   01GF-JACDCM 03GF.
musica, ed. Joseph Smits van
Waesberghe, Eddie Vetter, and Erik
Visser, Divitiae musicae artis, A/IXa
(Buren: Knuf, 1988), 21-46. Used by kind
permission of the Laaber-Verlag.

Author: Jacobus Leodiensis

Treatise: Tractatus de intonatione tonorum

Incipit: Tonus prout antiphona vel alter cantus totus alicuius toni dicitur, est plurium

File name: **JACDIT**	Data input by: Andreas Giger
File type: **TEXT**	Data checked by: Elisabeth Honn
MS: Print: **X**	Data approved by: Thomas J. Mathiesen

Filelist: 14th   File size: 39K   Annotations:

Source of data:
Jacobi Leodiensis Tractatus de consonantiis musicalibus, Tractatus de intonatione tonorum, Compendium de musica, ed. Joseph Smits van Waesberghe, Eddie Vetter, and Erik Visser, Divitiae musicae artis, A/IXa (Buren: Knuf, 1988), 47-87. Used by kind permission of the Laaber-Verlag.

Based on Brussels, Bibliothèque Royale Albert Ier, 10162/66, ff. 15v-22v. The graphics files for this treatise are JACDIT 01GF-JACDIT 12GF.

Author: Joannes Presbyter

Treatise: De musica antica et moderna

Incipit: In nomine domini incipit Michrologus id, est brevis sermo de Musica.

File name: **JOAMUS**	Data input by: John Csonka
File type: **TEXT**	Data checked by: Angela Mariani
MS: Print: **X**	Data approved by: Thomas J. Mathiesen

Filelist: 12th   File size: 19K   Annotations:

Source of data:
Adrien de la Fage, Essais de dipthérographie musicale (Paris: Legouix, 1864), 393-407.

The graphic file for this treatise is JOAMUS 01GF. Based on Monte Cassino, Arch. 318.

Author: Johannes Affligemensis

Treatise: De musica cum tonario

Incipit: Domino et patri suo venerabili Angelorum antistiti Fulgentio

File name: **JOHDEM**	Data input by: John Gray
File type: **TEXT**	Data checked by: Oliver Ellsworth & Luminita Aluas
MS: Print: **X**	Data approved by: Thomas J. Mathiesen

Filelist: 9th-11th   File size: 109K   Annotations:

Source of data:
Johannes Affligemensis, De musica cum tonario, ed. J. Smits van Waesberghe, Corpus scriptorum de musica, vol. 1 ([Rome]: American Institute of Musicology, 1950), 43-200. Used by permission.

The graphics files for this treatise are JOHDEM 01GF-JOHDEM 32GF. Cf. JOHMUS TEXT and JOHMU TEXT.

135

Author: Johannes Affligemensis
Treatise: Musica
Incipit: Domino et patri suo venerabili Angelorum antistiti Fulgentio

File name: **JOHMUS**	Data input by: Stephen E. Hayes
File type: **TEXT**	Data checked by: Peter Lefferts & Bradley Tucker
MS: Print: **X**	Data approved by: Thomas J. Mathiesen

Filelist: 9th-11th File size: 90K

Source of data:
  Scriptores ecclesiastici de musica sacra potissimum, 3 vols., ed. Martin Gerbert (St. Blaise: Typis San-Blasianis, 1784; reprint ed., Hildesheim: Olms, 1963), 2:230-65.

Annotations:
The graphics files for this treatise are JOHMUS 01GF-JOHMUS 08GF. Cf. JOHDEM TEXT and JOHMU TEXT.

Author: Johannes Affligemensis
Treatise: Musica
Incipit: Domino et Patri suo venerabili Anglorum antistiti Fulgentio

File name: **JOHMU**	Data input by: Stephen E. Hayes
File type: **TEXT**	Data checked by: Peter Slemon
MS: Print: **X**	Data approved by: Thomas J. Mathiesen

Filelist: 9th-11th File size: 91K

Source of data:
  Patrologia cursus completus, series latina, ed. J. P. Migne, 221 vols. (Paris: Garnier, 1844-1904), 150:1391-1430.

Annotations:
The graphics files for this treatise are JOHMU 01GF-JOHMU 08GF. Cf. JOHDEM TEXT and JOHMUS TEXT.

Author: Johannes de Garlandia
Treatise: De mensurabili musica
Incipit: Habito de ipsa plana musica, quae immensurabilis dicitur

File name: **GARDMM**	Data input by: Peter Slemon
File type: **TEXT**	Data checked by: Bradley Jon Tucker
MS: Print: **X**	Data approved by: Thomas J. Mathiesen

Filelist: 13th File size: 55K

Source of data:
  Erich Reimer, Johannes de Garlandia: De mensurabili musica, kritische Edition mit Kommentar und Interpretation der Notationslehre, 2 vols., Beihefte zum Archiv für Musikwissenschaft, vols. 10-11 (Wiesbaden: Steiner, 1972), 1:35-89 and 91-97. Used by permission.

Annotations:
The graphics files for this treatise are GARDMM 01GF-GARDMM 11GF. Cf. GARDEM TEXT, GARDEMP TEXT, GARDMMP TEXT, and GARDMP MPBN1666.

Author: Johannes de Garlandia

Treatise: De musica mensurabili

Incipit: Habito de ipsa plana musica que immensurabilis dicitur

File name: **GARDEM**

Data input by: John Snyder

File type: **TEXT**

Data checked by: Luminita Aluas

MS: Print: **X**

Data approved by: Thomas J. Mathiesen

Filelist: 13th   File size: 18K

Annotations:

Source of data:

Scriptorum de musica medii aevi nova series a Gerbertina altera, 4 vols., ed. Edmond de Coussemaker (Paris: Durand, 1864-76; reprint ed., Hildesheim: Olms, 1963), 1:175-82.

The graphics files for this treatise are GARDEM 01GF-GARDEM 02GF. Cf. GARDEMP TEXT, GARDMM TEXT, GARDMMP TEXT, and GARDMP MPBN1666.

Author: Johannes de Garlandia

Treatise: De musica mensurabili positio

Incipit: Habito inquit Iohannes de cognicione plane musice et omnium specierum soni

File name: **GARDMP**

Data input by: Sandra Pinegar

File type: **MPBN1666**

Data checked by: Michael W. Lundell

MS: **X**   Print:

Data approved by: Thomas J. Mathiesen

Filelist: 13th   File size: 50K

Annotations:

Source of data:

Paris, Bibliothèque nationale, lat. 16663, ff. 66r-76v.

=RISM BIII/1:124. The incipit is preceded by the introductory text: "Qua quia quedam naciones utuntur communiter uulgarem esse diximus. Sed qui defectuosa est ideo posicionem que Iohannis de Garlandia est: Subuetimus habito ...." The graphics files for this treatise are GARDMP 01GF-GARDMP 11GF. Cf. GARDEM TEXT, GARDEMP TEXT, GARDMMP TEXT, and GARDMM TEXT.

Author: Johannes de Garlandia

Treatise: De musica mensurabili positio

Incipit: Habito, inquit Johannes, de cognitione plane musice et omnium specierum soni

File name: **GARDEMP**

Data input by: Bradley Jon Tucker

File type: **TEXT**

Data checked by: Jan Herlinger

MS: Print: **X**

Data approved by: Thomas J. Mathiesen

Filelist: 13th   File size: 46K

Annotations:

Source of data:

Scriptorum de musica medii aevi nova series a Gerbertina altera, 4 vols., ed. Edmond de Coussemaker (Paris: Durand, 1864-76; reprint ed., Hildesheim: Olms, 1963), 1:97-117.

The graphics files for this treatise are GARDEMP 01GF-GARDEMP 12GF. Cf. GARDEM TEXT, GARDMM TEXT, GARDMMP TEXT, and GARDMP MPBN1666.

Author: Johannes de Garlandia
Treatise: De musica mensurabili positio
Incipit: Habito, inquit Johannes, de cognitione planae musicae et omnium specierum soni

File name: **GARDMMP**	Data input by: Stephen E. Hayes
File type: **TEXT**	Data checked by: Peter M. Lefferts & Andreas Giger
MS: Print: **X**	Data approved by: Thomas J. Mathiesen
Filelist: 13th File size: 46K	Annotations:

Source of data:
Hieronymus de Moravia, Tractatus de musica, ed. S. M. Cserba, Freiburger Studien zur Musikwissenschaft, vol. 2 (Regensburg: Pustet, 1935), 194-230.

The graphics files for this treatise are GARDMMP 01GF-GARDMMP 17GF. Cf. GARDEM TEXT, GARDMM TEXT, GARDEMP TEXT, and GARDMP MPBN1666.

Author: Johannes de Garlandia
Treatise: Optima introductio in contrapunctum pro rudibus
Incipit: Volentibus introduci in arte contrapunctus

File name: **GAROPT**	Data input by: C. Matthew Balensuela
File type: **TEXT**	Data checked by: Sandra Pinegar
MS: Print: **X**	Data approved by: Thomas J. Mathiesen
Filelist: 13th File size: 6K	Annotations:

Source of data:
Scriptorum de musica medii aevi nova series a Gerbertina altera, 4 vols., ed. Edmond de Coussemaker (Paris: Durand, 1864-76; reprint ed., Hildesheim: Olms, 1963), 3:12-13.

Author: Johannes de Grocheo
Treatise: De musica
Incipit: Quoniam quidam iuvenum, amici mei, me cum affectu rogaverunt, quatenus eis

File name: **GRODEM**	Data input by: Sergei Lebedev
File type: **TEXT**	Data checked by: Peter Slemon & Angela Mariani
MS: Print: **X**	Data approved by: Thomas J. Mathiesen
Filelist: 14th File size: 76K	Annotations:

Source of data:
Ernst Rohloff, Der Musiktraktat des Johannes de Grocheo nach den Quellen neu herausgegeben mit Übersetzung ins Deutsche und Revisionsbericht, Media latinitas musica, vol. 2 (Leipzig: Gebrüder Reinecke, 1943), 41-67.

Cf. GROTHE TEXT.

Author: Johannes de Grocheo

Treatise: Theoria

Incipit: Quoniam quidam iuvenum, amici mei, me cum affectu rogaverint, quatenus eis aliquid

File name: **GROTHE** Data input by: Bradley Jon Tucker

File type: **TEXT** Data checked by: Albert C. Rotola, S.J.

MS: Print: **X** Data approved by: Thomas J. Mathiesen

Filelist: 14th File size: 62K Annotations:

Source of data: Cf. GRODEM TEXT.

Johannes Wolf, "Die Musiklehre des Johannes de Grocheo," Sammelbände der Internationalen Musikgesellschaft 1 (1899-1900): 69-120.

Author: Johannes de Muris

Treatise: Ars contrapuncti

Incipit: Quilibet affectans scire contrapunctum ea scribat diligenter

File name: **MURARSC** Data input by: C. Matthew Balensuela

File type: **TEXT** Data checked by: Jan Herlinger

MS: Print: **X** Data approved by: Thomas J. Mathiesen

Filelist: 14th File size: 12K Annotations:

Source of data: The graphics files for this treatise are MURARSC 01GF-MURARSC 05GF. Although the treatise is "secundum Johannem de Muris," de Muris is no longer generally considered to be the author.

Scriptorum de musica medii aevi nova series a Gerbertina altera, 4 vols., ed. Edmond de Coussemaker (Paris: Durand, 1864-76; reprint ed., Hildesheim: Olms, 1963), 3:59-68.

Author: Johannes de Muris

Treatise: Ars discantus

Incipit: Ad sciendum artem discantus, primo est sciendum

File name: **MURARSD** Data input by: C. Matthew Balensuela

File type: **TEXT** Data checked by: Jan Herlinger

MS: Print: **X** Data approved by: Thomas J. Mathiesen

Filelist: 14th File size: 110K Annotations:

Source of data: The graphics files for this treatises are MURARSD 01GF-MURARSD 21GF. Although the treatise is "secundum Johannem de Muris," de Muris is no longer generally considered to be the author.

Scriptorum de musica medii aevi nova series a Gerbertina altera, 4 vols., ed. Edmond de Coussemaker (Paris: Durand, 1864-76; reprint ed., Hildesheim: Olms, 1963), 3:68-113.

Author: Johannes de Muris

Treatise: Ars discantus data a Magistro Iohanne de Muris abbreviando

Incipit: Princeps philosophorum Aristoteles ait in prooemio metaphysicae suae:

File name: **MURAD**   Data input by: Bradley Jon Tucker

File type: **TEXT**   Data checked by: Angela Mariani

MS: Print: **X**   Data approved by: Thomas J. Mathiesen

Filelist: 14th   File size: 7K   Annotations:

Source of data:

Scriptores ecclesiastici de musica sacra
potissimum, 3 vols., ed. Martin Gerbert
(St. Blaise: Typis San-Blasianis, 1784;
reprint ed., Hildesheim: Olms, 1963),
3:312-15.

The graphics file for this treatise is MURAD
01GF.

Author: Johannes de Muris

Treatise: Compendium musicae practicae

Incipit: Partes prolationis quot sunt? Quinque. Quae? Maxima, longa, brevis, semibrevis

File name: **MURCOM**   Data input by: Stephen E. Hayes

File type: **TEXT**   Data checked by: Peter Lefferts & Luminita Aluas

MS: Print: **X**   Data approved by: Thomas J. Mathiesen

Filelist: 14th   File size: 12K   Annotations:

Source of data:

Johannis de Muris Notitia artis musicae et
Compendium musicae practicae; Petrus
de Sancto Dionysio Tractatus de musica,
ed. Ulrich Michels, Corpus scriptorum de
musica, vol. 17 ([Rome]: American
Institute of Musicology, 1972), 119-45.
Used by permission.

The graphics file for this treatise is MURCOM
01GF.

Author: Johannes de Muris

Treatise: De numeris, qui musicas retinent consonantias, secundum Ptolomaeum de Parisius

Incipit: Et quia superius, cum de inventione musicae loqueremur

File name: **MURDEN**   Data input by: Sergei Lebedev

File type: **TEXT**   Data checked by: Angela Mariani

MS: Print: **X**   Data approved by: Thomas J. Mathiesen

Filelist: 14th   File size: 6K   Annotations:

Source of data:

Scriptores ecclesiastici de musica sacra
potissimum, 3 vols., ed. Martin Gerbert
(St. Blaise: Typis San-Blasianis, 1784;
reprint ed., Hildesheim: Olms, 1963),
3:284-86.

Although the treatise is included among the
treatises ascribed to Johannes de Muris by
Gerbert, de Muris is no longer generally
considered to be the author.

Author: Johannes de Muris

Treatise: De practica musica, seu de mensurabili

Incipit: Quoniam in antepositis sermonibus theoricam musicae leniter tetigimus et in brevi

File name: **MURPRA**   Data input by: Bradley Jon Tucker

File type: **TEXT**   Data checked by: Angela Mariani

  MS: Print: **X**   Data approved by: Thomas J. Mathiesen

Filelist: 14th   File size: 27K   Annotations:

Source of data: The graphics file for this treatise is MURPRA
  Scriptores ecclesiastici de musica sacra 01GF. See also MURDEP.
  potissimum, 3 vols., ed. Martin Gerbert
  (St. Blaise: Typis San-Blasianis, 1784;
  reprint ed., Hildesheim: Olms, 1963),
  3:292-301.

Author: Johannes de Muris

Treatise: De tonis

Incipit: Sequuntur numeri proportionales secundum Macrobium, qui quidem numeri

File name: **MURTON**   Data input by: Sergei Lebedev

File type: **TEXT**   Data checked by: Angela Mariani

  MS: Print: **X**   Data approved by: Thomas J. Mathiesen

Filelist: 14th   File size: 11K   Annotations:

Source of data: Continues MURQUAE.
  Scriptores ecclesiastici de musica sacra
  potissimum, 3 vols., ed. Martin Gerbert
  (St. Blaise: Typis San-Blasianis, 1784;
  reprint ed., Hildesheim: Olms, 1963),
  3:308-12.

Author: Johannes de Muris

Treatise: Libellus cantus mensurabilis

Incipit: Quilibet in arte pratica mensurabilis cantus erudiri

File name: **MURLIBF**   Data input by: Daniel Katz

File type: **MFAB1119**   Data checked by: Michael W. Lundell

  MS: **X**   Print: Data approved by: Thomas J. Mathiesen

Filelist: 14th   File size: 24K   Annotations:

Source of data: =RISM BIII/2:47-49. Cf. MURLIB TEXT and
  Florence, Biblioteca MURLIBV MVBM8-85.
  Medicea-Laurenziana, Ashburnham 1119,
  ff. 57r-63v.

Author: Johannes de Muris

Treatise: Libellus cantus mensurabilis

Incipit: Quilibet in arte pratica mensurabilis cantus erudiri

File name: **MURLIBV**   Data input by: Daniel Katz

File type: **MVBM8-85**   Data checked by: Michael W. Lundell

  MS: **X**   Print: Data approved by: Thomas J. Mathiesen

Filelist: 14th   File size: 28K   Annotations:

Source of data: =RISM BIII/2:128-29. The manuscript is
  Venice, Biblioteca Nazionale Marciana, dated 1464. The graphics file for this treatise
  lat. app. cl. VIII/85 (coll. 3579), ff. is MURLIBV 01GF. Cf. MURLIB TEXT and
  11r-23v. MURLIBF MFAB1119.

Author: Johannes de Muris

Treatise: Libellus cantus mensurabilis

Incipit: Quilibet in arte practica mensurabilis cantus erudiri

File name: **MURLIB**   Data input by: C. Matthew Balensuela

File type: **TEXT**   Data checked by: Luminita Aluas

MS: Print: **X**   Data approved by: Albert C. Rotola, S.J.

Filelist: 14th   File size: 24K   Annotations:

Source of data:

Scriptorum de musica medii aevi nova series a Gerbertina altera, 4 vols., ed. Edmond de Coussemaker (Paris: Durand, 1864-76; reprint ed., Hildesheim: Olms, 1963), 3:46-58.

The graphics file for this treatise is MURLIB 01GF. Cf. MURLIBF MFAB1119 and MURLIBV MVBM8-85.

Author: Johannes de Muris

Treatise: Notitia artis musicae

Incipit: Princeps philosophorum Aristoteles ait in prooemio Metaphysicae suae: Omnino

File name: **MURNOT**   Data input by: Stephen E. Hayes

File type: **TEXT**   Data checked by: Peter Lefferts & Luminita Aluas

MS: Print: **X**   Data approved by: Thomas J. Mathiesen

Filelist: 14th   File size: 40K   Annotations:

Source of data:

Johannis de Muris Notitia artis musicae et Compendium musicae practicae; Petrus de Sancto Dionysio Tractatus de musica, ed. Ulrich Michels, Corpus scriptorum de musica, vol. 17 ([Rome]: American Institute of Musicology, 1972), 47-107. Used by permission.

The graphics files for this treatise are MURNOT 01GF-MURNOT 03GF.

Author: Johannes de Muris

Treatise: Quaestiones super partes musicae

Incipit: Partes prolationis quot sunt? Quinque. Quae? maxima, longa, brevis, semibrevis

File name: **MURQUAE**   Data input by: Sergei Lebedev

File type: **TEXT**   Data checked by: Angela Mariani

MS: Print: **X**   Data approved by: Thomas J. Mathiesen

Filelist: 14th   File size: 18K   Annotations:

Source of data:

Scriptores ecclesiastici de musica sacra potissimum, 3 vols., ed. Martin Gerbert (St. Blaise: Typis San-Blasianis, 1784; reprint ed., Hildesheim: Olms, 1963), 3:301-8.

The graphics file for this treatise is MURQUAE 01GF. Continues in MURTON.

Author: Johannes de Muris

Treatise: Speculum musicae, Liber primus

Incipit: Libro tercio de phylosophica consolatione boethius uolens reddere causam

File name: **MURSPE**   Data input by: Peter Slemon

File type: **TEXT**   Data checked by: Kirk Ditzler

MS: Print: **X**   Data approved by: Thomas J. Mathiesen

Filelist: 14th   File size: 107K   Annotations:

Source of data:

Walter Grossmann, Die einleitenden Kapitel des Speculum Musicae von Johannes de Muris: Ein Beitrag zur Musikanschauung des Mittelalters (Leipzig: Breitkopf und Härtel, 1924; reprint ed., Nendeln/Liechtenstein: Kraus, 1976), 53-93.

Although attributed here to Johannes de Muris, the text is that of the treatise now attributed to Jacobus Leodiensis. Cf. JACSP1A TEXT.

Author: Johannes de Muris

Treatise: Summa

Incipit: Amicorum iusta et honesta petitio coactio reputatur, hac itaque me stimulante

File name: **MURSUM**   Data input by: Sergei Lebedev

File type: **TEXT**   Data checked by: Luminita Aluas

MS: Print: **X**   Data approved by: Thomas J. Mathiesen

Filelist: 14th   File size: 144K   Annotations:

Source of data:

Scriptores ecclesiastici de musica sacra potissimum, 3 vols., ed. Martin Gerbert (St. Blaise: Typis San-Blasianis, 1784; reprint ed., Hildesheim: Olms, 1963), 3:190-248.

The treatise is no longer generally attributed to Johannes de Muris. Cf. PEPESUM TEXT.

Author: Johannes de Muris

Treatise: Tractatus de musica

Incipit: Experimento multiplici colligi potest, quod musica promoveat affectiones animae

File name: **MURMUS**   Data input by: Sergei Lebedev

File type: **TEXT**   Data checked by: Angela Mariani

MS: Print: **X**   Data approved by: Thomas J. Mathiesen

Filelist: 14th   File size: 74K   Annotations:

Source of data:

Scriptores ecclesiastici de musica sacra potissimum, 3 vols., ed. Martin Gerbert (St. Blaise: Typis San-Blasianis, 1784; reprint ed., Hildesheim: Olms, 1963), 3:249-83.

The graphics files for this treatise are MURMUS 01GF-MURMUS 12GF.

Author: Johannes de Muris
Treatise: Tractatus de proportionibus
Incipit: Proportionum adipisci musicalium a venerandae memoriae magistro Iohanne de Muris
File name: **MURDEP**   Data input by: Sergei Lebedev
File type: **TEXT**   Data checked by: Bradley Jon Tucker
MS: Print: **X**   Data approved by: Charles M. Atkinson
Filelist: 14th   File size: 13K   Annotations:
Source of data: The graphics files for this treatise are
Scriptores ecclesiastici de musica sacra   MURDEP 01GF-MURDEP 02GF. "Secundus
potissimum, 3 vols., ed. Martin Gerbert   Liber" in MURPRA.
(St. Blaise: Typis San-Blasianis, 1784;
reprint ed., Hildesheim: Olms, 1963),
3:286-91.

Author: Johannes de Olomons
Treatise: Palma choralis
Incipit: Musica est enim scientia regularem docens notitiam ad canendi perfectionem
File name: **JOHPAL**   Data input by: Nigel Gwee
File type: **TEXT**   Data checked by: Peter Slemon
MS: Print: **X**   Data approved by: Thomas J. Mathiesen
Filelist: 15th   File size: 100K   Annotations:
Source of data: The graphics files for this treatise are
Johannes de Olomons, Palma choralis, ed.   JOHPAL 01GF-JOHPAL 26GF.
Albert Seay, Critical Texts, no. 6
(Colorado Springs: Colorado College
Music Press, 1977). Used by permission.

Author: Johannes dictus Balloce
Treatise: Abreviatio Magistri Franconis
Incipit: Gaudent brevitate moderni. Quandocunque punctus quadratus
File name: **BALABM**   Data input by: Peter Slemon
File type: **TEXT**   Data checked by: Bradley Jon Tucker
MS: Print: **X**   Data approved by: Thomas J. Mathiesen
Filelist: 13th   File size: 9K   Annotations:
Source of data: Based on Paris, Bibliothèque Nationale, lat.
Johannes dictus Balloce, Abreviatio   15128. The graphics file for this treatise is
magistri Franconis; Anonymus,   BALABM 01GF. Cf. ANOCBA MBAV5320,
Compendium musicae mensurabilis artis   ANOCMM TEXT, ANOCOM TEXT,
antiquae (Ms. Saint-Dié, Bibl.   ANOCOMM TEXT, ANOTDD TEXT,
Municipale, 42), ed. Gilbert Reaney;   ANO2TRA TEXT, ANO3DEC TEXT, and
Anonymus, Compendium musicae   BALABR TEXT.
mensurabilis artis antiquae (Ms. Wien,
Nationalbibl., 5003); Anonymus,
Tractatus artis antiquae cum explicatione
mensurae binariae (Ms. Wien,
Nationalbibl., 5003), ed. Heinz Ristory,
Corpus scriptorum de musica, vol. 34
(n.p.: American Institute of Musicology,
1987), 13-21. Used by permission.

Author: Johannes dictus Ballox

Treatise: Abreviatio Magistri Franconis

Incipit: Gaudent brevitate moderni. Quandocunque punctus quadratus

File name: **BALABR**   Data input by: Bradley Jon Tucker

File type: **TEXT**   Data checked by: Thomas J. Mathiesen

  MS: Print: **X**   Data approved by: Oliver B. Ellsworth

Filelist: 13th   File size: 8K   Annotations:

Source of data: The graphics file for this treatise is BALABR
  Scriptorum de musica medii aevi nova   01GF. Cf. ANOCBA MBAV5320,
  series a Gerbertina altera, 4 vols., ed. ANOCMM TEXT, ANOCOM TEXT,
  Edmond de Coussemaker (Paris: Durand, ANOCOMM TEXT, ANOTDD TEXT,
  1864-76; reprint ed., Hildesheim: Olms, ANO2TRA TEXT, ANO3DEC TEXT, and
  1963), 1:292-96.   BALABM TEXT.

Author: Johannes Gallicus

Treatise: Ritus canendi [Pars prima]

Incipit: Omnium quidem artium, etsi varia sit introductio

File name: **GALRC1**   Data input by: Stephen E. Hayes

File type: **TEXT**   Data checked by: Peter Slemon & Bradley Tucker

  MS: Print: **X**   Data approved by: Thomas J. Mathiesen

Filelist: 15th   File size: 133K   Annotations:

Source of data: The graphics files for this treatise are
  Johannes Gallicus, Ritus canendi [Pars GALRC1 01GF-GALRC1 18GF. Cf.
  prima], ed. Albert Seay, Critical Texts, GALRIT1 TEXT, GALRIT2 TEXT, and
  no. 13 (Colorado Springs: Colorado   GALRIT3 TEXT.
  College Music Press, 1981). Used by
  permission.

Author: Johannes Gallicus

Treatise: Ritus canendi [Pars secunda]

Incipit: Pauperibus ecclesiae Dei clericis, ac religiosis Deo laudes concinere

File name: **GALRC2**   Data input by: Stephen E. Hayes

File type: **TEXT**   Data checked by: Peter Slemon & Angela Mariani

  MS: Print: **X**   Data approved by: Thomas J. Mathiesen

Filelist: 15th   File size: 137K   Annotations:

Source of data: The graphics files for this treatise are
  Johannes Gallicus, Ritus canendi [Pars GALRC2 01GF-GALRC2 26GF. Cf.
  secunda], ed. Albert Seay, Critical Texts, GALRITS1 TEXT, GALRITS2 TEXT, and
  no. 14 (Colorado Springs: Colorado   GALRITS3 TEXT.
  College Music Press, 1981). Used by
  permission.

Author: Johannes Gallicus dictus Carthusiensis seu de Mantua
Treatise: Vera quamque facilis ad cantandum atque brevis introductio
Incipit: Pauperibus ecclesiae Dei clericis, ac religiosis Deo laudes concinere

File name: **GALRITS1**   Data input by: Stephen E. Hayes
File type: **TEXT**   Data checked by: Peter Lefferts & Luminita Aluas
  MS: Print: **X**   Data approved by: Thomas J. Mathiesen
Filelist: 15th   File size: 71K   Annotations:
Source of data: De ritu canendi. Secunda pars. Liber primus.
  Scriptorum de musica medii aevi nova   The graphics files for this treatise are
  series a Gerbertina altera, 4 vols., ed.   GALRITS1 01GF-GALRITS1 12GF.
  Edmond de Coussemaker (Paris: Durand,
  1864-76; reprint ed., Hildesheim: Olms,
  1963), 4:345-72.

Author: Johannes Gallicus dictus Carthusiensis seu de Mantua
Treatise: Incipit liber secundus de sex, ut, re, mi, fa, sol, la, sillabis
Incipit: Omnem ob sex sillabas et quinque vel sex modici decoris figuras

File name: **GALRITS2**   Data input by: Stephen E. Hayes
File type: **TEXT**   Data checked by: Peter Lefferts & Luminita Aluas
  MS: Print: **X**   Data approved by: Thomas J. Mathiesen
Filelist: 15th   File size: 35K   Annotations:
Source of data: De ritu canendi. Secunda pars. Liber secundus.
  Scriptorum de musica medii aevi nova   The graphics files for this treatise are
  series a Gerbertina altera, 4 vols., ed.   GALRITS2 01GF-GALRITS2 04GF.
  Edmond de Coussemaker (Paris: Durand,
  1864-76; reprint ed., Hildesheim: Olms,
  1963), 4:372-83.

Author: Johannes Gallicus dictus Carthusiensis seu de Mantua
Treatise: Incipit liber tertius de contrapuncto praefationcula
Incipit: Libet post editum de divino cantu quod pauperi clero sponte devoveram

File name: **GALRITS3**   Data input by: Stephen E. Hayes
File type: **TEXT**   Data checked by: Peter Lefferts & Luminita Aluas
  MS: Print: **X**   Data approved by: Thomas J. Mathiesen
Filelist: 15th   File size: 37K   Annotations:
Source of data: De ritu canendi. Secunda pars. Liber tertius.
  Scriptorum de musica medii aevi nova   The graphics files for this treatise are
  series a Gerbertina altera, 4 vols., ed.   GALRITS3 01GF-GALRITS3 08GF.
  Edmond de Coussemaker (Paris: Durand,
  1864-76; reprint ed., Hildesheim: Olms,
  1963), 4:383-96.

THESAURUS MUSICARUM LATINARUM: Canon of Data Files

Author: Johannes Gallicus dictus Carthusiensis seu de Mantua
Treatise: Incipit praefationcula in tam admirabilem quam tacitam et quietissimam novorum
Incipit: Etsi non parvum auribus humanis afferre soleant modi musici per ruritum

File name: **GALTRA**   Data input by: Stephen E. Hayes
File type: **TEXT**   Data checked by: Peter Lefferts & Bradley Tucker
MS: Print: **X**   Data approved by: Thomas J. Mathiesen
Filelist: 15th   File size: 43K   Annotations:

Source of data:
Scriptorum de musica medii aevi nova series a Gerbertina altera, 4 vols., ed. Edmond de Coussemaker (Paris: Durand, 1864-76; reprint ed., Hildesheim: Olms, 1963), 4:396-409.

Tractatus brevissimus de totis algorismi calculationibus. The graphics files for this treatise are GALTRA 01GF-GALTRA 03GF.

Author: Johannes Gallicus dictus Carthusiensis seu de Mantua
Treatise: Ritus canendi vetustissimus et novus, liber primus
Incipit: Omnium quidem artium, etsi varia sit introductio

File name: **GALRIT1**   Data input by: Stephen E. Hayes
File type: **TEXT**   Data checked by: Peter Lefferts & Luminita Aluas
MS: Print: **X**   Data approved by: Thomas J. Mathiesen
Filelist: 15th   File size: 42K   Annotations:

Source of data:
Scriptorum de musica medii aevi nova series a Gerbertina altera, 4 vols., ed. Edmond de Coussemaker (Paris: Durand, 1864-76; reprint ed., Hildesheim: Olms, 1963), 4:298-313.

The graphics files for this treatise are GALRIT1 01GF-GALRIT1 06GF. See also GALRIT2 and GALRIT3.

Author: Johannes Gallicus dictus Carthusiensis seu de Mantua
Treatise: Ritus canendi vetustissimus et novus, liber secundus
Incipit: Hoc expleto primo libro volens implere promissus ac in monocordo

File name: **GALRIT2**   Data input by: Stephen E. Hayes
File type: **TEXT**   Data checked by: Peter Lefferts & Luminita Aluas
MS: Print: **X**   Data approved by: Thomas J. Mathiesen
Filelist: 15th   File size: 50K   Annotations:

Source of data:
Scriptorum de musica medii aevi nova series a Gerbertina altera, 4 vols., ed. Edmond de Coussemaker (Paris: Durand, 1864-76; reprint ed., Hildesheim: Olms, 1963), 4:313-28.

The graphics files for this treatise are GALRIT2 01GF-GALRIT2 03GF. See also GALRIT1 and GALRIT3.

Author: Johannes Gallicus dictus Carthusiensis seu de Mantua

Treatise: Ritus canendi vetustissimus et novus, liber tertius

Incipit: His ista rite peractis ac quindecim philosophorum cordis in unum collectis

File name: **GALRIT3**   Data input by: Stephen E. Hayes

File type: **TEXT**   Data checked by: Peter Lefferts & Luminita Aluas

MS: Print: **X**   Data approved by: Thomas J. Mathiesen

Filelist: 15th   File size: 38K   Annotations:

Source of data:
Scriptorum de musica medii aevi nova
series a Gerbertina altera, 4 vols., ed.
Edmond de Coussemaker (Paris: Durand,
1864-76; reprint ed., Hildesheim: Olms,
1963), 4:328-45.

The graphics files for this treatise are
GALRIT3 01GF-GALRIT3 08GF. See also
GALRIT1 and GALRIT2.

Author: Johannes Gallicus dictus Carthusiensis seu de Mantua

Treatise: Tacita nunc inchoatur stupendaque numerorum musica

Incipit: Jam vero quisquis inquirere cupit a primis numeris

File name: **GALLIB**   Data input by: Stephen E. Hayes

File type: **TEXT**   Data checked by: Peter Lefferts & Bradley Tucker

MS: Print: **X**   Data approved by: Thomas J. Mathiesen

Filelist: 15th   File size: 38K   Annotations:

Source of data:
Scriptorum de musica medii aevi nova
series a Gerbertina altera, 4 vols., ed.
Edmond de Coussemaker (Paris: Durand,
1864-76; reprint ed., Hildesheim: Olms,
1963), 4:409-21.

Liber notabilis musicae Johannis Gallici. The
graphics files for this treatise are GALLIB
01GF-GALLIB 02GF.

Author: Johannes Verulus de Anagnia

Treatise: Liber de musica

Incipit: Cum igitur de arte musice tractare debeamus

File name: **VERDMPV**   Data input by: Oliver B. Ellsworth

File type: **MBAVB307**   Data checked by: P. Lefferts & J. Langford-Johnson

MS: **X**   Print: Data approved by: Thomas J. Mathiesen

Filelist: 14th   File size: 134K   Annotations:

Source of data:
Rome, Biblioteca Apostolica Vaticana,
Barberini lat. 307, ff. 1r-16v.

=RISM BIII/2:102-4. The graphics files for
this treatise are VERDMPV
01GF-VERDMPV 03GF. Cf. VERLDM
TEXT and VERLIB TEXT.

Author: Johannes Verulus de Anagnia

Treatise: Liber de musica

Incipit: Cum igitur de arte musice tractare debeamus

File name: **VERLIB**   Data input by: C. Matthew Balensuela

File type: **TEXT**   Data checked by: Luminita Aluas

MS: Print: **X**   Data approved by: Albert C. Rotola, S.J.

Filelist: 14th   File size: 127K   Annotations:

Source of data:
Scriptorum de musica medii aevi nova
series a Gerbertina altera, 4 vols., ed.
Edmond de Coussemaker (Paris: Durand,
1864-76; reprint ed., Hildesheim: Olms,
1963), 3:129-77.

The graphics files for this treatise are VERLIB
01GF-VERLIB 04GF. Cf. VERLDM TEXT.

Author: Johannes Verulus de Anagnia

Treatise: Liber de musica

Incipit: Cum igitur de arte musice tractare debeamus

File name: **VERLDM**   Data input by: Stephen E. Hayes

File type: **TEXT**   Data checked by: Peter M. Lefferts & Kirk Ditzler

  MS: Print: **X**   Data approved by: Thomas J. Mathiesen

Filelist: 14th   File size: 133K   Annotations:

Source of data:

  Liber de musica Iohannis Vetuli de
  Anagnia, ed. Frederick Hammond,
  Corpus scriptorum de musica, vol. 27
  (n.p.: American Institute of Musicology,
  1977), 26-97. Used by permission.

The graphics files for this treatise are
VERLDM 01GF-VERLDM 05GF. Cf.
VERLIB TEXT and VERDMPV
MBAVB307.

Author: Keck, Ioannes

Treatise: Introductorium musicae

Incipit: Musicam triplicem esse ferunt sapientes, metricam unam, rhythmicam alteram

File name: **KECKINMU**   Data input by: Sergei Lebedev

File type: **TEXT**   Data checked by: Bradley Jon Tucker

  MS: Print: **X**   Data approved by: Charles M. Atkinson

Filelist: 15th   File size: 28K   Annotations:

Source of data:

  Scriptores ecclesiastici de musica sacra
  potissimum, 3 vols., ed. Martin Gerbert
  (St. Blaise: Typis San-Blasianis, 1784;
  reprint ed., Hildesheim: Olms, 1963),
  3:319-29.

The treatise is preceded by a preface,
beginning: "Exultabunt labia mea, cum
cantavero tibi, inquit egregius ille musicus
regius ...." This is followed by the
"argumentum, beginning: "Introductorius in
musicam liber appellatur, quoniam omnium
sonorum proportiones mira brevitate
complectitur ...." Each of the five chapter
headings is then given prior to the formal
incipit, as transcribed above.

Author: Kilwardby, Robert

Treatise: De ortu et divisione philosophiae, Capitulum XVIII, De ortu et subiecto et proprio

Incipit: Jam tempus est de ortu aliarum mathematicarum aliquid dicere

File name: **KILDEO**   Data input by: Bradley Jon Tucker

File type: **TEXT**   Data checked by: Peter Slemon

  MS: Print: **X**   Data approved by: Thomas J. Mathiesen

Filelist: 13th   File size: 8K   Annotations:

Source of data:

  Walter Grossmann, Die einleitenden
  Kapitel des Speculum Musicae von
  Johannes de Muris: Ein Beitrag zur
  Musikanschauung des Mittelalters
  (Leipzig: Breitkopf und Härtel, 1924;
  reprint ed., Nendeln/Liechtenstein: Kraus,
  1976), 94-96.

Author: Kilwardby, Robert

Treatise: De ortu scientiarum

Incipit: Eodem etiam modo se habent ad invicem numerus de quo arithmetica et numerus

File name: **KILDOS**

File type: **TEXT**

MS: Print: **X**

Filelist: 13th   File size: 23K

Source of data:

Robert Kilwardby O.P, De ortu scientiarum, Auctores britannici medii aevi, vol. IV (London: The British Academy; Toronto: The Pontifical Institute of Mediaeval Studies, 1976), 46-47, 50-53, 55-60, 138, 144, 146, 167, and 224. Used by permission.

Data input by: John Gray

Data checked by: Oliver Ellsworth & Andreas Giger

Data approved by: Thomas J. Mathiesen

Annotations:

This file contains excerpts from De ortu scientiarum pertaining to music, including sections 112, 126-134 (i.e., Cap. XVIII [cf. KILDEO TEXT]), 138-51 (i.e., Capp. XX-XXI), 393 (i.e., Cap. XLII), 412, 417 (i.e., Cap. XLVI), 491, and 656.

Author: Kromer, Marcin

Treatise: De musica figurata

Incipit: Quae superiori libro diximus, non solum illa quidem ad planam musicam spectant

File name: **KRODEM**

File type: **TEXT**

MS: Print: **X**

Filelist: 16th   File size: 13K

Source of data:

Marcin Kromer, De musica figurata liber posterior, ed. Albert Seay, Texts/Translations, no. 3 (Colorado Springs: Colorado College Music Press, 1980), 2-34. Used by permission.

Data input by: Peter Slemon

Data checked by: Bradley Jon Tucker

Data approved by: Thomas J. Mathiesen

Annotations:

The graphics files for this treatise are KRODEM 01GF-KRODEM 05GF.

Author: Ladislaus de Zalka

Treatise: [Musica]

Incipit: Pro themate praesentis operis assigno Cassiodorum in quadam epistola sic

File name: **SZAMUS**

File type: **TEXT**

MS: Print: **X**

Filelist: 15th   File size: 128K

Source of data:

Dénes von Bartha, Das Musiklehrbuch einer ungarischen Klosterschule in der Handschrift von Fürstrimas Szalkai (1490), Musicologica hungarica, vol. 1 (Budapest: Magyar nemzeti múzeum, 1934), 63-128.

Data input by: Peter Slemon

Data checked by: Bradley Jon Tucker

Data approved by: Thomas J. Mathiesen

Annotations:

The graphics files for this treatise are SZAMUS 01GF-SZAMUS 19GF. SZAMUS 01GF, SZAMUS 04GF, SZAMUS 06GF, and SZAMUS 08GF-SZAMUS 10GF exhibit facsimiles of the original manuscript, Esztergom, Erzbischöfliche Bibliothek, II, 395.

Author: Liban, Jerzy

Treatise: De accentuum ecclesiasticorum exquisita ratione

Incipit: Quartam vtilitatem, Ecclesiae ministris noticia accentuum conferat.

File name: **LIBDEA**   Data input by: John Snyder

File type: **TEXT**   Data checked by: Andreas Giger

MS: Print: **X**   Data approved by: Thomas J. Mathiesen

Filelist: 16th   File size: 107K   Annotations:

Source of data:

De accentuum ecclesiasticorum exquisita ratione, scilicet Lectionali, Epistolari, et Euangelico, Libellus omnibus sacris iniciatis, Vicarijs et Ecclesiae Ministris, non minus Vtilis quam necessarius (Cracow: Scharffenberg, 1539; reprint ed., Cracow: Polskie Wydawnictwo Muzyczne, 1975).

The treatise is preceded by a long dedicatory preface, beginning: "Saepe mecum constitui Reuerende Domine congratulandi gratia, et cui ut bene praecarer, accedere Amplitudinem ...." The graphics files for this treatise are LIBDEA 01GF-LIBDEA 19GF.

Author: Liban, Jerzy

Treatise: De musicae laudibus oratio

Incipit: Animaduerti quam plurimos iam pridem Adolescentulos, iucundissimae Musices

File name: **LIBDEM**   Data input by: John Snyder

File type: **TEXT**   Data checked by: Andreas Giger

MS: Print: **X**   Data approved by: Thomas J. Mathiesen

Filelist: 16th   File size: 76K   Annotations:

Source of data:

De musicae laudibus oratio seu adhortatio quaedam, ad musicae studiosos: cui annexa est, quae in scalis et musica tractantur, multorum vocabulorum graecorum interpretatio, cum octo tonorum proprietatibus, et totidem eorum melodijs, tetraphonis haud inconcinnis Atque alia nonnulla, quae sequens ostendit paginula. His octo tonis, tanquam auctarium additur Peregrinus, quasi post liminio reuersus, qui cum coeteris tonis fratribus suis, in pristinam redit noticiam (Cracow: Halicz, 1540; reprint ed., Cracow: Polskie Wydawnictwo Muzyczne, 1975).

The treatise is preceded by a table of contents and a long dedicatory preface, beginning: "Magnus orator et eloquentiae parens Cicero [<en> arche ton protou ton kathekon]. his verbis alloquitur filium suum ...." The graphics files for this treatise are LIBDEM 01GF-LIBDEM 09GF.

THESAURUS MUSICARUM LATINARUM: Canon of Data Files

Author: Liban, Jerzy
Treatise: De philosophiae laudibus oratio
Incipit: Veror nimirum magnifice domine Rector, Doctores Celebres, Magistri insignes

File name: **LIBDEP**   Data input by: John Snyder
File type: **TEXT**   Data checked by: Andreas Giger
  MS: Print: **X**   Data approved by: Thomas J. Mathiesen
Filelist: 16th   File size: 31K   Annotations:

Source of data: The treatise is preceded by a long dedicatory
De philosophiae laudibus oratio in qua   preface, beginning: "Cum indies fere mecum
singularum artium fere liberalium, laus et   animo reuoluerem Reuerende pater,
decorum continetur et utilitas, a   pulcherrima illa tua a plusculis annis in me
doctissimorum sententiis philosphorum,   collata ...."
non abhorrens, eme, lege, et adficiere
(Cracow: Scharffenberg, 1537; reprint
ed., Cracow: Polskie Wydawnictwo
Muzyczne, 1975).

Author: Lippus, junior, Raphael Brandolinus
Treatise: De musica et poetica opusculum in quo Conradolum Stangam prothonotarium
Incipit: Patrum nostrorum memoria et Alphonsus, splendidissimus ille Aragonum rex

File name: **LIPDEM**   Data input by: John Csonka
File type: **TEXT**   Data checked by: Bradley Jon Tucker
  MS: Print: **X**   Data approved by: Thomas J. Mathiesen
Filelist: 16th   File size: 11K   Annotations:

Source of data: Based on Rome, Biblioteca Casanatense,
Adrien de la Fage, Essais de   c.V,3.
dipthérographie musicale (Paris: Legouix,
1864), 62-65.

Author: Ludovicus Sanctus
Treatise: Sentencia in musica sonora subiecti
Incipit: Omnes homines sicut dicit philosophus naturaliter scire desiderant.

File name: **LUDSENT**   Data input by: Andreas Giger
File type: **MFAB1051**   Data checked by: Michael W. Lundell
  MS: **X**   Print: Data approved by: Thomas J. Mathiesen
Filelist: 14th   File size: 4K   Annotations:

Source of data: The text is also transcribed in Henry Cochin,
Florence, Biblioteca   "Sur le Socrate de Pétrarque," Mélanges
Medicea-Laurenziana, Ashburnham 1051,   d'archéologie et d'histoire 37 (1918-1919):
f. 170r.   31-32. Cf. LUDSEN TEXT.

Author: Ludovicus Sanctus
Treatise: Sentencia in musica sonora subiecti
Incipit: Omnes homines, sicut dicit philosophus, naturaliter scire desiderant

File name: **LUDSEN**   Data input by: Andreas Giger
File type: **TEXT**   Data checked by: Andreas Giger
  MS: Print: **X**   Data approved by: Thomas J. Mathiesen
Filelist: 14th   File size: 4K   Annotations:
Source of data: Based on Florence, Biblioteca
  Ambrogio Abbate Amelli, O.S.B., "Di   Medicea-Laurenziana, Ashburnham 1051. Cf.
  uno scritto inedito di S. Lodovico   LUDSENT MFAB1051.
  vescovo di Tolosa intorno alla musica,"
  Archivum franciscanum historicum 2
  (1909): 379-80.

Author: Magister de Garlandia
Treatise: Introductio musice
Incipit: Introductiones in arte musice. Primo videndum est quod sit introductio

File name: **GARINT**   Data input by: Bradley Jon Tucker
File type: **TEXT**   Data checked by: Thomas J. Mathiesen
  MS: Print: **X**   Data approved by: Peter M. Lefferts
Filelist: 13th   File size: 36K   Annotations:
Source of data: The graphics files for this treatise are
  Scriptorum de musica medii aevi nova   GARINT 01GF-GARINT 13GF. The author
  series a Gerbertina altera, 4 vols., ed.   of this treatise is the hypothetical "Garlandia
  Edmond de Coussemaker (Paris: Durand,   the Younger," but most scholars no longer
  1864-76; reprint ed., Hildesheim: Olms,   accept the hypothesis.
  1963), 1:157-75.

Author: Marchetus de Padua
Treatise: Brevis compilatio in arte musicae mensuratae
Incipit: Quoniam omnis cantus mesuratus dicitur eo quod tempore mensuratur

File name: **MARBRE**   Data input by: C. Matthew Balensuela
File type: **TEXT**   Data checked by: Stephen E. Hayes
  MS: Print: **X**   Data approved by: Peter M. Lefferts
Filelist: 14th   File size: 22K   Annotations:
Source of data:
  Scriptorum de musica medii aevi nova
  series a Gerbertina altera, 4 vols., ed.
  Edmond de Coussemaker (Paris: Durand,
  1864-76; reprint ed., Hildesheim: Olms,
  1963), 3:1-12.

Author: Marchetus de Padua

Treatise: Lucidarium, tractatus primus

Incipit: Qualiter Pytagoras adinvenit musicam, memorat Macrobius

File name: **MARLU1**   Data input by: Bradley Jon Tucker

File type: **TEXT**   Data checked by: Angela Mariani

  MS: Print: **X**   Data approved by: Thomas J. Mathiesen

Filelist: 14th   File size: 15K   Annotations:

Source of data:

Scriptores ecclesiastici de musica sacra potissimum, 3 vols., ed. Martin Gerbert (St. Blaise: Typis San-Blasianis, 1784; reprint ed., Hildesheim: Olms, 1963), 3:64-70.

The treatise is preceded by a letter, beginning: "Magnifico militi et potenti domino suo, domino Raynerio domini Zachariae de Urbe veteri, ..." See also files MARLU2 through MARLU16; and all the files of MARLUC.

Author: Marchetus de Padua

Treatise: Lucidarium, tractatus secundus

Incipit: Ad huius evidentiam est sciendum, quod secundum Remigium

File name: **MARLU2**   Data input by: Bradley Jon Tucker

File type: **TEXT**   Data checked by: Angela Mariani

  MS: Print: **X**   Data approved by: Thomas J. Mathiesen

Filelist: 14th   File size: 18K   Annotations:

Source of data:

Scriptores ecclesiastici de musica sacra potissimum, 3 vols., ed. Martin Gerbert (St. Blaise: Typis San-Blasianis, 1784; reprint ed., Hildesheim: Olms, 1963), 3:70-76.

The graphics file for this treatise is MARLU2 01GF. See also files MARLU1 and MARLU3 through MARLU16; and all the files of MARLUC.

Author: Marchetus de Padua

Treatise: Lucidarium, tractatus tertius

Incipit: Ad videndum autem de numeris musicalibus

File name: **MARLU3**   Data input by: Bradley Jon Tucker

File type: **TEXT**   Data checked by: Angela Mariani

  MS: Print: **X**   Data approved by: Thomas J. Mathiesen

Filelist: 14th   File size: 5K   Annotations:

Source of data:

Scriptores ecclesiastici de musica sacra potissimum, 3 vols., ed. Martin Gerbert (St. Blaise: Typis San-Blasianis, 1784; reprint ed., Hildesheim: Olms, 1963), 3:76-78.

See also files MARLU1 through MARLU2 and MARLU4 through MARLU16; and all the files of MARLUC.

Author: Marchetus de Padua

Treatise: Lucidarium, tractatus quartus

Incipit: Proportio est quaedam habitudo duorum terminorum

File name: **MARLU4**　　Data input by: Bradley Jon Tucker

File type: **TEXT**　　Data checked by: Angela Mariani

　MS:　　Print: **X**　　Data approved by: Thomas J. Mathiesen

Filelist: 14th　　File size: 5K　　Annotations:

Source of data:　　　　　　　See also files MARLU1 through MARLU3
　Scriptores ecclesiastici de musica sacra　and MARLU5 through MARLU16; and all the
　potissimum, 3 vols., ed. Martin Gerbert　files of MARLUC.
　(St. Blaise: Typis San-Blasianis, 1784;
　reprint ed., Hildesheim: Olms, 1963),
　3:78-80.

Author: Marchetus de Padua

Treatise: Lucidarium, tractatus quintus

Incipit: Sequitur videre de consonantia, de qua primo videbimus

File name: **MARLU5**　　Data input by: Bradley Jon Tucker

File type: **TEXT**　　Data checked by: Angela Mariani

　MS:　　Print: **X**　　Data approved by: Thomas J. Mathiesen

Filelist: 14th　　File size: 9K　　Annotations:

Source of data:　　　　　　　The graphics file for this treatise is MARLU5
　Scriptores ecclesiastici de musica sacra　01GF. See also files MARLU1 through
　potissimum, 3 vols., ed. Martin Gerbert　MARLU4 and MARLU6 through MARLU16;
　(St. Blaise: Typis San-Blasianis, 1784;　and all the files of MARLUC.
　reprint ed., Hildesheim: Olms, 1963),
　3:80-83.

Author: Marchetus de Padua

Treatise: Lucidarium, tractatus sextus

Incipit: Quaeritur, quare una consonantia magis concordet quam altera

File name: **MARLU6**　　Data input by: Bradley Jon Tucker

File type: **TEXT**　　Data checked by: Angela Mariani

　MS:　　Print: **X**　　Data approved by: Thomas J. Mathiesen

Filelist: 14th　　File size: 12K　　Annotations:

Source of data:　　　　　　　See also files MARLU1 through MARLU5
　Scriptores ecclesiastici de musica sacra　and MARLU7 through MARLU16; and all the
　potissimum, 3 vols., ed. Martin Gerbert　files of MARLUC.
　(St. Blaise: Typis San-Blasianis, 1784;
　reprint ed., Hildesheim: Olms, 1963),
　3:83-87.

Author: Marchetus de Padua

Treatise: Lucidarium, tractatus septimus

Incipit: Genera inaequalitatis quinque sunt, scilicet multiplex

File name: **MARLU7**   Data input by: Bradley Jon Tucker

File type: **TEXT**   Data checked by: Angela Mariani

　MS:　　　Print: **X**   Data approved by: Thomas J. Mathiesen

Filelist: 14th　　File size: 4K   Annotations:

Source of data:

Scriptores ecclesiastici de musica sacra potissimum, 3 vols., ed. Martin Gerbert (St. Blaise: Typis San-Blasianis, 1784; reprint ed., Hildesheim: Olms, 1963), 3:87-88.

See also files MARLU1 through MARLU6 and MARLU8 through MARLU16; and all the files of MARLUC.

Author: Marchetus de Padua

Treatise: Lucidarium, tractatus octavus

Incipit: Quoniam omnis tonus et semitonium in voce consistit

File name: **MARLU8**   Data input by: Bradley Jon Tucker

File type: **TEXT**   Data checked by: Angela Mariani

　MS:　　　Print: **X**   Data approved by: Thomas J. Mathiesen

Filelist: 14th　　File size: 10K   Annotations:

Source of data:

Scriptores ecclesiastici de musica sacra potissimum, 3 vols., ed. Martin Gerbert (St. Blaise: Typis San-Blasianis, 1784; reprint ed., Hildesheim: Olms, 1963), 3:88-92.

The graphics files for this treatise are MARLU8 01GF-MARLU8 02GF. See also files MARLU1 through MARLU7 and MARLU9 through MARLU16; and all the files of MARLUC.

Author: Marchetus de Padua

Treatise: Lucidarium, tractatus nonus

Incipit: Coniunctio in musica est dispositio sive ordinatio sonorum

File name: **MARLU9**   Data input by: Bradley Jon Tucker

File type: **TEXT**   Data checked by: Angela Mariani

　MS:　　　Print: **X**   Data approved by: Thomas J. Mathiesen

Filelist: 14th　　File size: 14K   Annotations:

Source of data:

Scriptores ecclesiastici de musica sacra potissimum, 3 vols., ed. Martin Gerbert (St. Blaise: Typis San-Blasianis, 1784; reprint ed., Hildesheim: Olms, 1963), 3:92-100.

The graphics files for this treatise are MARLU9 01GF-MARLU9 06GF. See also files MARLU1 through MARLU8 and MARLU10 through MARLU16; and all the files of MARLUC.

Author: Marchetus de Padua

Treatise: Lucidarium, tractatus decimus

Incipit: Mensura in musica est ordo cantuum mensuratorum

File name: **MARLU10**   Data input by: Bradley Jon Tucker

File type: **TEXT**   Data checked by: Angela Mariani

MS: Print: **X**   Data approved by: Thomas J. Mathiesen

Filelist: 14th   File size: 2K   Annotations:

Source of data:

Scriptores ecclesiastici de musica sacra potissimum, 3 vols., ed. Martin Gerbert (St. Blaise: Typis San-Blasianis, 1784; reprint ed., Hildesheim: Olms, 1963), 3:100.

See also files MARLU1 through MARLU9 and MARLU11 through MARLU16; and all the files of MARLUC.

Author: Marchetus de Padua

Treatise: Lucidarium, tractatus undecimus

Incipit: Tonus, tropus, sive modus, secundum dicta Boetii

File name: **MARLU11**   Data input by: Bradley Jon Tucker

File type: **TEXT**   Data checked by: Angela Mariani

MS: Print: **X**   Data approved by: Thomas J. Mathiesen

Filelist: 14th   File size: 32K   Annotations:

Source of data:

Scriptores ecclesiastici de musica sacra potissimum, 3 vols., ed. Martin Gerbert (St. Blaise: Typis San-Blasianis, 1784; reprint ed., Hildesheim: Olms, 1963), 3:100-117.

The graphics files for this treatise are MARLU11 01GF-MARLU11 08GF. See also files MARLU1 through MARLU10 and MARLU12 through MARLU16; and all the files of MARLUC.

Author: Marchetus de Padua

Treatise: Lucidarium, tractatus duodecimus

Incipit: Ostenso superius de tonis, quomodo per species formentur

File name: **MARLU12**   Data input by: Bradley Jon Tucker

File type: **TEXT**   Data checked by: Angela Mariani

MS: Print: **X**   Data approved by: Thomas J. Mathiesen

Filelist: 14th   File size: 5K   Annotations:

Source of data:

Scriptores ecclesiastici de musica sacra potissimum, 3 vols., ed. Martin Gerbert (St. Blaise: Typis San-Blasianis, 1784; reprint ed., Hildesheim: Olms, 1963), 3:117-19.

The graphics file for this treatise is MARLU12 01GF. See also files MARLU1 through MARLU11 and MARLU13 through MARLU16; and all the files of MARLUC.

Author: Marchetus de Padua

Treatise: Lucidarium, tractatus decimustertius

Incipit: Sequitur videre de pausis, scilicet quo modo in cantu plano

File name: **MARLU13**   Data input by: Bradley Jon Tucker

File type: **TEXT**   Data checked by: Angela Mariani

  MS: Print: **X**   Data approved by: Thomas J. Mathiesen

Filelist: 14th   File size: 2K   Annotations:

Source of data:

  Scriptores ecclesiastici de musica sacra   See also files MARLU1 through MARLU12
potissimum, 3 vols., ed. Martin Gerbert   and MARLU14 through MARLU16; and all
(St. Blaise: Typis San-Blasianis, 1784;   the files of MARLUC.
reprint ed., Hildesheim: Olms, 1963),
3:119.

Author: Marchetus de Padua

Treatise: Lucidarium, tractatus decimusquartus

Incipit: Clavis est reseratio notarum in cantu quolibet signatarum

File name: **MARLU14**   Data input by: Bradley Jon Tucker

File type: **TEXT**   Data checked by: Angela Mariani

  MS: Print: **X**   Data approved by: Thomas J. Mathiesen

Filelist: 14th   File size: 3K   Annotations:

Source of data: See also files MARLU1 through MARLU13

  Scriptores ecclesiastici de musica sacra   and MARLU15 through MARLU16; and all
potissimum, 3 vols., ed. Martin Gerbert   the files of MARLUC.
(St. Blaise: Typis San-Blasianis, 1784;
reprint ed., Hildesheim: Olms, 1963),
3:120.

Author: Marchetus de Padua

Treatise: Lucidarium, tractatus decimusquintus

Incipit: A. Proslambanosmenos, B. Hypate hypaton

File name: **MARLU15**   Data input by: Bradley Jon Tucker

File type: **TEXT**   Data checked by: Angela Mariani

  MS: Print: **X**   Data approved by: Thomas J. Mathiesen

Filelist: 14th   File size: 1K   Annotations:

Source of data: See also files MARLU1 through MARLU14

  Scriptores ecclesiastici de musica sacra   and MARLU16; and all the files of
potissimum, 3 vols., ed. Martin Gerbert   MARLUC.
(St. Blaise: Typis San-Blasianis, 1784;
reprint ed., Hildesheim: Olms, 1963),
3:120.

Author: Marchetus de Padua

Treatise: Lucidarium, tractatus decimussextus

Incipit: Musicus dicitur ille, testante Boetio, cui adest facultas

File name: **MARLU16**   Data input by: Bradley Jon Tucker

File type: **TEXT**   Data checked by: Angela Mariani

  MS: Print: **X**   Data approved by: Thomas J. Mathiesen

Filelist: 14th   File size: 2K   Annotations:

Source of data: See also files MARLU1 through MARLU15;

Scriptores ecclesiastici de musica sacra   and all the files of MARLUC.
potissimum, 3 vols., ed. Martin Gerbert
(St. Blaise: Typis San-Blasianis, 1784;
reprint ed., Hildesheim: Olms, 1963),
3:121.

Author: Marchetus de Padua

Treatise: Lucidarium, tractatus primus

Incipit: Qualiter Pytagoras adinvenit musicam memorat Macrobius

File name: **MARLUC1**   Data input by: Stephen E. Hayes

File type: **TEXT**   Data checked by: Peter M. Lefferts

  MS: Print: **X**   Data approved by: Thomas J. Mathiesen

Filelist: 14th   File size: 16K   Annotations:

Source of data: The treatise is preceded by a letter, beginning:

The Lucidarium of Marchetto of Padua: "Magnifico militi et potenti, domino suo,
A Critical Edition, Translation, and   Domino Raynerio Domini Zacharie de
Commentary, ed. and trans. by Jan W.   Urbeveteri, ..." See also files MARLUC2
Herlinger (Chicago and London: The   through MARLUC16; and all the files of
University of Chicago Press, 1985),   MARLU.
68-106. Used by permission.

Author: Marchetus de Padua

Treatise: Lucidarium, tractatus secundus

Incipit: Ad huius evidentiam est sciendum quod, secundum Remigium

File name: **MARLUC2**   Data input by: Stephen E. Hayes

File type: **TEXT**   Data checked by: Peter M. Lefferts

  MS: Print: **X**   Data approved by: Thomas J. Mathiesen

Filelist: 14th   File size: 20K   Annotations:

Source of data: The graphics file for this treatise is

The Lucidarium of Marchetto of Padua: MARLUC2 01GF. See also files MARLUC1
A Critical Edition, Translation, and   and MARLUC3 through MARLUC16; and all
Commentary, ed. and trans. by Jan W.   the files of MARLU.
Herlinger (Chicago and London: The
University of Chicago Press, 1985),
106-66. Used by permission.

Author: Marchetus de Padua

Treatise: Lucidarium, tractatus tercius

Incipit: Ad videndum autem de numeris musicalibus

File name: **MARLUC3**   Data input by: Stephen E. Hayes

File type: **TEXT**   Data checked by: Peter M. Lefferts

MS: Print: **X**   Data approved by: Thomas J. Mathiesen

Filelist: 14th   File size: 6K   Annotations:

Source of data:
The Lucidarium of Marchetto of Padua: A Critical Edition, Translation, and Commentary, ed. and trans. by Jan W. Herlinger (Chicago and London: The University of Chicago Press, 1985), 168-80. Used by permission.

See also files MARLUC1 through MARLUC2 and MARLUC4 through MARLUC16; and all the files of MARLU.

Author: Marchetus de Padua

Treatise: Lucidarium, tractatus quartus

Incipit: Proportio est quedam habitudo duorum terminorum

File name: **MARLUC4**   Data input by: Stephen E. Hayes

File type: **TEXT**   Data checked by: Peter M. Lefferts

MS: Print: **X**   Data approved by: Thomas J. Mathiesen

Filelist: 14th   File size: 6K   Annotations:

Source of data:
The Lucidarium of Marchetto of Padua: A Critical Edition, Translation, and Commentary, ed. and trans. by Jan W. Herlinger (Chicago and London: The University of Chicago Press, 1985), 182-94. Used by permission.

See also files MARLUC1 through MARLUC3 and MARLUC5 through MARLUC16; and all the files of MARLU.

Author: Marchetus de Padua

Treatise: Lucidarium, tractatus quintus

Incipit: Sequitur videre de consonantia, de qua primo videbimus

File name: **MARLUC5**   Data input by: Stephen E. Hayes

File type: **TEXT**   Data checked by: Peter M. Lefferts

MS: Print: **X**   Data approved by: Thomas J. Mathiesen

Filelist: 14th   File size: 10K   Annotations:

Source of data:
The Lucidarium of Marchetto of Padua: A Critical Edition, Translation, and Commentary, ed. and trans. by Jan W. Herlinger (Chicago and London: The University of Chicago Press, 1985), 196-222. Used by permission.

The graphics file for this treatise is MARLUC5 01GF. See also files MARLUC1 through MARLUC4 and MARLUC6 through MARLUC16; and all the files of MARLU.

Author: Marchetus de Padua

Treatise: Lucidarium, tractatus sextus

Incipit: Queritur quare una consonantia magis concordet quam altera

File name: **MARLUC6**   Data input by: Stephen E. Hayes

File type: **TEXT**   Data checked by: Peter M. Lefferts

MS: Print: **X**   Data approved by: Thomas J. Mathiesen

Filelist: 14th   File size: 12K   Annotations:

Source of data:

The Lucidarium of Marchetto of Padua: A Critical Edition, Translation, and Commentary, ed. and trans. by Jan W. Herlinger (Chicago and London: The University of Chicago Press, 1985), 224-56. Used by permission.

See also files MARLUC1 through MARLUC5 and MARLUC7 through MARLUC16; and all the files of MARLU.

Author: Marchetus de Padua

Treatise: Lucidarium, tractatus septimus

Incipit: Genera inequalitatis quinque sunt, scilicet multiplex

File name: **MARLUC7**   Data input by: Stephen E. Hayes

File type: **TEXT**   Data checked by: Peter M. Lefferts

MS: Print: **X**   Data approved by: Thomas J. Mathiesen

Filelist: 14th   File size: 6K   Annotations:

Source of data:

The Lucidarium of Marchetto of Padua: A Critical Edition, Translation, and Commentary, ed. and trans. by Jan W. Herlinger (Chicago and London: The University of Chicago Press, 1985), 256-66. Used by permission.

See also files MARLUC1 through MARLUC6 and MARLUC8 through MARLUC16; and all the files of MARLU.

Author: Marchetus de Padua

Treatise: Lucidarium, tractatus octavus

Incipit: Quoniam omnis tonus et semitonium in voce consistit

File name: **MARLUC8**   Data input by: Stephen E. Hayes

File type: **TEXT**   Data checked by: Peter M. Lefferts

MS: Print: **X**   Data approved by: Thomas J. Mathiesen

Filelist: 14th   File size: 12K   Annotations:

Source of data:

The Lucidarium of Marchetto of Padua: A Critical Edition, Translation, and Commentary, ed. and trans. by Jan W. Herlinger (Chicago and London: The University of Chicago Press, 1985), 268-306. Used by permission.

The graphics file for this treatise is MARLUC8 01GF. See also files MARLUC1 through MARLUC7 and MARLUC9 through MARLUC16; and all the files of MARLU.

Author: Marchetus de Padua

Treatise: Lucidarium, tractatus nonus

Incipit: Coniunctio in musica est dispositio sive ordinatio sonorum

File name: **MARLUC9**   Data input by: Stephen E. Hayes

File type: **TEXT**   Data checked by: Peter M. Lefferts

MS: Print: **X**   Data approved by: Thomas J. Mathiesen

Filelist: 14th   File size: 18K   Annotations:

Source of data: See also files MARLUC1 through MARLUC8
The Lucidarium of Marchetto of Padua: and MARLUC10 through MARLUC16; and
A Critical Edition, Translation, and   all the files of MARLU.
Commentary, ed. and trans. by Jan W.
Herlinger (Chicago and London: The
University of Chicago Press, 1985),
306-66. Used by permission.

Author: Marchetus de Padua

Treatise: Lucidarium, tractatus decimus

Incipit: Mensura in musica est ordo cantuum mensuratorum

File name: **MARLUC10**   Data input by: Stephen E. Hayes

File type: **TEXT**   Data checked by: Peter M. Lefferts

MS: Print: **X**   Data approved by: Thomas J. Mathiesen

Filelist: 14th   File size: 2K   Annotations:

Source of data: See also files MARLUC1 through MARLUC9
The Lucidarium of Marchetto of Padua: and MARLUC11 through MARLUC16; and
A Critical Edition, Translation, and   all the files of MARLU.
Commentary, ed. and trans. by Jan W.
Herlinger (Chicago and London: The
University of Chicago Press, 1985), 368.
Used by permission.

Author: Marchetus de Padua

Treatise: Lucidarium, tractatus undecimus

Incipit: Tonus, tropus, sive modus, secundum dicta Boetii

File name: **MARLUC11**   Data input by: Stephen E. Hayes

File type: **TEXT**   Data checked by: Peter M. Lefferts

MS: Print: **X**   Data approved by: Thomas J. Mathiesen

Filelist: 14th   File size: 36K   Annotations:

Source of data: The graphics file for this treatise is
The Lucidarium of Marchetto of Padua: MARLUC11 01GF-MARLUC11 06GF. See
A Critical Edition, Translation, and   also files MARLUC1 through MARLUC10
Commentary, ed. and trans. by Jan W.   and MARLUC12 through MARLUC16; and
Herlinger (Chicago and London: The   all the files of MARLU.
University of Chicago Press, 1985),
370-518. Used by permission.

Author: Marchetus de Padua
Treatise: Lucidarium, tractatus duodecimus
Incipit: Ostenso superius de tonis quomodo per species formentur

File name: **MARLUC12**	Data input by: Stephen E. Hayes
File type: **TEXT**	Data checked by: Peter M. Lefferts
MS: Print: **X**	Data approved by: Thomas J. Mathiesen
Filelist: 14th File size: 6K	Annotations:

Source of data:
The Lucidarium of Marchetto of Padua: A Critical Edition, Translation, and Commentary, ed. and trans. by Jan W. Herlinger (Chicago and London: The University of Chicago Press, 1985), 518-32. Used by permission.

Annotations:
The graphics file for this treatise is MARLUC12 01GF. See also files MARLUC1 through MARLUC11 and MARLUC13 through MARLUC16; and all the files of MARLU.

Author: Marchetus de Padua
Treatise: Lucidarium, tractatus tercius decimus
Incipit: Sequitur videre de pausis, scilicet quomodo in cantu plano

File name: **MARLUC13**	Data input by: Stephen E. Hayes
File type: **TEXT**	Data checked by: Peter M. Lefferts
MS: Print: **X**	Data approved by: Thomas J. Mathiesen
Filelist: 14th File size: 4K	Annotations:

Source of data:
The Lucidarium of Marchetto of Padua: A Critical Edition, Translation, and Commentary, ed. and trans. by Jan W. Herlinger (Chicago and London: The University of Chicago Press, 1985), 534-38. Used by permission.

Annotations:
See also files MARLUC1 through MARLUC12 and MARLUC14 through MARLUC16; and all the files of MARLU.

Author: Marchetus de Padua
Treatise: Lucidarium, tractatus quartus decimus
Incipit: Clavis est reseratio notarum in cantu quolibet signatarum

File name: **MARLUC14**	Data input by: Stephen E. Hayes
File type: **TEXT**	Data checked by: Peter M. Lefferts
MS: Print: **X**	Data approved by: Thomas J. Mathiesen
Filelist: 14th File size: 4K	Annotations:

Source of data:
The Lucidarium of Marchetto of Padua: A Critical Edition, Translation, and Commentary, ed. and trans. by Jan W. Herlinger (Chicago and London: The University of Chicago Press, 1985), 538-42. Used by permission.

Annotations:
See also files MARLUC1 through MARLUC13 and MARLUC15 through MARLUC16; and all the files of MARLU.

Author: Marchetus de Padua

Treatise: Lucidarium, tractatus quintus decimus

Incipit: A. Proslambanosmenos, [sqb]. Ypate ypaton

File name: **MARLUC15**   Data input by: Stephen E. Hayes

File type: **TEXT**   Data checked by: Peter M. Lefferts

MS: Print: **X**   Data approved by: Thomas J. Mathiesen

Filelist: 14th   File size: 2K   Annotations:

Source of data:

The Lucidarium of Marchetto of Padua: A Critical Edition, Translation, and Commentary, ed. and trans. by Jan W. Herlinger (Chicago and London: The University of Chicago Press, 1985), 544-46. Used by permission.

See also files MARLUC1 through MARLUC14 and MARLUC16; and all the files of MARLU.

Author: Marchetus de Padua

Treatise: Lucidarium, tractatus sextus decimus

Incipit: Musicus dicitur ille, testante Boetio, cui adest facultas

File name: **MARLUC16**   Data input by: Stephen E. Hayes

File type: **TEXT**   Data checked by: Peter M. Lefferts

MS: Print: **X**   Data approved by: Thomas J. Mathiesen

Filelist: 14th   File size: 2K   Annotations:

Source of data:

The Lucidarium of Marchetto of Padua: A Critical Edition, Translation, and Commentary, ed. and trans. by Jan W. Herlinger (Chicago and London: The University of Chicago Press, 1985), 546-50. Used by permission.

See also files MARLUC1 through MARLUC15; and all the files of MARLU.

Author: Marchetus de Padua

Treatise: Pomerium

Incipit: Quoniam dicente philosopho inde omnia accidentia multum conferunt

File name: **MARPOM**   Data input by: Bradley Jon Tucker

File type: **TEXT**   Data checked by: Angela Mariani

MS: Print: **X**   Data approved by: Thomas J. Mathiesen

Filelist: 14th   File size: 185K   Annotations:

Source of data:

Scriptores ecclesiastici de musica sacra potissimum, 3 vols., ed. Martin Gerbert (St. Blaise: Typis San-Blasianis, 1784; reprint ed., Hildesheim: Olms, 1963), 3:121-88.

The graphics file for this treatise is MARPOM 01GF. A long introduction precedes the treatise proper, beginning: "Analysis operis, prout in dicto codice eidem praeponitur. Quatuor sunt causae ...." Then, a dedicatory letter follows, beginning: "Praeclarissimo Principum domino Roberto Dei gratia Ierusalem et Siciliae Regi Marchetus de Padua ...." Cf. MARPOME TEXT.

THESAURUS MUSICARUM LATINARUM: Canon of Data Files

Author: Marchetus de Padua

Treatise: Pomerium

Incipit: Quoniam, dicente Philosopho in prooemio de Anima, accidentia multum conferunt

File name: **MARPOME**   Data input by: John Gray

File type: **TEXT**   Data checked by: Oliver Ellsworth & Bradley Tucker

MS: Print: **X**   Data approved by: Thomas J. Mathiesen

Filelist: 14th   File size: 193K   Annotations:

Source of data:
Marcheti de Padua Pomerium, ed. Ioseph Vecchi, Corpus scriptorum de musica, vol. 6 ([Rome]: American Institute of Musicology, 1961), 31-210. Used by permission.

A long introduction precedes the treatise proper, beginning: "Frimae partis primi libri divisiones praemittuntur. Quattuor sunt causae ...." Then, a dedicatory letter follows, beginning: "Praeclarissimo principum, domino Roberto, Dei gratia Jerusalem et Siciliae regi, Marchetus de Padua . .." The graphics files for this treatise are MARPOME 01GF-MARPOME 02GF. Cf. MARPOM TEXT.

Author: Marchetus de Padua, Ciconia, and Anonymous

Treatise: Lucidarium, Regulae de tonis, Tractatus figurarum, and Nova musica

Incipit: [See annotations below]

File name: **LAFVAR**   Data input by: John Csonka

File type: **TEXT**   Data checked by: Angela Mariani

MS: Print: **X**   Data approved by: Thomas J. Mathiesen

Filelist: 15th   File size: 5K   Annotations:

Source of data:
Adrien de la Fage, Essais de dipthérographie musicale (Paris: Legouix, 1864), 385-88.

Based on Pisa, Biblioteca universitaria, IV,9. La Fage prints short excerpts beginning as follows: "Incipit quidam extractus. Marchetti de Padua de Tonis. Divna auxiliante gratia, breve tractatum compilare intendo de arte musicali plana" (385); "Quaedam regulae de tonis secundum illorum de Francia" (386); "Incipit Tractatus figurarum per quas diversimode [fit] discanus per aliquas non sequentes modum tenoris" (386); "De proportionibus. Venerabili viro et egregio domino presbytero Johanni Gasparo canonico Vicentino" (387); "Auctores diversi. Sunt precipue magister francho de colonia prothonotarius Johannes de Muris et Marchettus de Padua" (337); and "Quoniam de canendi scientia doctrinam sumus facturi" (388).

Author: Martianus Capella

Treatise: De nuptiis Philologiae et Mercurii, Liber IX, De harmonia

Incipit: Iam facibus lassos spectans marcentibus ignes instaurare iubet tunc hymenea Venus

File name: **MARDEN9**   Data input by: Bradley Tucker

File type: **TEXT**   Data checked by: Angela Mariani

MS: Print: **X**   Data approved by: Thomas J. Mathiesen

Filelist: 4th-5th   File size: 63K   Annotations:

Source of data:
Martianus Capella, ed. Adolfus Dick (Leipzig: B. G. Teubner, 1925), 469-535.

Cf. MARDNP9 TEXT.

Author: Martianus Capella
Treatise: De nuptiis Philologiae et Mercurii, Liber IX, De musica
Incipit: Iam facibus lassos spectans marcentibus ignes instaurare jubet. tunc hymenea Venus;

File name: **MARDNP9**   Data input by: Stephen E. Hayes
File type: **TEXT**   Data checked by: Peter Lefferts & Angela Mariani
MS: Print: **X**   Data approved by: Thomas J. Mathiesen
Filelist: 4th-5th   File size: 64K   Annotations:
Source of data: Cf. MARDEN9 TEXT.
  Antiquae musicae auctores septem.
  Graece et Latine, Marcus Meibomius
  restituit ac notis explicavit, 2 vols.
  (Amstelodami, apud Ludovicum
  Elzevirium, 1652), 2:165-98.

Author: Monachus Carthusiensis
Treatise: Tractatus de musica plana
Incipit: Etsi multi musici his tribus vocabulis: tropus, modus et tonus, quasi sinonimis

File name: **CARTRA**   Data input by: Stephen E. Hayes
File type: **TEXT**   Data checked by: Peter Lefferts & Angela Mariani
MS: Print: **X**   Data approved by: Thomas J. Mathiesen
Filelist: 15th   File size: 130K   Annotations:
Source of data: The ascription of authorship to "A Certain
  Scriptorum de musica medii aevi nova   Carthusian Monk" is Coussemaker's. The text
  series a Gerbertina altera, 4 vols., ed.   is based on Gent, Universiteitsbibliotheek 70
  Edmond de Coussemaker (Paris: Durand,   (71). The graphics files for this treatise are
  1864-76; reprint ed., Hildesheim: Olms,   CARTRA 01GF-CARTRA 20GF.
  1963), 2:434-83.

Author: Nicetius, episcopus
Treatise: De laude et utilitate spiritualium canticorum, quae fiunt in ecclesia Christiana; seu de
Incipit: Dicamus, quae nobis Deus donare dignatur, quando fit grata et acceptabilis Deo

File name: **NICLAU**   Data input by: Stephen E. Hayes
File type: **TEXT**   Data checked by: Peter Lefferts & Angela Mariani
MS: Print: **X**   Data approved by: Thomas J. Mathiesen
Filelist: 6th-8th   File size: 13K   Annotations:
Source of data:
  Scriptores ecclesiastici de musica sacra
  potissimum, 3 vols., ed. Martin Gerbert
  (St. Blaise: Typis San-Blasianis, 1784;
  reprint ed., Hildesheim: Olms, 1963),
  1:9-14.

Author: Nicolaus de Senis
Treatise: Tractatus de musica
Incipit: Notandum primo, quod quatuor sunt uoces supra tenorem consonantiam facientes

File name: **NICTRA**   Data input by: Stephen E. Hayes
File type: **TEXT**   Data checked by: Peter Lefferts & Luminita Aluas
  MS: Print: **X**   Data approved by: Thomas J. Mathiesen
Filelist: 15th   File size: 5K   Annotations:

Source of data:
Higini Angles, "Dos tractats medievals de musica figurada," in Musikwissenschaftliche Beiträge: Festschrift für Johannes Wolf zu seinem sechzigsten Geburtstag, ed. W. Lott, H. Osthoff, and W. Wolffheim (Berlin: Breslauer, 1929), 10-12.

Sometimes known as Angles Anonymous 1929; based on Sevilla, Biblioteca Capitular y Colombina 5.II.25 [in Catedral metropolitana]. The graphics file for this treatise is NICTRA 01GF.

Author: Notker
Treatise: [De musica]
Incipit: Quid singulae litterae in superscriptione significent cantilenae

File name: **NOTDEMU**   Data input by: John Gray
File type: **TEXT**   Data checked by: Oliver Ellsworth & Andreas Giger
  MS: Print: **X**   Data approved by: Thomas J. Mathiesen
Filelist: 9th-11th File size: 12K   Annotations:

Source of data:
Patrologia cursus completus, series latina, ed. J. P. Migne, 221 vols. (Paris: Garnier, 1844-1904), 131:1171-78.

The incipit is preceded by the salutation "Notker Lamberto fratri salutem." Beginning with the heading "De octo tonis," the odd-numbered columns provide the text in Althochdeutsch, with the even-numbered columns providing the "Latin interpretation." Only the even-numbered columns have been included from that point to the end of this file. Cf. NOTDEM TEXT.

Author: Notker
Treatise: De musica
Incipit: Quid singulae litterae in superscriptione significent cantilenae

File name: **NOTDEM**   Data input by: Stephen E. Hayes
File type: **TEXT**   Data checked by: Peter M. Lefferts
  MS: Print: **X**   Data approved by: Thomas J. Mathiesen
Filelist: 9th-11th File size: 11K   Annotations:

Source of data:
Scriptores ecclesiastici de musica sacra potissimum, 3 vols., ed. Martin Gerbert (St. Blaise: Typis San-Blasianis, 1784; reprint ed., Hildesheim: Olms, 1963), 1:95-102.

The incipit is preceded by the salutation "Notker Lamberto fratri salutem." Cf. NOTDEMU TEXT.

THESAURUS MUSICARUM LATINARUM: Canon of Data Files

Author: Odington, Walter

Treatise: De speculatione musice

Incipit: Plura quam digna de musice speculatione et musice speculatoribus perutilia brevi

File name: **ODIDES**   Data input by: John Snyder

File type: **TEXT**   Data checked by: Luminita Aluas

  MS: Print: **X**   Data approved by: Thomas J. Mathiesen

Filelist: 14th   File size: 149K   Annotations:

Source of data: The graphics files for this treatise are ODIDES
  Scriptorum de musica medii aevi nova   01GF-ODIDES 36GF. See also ODISUM.
  series a Gerbertina altera, 4 vols., ed.
  Edmond de Coussemaker (Paris: Durand,
  1864-76; reprint ed., Hildesheim: Olms,
  1963), 1:182-250.

Author: Odington, Walter

Treatise: Summa de speculatione musice

Incipit: Plura quam digna de musicae speculatione et musicae speculatoribus perutilia brevi

File name: **ODISUM**   Data input by: Stephen E. Hayes

File type: **TEXT**   Data checked by: Peter Lefferts & Bradley Tucker

  MS: Print: **X**   Data approved by: Thomas J. Mathiesen

Filelist: 14th   File size: 149K   Annotations:

Source of data: The graphics files for this treatise are
  Walteri Odington, Summa de   ODISUM 01GF-ODISUM 42GF. See also
  speculatione musicae, ed. Frederick F.   ODIDES.
  Hammond, Corpus scriptorum de musica,
  vol. 14 ([Rome]: American Institute of
  Musicology, 1970), 42-146. Used by
  permission.

Author: Odo

Treatise: De musica

Incipit: Musicae artis disciplina summo studio appetenda est, et maxime his, qui communi

File name: **ODOMUS**   Data input by: Stephen E. Hayes

File type: **TEXT**   Data checked by: Peter Lefferts & Bradley Tucker

  MS: Print: **X**   Data approved by: Thomas J. Mathiesen

Filelist: 9th-11th File size: 49K   Annotations:

Source of data: The graphics files for this treatise are
  Scriptores ecclesiastici de musica sacra   ODOMUS 01GF-ODOMUS 05GF. See also
  potissimum, 3 vols., ed. Martin Gerbert   ODOMU.
  (St. Blaise: Typis San-Blasianis, 1784;
  reprint ed., Hildesheim: Olms, 1963),
  1:265-84.

Author: Odo

Treatise: De musica

Incipit: Musicae artis disciplina summo studio appetenda est, et maxime his qui communi

File name: **ODOMU**   Data input by: Stephen E. Hayes

File type: **TEXT**   Data checked by: Peter Lefferts & Peter Slemon

  MS: Print: **X**   Data approved by: Thomas J. Mathiesen

Filelist: 9th-11th File size: 52K   Annotations:

Source of data: See also ODOMUS. The graphics files for this
  Patrologia cursus completus, series latina,   treatise are ODOMU 01GF-ODOMU 07GF.
  ed. J. P. Migne, 221 vols. (Paris: Garnier,
  1844-1904), 133:773-96.

Author: Odo

Treatise: Dialogus de musica

Incipit: Petistis obnixe, Carissimi Fratres! quatenus paucas vobis de Musica regulas traderem

File name: **ODODIA**   Data input by: Stephen E. Hayes

File type: **TEXT**   Data checked by: Peter Lefferts & Angela Mariani

  MS: Print: **X**   Data approved by: Thomas J. Mathiesen

Filelist: 9th-11th File size: 37K   Annotations:

Source of data: The graphics file for this treatise is ODODIA
  Scriptores ecclesiastici de musica sacra   01GF. See also ODODI.
  potissimum, 3 vols., ed. Martin Gerbert
  (St. Blaise: Typis San-Blasianis, 1784;
  reprint ed., Hildesheim: Olms, 1963),
  1:251-64.

Author: Odo

Treatise: Dialogus de musica

Incipit: Petistis obnixe, charissimi fratres, quatenus paucas vobis de Musica regulas traderem

File name: **ODODI**   Data input by: Stephen E. Hayes

File type: **TEXT**   Data checked by: Peter Slemon

  MS: Print: **X**   Data approved by: Thomas J. Mathiesen

Filelist: 9th-11th File size: 37K   Annotations:

Source of data: The graphics file for this treatise is ODODI
  Patrologia cursus completus, series latina,   01GF. See also ODODIA.
  ed. J. P. Migne, 221 vols. (Paris: Garnier,
  1844-1904), 133:757-74.

Author: Odo

Treatise: Intonarium

Incipit: Incipit intonarium a Domno Octone abbate diligenter examinatum et ordinatum

File name: **ODOINT**   Data input by: Firoozeh Khazrai

File type: **TEXT**   Data checked by: Angela Mariani & Bradley Tucker

  MS: Print: **X**   Data approved by: Thomas J. Mathiesen

Filelist: 9th-11th File size: 35K   Annotations:

Source of data: The graphics files for this treatise are
  Scriptorum de musica medii aevi nova   ODOINT 01GF-ODOINT 30GF.
  series a Gerbertina altera, 4 vols., ed.
  Edmond de Coussemaker (Paris: Durand,
  1864-76; reprint ed., Hildesheim: Olms,
  1963), 2:117-49.

Author: Odo

Treatise: Quomodo organistrum construatur

Incipit: In primis a capite iuxta primum plectrum, infra usque ad aliud plectrum

File name: **ODOORG** Data input by: Stephen E. Hayes

File type: **TEXT** Data checked by: Peter Lefferts & Bradley Tucker

MS: Print: **X** Data approved by: Thomas J. Mathiesen

Filelist: 9th-11th File size: 2K Annotations:

Source of data: See also ODOOR.
  Scriptores ecclesiastici de musica sacra
  potissimum, 3 vols., ed. Martin Gerbert
  (St. Blaise: Typis San-Blasianis, 1784;
  reprint ed., Hildesheim: Olms, 1963),
  1:303.

Author: Odo

Treatise: Quomodo organistrum construatur

Incipit: In primis a capite juxta primum plectrum, infra usque ad aliud plectrum

File name: **ODOOR** Data input by: Stephen E. Hayes

File type: **TEXT** Data checked by: Peter Lefferts & Peter Slemon

MS: Print: **X** Data approved by: Thomas J. Mathiesen

Filelist: 9th-11th File size: 2K Annotations:

Source of data: See also ODOORG.
  Patrologia cursus completus, series latina,
  ed. J. P. Migne, 221 vols. (Paris: Garnier,
  1844-1904), 133:815-16.

Author: Odo

Treatise: Regulae de rhythmimachia

Incipit: Sesquialtera proportio est, quando numerus maior continet in se totum numerum

File name: **ODORHY** Data input by: Stephen E. Hayes

File type: **TEXT** Data checked by: Peter Lefferts & Angela Mariani

MS: Print: **X** Data approved by: Thomas J. Mathiesen

Filelist: 9th-11th File size: 28K Annotations:

Source of data: The graphics files for this treatise are
  Scriptores ecclesiastici de musica sacra ODORHY 01GF-ODORHY 03GF. Cf.
  potissimum, 3 vols., ed. Martin Gerbert ODORH TEXT.
  (St. Blaise: Typis San-Blasianis, 1784;
  reprint ed., Hildesheim: Olms, 1963),
  1:285-95.

Author: Odo

Treatise: Regulae de rhythmimachia

Incipit: Sesquialtera proportio est, quando numerus major continet in se totum numerum

File name: **ODORH** Data input by: Stephen E. Hayes

File type: **TEXT** Data checked by: Peter Lefferts & Bradley Tucker

MS: Print: **X** Data approved by: Thomas J. Mathiesen

Filelist: 9th-11th File size: 28K Annotations:

Source of data: The graphics files for this treatise are ODORH
  Patrologia cursus completus, series latina, 01GF-ODORH 03GF. Cf. ODORHY TEXT.
  ed. J. P. Migne, 221 vols. (Paris: Garnier,
  1844-1904), 133:795-808.

Author: Odo

Treatise: Regulae super abacum

Incipit: Si quis notitiam abaci habere desiderat, necesse est, ut in consideratione numeri

File name: **ODOREG** Data input by: Stephen E. Hayes

File type: **TEXT** Data checked by: Peter Lefferts & Angela Mariani

 MS: Print: **X** Data approved by: Thomas J. Mathiesen

Filelist: 9th-11th File size: 20K Annotations:

Source of data: See also ODORE.
 Scriptores ecclesiastici de musica sacra
 potissimum, 3 vols., ed. Martin Gerbert
 (St. Blaise: Typis San-Blasianis, 1784;
 reprint ed., Hildesheim: Olms, 1963),
 1:296-302.

Author: Odo

Treatise: Regulae super abacum

Incipit: Si quis notitiam abaci habere desiderat, necesse est ut in consideratione numeri

File name: **ODORE** Data input by: Stephen E. Hayes

File type: **TEXT** Data checked by: Peter Lefferts & Peter Slemon

 MS: Print: **X** Data approved by: Thomas J. Mathiesen

Filelist: 9th-11th File size: 20K Annotations:

Source of data: See also ODOREG.
 Patrologia cursus completus, series latina,
 ed. J. P. Migne, 221 vols. (Paris: Garnier,
 1844-1904), 133:807-14.

Author: Odo

Treatise: Tonarium

Incipit: Incipit formula super tonos, qualiter unusquisque cantor in Ecclesia agere debeat.

File name: **ODOTON** Data input by: Stephen E. Hayes

File type: **TEXT** Data checked by: Peter Lefferts & Angela Mariani

 MS: Print: **X** Data approved by: Thomas J. Mathiesen

Filelist: 9th-11th File size: 8K Annotations:

Source of data: See also ODOTO.
 Scriptores ecclesiastici de musica sacra
 potissimum, 3 vols., ed. Martin Gerbert
 (St. Blaise: Typis San-Blasianis, 1784;
 reprint ed., Hildesheim: Olms, 1963),
 1:247-50.

Author: Odo

Treatise: Tonarium

Incipit: Incipit formula super tonos, qualiter unusquisque cantor in ecclesia agere debeat.

File name: **ODOTO** Data input by: Stephen E. Hayes

File type: **TEXT** Data checked by: Peter Lefferts & Peter Slemon

 MS: Print: **X** Data approved by: Thomas J. Mathiesen

Filelist: 9th-11th File size: 8K Annotations:

Source of data: See also ODOTON.
 Patrologia cursus completus, series latina,
 ed. J. P. Migne, 221 vols. (Paris: Garnier,
 1844-1904), 133:755-58.

Author: Odorannus de Sens

Treatise: Liber opusculorum, capitula V-VI

Incipit: Dimidiae parti animae suae fratri et consacerdoti Rotberto, peccatis maximis

File name: **ODOSENS**   Data input by: Andreas Giger

File type: **TEXT**   Data checked by: Elisabeth Honn

MS: Print: **X**   Data approved by: Thomas J. Mathiesen

Filelist: 9th-11th File size: 39K   Annotations:

Source of data:

Odorannus de Sens, Opera omnia: Textes édités, traduits et annotés par Robert-Henri Bautier et Monique Gilles, et, pour la partie musicologique, par Marie-Elisabeth Duchez et Michel Huglo (Paris: Centre national de la recherche scientifique, 1972), 150-225. Used by permission.

Based on Rome, Biblioteca Apostolica Vaticana, Reginensis lat. 577. The graphics files for this treatise are ODOSENS 01GF-ODOSENS 48GF.

Author: Osbernus Cantuariensis (?)

Treatise: De vocum consonantiis

Incipit: Ars est iam utillima, a philosophis composita, ars est vocata Musica

File name: **OSBMUS**   Data input by: Andreas Giger

File type: **TEXT**   Data checked by: Elisabeth Honn

MS: Print: **X**   Data approved by: Thomas J. Mathiesen

Filelist: 9th-11th File size: 29K   Annotations:

Source of data:

Codex Oxoniensis Bibl. Bodl. Rawl. C 270: Pars A, "De vocum consonantiis" ac "De re musica" (Osberni Cantuariensis?), ed. Joseph Smits van Waesberghe, Divitiae musicae artis, A/Xa (Buren: Knuf, 1979), 14-38. Used by kind permission of the Laaber-Verlag.

Based on Oxford, Bodleian Library, Rawl. C 270, ff. 1r-9v; and Rome, Biblioteca Apostolica Vaticana, Reg. lat. 1146, ff. 9v-16v. The graphics files for this treatise are OSBMUS 01GF-OSBMUS 03GF.

Author: Pambo, Abbas

Treatise: [Gerontikon]

Incipit: Abbas Pambo misit discipulum suum in Alexandriam, ut eorum manufacta venderet.

File name: **PAMGER**   Data input by: Stephen E. Hayes

File type: **TEXT**   Data checked by: Peter Lefferts & Angela Mariani

MS: Print: **X**   Data approved by: Thomas J. Mathiesen

Filelist: 6th-8th   File size: 3K   Annotations:

Source of data:

Scriptores ecclesiastici de musica sacra potissimum, 3 vols., ed. Martin Gerbert (St. Blaise: Typis San-Blasianis, 1784; reprint ed., Hildesheim: Olms, 1963), 1:1-4.

Author: Paulirinus, Paulus

Treatise: Tractatus de musica

Incipit: Mutetus est cantus mensuralis per triplum vadens in quo discantus habet textum

File name: **PAUTRA**

File type: **TEXT**

MS: Print: **X**

Filelist: 15th File size: 11K

Data input by: Stephen E. Hayes

Data checked by: Peter Lefferts & Angela Mariani

Data approved by: Thomas J. Mathiesen

Annotations:

Source of data:

Josef Reiss, "Pauli Paulirini de Praga Tractatus de musica (etwa 1460)," Zeitschrift für Musikwissenschaft 7 (1924-25): 261-64.

The treatise is preserved in Codex 257 of the Jagellonian Library in Cracow. Only excerpts from Parts 2 and 3 of Paulirinus's Tractatus are included in this article.

Author: Perseus and Petrus

Treatise: Summa musice

Incipit: Amicorum iusta et honesta petitio coactio reputatur. Hac itaque me stimulante

File name: **PEPESUM**

File type: **TEXT**

MS: Print: **X**

Filelist: 13th File size: 143K

Data input by: Andreas Giger

Data checked by: Elisabeth Honn

Data approved by: Thomas J. Mathiesen

Annotations:

Source of data:

The Summa Musice: A Thirteenth-Century Manual for Singers, ed. Christopher Page, Cambridge Musical Texts and Monographs (Cambridge: Cambridge University Press, 1991), 139-211. Used by permission.

The graphics file for this treatise is PEPESUM 01GF. Cf. MURSUM TEXT.

Author: Person, Gobelinus

Treatise: Tractatus musicae scientiae

Incipit: Quamvis inter artes liberales musica sit digne numerata, ipsa tamen quorundam

File name: **PERTRA**

File type: **TEXT**

MS: Print: **X**

Filelist: 15th File size: 65K

Data input by: Peter Slemon

Data checked by: Sandra Pinegar

Data approved by: Thomas J. Mathiesen

Annotations:

Source of data:

Hermann Müller, "Der tractatus musicae scientiae des Gobelinus Person," Kirchenmusikalisches Jahrbuch 20 (1907): 180-96.

Author: Petrus de Cruce Ambianensis
Treatise: Tractatus de tonis
Incipit: Dicturi de tonis: primo videndum est quid sit tonus et unde dicatur.

File name: **PETTRA**   Data input by: Bradley Jon Tucker
File type: **TEXT**   Data checked by: Thomas J. Mathiesen
MS: Print: **X**   Data approved by: Oliver B. Ellsworth
Filelist: 13th   File size: 10K   Annotations:

Source of data: The graphics files for this treatise are
Scriptorum de musica medii aevi nova   PETTRA 01GF-PETTRA 10GF. Cf.
series a Gerbertina altera, 4 vols., ed. PETTRAC TEXT.
Edmond de Coussemaker (Paris: Durand,
1864-76; reprint ed., Hildesheim: Olms,
1963), 1:282-92.

Author: Petrus de Cruce Ambianensis
Treatise: Tractatus de tonis
Incipit: Dicturi de tonis, primo videndum est quid sit tonus et unde dicatur.

File name: **PETTRAC**   Data input by: Peter Slemon
File type: **TEXT**   Data checked by: Angela Mariani
MS: Print: **X**   Data approved by: Thomas J. Mathiesen
Filelist: 13th   File size: 10K   Annotations:

Source of data: The graphics files for this treatise are
Petrus de Cruce Ambianensi Tractatus de PETTRAC 01GF-PETTRAC 17GF. Cf.
tonis, ed. Denis Harbison, Corpus   PETTRA TEXT.
scriptorum de musica, vol. 29 (n.p.:
American Institute of Musicology, 1976),
vi-xxv. Used by permission.

Author: Petrus de Sancto Dionysio
Treatise: Tractatus de Musica
Incipit: Incipit tractatus fratris Petri de Sancto Dionysio, qui est in duas partes divisus

File name: **PSDTRA**   Data input by: Stephen E. Hayes
File type: **TEXT**   Data checked by: Peter Lefferts & Bradley Tucker
MS: Print: **X**   Data approved by: Thomas J. Mathiesen
Filelist: 14th   File size: 19K   Annotations:

Source of data: A glossed version of MURNOT. The editor
Johannis de Muris Notitia artis musicae et   has provided only the additions of Petrus, with
Compendium musicae practicae; Petrus   parenthetical references (referring to book,
de Sancto Dionysio Tractatus de musica, chapter and sentence numbers) to orient the
ed. Ulrich Michels, Corpus scriptorum de reader to the appropriate sections of the de
musica, vol. 17 ([Rome]: American   Muris Notitia artis musicae as edited in CSM,
Institute of Musicology, 1972), 147-59. vol 17. The graphics files for this treatise are
Used by permission.   PSDTRA 01GF-PSDTRA 02GF.

Author: Petrus dictus Palma ociosa

Treatise: Compendium de discantu mensurabili

Incipit: Ad honorem Sanctae et Individuae Trinitatis et intemeratae viriginis Mariae

File name: **PETCOM**　　Data input by: Stephen E. Hayes

File type: **TEXT**　　　Data checked by: Peter Lefferts & Luminita Aluas

　MS:　　Print: **X**　　Data approved by: Thomas J. Mathiesen

Filelist: 14th　　File size: 37K　　Annotations:

Source of data:　　　　　　　　The graphics files for this treatise are
Johannes Wolf, "Ein Beitrag zur　　PETCOM 01GF-PETCOM 19GF.
Diskantlehre des 14. Jahrhunderts,"
Sammelbände der Internationalen
Musikgesellschaft 15 (1913-14): 505-34.

Author: Petrus Picardus

Treatise: Ars motettorum compilata breviter

Incipit: Quoniam nonnulli, maxime novi auditores, compendiosa brevitate letantur

File name: **PETARS**　　Data input by: Stephen E. Hayes

File type: **TEXT**　　　Data checked by: Peter Lefferts & Bradley Tucker

　MS:　　Print: **X**　　Data approved by: Thomas J. Mathiesen

Filelist: 13th　　File size: 12K　　Annotations:

Source of data:　　　　　　　　The graphics files for this treatise are
Petrus Picardus, Ars motettorum　　PETARS 01GF-PETARS 03GF. See also
compilata breviter, ed. F. Alberto Gallo;　PETMUS, PETMUSM, and PETMM
Anonymus, Ars musicae mensurabilis　MPBN1666.
secundum Franconem (Mss. Paris, Bibl.
Nat., lat. 15129; Uppsala,
Universiteitsbibl., C 55), ed. Gilbert
Reaney and André Gilles; Anonymus,
Compendium musicae mensurabilis artis
antiquae (Ms. Faenza, Biblioteca
Comunale 117), ed. F. Alberto Gallo,
Corpus scriptorum de musica, vol. 15
([Rome]: American Institute of
Musicology, 1971), 16-24. Used by
permission.

Author: Petrus Picardus

Treatise: Musica mensurabilis

Incipit: Quoniam non nulli maxime noui auditores compendiosa breuitate letantur

File name: **PETMM**　　Data input by: Sandra Pinegar

File type: **MPBN1666**　　Data checked by: Michael W. Lundell

　MS: **X**　　Print:　　Data approved by: Thomas J. Mathiesen

Filelist: 13th　　File size: 8K　　Annotations:

Source of data:　　　　　　　　=RISM BIII/1:124. The incipit is preceded by
Paris, Bibliothèque nationale, lat. 16663,　the introductory text: "Que quidem quasi
ff. 83r-84v.　　　　　　　　　epilogando sed abreuiando Petrus Picardus
　　　　　　　　　　　　　　　scribens ait." Cf. PETARS TEXT, PETMUS
　　　　　　　　　　　　　　　TEXT, and PETMUSM TEXT.

Author: Petrus Picardus

Treatise: Musica mensurabilis

Incipit: Quoniam nonnulli maxime novi auditores compendiosa brevitate letantur

File name: **PETMUS**	Data input by: Bradley Jon Tucker
File type: **TEXT**	Data checked by: Thomas J. Mathiesen
MS: Print: **X**	Data approved by: Albert C. Rotola, S.J.

Filelist: 13th   File size: 7K   Annotations:

Source of data: See also PETARS, PETMUSM, and PETMM
 Scriptorum de musica medii aevi nova   MPBN1666.
 series a Gerbertina altera, 4 vols., ed.
 Edmond de Coussemaker (Paris: Durand,
 1864-76; reprint ed., Hildesheim: Olms,
 1963), 1:136-39.

Author: Petrus Picardus

Treatise: Musica mensurabilis

Incipit: Quoniam nonnulli, maxime novi auditores, compendiosa brevitate laetantur

File name: **PETMUSM**	Data input by: Stephen E. Hayes
File type: **TEXT**	Data checked by: Peter M. Lefferts & Kirk Ditzler
MS: Print: **X**	Data approved by: Thomas J. Mathiesen

Filelist: 13th   File size: 7K   Annotations:

Source of data: See also PETARS, PETMUS, and PETMM
 Hieronymus de Moravia, Tractatus de   MPBN1666.
 musica, ed. S. M. Cserba, Freiburger
 Studien zur Musikwissenschaft, vol. 2
 (Regensburg: Pustet, 1935), 259-63.

Author: Philippe de Vitry

Treatise: Ars contrapunctus

Incipit: Volentibus introduci in artem contrapuncti

File name: **VITARSC**	Data input by: C. Matthew Balensuela
File type: **TEXT**	Data checked by: Oliver B. Ellsworth
MS: Print: **X**	Data approved by: Thomas J. Mathiesen

Filelist: 14th   File size: 14K   Annotations:

Source of data: Although the treatise is "secundum Philippum
 Scriptorum de musica medii aevi nova   de Vitriaco," de Vitry is no longer generally
 series a Gerbertina altera, 4 vols., ed. considered to be the author. The graphics file
 Edmond de Coussemaker (Paris: Durand,   for this treatise is VITARSC 01GF.
 1864-76; reprint ed., Hildesheim: Olms,
 1963), 3:23-27.

Author: Philippe de Vitry

Treatise: Ars nova

Incipit: Musice tria sunt genera Mundanum humanum et instrumentalem

File name: **VITANV**	Data input by: John Gray
File type: **MBAVB307**	Data checked by: Oliver Ellsworth & M. W. Lundell
MS: **X** Print:	Data approved by: Thomas J. Mathiesen

Filelist: 14th   File size: 29K   Annotations:

Source of data: =RISM BIII/2:102-4. The graphics files for
 Rome, Biblioteca Apostolica Vaticana,   this treatise are VITANV 01GF-VITANV
 Barberini lat. 307, ff. 17r-20v.   02GF. Cf. VITARSN TEXT, VITARN TEXT,
                                          and VITARNO TEXT.

Author: Philippe de Vitry

Treatise: Ars nova

Incipit: Musice tria sunt genera: mundanum, humanum, et instrumentale

File name: **VITARSN**   Data input by: C. Matthew Balensuela

File type: **TEXT**   Data checked by: Oliver B. Ellsworth

MS: Print: **X**   Data approved by: Thomas J. Mathiesen

Filelist: 14th   File size: 28K   Annotations:

Source of data: The graphics file for this treatise is VITARSN
Scriptorum de musica medii aevi nova   01GF. Cf. VITANV MBAVB307, VITARNO
series a Gerbertina altera, 4 vols., ed.   TEXT, and VITARN TEXT.
Edmond de Coussemaker (Paris: Durand,
1864-76; reprint ed., Hildesheim: Olms,
1963), 3:13-22.

Author: Philippe de Vitry

Treatise: Ars nova

Incipit: Musicae tria sunt genera: mundanum, humanum et instrumentale

File name: **VITARNO**   Data input by: Stephen E. Hayes

File type: **TEXT**   Data checked by: Peter Lefferts & Luminita Aluas

MS: Print: **X**   Data approved by: Thomas J. Mathiesen

Filelist: 14th   File size: 30K   Annotations:

Source of data: The graphics file for this treatise is VITARNO
Philippi de Vitriaco Ars nova, ed. Gilbert   01GF. Cf. VITANV MBAVB307, VITARSN
Reaney, André Gilles, and Jean Maillard,   TEXT, and VITARN TEXT.
Corpus scriptorum de musica, vol. 8
([Rome]: American Institute of
Musicology, 1964), 13-31. Used by
permission.

Author: Philippe de Vitry

Treatise: Ars nova

Incipit: Musicae tria sunt genera: mundanum, humanum et instrumentale

File name: **VITARN**   Data input by: Stephen E. Hayes

File type: **TEXT**   Data checked by: Hannah Jo Smith & Andreas Giger

MS: Print: **X**   Data approved by: Thomas J. Mathiesen

Filelist: 14th   File size: 32K   Annotations:

Source of data: The graphics file for this treatise is VITARN
Gilbert Reaney, André Gilles, and Jean   01GF. Cf. VITANV MBAVB307, VITARSN
Maillard, "The 'Ars nova' of Philippe de   TEXT, and VITARNO TEXT.
Vitry," Musica disciplina 10 (1956):
13-32. Used by permission of the
American Institute of Musicology
(Tempo Music Publications, 3773 West
95th Street, Leawood, KS 66206).

Author: Philippe de Vitry
Treatise: Ars perfecta in musica
Incipit: Septem sunt species consonantiarum in discantu

File name: **VITARSP**	Data input by: C. Matthew Balensuela
File type: **TEXT**	Data checked by: Dolores Pesce
MS: Print: **X**	Data approved by: Thomas J. Mathiesen

Filelist: 14th   File size: 20K   Annotations:

Source of data:
  Scriptorum de musica medii aevi nova
series a Gerbertina altera, 4 vols., ed.
Edmond de Coussemaker (Paris: Durand,
1864-76; reprint ed., Hildesheim: Olms,
1963), 3:28-35.

The graphics files for this treatise are VITARSP 01GF-VITARSP 02GF.

Author: Philippe de Vitry
Treatise: Liber musicalium
Incipit: Quoniam de arte mensurabili tractare proponimus

File name: **VITLIBM**	Data input by: C. Matthew Balensuela
File type: **TEXT**	Data checked by: Luminita Aluas
MS: Print: **X**	Data approved by: Albert C. Rotola, S.J.

Filelist: 14th   File size: 26K   Annotations:

Source of data:
  Scriptorum de musica medii aevi nova
series a Gerbertina altera, 4 vols., ed.
Edmond de Coussemaker (Paris: Durand,
1864-76; reprint ed., Hildesheim: Olms,
1963), 3:35-46.

The graphics files for this treatise are VITLIBM 01GF-VITLIBM 03GF.

Author: Philippus de Caserta
Treatise: Tractatus de diversis figuris
Incipit: Quoniam sicut domino placuit scientiam musice

File name: **CASTRA**	Data input by: C. Matthew Balensuela
File type: **TEXT**	Data checked by: Oliver B. Ellsworth
MS: Print: **X**	Data approved by: Thomas J. Mathiesen

Filelist: 14th   File size: 14K   Annotations:

Source of data:
  Scriptorum de musica medii aevi nova
series a Gerbertina altera, 4 vols., ed.
Edmond de Coussemaker (Paris: Durand,
1864-76; reprint ed., Hildesheim: Olms,
1963), 3:118-24.

The graphics file for this treatise is CASTRA 01GF. Cf. TRAFIG TEXT.

Author: Phillipotus Andrea

Treatise: De contrapuncto quaedam regulae utiles

Incipit: Versus Post octavam quinta, si note tendunt

File name: **ANDCON**	Data input by: C. Matthew Balensuela
File type: **TEXT**	Data checked by: Oliver B. Ellsworth
MS: Print: **X**	Data approved by: Thomas J. Mathiesen
Filelist: 14th File size: 4K	Annotations:

Source of data:

Scriptorum de musica medii aevi nova series a Gerbertina altera, 4 vols., ed. Edmond de Coussemaker (Paris: Durand, 1864-76; reprint ed., Hildesheim: Olms, 1963), 3:116-18.

The graphics files for this treatise are ANDCON 01GF-ANDCON 03GF.

Author: Prosdocimo de' Beldomandi

Treatise: Brevis summula proportionum

Incipit: Tibi, dilecte frater, tuus Prosdocimus de Beldemandis

File name: **PROBRE2**	Data input by: C. Matthew Balensuela
File type: **TEXT**	Data checked by: Thomas J. Mathiesen
MS: Print: **X**	Data approved by: Benito V. Rivera
Filelist: 15th File size: 14K	Annotations:

Source of data:

Scriptorum de musica medii aevi nova series a Gerbertina altera, 4 vols., ed. Edmond de Coussemaker (Paris: Durand, 1864-76; reprint ed., Hildesheim: Olms, 1963), 3:258-61.

Cf. PROBRE1 TEXT.

Author: Prosdocimo de' Beldomandi

Treatise: Brevis summula proportionum quantum ad musicam pertinet

Incipit: Adsit principio Virgo Maria meo. Tibi, dilecte frater

File name: **PROBRE1**	Data input by: Malcolm Litchfield
File type: **TEXT**	Data checked by: Jan Herlinger & Anne Stone
MS: Print: **X**	Data approved by: Thomas J. Mathiesen
Filelist: 15th File size: 14K	Annotations:

Source of data:

Prosdocimo de' Beldomandi, Brevis summula proportionum quantum ad musicam pertinet and Parvus tractatulus de modo monacordum dividendi, ed. and trans. by Jan Herlinger, Greek and Latin Music Theory, vol. 4 (Lincoln: University of Nebraska Press, 1987), 46-62. Used by permission.

Cf. PROBRE2 TEXT.

Author: Prosdocimo de' Beldomandi

Treatise: Contrapunctus

Incipit: Scribit Aristotiles secundo Elenchorum, capitulo ultimo

File name: **PROCON**   Data input by: Jan Herlinger

File type: **TEXT**   Data checked by: C. Matthew Balensuela

  MS: Print: **X**   Data approved by: Thomas J. Mathiesen

Filelist: 15th   File size: 22K   Annotations:

Source of data: The graphics file for this treatise is PROCON
  Prosdocimo de' Beldomandi,   01GF. Cf. PROTRAC TEXT.
  Contrapunctus, ed. and trans. by Jan
  Herlinger, Greek and Latin Music
  Theory, vol. 1 (Lincoln: University of
  Nebraska Press, 1984), 26-94. Used by
  permission.

Author: Prosdocimo de' Beldomandi

Treatise: Libellus monocordi

Incipit: Etsi facile sit inventis addere

File name: **PROLIB**   Data input by: C. Matthew Balensuela

File type: **TEXT**   Data checked by: John Snyder

  MS: Print: **X**   Data approved by: Thomas J. Mathiesen

Filelist: 15th   File size: 34K   Annotations:

Source of data: The graphics file for this treatise is PROLIB
  Scriptorum de musica medii aevi nova   01GF. Cf. PROPAR TEXT.
  series a Gerbertina altera, 4 vols., ed.
  Edmond de Coussemaker (Paris: Durand,
  1864-76; reprint ed., Hildesheim: Olms,
  1963), 3:248-58.

Author: Prosdocimo de' Beldomandi

Treatise: Parvus tractatulus de modo monacordum dividendi

Incipit: Etsi facile sit inventis addere

File name: **PROPAR**   Data input by: Malcolm Litchfield

File type: **TEXT**   Data checked by: Jan Herlinger & Anne Stone

  MS: Print: **X**   Data approved by: Thomas J. Mathiesen

Filelist: 15th   File size: 34K   Annotations:

Source of data: The graphics file for this treatise is PROPAR
  Prosdocimo de' Beldomandi, Brevis   01GF. Cf. PROLIB TEXT.
  summula proportionum quantum ad
  musicam pertinet and Parvus tractatulus
  de modo monacordum dividendi, ed. and
  trans. by Jan Herlinger, Greek and Latin
  Music Theory, vol. 4 (Lincoln: University
  of Nebraska Press, 1987), 64-118. Used
  by permission.

Author: Prosdocimo de' Beldomandi
Treatise: Tractatus de contrapuncto
Incipit: Scribit Aristoteles, secundo Elencorum capitulo ultimo

File name: **PROTRAC**	Data input by: C. Matthew Balensuela
File type: **TEXT**	Data checked by: Dolores Pesce
MS: Print: **X**	Data approved by: Thomas J. Mathiesen

Filelist: 15th   File size: 22K   Annotations:

Source of data:
   Scriptorum de musica medii aevi nova series a Gerbertina altera, 4 vols., ed. Edmond de Coussemaker (Paris: Durand, 1864-76; reprint ed., Hildesheim: Olms, 1963), 3:193-99.

The graphics file for this treatise is PROTRAC 01GF. Cf. PROCON TEXT.

Author: Prosdocimo de' Beldomandi
Treatise: Tractatus musice speculative
Incipit: Dum quidam mihi carus ac uti frater intimus lucas nomine de castro lendenarie

File name: **PROSPE**	Data input by: Jessica Burr
File type: **TEXT**	Data checked by: Angela Mariani & Bradley Tucker
MS: Print: **X**	Data approved by: Thomas J. Mathiesen

Filelist: 15th   File size: 90K   Annotations:

Source of data:
   D. Raffaello Baralli and Luigi Torri, "Il Trattato di Prosdocimo de' Beldomandi contro il Lucidario di Marchetto da Padova per la prima volta trascritto e illustrato," Rivista musicale italiana 20 (1913): 731-62.

A single graphic is contained in PROSPE 01GF.

Author: Prosdocimo de' Beldomandi
Treatise: Tractatus practice de musica mensurabili
Incipit: Quoniam multitudo scripture lectoris animo sepius fastidium non parum infert

File name: **PROTRAP1**	Data input by: C. Matthew Balensuela
File type: **TEXT**	Data checked by: Stephen E. Hayes
MS: Print: **X**	Data approved by: Peter M. Lefferts

Filelist: 15th   File size: 92K   Annotations:

Source of data:
   Scriptorum de musica medii aevi nova series a Gerbertina altera, 4 vols., ed. Edmond de Coussemaker (Paris: Durand, 1864-76; reprint ed., Hildesheim: Olms, 1963), 3:200-228.

Author: Prosdocimo de' Beldomandi
Treatise: Tractatus practice de musica mensurabili ad modum italicorum
Incipit: Ars pratice cantus mensurabilis duplex reperitu
File name: **PROTRAP2**   Data input by: C. Matthew Balensuela
File type: **TEXT**   Data checked by: Walter Kreyszig
MS: Print: **X**   Data approved by: Thomas J. Mathiesen
Filelist: 15th   File size: 64K   Annotations:
Source of data: The graphics files for this treatise are
Scriptorum de musica medii aevi nova   PROTRAP2 01GF-PROTRAP2 03GF.
series a Gerbertina altera, 4 vols., ed.
Edmond de Coussemaker (Paris: Durand,
1864-76; reprint ed., Hildesheim: Olms,
1963), 3:228-48.

Author: Rabanus Maurus
Treatise: De origine rerum
Incipit: Musica est peritia modulationis sono cantuque consistens et dicta musica
File name: **MAUMUS**   Data input by: John Csonka
File type: **TEXT**   Data checked by: Angela Mariani
MS: Print: **X**   Data approved by: Thomas J. Mathiesen
Filelist: 9th-11th File size: 16K   Annotations:
Source of data: Based on Monte-Cassino, Arch. 132. Cf.
Adrien de la Fage, Essais de   MAUDEU TEXT.
dipthérographie musicale (Paris: Legouix,
1864), 365-72.

Author: Rabanus Maurus
Treatise: De universo, liber XVIII, caput IV
Incipit: Musica est peritia modulationis sono cantuque consistens; et dicta musica
File name: **MAUDEU**   Data input by: John Gray
File type: **TEXT**   Data checked by: Oliver Ellsworth & Andreas Giger
MS: Print: **X**   Data approved by: Thomas J. Mathiesen
Filelist: 9th-11th File size: 16K   Annotations:
Source of data: Cf. MAUMUS TEXT.
Patrologia cursus completus, series latina,
ed. J. P. Migne, 221 vols. (Paris: Garnier,
1844-1904), 111:495-500.

Author: Ramus de Pareia, Bartholomeus

Treatise: Musica practica, prima pars, tractatus primus

Incipit: Boetii musices disciplina quinque voluminibus comprehensa quoniam profundissimis

File name: **RAMMP1T1**   Data input by: Jingfa Sun

File type: **TEXT**   Data checked by: Peter Slemon

MS: Print: **X**   Data approved by: Thomas J. Mathiesen

Filelist: 15th   File size: 44K   Annotations:

Source of data:

Johannes Wolf, Musica practica Bartolomei Rami de Pareia Bononiae, impressa opere et industria ac expensis magistri Baltasaris de Hiriberia MCCCCLXXXII: Nach den Originaldrucken des Liceo musicale mit Genehmigung der Commune von Bologna, Publikationen der Internationalen Musikgesellschaft, Beihefte, Heft 2 (Leipzig: Breitkopf und Härtel, 1901), 1-24.

See also RAMMP1T2, RAMMP1T3, RAMMP2, RAMMP3T1, and RAMMP3T2. The graphics files for this treatise are RAMMP 01GF-RAMMP 08GF.

Author: Ramus de Pareia, Bartholomeus

Treatise: Musica practica, prima pars, tractatus secundus

Incipit: Etiam nunc voces musicas distinguamus. Vox est aeris repercussio indissoluta

File name: **RAMMP1T2**   Data input by: Jingfa Sun

File type: **TEXT**   Data checked by: Peter Slemon

MS: Print: **X**   Data approved by: Thomas J. Mathiesen

Filelist: 15th   File size: 51K   Annotations:

Source of data:

Johannes Wolf, Musica practica Bartolomei Rami de Pareia Bononiae, impressa opere et industria ac expensis magistri Baltasaris de Hiriberia MCCCCLXXXII: Nach den Originaldrucken des Liceo musicale mit Genehmigung der Commune von Bologna, Publikationen der Internationalen Musikgesellschaft, Beihefte, Heft 2 (Leipzig: Breitkopf und Härtel, 1901), 25-51.

See also RAMMP1T1, RAMMP1T3, RAMMP2, RAMMP3T1, and RAMMP3T2. The graphics files for this treatise are RAMMP 01GF-RAMMP 08GF.

Author: Ramus de Pareia, Bartholomeus
Treatise: Musica practica, prima pars, tractatus tertius
Incipit: Redeamus igitur ad ipsam musicae speciem, quae totam harmoniae vim dicitur

File name: **RAMMP1T3**   Data input by: Jingfa Sun
File type: **TEXT**   Data checked by: Peter Slemon
MS: Print: **X**   Data approved by: Thomas J. Mathiesen
Filelist: 15th   File size: 20K   Annotations:
Source of data: See also RAMMP1T1, RAMMP1T2,
Johannes Wolf, Musica practica   RAMMP2, RAMMP3T1, and RAMMP3T2.
Bartolomei Rami de Pareia Bononiae,   The graphics files for this treatise are
impressa opere et industria ac expensis   RAMMP 01GF-RAMMP 08GF.
magistri Baltasaris de Hiriberia
MCCCCLXXXII: Nach den
Originaldrucken des Liceo musicale mit
Genehmigung der Commune von
Bologna, Publikationen der
Internationalen Musikgesellschaft,
Beihefte, Heft 2 (Leipzig: Breitkopf und
Härtel, 1901), 52-61.

Author: Ramus de Pareia, Bartholomeus
Treatise: Musica practica, secunda pars, tractatus primus
Incipit: Taliter hucusque prosecuti fuimus, ut tantum de vocibus successive prolatis

File name: **RAMMP2**   Data input by: Jingfa Sun
File type: **TEXT**   Data checked by: Peter Slemon
MS: Print: **X**   Data approved by: Thomas J. Mathiesen
Filelist: 15th   File size: 32K   Annotations:
Source of data: See also RAMMP1T1, RAMMP1T2,
Johannes Wolf, Musica practica   RAMMP1T3, RAMMP3T1, and
Bartolomei Rami de Pareia Bononiae,   RAMMP3T2. The graphics files for this
impressa opere et industria ac expensis   treatise are RAMMP 01GF-RAMMP 08GF.
magistri Baltasaris de Hiriberia
MCCCCLXXXII: Nach den
Originaldrucken des Liceo musicale mit
Genehmigung der Commune von
Bologna, Publikationen der
Internationalen Musikgesellschaft,
Beihefte, Heft 2 (Leipzig: Breitkopf und
Härtel, 1901), 62-76.

Author: Ramus de Pareia, Bartholomeus

Treatise: Musica practica, tertia pars, tractatus primus

Incipit: Binas longas maximam binasque breves longam atque brevem duas semibreves

File name: **RAMMP3T1**　　Data input by: Jingfa Sun

File type: **TEXT**　　Data checked by: Peter Slemon

　MS:　　Print: **X**　　Data approved by: Thomas J. Mathiesen

Filelist: 15th　　File size: 31K　　Annotations:

Source of data:

Johannes Wolf, Musica practica Bartolomei Rami de Pareia Bononiae, impressa opere et industria ac expensis magistri Baltasaris de Hiriberia MCCCCLXXXII: Nach den Originaldrucken des Liceo musicale mit Genehmigung der Commune von Bologna, Publikationen der Internationalen Musikgesellschaft, Beihefte, Heft 2 (Leipzig: Breitkopf und Härtel, 1901), 77-92.

See also RAMMP1T1, RAMMP1T2, RAMMP1T3, RAMMP2, and RAMMP3T2. The graphics files for this treatise are RAMMP 01GF-RAMMP 08GF.

Author: Ramus de Pareia, Bartholomeus

Treatise: Musica practica, tertia pars, tractatus secundus

Incipit: Sicut igitur ex numerorum multiplicatione relata proportionum genera redundarunt

File name: **RAMMP3T2**　　Data input by: Jingfa Sun

File type: **TEXT**　　Data checked by: Peter Slemon

　MS:　　Print: **X**　　Data approved by: Thomas J. Mathiesen

Filelist: 15th　　File size: 42K　　Annotations:

Source of data:

Johannes Wolf, Musica practica Bartolomei Rami de Pareia Bononiae, impressa opere et industria ac expensis magistri Baltasaris de Hiriberia MCCCCLXXXII: Nach den Originaldrucken des Liceo musicale mit Genehmigung der Commune von Bologna, Publikationen der Internationalen Musikgesellschaft, Beihefte, Heft 2 (Leipzig: Breitkopf und Härtel, 1901), 93-112.

See also RAMMP1T1, RAMMP1T2, RAMMP1T3, RAMMP2, and RAMMP3T1. The graphics files for this treatise are RAMMP 01GF-RAMMP 08GF. This file also includes the Anhang that forms a part of Wolf's edition, containing excerpts from Burtius, Hothby, and Gaffurio.

Author: Regino Prumiensis

Treatise: De harmonica institutione

Incipit: Cum frequenter in Ecclesiae vestrae dioecesibus chorus psallentium psalmorum

File name: **REGHARI**　　Data input by: Stephen E. Hayes

File type: **TEXT**　　Data checked by: Peter Slemon

　MS:　　Print: **X**　　Data approved by: Thomas J. Mathiesen

Filelist: 9th-11th　　File size: 52K　　Annotations:

Source of data:

Patrologia cursus completus, series latina, ed. J. P. Migne, 221 vols. (Paris: Garnier, 1844-1904), 132:483-502.

The incipit is preceded by the address "Excellentissimo domino Radbodo, sanctae Treverensis Ecclesiae archiepiscopo. Regino devotum obsequium in perpetuum." Cf. REGDHI TEXT and REGHAR TEXT.

Author: Regino Prumiensis
Treatise: De harmonica institutione
Incipit: Cum frequenter in ecclesiae vestrae dioecesibus chorus psallentium psalmorum

File name: **REGDHI**   Data input by: Angela Mariani
File type: **TEXT**   Data checked by: Bradley Jon Tucker
MS: Print: **X**   Data approved by: Thomas J. Mathiesen
Filelist: 9th-11th   File size: 51K   Annotations:

Source of data:
Edna Marie Le Roux, RSM, "The De harmonica and Tonarius of Regino of Prüm" (Ph.D. dissertation, Catholic University of America, 1965), 22-84. Used by permission.

The incipit is preceded by the address "Excellentissimo domino Rathbodo sanctae Treverensis ecclesiae Archiepiscopo, Regino devotum obsequium in perpetuum." The editor of this text indicated the folio numbers for Leipzig, Universitätsbibliothek, lat. 169 in brackets and the page numbers for the Gerbert edition (see REGHAR) in parentheses throughout the text. Each indication is preceded by a virgule (/). Cf. REGHAR TEXT and REGHARI TEXT.

Author: Regino Prumiensis
Treatise: Epistola de harmonica institutione
Incipit: Cum frequenter in ecclesiae vestrae dioecesibus chorus psallentium psalmorum

File name: **REGHAR**   Data input by: Stephen E. Hayes
File type: **TEXT**   Data checked by: Peter Lefferts & Angela Mariani
MS: Print: **X**   Data approved by: Thomas J. Mathiesen
Filelist: 9th-11th   File size: 51K   Annotations:

Source of data:
Scriptores ecclesiastici de musica sacra potissimum, 3 vols., ed. Martin Gerbert (St. Blaise: Typis San-Blasianis, 1784; reprint ed., Hildesheim: Olms, 1963), 1:230-47.

The incipit is preceded by the address "Excellentessimo domino Rathbodo sanctae Treverensis ecclesiae Archiepiscopo, Regino devotum obsequium in perpetuum." Cf. REGDHI TEXT and REGHARI TEXT.

Author: Regino Prumiensis
Treatise: Tonarius
Incipit: Incipiunt octo toni musicae artis cum suis differentiis authenticus protus

File name: **REGTONA**   Data input by: Angela Mariani
File type: **TEXT**   Data checked by: Andreas Giger
MS: Print: **X**   Data approved by: Thomas J. Mathiesen
Filelist: 9th-11th   File size: 240K   Annotations:

Source of data:
Edna Marie Le Roux, RSM, "The De harmonica and Tonarius of Regino of Prüm" (Ph.D. dissertation, Catholic University of America, 1965), 137-294 and (left column only) 303-5. Used by permission.

The editor of this text indicated the folio numbers for Leipzig, Universitätsbibliothek, lat. 169 in brackets throughout the text. Cf. REGTON TEXT.

THESAURUS MUSICARUM LATINARUM: Canon of Data Files

Author: Regino Prumiensis
Treatise: Tonarius
Incipit: Ignatius Antiochie Syrie tertius post apostolum Petrum Episcopus,

File name: **REGTON**	Data input by: Firoozeh Khazrai
File type: **TEXT**	Data checked by: Bradley Jon Tucker
MS:　　Print: **X**	Data approved by: Thomas J. Mathiesen

Filelist: 9th-11th File size: 49K　　Annotations:

Source of data:　　　　　　　　　The graphics files for this treatise are
Scriptorum de musica medii aevi nova　REGTON 01GF-REGTON 35GF. Cf.
series a Gerbertina altera, 4 vols., ed.　REGTONA TEXT.
Edmond de Coussemaker (Paris: Durand,
1864-76; reprint ed., Hildesheim: Olms,
1963), 2:1-73.

Author: Remigius Altisiodorensis
Treatise: Musica
Incipit: Omnis ars Musica proportionibus constat, id est consonantiis. (Dico, quidquid recte

File name: **REMMUS**	Data input by: Stephen E. Hayes
File type: **TEXT**	Data checked by: Peter Lefferts & Angela Mariani
MS:　　Print: **X**	Data approved by: Thomas J. Mathiesen

Filelist: 9th-11th File size: 90K　　Annotations:

Source of data:　　　　　　　　　Cf. REMMUSI TEXT.
Scriptores ecclesiastici de musica sacra
potissimum, 3 vols., ed. Martin Gerbert
(St. Blaise: Typis San-Blasianis, 1784;
reprint ed., Hildesheim: Olms, 1963),
1:63-94.

Author: Remigius Altisiodorensis
Treatise: Musica
Incipit: Omnis ars musica proportionibus constat, id est consonantiis. (Dico, quidquid recte

File name: **REMMUSI**	Data input by: John Gray
File type: **TEXT**	Data checked by: Oliver Ellsworth & Andreas Giger
MS:　　Print: **X**	Data approved by: Thomas J. Mathiesen

Filelist: 9th-11th File size: 90K　　Annotations:

Source of data:　　　　　　　　　Cf. REMMUS TEXT.
Patrologia cursus completus, series latina,
ed. J. P. Migne, 221 vols. (Paris: Garnier,
1844-1904), 131:931-64.

Author: Rhau, Georg

Treatise: Enchiridion utriusque musicae practicae

Incipit: Musicam artem multis retro seculis floruisse, nemo est qui neget.

File name: **RHAENC**   Data input by: Peter Slemon

File type: **TEXT**   Data checked by: Angela Mariani

  MS: Print: **X**   Data approved by: Thomas J. Mathiesen

Filelist: 16th   File size: 58K   Annotations:

Source of data:

Enchiridion utriusque musicae practicae a Georgio Rhau ex varijs musicorum libris, pro pueris in schola Vitebergensi congestum (Wittemberg: Georg Rhau, 1538; reprint ed., Kassel: Bärenreiter, 1951).

The text proper is preceded by a pedagogical epigram, a dedicatory letter (beginning "Omnes eruditi homines, qui vel antiquis illis temporibus ..."), and a note Ad pueros (beginning "Non miremini optimi pueri ..."). The graphics files for this treatise are RHAENC 01GF-RHAENC 27GF.

Author: Robertus de Handlo

Treatise: Regulae

Incipit: Incipiunt regule cum maximis magistri Franconis, cum additionibus aliorum

File name: **HANREGU**   Data input by: Peter M. Lefferts

File type: **TEXT**   Data checked by: Bradley Jon Tucker

  MS: Print: **X**   Data approved by: Thomas J. Mathiesen

Filelist: 14th   File size: 44K   Annotations:

Source of data:

Scriptorum de musica medii aevi nova series a Gerbertina altera, 4 vols., ed. Edmond de Coussemaker (Paris: Durand, 1864-76; reprint ed., Hildesheim: Olms, 1963), 1:383-403.

The graphics files for this treatise are HANREGU 01GF-HANREGU 02GF. Cf. HANREG TEXT.

Author: Robertus de Handlo

Treatise: Regule

Incipit: Incipiunt regule cum maximis magistri Franconis cum additionibus aliorum

File name: **HANREG**   Data input by: Peter M. Lefferts

File type: **TEXT**   Data checked by: Luminita Aluas

  MS: Print: **X**   Data approved by: Thomas J. Mathiesen

Filelist: 14th   File size: 44K   Annotations:

Source of data:

Robertus de Handlo, Regule, and Johannes Hanboys, Summa, ed. and trans. by Peter M. Lefferts, Greek and Latin Music Theory, vol. 7 (Lincoln: University of Nebraska Press, 1991), 80-178. Used by permission.

The graphics files for this treatise are HANREG 01GF-HANREG 02GF. Cf. HANREGU TEXT.

Author: Roffredi, Guglielmo
Treatise: Summa musicae artis
Incipit: Musica est motus vocum, id est, per arsyn et thesyn. Est etiam veraciter canendi

File name: **ROFFSUM**　　Data input by: Stephen E. Hayes
File type: **TEXT**　　　　Data checked by: Peter M. Lefferts & Andreas Giger
MS:　　　Print: **X**　　Data approved by: Thomas J. Mathiesen
Filelist: 12th　　File size: 15K　　Annotations:

Source of data:
Albert Seay, "Guglielmo Roffredi's Summa musicae artis," Musica disciplina 24 (1970): 71-77. Used by permission of the American Institute of Musicology (Tempo Music Publications, 3773 West 95th Street, Leawood, KS 66206).

Based by Lucca, Biblioteca arcivescovile, 614, ff. 211v-212r. The graphics file for this treatise is ROFFSUM 01GF.

Author: Rossetti, Biagio
Treatise: Libellus de rudimentis musices: Compendium musicae
Incipit: Musica est ars Deo placens ac hominibus, omne quod canitur discernens

File name: **ROSLIB1**　　Data input by: Nigel Gwee
File type: **TEXT**　　　　Data checked by: Bradley Jon Tucker
MS:　　　Print: **X**　　Data approved by: Thomas J. Mathiesen
Filelist: 16th　　File size: 111K　　Annotations:

Source of data:
Biagio Rossetti, Libellus de rudimentis musices, ed. Albert Seay, Critical Texts, no. 12 (Colorado Springs: Colorado College Music Press, 1981), 1-60. Used by permission.

The incipit is preceded by various dedicatory poems. The graphics files for this treatise are ROSLIB1 01GF-ROSLIB1 06GF. Cf. ROSLIB2 TEXT.

Author: Rossetti, Biagio
Treatise: Libellus de rudimentis musices: De choro et organo compendium
Incipit: Habitis itaque atque utcumque enucleatis musices rudimentis quibus pueri

File name: **ROSLIB2**　　Data input by: Nigel Gwee
File type: **TEXT**　　　　Data checked by: Bradley Jon Tucker
MS:　　　Print: **X**　　Data approved by: Thomas J. Mathiesen
Filelist: 16th　　File size: 68K　　Annotations:

Source of data:
Biagio Rossetti, Libellus de rudimentis musices, ed. Albert Seay, Critical Texts, no. 12 (Colorado Springs: Colorado College Music Press, 1981), 62-94. Used by permission.

The graphics files for this treatise are ROSLIB2 01GF-ROSLIB2 03GF. Cf. ROSLIB1 TEXT.

Author: Rudolf of St. Trond

Treatise: Quaestiones in musica

Incipit: Quare non possint esse plura quam septem vocum discrimina. Natura omnium rerum

File name: **RUDQUA**   Data input by: Angela Mariani

File type: **TEXT**   Data checked by: Bradley Jon Tucker

MS: Print: **X**   Data approved by: Thomas J. Mathiesen

Filelist: 12th   File size: 116K   Annotations:

Source of data: The graphics files for this treatise are
Rudolf Steglich, ed., Die Quaestiones in   RUDQUA 01GF-RUDQUA 19GF.
musica: Ein Choraltraktat des zentralen
Mittelalters und ihr mutmasslicher
Verfasser Rudolf von St. Trond
(1070-1138) (Leipzig: Breitkopf und
Härtel, 1911), 12-99.

Author: Sadze de Flandria, Christianus

Treatise: Tractatus modi, temporis et prolationis

Incipit: Omnem scientiam omnemque philosophiam credimus et profitemur de externo fonte

File name: **FLATRA**   Data input by: C. Matthew Balensuela

File type: **TEXT**   Data checked by: Thomas J. Mathiesen

MS: Print: **X**   Data approved by: Benito V. Rivera

Filelist: 15th   File size: 14K   Annotations:

Source of data: The graphics files for this treatise are
Scriptorum de musica medii aevi nova   FLATRA 01GF-FLATRA 07GF.
series a Gerbertina altera, 4 vols., ed.
Edmond de Coussemaker (Paris: Durand,
1864-76; reprint ed., Hildesheim: Olms,
1963), 3:264-73.

Author: Saess, Heinrich

Treatise: Musica plana atque mensurabilis una cum nonnullis solmisationis regulis certissimis

Incipit: Musicae artis non unum tantum, sed plures diversis saeculis et coeli plagis

File name: **SAEMUS**   Data input by: Elisabeth Honn

File type: **TEXT**   Data checked by: Andreas Giger

MS: Print: **X**   Data approved by: Thomas J. Mathiesen

Filelist: 16th   File size: 58K   Annotations:

Source of data: The incipit is preceded by a two laudatory
Renate Federhofer-Königs, "Die Musica   poems, beginning: "Quisquis ad Orpheum
plana atque mensurabilis von Heinrich   velis applicuisse leporem..." and "Dulcisona
Saess," Kirchenmusikalisches Jahrbuch   lector qui vis complectier arte ..."; and a
48 (1964): 64-94. Used by permission.   dedicatory preface, beginning: "Deos placatos
pietas efficiet et sanctitas ...." The graphics
files for this treatise are SAEMUS
01GF-SAEMUS 21GF.

Author: Salinas, Franciscus

Treatise: De musica, liber primus

Incipit: Inter omnium animantium voces merito vox humana principem locum obtinere

File name: **SALMUS1**   Data input by: Stephen E. Hayes

File type: **TEXT**   Data checked by: Peter M. Lefferts & Andreas Giger

MS: Print: **X**   Data approved by: Thomas J. Mathiesen

Filelist: 16th   File size: 189K   Annotations:

Source of data:

Francisci Salinae Burgensis Abbatis Sancti Pancratii de Rocca Scalegna in regno Neapolitano, et in Academia Salmanticensi Musicae Professoris, de Musica libri Septem, in quibus eius doctrinae veritas tam quae ad Harmoniam, quam quae ad Rhythmum pertinet, iuxta sensus ac rationis iudicium ostenditur, et demonstratur (Salamanca: Mathias Gastius, 1577), ff. 1r-8v and pp. 1-45.

The incipit is preceded by the imprimatur, several dedicatory verses, and a dedicatory preface. The graphics files for this treatise are SALMUS1 01GF-SALMUS1 13GF. See also SALMUS2 TEXT, SALMUS3 TEXT, SALMUS4 TEXT, SALMUS5 TEXT, SALMUS6 TEXT, and SALMUS7 TEXT.

Author: Salinas, Franciscus

Treatise: De musica, liber secundus

Incipit: De Numeris, et Proportionibus, quae ex numerorum comparationibus oriuntur,

File name: **SALMUS2**   Data input by: Bradley Tucker & Andreas Giger

File type: **TEXT**   Data checked by: Albert C. Rotola, S.J.

MS: Print: **X**   Data approved by: Thomas J. Mathiesen

Filelist: 16th   File size: 175K   Annotations:

Source of data:

Francisci Salinae Burgensis Abbatis Sancti Pancratii de Rocca Scalegna in regno Neapolitano, et in Academia Salmanticensi Musicae Professoris, de Musica libri Septem, in quibus eius doctrinae veritas tam quae ad Harmoniam, quam quae ad Rhythmum pertinet, iuxta sensus ac rationis iudicium ostenditur, et demonstratur (Salamanca: Mathias Gastius, 1577), 46-100.

The incipit is preceded by the chapter title: "Qvod non nvmervs per se, neqve sonvs ab harmonico considerandus sit, sed vterque simul: et quot modis Soni nomen accipiatur." The graphics files for this treatise are SALMUS2 01GF-SALMUS2 19GF. See also SALMUS1 TEXT, SALMUS3 TEXT, SALMUS4 TEXT, SALMUS5 TEXT, SALMUS6 TEXT, and SALMUS7 TEXT.

Author: Salinas, Franciscus
Treatise: De musica, liber tertius
Incipit: Libro superiore satis atque abunde de consonantijs, et minoribus interuallis

File name: **SALMUS3**　Data input by: Claudia Di Luca
File type: **TEXT**　Data checked by: Andreas Giger
　MS:　Print: **X**　Data approved by: Thomas J. Mathiesen
Filelist: 16th　File size: 240K

Source of data:

Francisci Salinae Burgensis Abbatis Sancti Pancratii de Rocca Scalegna in regno Neapolitano, et in Academia Salmanticensi Musicae Professoris, de Musica libri Septem, in quibus eius doctrinae veritas tam quae ad Harmoniam, quam quae ad Rhythmum pertinet, iuxta sensus ac rationis iudicium ostenditur, et demonstratur (Salamanca: Mathias Gastius, 1577), 101-75.

Annotations:

The incipit is preceded by the chapter title: "Qvid sit genvs in mvsica: et quot sunt Genera melodiarum." The graphics files for this treatise are SALMUS3 01GF-SALMUS3 21GF. See also SALMUS1 TEXT, SALMUS2 TEXT, SALMUS4 TEXT, SALMUS5 TEXT, SALMUS6 TEXT, and SALMUS7 TEXT.

Author: Salinas, Franciscus
Treatise: De musica, liber quartus
Incipit: Postquam tribus superioribus libris absoluimus omnia, quae ad compositionem

File name: **SALMUS4**　Data input by: Andreas Giger
File type: **TEXT**　Data checked by: Andre Barbera
　MS:　Print: **X**　Data approved by: Thomas J. Mathiesen
Filelist: 16th　File size: 207K

Source of data:

Francisci Salinae Burgensis Abbatis Sancti Pancratii de Rocca Scalegna in regno Neapolitano, et in Academia Salmanticensi Musicae Professoris, de Musica libri Septem, in quibus eius doctrinae veritas tam quae ad Harmoniam, quam quae ad Rhythmum pertinet, iuxta sensus ac rationis iudicium ostenditur, et demonstratur (Salamanca: Mathias Gastius, 1577), 176-234.

Annotations:

The incipit is preceded by the chapter title: "Qvid sit species in mvsica, et quomodo differat a genere, et de speciebus consonantiarum iuxta Euclidis, et Ptolemaei, ac Boetij positiones." The graphics files for this treatise are SALMUS4 01GF-SALMUS4 10GF. See also SALMUS1 TEXT, SALMUS2 TEXT, SALMUS3 TEXT, SALMUS5 TEXT, SALMUS6 TEXT, and SALMUS7 TEXT.

Author: Salinas, Franciscus

Treatise: De musica, liber quintus

Incipit: Qvatuor superioribus libris a nobis tractatum est de priore Musicae parte

File name: **SALMUS5**   Data input by: Andreas Giger

File type: **TEXT**   Data checked by: Albert C. Rotola, S.J.

MS: Print: **X**   Data approved by: Thomas J. Mathiesen

Filelist: 16th   File size: 185K   Annotations:

Source of data:

Francisci Salinae Burgensis Abbatis Sancti Pancratii de Rocca Scalegna in regno Neapolitano, et in Academia Salmanticensi Musicae Professoris, de Musica libri Septem, in quibus eius doctrinae veritas tam quae ad Harmoniam, quam quae ad Rhythmum pertinet, iuxta sensus ac rationis iudicium ostenditur, et demonstratur (Salamanca: Mathias Gastius, 1577), 235-85.

The incipit is preceded by the chapter title: "Qvid sit rhythmvs, a quo altera Musicae pars Rhythmica nominatur, iuxta Philoxeni et Platonis, et aliorum definitiones, et quo pacto Rhythmus Oratorius, et Poeticus a Musico differant." The graphics file for this treatise is SALMUS5 01GF. See also SALMUS1 TEXT, SALMUS2 TEXT, SALMUS3 TEXT, SALMUS4 TEXT, SALMUS6 TEXT, and SALMUS7 TEXT.

Author: Salinas, Franciscus

Treatise: De musica, liber sextus

Incipit: Svperest nunc vt de metris ac versibus ac eorum canoris differentijs dicamus

File name: **SALMUS6**   Data input by: Andreas Giger

File type: **TEXT**   Data checked by: Benito V. Rivera

MS: Print: **X**   Data approved by: Thomas J. Mathiesen

Filelist: 16th   File size: 271K   Annotations:

Source of data:

Francisci Salinae Burgensis Abbatis Sancti Pancratii de Rocca Scalegna in regno Neapolitano, et in Academia Salmanticensi Musicae Professoris, de Musica libri Septem, in quibus eius doctrinae veritas tam quae ad Harmoniam, quam quae ad Rhythmum pertinet, iuxta sensus ac rationis iudicium ostenditur, et demonstratur (Salamanca: Mathias Gastius, 1577), 286-373.

The incipit is preceded by the chapter title: "Qvod non ponenda sit tertia Musicae pars, quae metrica nominatur, sed ad rhythmicam metrorum tractatio pertineat: et vtrum plus laudis mereantur, qui tenorem vnius vocis metrica lege constantem inuenerint, an qui inuentum artificioso plurium vocum cantu composuerint." The graphics file for this treatise is SALMUS6 01GF. See also SALMUS1 TEXT, SALMUS2 TEXT, SALMUS3 TEXT, SALMUS4 TEXT, SALMUS5 TEXT, and SALMUS7 TEXT.

Author: Salinas, Franciscus
Treatise: De musica, liber septimus
Incipit: Traditis iam et expositis, quae ad rhythmorum et metrorum compositionem visa sunt

File name: **SALMUS7**   Data input by: Andreas Giger
File type: **TEXT**   Data checked by: Albert C. Rotola, S.J.
MS: Print: **X**   Data approved by: Thomas J. Mathiesen
Filelist: 16th   File size: 184K   Annotations:

Source of data:
Francisci Salinae Burgensis Abbatis Sancti Pancratii de Rocca Scalegna in regno Neapolitano, et in Academia Salmanticensi Musicae Professoris, de Musica libri Septem, in quibus eius doctrinae veritas tam quae ad Harmoniam, quam quae ad Rhythmum pertinet, iuxta sensus ac rationis iudicium ostenditur, et demonstratur (Salamanca: Mathias Gastius, 1577) 374-438.

The incipit is preceded by the chapter title: "De metri et versus differentia, et de versus nominis etymologia." The graphics file for this treatise is SALMUS7 01GF. See also SALMUS1 TEXT, SALMUS2 TEXT, SALMUS3 TEXT, SALMUS4 TEXT, SALMUS5 TEXT, and SALMUS6 TEXT.

Author: Salomo, Elias
Treatise: Scientia artis musicae
Incipit: Sciendum est, quod ars musicae septenario numero litterarum contenta est

File name: **SALSCI**   Data input by: Angela Mariani
File type: **TEXT**   Data checked by: Bradley Jon Tucker
MS: Print: **X**   Data approved by: Thomas J. Mathiesen
Filelist: 13th   File size: 105K   Annotations:

Source of data:
Scriptores ecclesiastici de musica sacra potissimum, 3 vols., ed. Martin Gerbert (St. Blaise: Typis San-Blasianis, 1784; reprint ed., Hildesheim: Olms, 1963), 3:16-64.

A long preface precedes the treatise, beginning: "Quoniam veritas et claritas scientiae artis musicae ubique partium mundi, super quem fundamentalis universalis ecclesiae quasi post fidem orthodoxam consistit, ..." The graphics files for this treatise are SALSCI 01GF-SALSCI 16GF.

Author: Sebastianus de Felstin
Treatise: Modus regulariter accentuandi lectiones Matutinales, prophetias necnon epistolas et
Incipit: Cum regularis debitaque pronunciatio vniuscuiusque vocis (que finis grammatice

File name: **FELMOD**   Data input by: Sergei Lebedev
File type: **TEXT**   Data checked by: Andreas Giger
MS: Print: **X**   Data approved by: Thomas J. Mathiesen
Filelist: 16th   File size: 27K   Annotations:

Source of data:
Modus regulariter accentuandi lectiones Matutinales, prophetias necnon epistolas et euangelia ([Cracow: Jan Haller, 1518]; reprint ed., Cracow: Polskie Wydawnictwo Muzyczne, 1979).

The incipit is preceded by an ad lectorem, beginning: "Si quid in hoc vicij, cernas pugnare libello ...." The graphics files for this treatise are FELMOD 01GF-FELMOD 14GF.

Author: Sebastianus de Felstin
Treatise: Opusculum musice
Incipit: In laudem pulcherrime artis musicae assummo dictum diuini Dauid

File name: **FELOP**
File type: **TEXT**
MS: Print: **X**
Filelist: 16th   File size: 34K

Data input by: Sergei Lebedev & Olga Lebedeva
Data checked by: Andreas Giger
Data approved by: Thomas J. Mathiesen
Annotations:

Source of data:
Opusculum musice compilatum nouiter per dominum Sebastianum presbiterum de Felstin. Pro institutione adolescentum in cantu Simplici seu Gregoriano ([Cracow: Jan Haller, 1517]; reprint ed., Cracow: Polskie Wydawnictwo Muzyczne, 1979).

The graphics files for this treatise are FELOP 01GF-FELOP16GF.

Author: Stoquerus, Gaspar
Treatise: De modo, tempore, et prolatione
Incipit: Quae nominibus tria proponuntur, re vera quatuor sunt.

File name: **STOMTP**
File type: **MMBN6486**
MS: **X**   Print:
Filelist: 16th   File size: 7K

Data input by: Albert C. Rotola, S.J.
Data checked by: Andreas Giger
Data approved by: Thomas J. Mathiesen
Annotations:

Source of data:
Madrid, Biblioteca nacional 6486, ff. 46v-49r.

This treatise follows Stoquerus's De vera solfizationis (cf. STOVERA MMBN6486) and De musica verbali (cf. STODEM TEXT) in the manuscript. The graphics file for this treatise is STOMTP 01GF.

Author: Stoquerus, Gaspar
Treatise: De musica verbali libri duo
Incipit: Ociosum me nec gravioribus additum studiis

File name: **STODEM**
File type: **TEXT**
MS: Print: **X**
Filelist: 16th   File size: 96K

Data input by: Albert C. Rotola, S.J.
Data checked by: Anne Stone
Data approved by: Thomas J. Mathiesen
Annotations:

Source of data:
Gaspar Stoquerus, De musica verbali libri duo, ed. and trans. by Albert C. Rotola, S.J., Greek and Latin Music Theory, vol. 5 (Lincoln: University of Nebraska Press, 1988), 100-254. Used by permission.

The graphics file for this treatise is STODEM 01GF.

Author: Stoquerus, Gaspar
Treatise: De vera solfizationis
Incipit: Quam stulte faciant, qui Solfizandi rationem pueros ex Guidonis scala docere conantur

File name: **STOVERA**
File type: **MMBN6486**
MS: **X**   Print:
Filelist: 16th   File size: 12K

Data input by: Albert C. Rotola, S.J.
Data checked by: Andreas Giger
Data approved by: Thomas J. Mathiesen
Annotations:

Source of data:
Madrid, Biblioteca nacional 6486, ff. 41r-45v.

This treatise follows Stoquerus's De musica verbali (cf. STODEM TEXT) in the manuscript.

Author: Tallanderius, Petrus

Treatise: Lectura

Incipit: Incipit lectura per Petrum Tallanderii ordinata tam super cantu mensurabili

File name: **TALLEC**	Data input by: Peter Slemon
File type: **TEXT**	Data checked by: Angela Mariani
MS: Print: **X**	Data approved by: Thomas J. Mathiesen

Filelist: 15th   File size: 23K   Annotations:

Source of data:
Petrus Tallanderius, Lectura, ed. Albert Seay, Critical Texts, no. 4 (Colorado Springs: Colorado College Music Press, 1977). Used by permission.

The graphics files for this treatise are TALLEC 01GF-TALLEC 11GF.

Author: Theinredus Doverensis

Treatise: Musica, liber primus

Incipit: Quoniam musicorum de hijs cantibus frequens est dissensio. qui in uno octo chordo

File name: **TDMUS1**	Data input by: John Snyder
File type: **MOBB842**	Data checked by: Peter M. Lefferts
MS: **X** Print:	Data approved by: Thomas J. Mathiesen

Filelist: 12th   File size: 44K   Annotations:

Source of data:
Oxford, Bodleian Library, Bodley 842 (S.C. 2575), ff. 1r-18v.

=RISM BIII/4:110-15. The graphics files for this treatise are TDMUS1 01GF-TDMUS1 12GF. Continues in TDMUS2 and TDMUS3.

Author: Theinredus Doverensis

Treatise: Musica, liber secundus

Incipit: Raciones autem musicarum consonanciarum hee sunt uniuersi generis arithmetici

File name: **TDMUS2**	Data input by: John Snyder
File type: **MOBB842**	Data checked by: Peter M. Lefferts
MS: **X** Print:	Data approved by: Thomas J. Mathiesen

Filelist: 12th   File size: 8K   Annotations:

Source of data:
Oxford, Bodleian Library, Bodley 842 (S.C. 2575), ff. 18v-21r.

=RISM BIII/4:110-15. The graphics file for this treatise is TDMUS2 01GF. Continued from TDMUS1 and in TDMUS3.

Author: Theinredus Doverensis

Treatise: Musica, liber tercius

Incipit: Consonanciarum igitur racionibus perspectis; ad species earum perspiciendas

File name: **TDMUS3**	Data input by: John Snyder
File type: **MOBB842**	Data checked by: Peter M. Lefferts
MS: **X** Print:	Data approved by: Thomas J. Mathiesen

Filelist: 12th   File size: 51K   Annotations:

Source of data:
Oxford, Bodleian Library, Bodley 842 (S.C. 2575), ff. 21r-44v.

=RISM BIII/4:110-15. Note: this file employs the following special codes:[ddem] = a "d" with a leaning stem; [der] = a "d" with a straight stem; [ddup] = a "d" with a double loop; [dt] = an edh; [roe] = an "e rotundum"; [lgs] = a long "s"; [sqd] = "d quadratum"; [sts] = a short "s." The graphics files for this treatise are TDMUS3 01GF-TDMUS3 28GF. Continued from TDMUS1 and TDMUS2.

THESAURUS MUSICARUM LATINARUM: Canon of Data Files

Author: Theodoricus de Campo

Treatise: De musica mensurabili

Incipit: Omnis ars sive doctrina honorabiliorem habet rationem

File name: **CAMDEM**   Data input by: C. Matthew Balensuela

File type: **TEXT**   Data checked by: Stephen E. Hayes

  MS: Print: **X**   Data approved by: Peter M. Lefferts

Filelist: 14th   File size: 48K   Annotations:

Source of data: The graphics file for this treatise is CAMDEM
  Scriptorum de musica medii aevi nova   01GF. See also ANODEM.
  series a Gerbertina altera, 4 vols., ed.
  Edmond de Coussemaker (Paris: Durand,
  1864-76; reprint ed., Hildesheim: Olms,
  1963), 3:177-93.

Author: Theogerus Metensis

Treatise: Musica

Incipit: Pythagoras philosophus primus apud Graecos musicae artis repertor legitur.

File name: **THEMUS**   Data input by: Sean Ferguson

File type: **TEXT**   Data checked by: Charles Atkinson & Angela Mariani

  MS: Print: **X**   Data approved by: Thomas J. Mathiesen

Filelist: 9th-11th File size: 37K   Annotations:

Source of data: In the first paragraph,there are two annotations
  Scriptores ecclesiastici de musica sacra   in parentheses beginning with the initial P.
  potissimum, 3 vols., ed. Martin Gerbert   According to the material prefatory to this
  (St. Blaise: Typis San-Blasianis, 1784;   text, these are variant readings contributed by
  reprint ed., Hildesheim: Olms, 1963),   the Abbot Philippus Jacobus. The graphics
  2:183-96.   files for this treatise are THEMUS
                          01GF-THEMUS 03GF. Cf. THEMUSI TEXT.

Author: Theogerus Metensis

Treatise: Musica

Incipit: Pythagoras philosophus primus apud Graecos musicae artis repertor legitur.

File name: **THEMUSI**   Data input by: John Gray

File type: **TEXT**   Data checked by: Oliver Ellsworth & Andreas Giger

  MS: Print: **X**   Data approved by: Thomas J. Mathiesen

Filelist: 9th-11th File size: 37K   Annotations:

Source of data: In the first paragraph,there are two annotations
  Patrologia cursus completus, series latina,   in parentheses beginning with the initial P.
  ed. J. P. Migne, 221 vols. (Paris: Garnier,   According to the material prefatory to this
  1844-1904), 163:777-92.   text, these are variant readings contributed by
                          the Abbot Philippus Jacobus. The graphics for
                          this treatise are THEMUSI 01GF-THEMUSI
                          02GF. Cf. THEMUS TEXT.

Author: Tinctoris, Johannes
Treatise: Complexus effectuum musices
Incipit: Effectus primus est iste: Musica Deum delectat. Proprium etenim est cujuslibet

File name: **TINCOM**	Data input by: Stephen E. Hayes
File type: **TEXT**	Data checked by: Peter M. Lefferts
MS: Print: **X**	Data approved by: Jan W. Herlinger
Filelist: 15th File size: 22K	Annotations:

Source of data:
Johannis Tinctoris Opera theoretica, ed. Albert Seay, 3 vols. in 2, Corpus scriptorum de musica, vol. 22 ([Rome]: American Institute of Musicology, 1975-78), 2:165-77. Used by permission.

Annotations:
The incipit is preceded by a dedicatory prologue beginning: "Illustrissimae dominae Beatrici de Aragonia ...." Cf. TINCOM1 TEXT and TINCOM2 TEXT.

Author: Tinctoris, Johannes
Treatise: Complexus effectuum musices
Incipit: Primo, Musica Deum delectat. Proprium etenim est cujuslibet artificis

File name: **TINCOM1**	Data input by: Stephen E. Hayes
File type: **TEXT**	Data checked by: Peter Lefferts & Luminita Aluas
MS: Print: **X**	Data approved by: Thomas J. Mathiesen
Filelist: 15th File size: 11K	Annotations:

Source of data:
Scriptorum de musica medii aevi nova series a Gerbertina altera, 4 vols., ed. Edmond de Coussemaker (Paris: Durand, 1864-76; reprint ed., Hildesheim: Olms, 1963), 4:191-95.

Annotations:
Cf. TINCOM TEXT and TINCOM2 TEXT.

Author: Tinctoris, Johannes
Treatise: Complexus viginti effectuum nobilis artis musices
Incipit: Effectus primus est iste: Musica Deum delectat.--Proprium etenim est: cujuslibet

File name: **TINCOM2**	Data input by: Stephen E. Hayes
File type: **TEXT**	Data checked by: Peter Lefferts & Luminita Aluas
MS: Print: **X**	Data approved by: Thomas J. Mathiesen
Filelist: 15th File size: 19K	Annotations:

Source of data:
Scriptorum de musica medii aevi nova series a Gerbertina altera, 4 vols., ed. Edmond de Coussemaker (Paris: Durand, 1864-76; reprint ed., Hildesheim: Olms, 1963), 4:195-200.

Annotations:
Cf. TINCOM TEXT and TINCOM1 TEXT.

Author: Tinctoris, Johannes

Treatise: De inventione et usu musice

Incipit: Cantores quibus ars uox quoque dulcis est

File name: **TININV2**   Data input by: Stephen E. Hayes

File type: **TEXT**   Data checked by: Peter Lefferts & Elisabeth Honn

MS: Print: **X**   Data approved by: Thomas J. Mathiesen

Filelist: 15th   File size: 17K   Annotations:

Source of data: Based on Cambrai, Bibliothèque municipale,
Ronald Woodley, "The Printing and   A 416, ff. 8v-12v.
Scope of Tinctoris's Fragmentary Treatise
De inventione et vsv mvsice," Early
Music History 5 (1985): 259-68. Used by
permission.

Author: Tinctoris, Johannes

Treatise: De inventione et usu musicae

Incipit: Quid sit lyra populariter leutum dicta: quid etiam quelibet instrumentalis species

File name: **TININV4**   Data input by: Stephen E. Hayes

File type: **TEXT**   Data checked by: Peter M. Lefferts

MS: Print: **X**   Data approved by: Jan W. Herlinger

Filelist: 15th   File size: 7K   Annotations:

Source of data: See also TININV.
Karl Weinmann, "Ein unbekannter
Traktat des Johannes Tinctoris," in
Riemann-Festschrift: Gesammelte
Studien: Hugo Riemann zum sechzigsten
Geburtstage überreicht von Freunden und
Schülern (Leipzig: Hesse, 1909), 269-71.

Author: Tinctoris, Johannes

Treatise: De inventione et usu musicae

Incipit: De hoc autem instrumento naturali ac prestantissimo id est voce:

File name: **TININV**   Data input by: Stephen E. Hayes

File type: **TEXT**   Data checked by: Peter Lefferts & Angela Mariani

MS: Print: **X**   Data approved by: Thomas J. Mathiesen

Filelist: 15th   File size: 41K   Annotations:

Source of data: See also TININV4.
Karl Weinmann, ed., Johannes Tinctoris
(1445-1511) und sein unbekannter
Traktat "De inventione et usu musicae"
(Regensburg: F. Pustet, 1917), 27-46.

THESAURUS MUSICARUM LATINARUM: Canon of Data Files

Author: Tinctoris, Johannes

Treatise: Diffinitorium musicae

Incipit: A est clavis locorum A re et utriusque A la mi re. Acutae claves, acuta loca

File name: **TINDIF**   Data input by: Stephen E. Hayes

File type: **TEXT**   Data checked by: Peter Lefferts & Bradley Tucker

MS: Print: **X**   Data approved by: Thomas J. Mathiesen

Filelist: 15th   File size: 40K   Annotations:

Source of data:
Scriptorum de musica medii aevi nova
series a Gerbertina altera, 4 vols., ed.
Edmond de Coussemaker (Paris: Durand,
1864-76; reprint ed., Hildesheim: Olms,
1963), 4:177-91.

Author: Tinctoris, Johannes

Treatise: Expositio manus

Incipit: Manus est brevis et utilis doctrina ostendens compendiose qualitates vocum musicae

File name: **TINEM**   Data input by: Stephen E. Hayes

File type: **TEXT**   Data checked by: Peter Lefferts & Angela Mariani

MS: Print: **X**   Data approved by: Thomas J. Mathiesen

Filelist: 15th   File size: 40K   Annotations:

Source of data: The graphics files for this treatise are TINEM
Johannis Tinctoris Opera theoretica, ed.   01GF-TINEM 10GF. Cf. TINEXP TEXT.
Albert Seay, 3 vols. in 2, Corpus
scriptorum de musica, vol. 22 ([Rome]:
American Institute of Musicology,
1975-78), 2:31-57. Used by permission.

Author: Tinctoris, Johannes

Treatise: Expositio manus

Incipit: Manus est brevis et utilis doctrina ostendens compendiose qualitates vocum musicae

File name: **TINEXP**   Data input by: Stephen E. Hayes

File type: **TEXT**   Data checked by: Peter Lefferts & Luminita Aluas

MS: Print: **X**   Data approved by: Thomas J. Mathiesen

Filelist: 15th   File size: 40K   Annotations:

Source of data: The graphics files for this treatise are TINEXP
Scriptorum de musica medii aevi nova   01GF-TINEXP 08GF. Cf. TINEM TEXT.
series a Gerbertina altera, 4 vols., ed.
Edmond de Coussemaker (Paris: Durand,
1864-76; reprint ed., Hildesheim: Olms,
1963), 4:1-16.

Author: Tinctoris, Johannes

Treatise: Liber de arte contrapuncti, Liber primus

Incipit: Contrapuncto daturos operam quid sit ac unde descendat scire primum oportet.

File name: **TINCON1**	Data input by: Stephen E. Hayes
File type: **TEXT**	Data checked by: Peter Lefferts & Luminita Aluas
MS: Print: **X**	Data approved by: Thomas J. Mathiesen
Filelist: 15th File size: 91K	Annotations:

Source of data:
Scriptorum de musica medii aevi nova series a Gerbertina altera, 4 vols., ed. Edmond de Coussemaker (Paris: Durand, 1864-76; reprint ed., Hildesheim: Olms, 1963), 4:76-119.

The incipit is preceded by dedicatory prologue, beginning: "Sacratissimo gloriosissimoque principi Ferdinando, Dei gratia Jerusalem ac Siciliae regi ...." The graphics files for this treatise are TINCON1 01GF-TINCON1 36GF. See also TINCON2 and TINCON3. Cf. TINCPT1 TEXT.

Author: Tinctoris, Johannes

Treatise: Liber de arte contrapuncti, Liber secundus

Incipit: Postquam superiori libro de concordantiis tractatum est, ut nunc de discordantiis

File name: **TINCON2**	Data input by: Stephen E. Hayes
File type: **TEXT**	Data checked by: Peter Lefferts & Luminita Aluas
MS: Print: **X**	Data approved by: Thomas J. Mathiesen
Filelist: 15th File size: 45K	Annotations:

Source of data:
Scriptorum de musica medii aevi nova series a Gerbertina altera, 4 vols., ed. Edmond de Coussemaker (Paris: Durand, 1864-76; reprint ed., Hildesheim: Olms, 1963), 4:119-47.

The graphics files for this treatise are TINCON2 01GF-TINCON2 23GF. See also TINCON1 and TINCON3. Cf. TINCPT2 TEXT.

Author: Tinctoris, Johannes

Treatise: Liber de arte contrapuncti, Liber tertius

Incipit: Quoniam autem hucusque de usu concordantiarum praemissuque discordantiarum

File name: **TINCON3**	Data input by: Stephen E. Hayes
File type: **TEXT**	Data checked by: Peter Lefferts & Luminita Aluas
MS: Print: **X**	Data approved by: Thomas J. Mathiesen
Filelist: 15th File size: 12K	Annotations:

Source of data:
Scriptorum de musica medii aevi nova series a Gerbertina altera, 4 vols., ed. Edmond de Coussemaker (Paris: Durand, 1864-76; reprint ed., Hildesheim: Olms, 1963), 4:147-53.

The graphics files for this treatise are TINCON3 01GF-TINCON3 05GF. See also TINCON1 and TINCON2. Cf. TINCPT3 TEXT.

Author: Tinctoris, Johannes

Treatise: Liber de arte contrapuncti, Liber primus

Incipit: Contrapuncto daturos operam quid sit ac unde descendat scire primum oportet.

File name: **TINCPT1**   Data input by: Stephen E. Hayes

File type: **TEXT**   Data checked by: Peter Lefferts & Bradley Tucker

MS: Print: **X**   Data approved by: Thomas J. Mathiesen

Filelist: 15th   File size: 91K   Annotations:

Source of data: The graphics files for this treatise are
Johannis Tinctoris Opera theoretica, ed.   TINCPT1 01GF-TINCPT1 34GF. Cf.
Albert Seay, 3 vols. in 2, Corpus   TINCON1 TEXT.
scriptorum de musica, vol. 22 ([Rome]:
American Institute of Musicology,
1975-78), 2:11-89. Used by permission.

Author: Tinctoris, Johannes

Treatise: Liber de arte contrapuncti, Liber secundus

Incipit: Postquam superiori libro de concordantiis tractatum est, ut nunc de discordantiis

File name: **TINCPT2**   Data input by: Stephen E. Hayes

File type: **TEXT**   Data checked by: Peter Lefferts & Angela Mariani

MS: Print: **X**   Data approved by: Thomas J. Mathiesen

Filelist: 15th   File size: 46K   Annotations:

Source of data: The graphics files for this treatise are
Johannis Tinctoris Opera theoretica, ed.   TINCPT2 01GF-TINCPT2 40GF. Cf.
Albert Seay, 3 vols. in 2, Corpus   TINCON2 TEXT.
scriptorum de musica, vol. 22 ([Rome]:
American Institute of Musicology,
1975-78), 2:90-145. Used by permission.

Author: Tinctoris, Johannes

Treatise: Liber de arte contrapuncti, Liber tertius

Incipit: Quoniam autem huc usque de usu concordantiarum permissuque discordantiarum

File name: **TINCPT3**   Data input by: Stephen E. Hayes

File type: **TEXT**   Data checked by: Peter M. Lefferts

MS: Print: **X**   Data approved by: Jan W. Herlinger

Filelist: 15th   File size: 12K   Annotations:

Source of data: The graphics files for this treatise are
Johannis Tinctoris Opera theoretica, ed.   TINCPT3 01GF-TINCPT3 07GF. Cf.
Albert Seay, 3 vols. in 2, Corpus   TINCON3 TEXT.
scriptorum de musica, vol. 22 ([Rome]:
American Institute of Musicology,
1975-78), 2:146-57. Used by permission.

Author: Tinctoris, Johannes
Treatise: Liber de natura et proprietate tonorum
Incipit: Secundum Ciceronis praeceptum in eo libro quem de Officiis inscripsit

File name: **TINNAT**	Data input by: Stephen E. Hayes
File type: **TEXT**	Data checked by: Peter Lefferts & Bradley Tucker
MS: Print: **X**	Data approved by: Thomas J. Mathiesen

Filelist: 15th   File size: 64K   Annotations:

Source of data:
Scriptorum de musica medii aevi nova series a Gerbertina altera, 4 vols., ed. Edmond de Coussemaker (Paris: Durand, 1864-76; reprint ed., Hildesheim: Olms, 1963), 4:16-41.

The graphics files for this treatise are TINNAT 01GF-TINNAT 14GF. Cf. TINLDN TEXT.

Author: Tinctoris, Johannes
Treatise: Liber de natura et proprietate tonorum
Incipit: Secundum Ciceronis praeceptum in eo libro quem de officiis inscripsit

File name: **TINLDN**	Data input by: Stephen E. Hayes
File type: **TEXT**	Data checked by: Peter Lefferts & Angela Mariani
MS: Print: **X**	Data approved by: Thomas J. Mathiesen

Filelist: 15th   File size: 64K   Annotations:

Source of data:
Johannis Tinctoris Opera theoretica, ed. Albert Seay, 3 vols. in 2, Corpus scriptorum de musica, vol. 22 ([Rome]: American Institute of Musicology, 1975-78), 1:65-104. Used by permission.

A long prologue precedes the treatise, beginning: "Praestantissimis ac celeberrimis artis musicae professoribus Domino Johanni Okeghem, christianissimi regis Francorum ...." The graphics files for this treatise are TINLDN 01GF-TINLDN 15GF. Cf. TINNAT TEXT.

Author: Tinctoris, Johannes
Treatise: Liber imperfectionum notarum musicalium
Incipit: Tractaturus autem de ipsis notarum musicalium imperfectionibus

File name: **TINLIB**	Data input by: Stephen E. Hayes
File type: **TEXT**	Data checked by: Peter Lefferts & Luminita Aluas
MS: Print: **X**	Data approved by: Thomas J. Mathiesen

Filelist: 15th   File size: 34K   Annotations:

Source of data:
Scriptorum de musica medii aevi nova series a Gerbertina altera, 4 vols., ed. Edmond de Coussemaker (Paris: Durand, 1864-76; reprint ed., Hildesheim: Olms, 1963), 4:54-66.

The graphics file for this treatise is TINLIB 01GF. Cf. TINLIMP TEXT.

Author: Tinctoris, Johannes

Treatise: Liber imperfectionum notarum musicalium

Incipit: Tractaturus autem de ipsis notarum musicalium imperfectionibus

File name: **TINLIMP**   Data input by: Stephen E. Hayes

File type: **TEXT**   Data checked by: Peter Lefferts & Bradley Tucker

MS: Print: **X**   Data approved by: Thomas J. Mathiesen

Filelist: 15th   File size: 34K   Annotations:

Source of data:

Johannis Tinctoris Opera theoretica, ed. Albert Seay, 3 vols. in 2, Corpus scriptorum de musica, vol. 22 ([Rome]: American Institute of Musicology, 1975-78), 1:143-67. Used by permission.

A long prologue precedes the treatise, beginning: "Artis musicae studiosissimo iuveni Jacobo Frontin, Johannes, Tinctoris eiusdem artis professor minimus ...." The graphics file for this treatise is TINLIMP 01GF. Cf. TINLIB TEXT.

Author: Tinctoris, Johannes

Treatise: Proportionale musices

Incipit: Proportio est duorum terminorum ad invicem habitudo. Haec autem diffinitio

File name: **TINPRO**   Data input by: Stephen E. Hayes

File type: **TEXT**   Data checked by: Peter Lefferts & Bradley Tucker

MS: Print: **X**   Data approved by: Thomas J. Mathiesen

Filelist: 15th   File size: 49K   Annotations:

Source of data:

Scriptorum de musica medii aevi nova series a Gerbertina altera, 4 vols., ed. Edmond de Coussemaker (Paris: Durand, 1864-76; reprint ed., Hildesheim: Olms, 1963), 4:153-77.

The graphics files for this treatise are TINPRO 01GF-TINPRO 19GF. Cf. TINPROM TEXT.

Author: Tinctoris, Johannes

Treatise: Proportionale musices

Incipit: Proportio est duorum terminorum ad invicem habitudo. Haec autem diffinitio

File name: **TINPROM**   Data input by: Stephen E. Hayes

File type: **TEXT**   Data checked by: Peter Lefferts & Angela Mariani

MS: Print: **X**   Data approved by: Thomas J. Mathiesen

Filelist: 15th   File size: 50K   Annotations:

Source of data:

Johannis Tinctoris Opera theoretica, ed. Albert Seay, 3 vols. in 2, Corpus scriptorum de musica, vol. 22 ([Rome]: American Institute of Musicology, 1975-78), 2a:9-60. Used by permission.

A long prologue precedes the treatise, beginning: "Sacratissimo ac invictissimo principi divo Ferdinando, regis regum dominique dominantium providentia regi Siciliae, Jherusalem et Ungariae, Johannes Tinctoris, inter musicae professores suosque capellanos minimus ...." The graphics files for this treatise are TINPROM 01GF-TINPRM 27GF. Cf. TINPRO TEXT.

Author: Tinctoris, Johannes

Treatise: Tractatus alterationum

Incipit: Alteratio est proprii valoris alicujus notae duplicatio. Notam enim alterari

File name: **TINTRALT** Data input by: Stephen E. Hayes

File type: **TEXT** Data checked by: Peter Lefferts & Luminita Aluas

MS: Print: **X** Data approved by: Thomas J. Mathiesen

Filelist: 15th File size: 10K Annotations:

Source of data: Cf. TINTRAL TEXT.
Scriptorum de musica medii aevi nova series a Gerbertina altera, 4 vols., ed. Edmond de Coussemaker (Paris: Durand, 1864-76; reprint ed., Hildesheim: Olms, 1963), 4:66-70.

Author: Tinctoris, Johannes

Treatise: Tractatus alterationum

Incipit: Alteratio est proprii valoris alicuius notae duplicatio. Notam etenim alterari

File name: **TINTRAL** Data input by: Stephen E. Hayes

File type: **TEXT** Data checked by: Peter Lefferts & Angela Mariani

MS: Print: **X** Data approved by: Thomas J. Mathiesen

Filelist: 15th File size: 10K Annotations:

Source of data: Cf. TINTRALT TEXT.
Johannis Tinctoris Opera theoretica, ed. Albert Seay, 3 vols. in 2, Corpus scriptorum de musica, vol. 22 ([Rome]: American Institute of Musicology, 1975-78), 1:173-79. Used by permission.

Author: Tinctoris, Johannes

Treatise: Tractatus de notis et pausis

Incipit: Primum igitur de notis, postmodum de pausis tractemus. Nota est signum vocis certi

File name: **TINTRAN** Data input by: Stephen E. Hayes

File type: **TEXT** Data checked by: Peter Lefferts & Luminita Aluas

MS: Print: **X** Data approved by: Thomas J. Mathiesen

Filelist: 15th File size: 15K Annotations:

Source of data: The graphics file for this treatise is TINTRAN
Scriptorum de musica medii aevi nova series a Gerbertina altera, 4 vols., ed. Edmond de Coussemaker (Paris: Durand, 1864-76; reprint ed., Hildesheim: Olms, 1963), 4:41-46. 01GF. Cf. TINTDN TEXT.

Author: Tinctoris, Johannes

Treatise: Tractatus de notis et pausis

Incipit: Primum igitur de notis, postmodum de pausis tractemus. Nota est signum vocis certi

File name: **TINTDN**   Data input by: Stephen E. Hayes

File type: **TEXT**   Data checked by: Peter Lefferts & Angela Mariani

  MS: Print: **X**   Data approved by: Thomas J. Mathiesen

Filelist: 15th   File size: 15K   Annotations:

Source of data: The graphics file for this treatise is TINTDN
  Johannis Tinctoris Opera theoretica, ed.   01GF. Cf. TINTRAN TEXT.
  Albert Seay, 3 vols. in 2, Corpus
  scriptorum de musica, vol. 22 ([Rome]:
  American Institute of Musicology,
  1975-78), 1:109-20. Used by permission.

Author: Tinctoris, Johannes

Treatise: Tractatus de punctis

Incipit: Punctus est minimum signum quod notae appositum eam dividit, aut augmentat

File name: **TINTDP**   Data input by: Stephen E. Hayes

File type: **TEXT**   Data checked by: Peter Lefferts & Angela Mariani

  MS: Print: **X**   Data approved by: Thomas J. Mathiesen

Filelist: 15th   File size: 19K   Annotations:

Source of data: The graphics files for this treatise are TINTDP
  Johannis Tinctoris Opera theoretica, ed.   01GF-TINTDP 02GF. Cf. TINTRAP TEXT.
  Albert Seay, 3 vols. in 2, Corpus
  scriptorum de musica, vol. 22 ([Rome]:
  American Institute of Musicology,
  1975-78), 1:185-98. Used by permission.

Author: Tinctoris, Johannes

Treatise: Tractatus de regulari valore notarum

Incipit: Quamquam in plerisque opusculis nostris quot et quae notae sint explicaverimus

File name: **TINTRAR**   Data input by: Stephen E. Hayes

File type: **TEXT**   Data checked by: Peter Lefferts & Luminita Aluas

  MS: Print: **X**   Data approved by: Thomas J. Mathiesen

Filelist: 15th   File size: 20K   Annotations:

Source of data: Cf. TINTDR TEXT.
  Scriptorum de musica medii aevi nova
  series a Gerbertina altera, 4 vols., ed.
  Edmond de Coussemaker (Paris: Durand,
  1864-76; reprint ed., Hildesheim: Olms,
  1963), 4:46-53.

Author: Tinctoris, Johannes

Treatise: Tractatus de regulari valore notarum

Incipit: Quamquam in plerisque opusculis nostris quot et quae notae sint explicaverimus

File name: **TINTDR**   Data input by: Stephen E. Hayes

File type: **TEXT**   Data checked by: Peter Lefferts & Angela Mariani

MS: Print: **X**   Data approved by: Thomas J. Mathiesen

Filelist: 15th   File size: 20K   Annotations:

Source of data: Cf. TINTRAR TEXT.

Johannis Tinctoris Opera theoretica, ed. Albert Seay, 3 vols. in 2, Corpus scriptorum de musica, vol. 22 ([Rome]: American Institute of Musicology, 1975-78), 1:125-38. Used by permission.

Author: Tinctoris, Johannes

Treatise: Tractatus super punctis musicalibus

Incipit: Punctus est minimum signum quod notae appositum eam dividit, aut augmentat

File name: **TINTRAP**   Data input by: Stephen E. Hayes

File type: **TEXT**   Data checked by: Peter Lefferts & Luminita Aluas

MS: Print: **X**   Data approved by: Thomas J. Mathiesen

Filelist: 15th   File size: 17K   Annotations:

Source of data: The graphics file for this treatise is TINTRAP

Scriptorum de musica medii aevi nova series a Gerbertina altera, 4 vols., ed. Edmond de Coussemaker (Paris: Durand, 1864-76; reprint ed., Hildesheim: Olms, 1963), 4:70-76.

01GF. Cf. TINTDP TEXT.

Author: Torkesey, Johannes

Treatise: Declaratio et expositio

Incipit: Ad habendam perfectam noticiam actus musice mensurabilis

File name: **TORKDEC**   Data input by: Peter M. Lefferts

File type: **MLBLL763**   Data checked by: Michael W. Lundell

MS: **X**   Print: Data approved by: Thomas J. Mathiesen

Filelist: 14th   File size: 18K   Annotations:

Source of data: =RISM BIII/4:87-91. The incipit is preceded

London, British Library, Lansdowne 763, ff. 89v-94v.

by the "triangle" figures. The graphics files for this treatise are TORKDEC 01GF-TORKDEC 05GF. See also TORTRI TEXT and TORTRIL MLBL2145.

Author: Torkesey, Johannes
Treatise: Septem sunt species
Incipit: Septem sunt species discantus secundum modernos, videlicet unisonus

File name: **TORKSEP**   Data input by: Peter M. Lefferts
File type: **TEXT**   Data checked by: Elisabeth Honn
MS: Print: **X**   Data approved by: Thomas J. Mathiesen
Filelist: 14th   File size: 3K   Annotations:
Source of data: Edited from London, British Library,
  Manfred Bukofzer, Geschichte des   Lansdowne 763, f. 94. Cf. TORKDEC
  englischen Diskants und des   MLBLL763.
  Fauxbourdons nach den theoretischen
  Quellen, Sammlung
  musikwissenschaftlicher Abhandlungen,
  Band 21 (Strassbourg: Heitz, 1936),
  136-37.

Author: Torkesey, Johannes
Treatise: Trianguli et scuti declaratio
Incipit: Ad habendam noticiam perfectam arte musice mensurabilis

File name: **TORTRIL**   Data input by: Peter M. Lefferts
File type: **MLBL2145**   Data checked by: Michael W. Lundell
MS: **X**   Print: Data approved by: Thomas J. Mathiesen
Filelist: 14th   File size: 6K   Annotations:
Source of data: =RISM BIII/4:46-47. The graphics file for this
  London, British Library, Additional   treatise is TORTRIL 01GF. See also TORTRI
  21455, ff. 7r-8v.   TEXT and TORKDEC MLBLL763.

Author: Torkesey, Johannes
Treatise: Trianguli et scuti declaratio de proportionibus musicae mensurabilis
Incipit: Ad habendam notitiam perfectam artis musicae mensurabilis

File name: **TORTRI**   Data input by: Stephen E. Hayes
File type: **TEXT**   Data checked by: Peter Lefferts & Bradley Tucker
MS: Print: **X**   Data approved by: Thomas J. Mathiesen
Filelist: 14th   File size: 7K   Annotations:
Source of data: The graphics files for this treatise are TORTRI
  Ms. Oxford, Bodley 842 (Willelmus),   01GF-TORTRI 02GF. See also TORTRIL and
  Breviarium regulare musicae; Ms. British   TORKDEC.
  Museum, Royal 12. C. VI., Tractatus de
  figuris sive de notis; Johannes Torkesey,
  Declaratio trianguli et scuti, ed. Gilbert
  Reaney and André Gilles, Corpus
  scriptorum de musica, vol. 12 ([Rome]:
  American Institute of Musicology, 1966),
  58-61. Used by permission.

Author: Ugolino Urbevetanis
Treatise: Declaratio musicae disciplinae, liber primus
Incipit: Potentiarum animae nobilissima esse noscitur intellectiva potentia, nam anima
File name: **UGODEC1A** Data input by: John Gray
File type: **TEXT**   Data checked by: Oliver Ellsworth & Bradley Tucker
  MS: Print: **X**   Data approved by: Thomas J. Mathiesen
Filelist: 15th   File size: 221K   Annotations:
Source of data: The graphics files for this treatise are
  Ugolini Urbevetanis Declaratio musicae   UGODEC1A 01GF-UGODEC1A 14GF.
  disciplinae, ed. Albert Seay, Corpus   Continues in UGODEC1B. See also
  scriptorum de musica, vol. 7/1 ([Rome]:   UGODEC2, UGODEC3A, UGODEC3B,
  American Institute of Musicology, 1959),   UGODEC4, and UGODEC5.
  13-121. Used by permission.

Author: Ugolino Urbevetanis
Treatise: Declaratio musicae disciplinae, liber primus
Incipit: Tertia differentia huius quarti tropi cum secunda conformem habet modum
File name: **UGODEC1B** Data input by: John Gray
File type: **TEXT**   Data checked by: Oliver Ellsworth & Bradley Tucker
  MS: Print: **X**   Data approved by: Thomas J. Mathiese
Filelist: 15th   File size: 238K   Annotations:
Source of data: The incipit is preceded by the headings:
  Ugolini Urbevetanis Declaratio musicae   "Capitulum LXXXI. De tertia differentia."
  disciplinae, ed. Albert Seay, Corpus   The graphics files for this treatise are
  scriptorum de musica, vol. 7/1 ([Rome]:   UGODEC1B 01GF-UGODEC1B 19GF.
  American Institute of Musicology, 1959),   Continued from UGODEC1A. See also
  121-230. Used by permission.   UGODEC2, UGODEC3A, UGODEC3B,
                  UGODEC4, and UGODEC5.

Author: Ugolino Urbevetanis
Treatise: Declaratio musicae disciplinae, liber secundus
Incipit: Homo dicitur esse liber qui sui ipsius causa est et in ratione causae moventis
File name: **UGODEC2** Data input by: John Gray
File type: **TEXT**   Data checked by: Oliver Ellsworth & Bradley Tucker
  MS: Print: **X**   Data approved by: Thomas J. Mathiesen
Filelist: 15th   File size: 113K   Annotations:
Source of data: The graphics files for this treatise are
  Ugolini Urbevetanis Declaratio musicae   UGODEC2 01GF-UGODEC2 13GF. See also
  disciplinae, ed. Albert Seay, Corpus   UGODEC1A, UGODEC1B, UGODEC3A,
  scriptorum de musica, vol. 7/2 ([Rome]:   UGODEC3B, UGODEC4, and UGODEC5.
  American Institute of Musicology, 1960),
  1-53. Used by permission.

Author: Ugolino Urbevetanis
Treatise: Declaratio musicae disciplinae, liber tertius
Incipit: Aristoteles in elenchis persuadens erudiri iuvenes et assuefieri virtutibus
File name: **UGODEC3A** Data input by: John Gray
File type: **TEXT** Data checked by: Oliver Ellsworth & Bradley Tucker
MS: Print: **X** Data approved by: Thomas J. Mathiesen
Filelist: 15th File size: 277K Annotations:
Source of data: The graphics files for this treatise are
Ugolini Urbevetanis Declaratio musicae UGODEC3A 01GF-UGODEC3A 04GF.
disciplinae, ed. Albert Seay, Corpus Continues in UGODEC3B. See also
scriptorum de musica, vol. 7/2 ([Rome]: UGODEC1A, UGODEC1B, UGODEC2,
American Institute of Musicology, 1960), UGODEC4, and UGODEC5.
54-167. Used by permission.

Author: Ugolino Urbevetanis
Treatise: Declaratio musicae disciplinae, liber tertius
Incipit: Sequitur de alteratione unde alteratio in musica est proprii valoris secundum notae
File name: **UGODEC3B** Data input by: John Gray
File type: **TEXT** Data checked by: Oliver Ellsworth & Peter Slemon
MS: Print: **X** Data approved by: Thomas J. Mathiesen
Filelist: 15th File size: 239K Annotations:
Source of data: The incipit is preceded by the headings:
Ugolini Urbevetanis Declaratio musicae "Capitulum IV. Capitulum quartum de
disciplinae, ed. Albert Seay, Corpus alteratione." The graphics files for this treatise
scriptorum de musica, vol. 7/2 ([Rome]: are UGODEC3B 01GF-UGODEC3B 03GF.
American Institute of Musicology, 1960), Continued from UGODEC3A. See also
167-266. Used by permission. UGODEC1A, UGODEC1B, UGODEC2,
  UGODEC4, and UGODEC5.

Author: Ugolino Urbevetanis
Treatise: Declaratio musicae disciplinae, liber quartus
Incipit: Tres esse musicas, mundanam, scilicet, humanam et instrumentalem, ex prioris
File name: **UGODEC4** Data input by: John Gray
File type: **TEXT** Data checked by: Oliver Ellsworth & Peter Slemon
MS: Print: **X** Data approved by: Thomas J. Mathiesen
Filelist: 15th File size: 152K Annotations:
Source of data: See also UGODEC1A, UGODEC1B,
Ugolini Urbevetanis Declaratio musicae UGODEC2, UGODEC3A, UGODEC3B, and
disciplinae, ed. Albert Seay, Corpus UGODEC5.
scriptorum de musica, vol. 7/3 ([Rome]:
American Institute of Musicology, 1962),
1-84. Used by permission.

Author: Ugolino Urbevetanis

Treatise: Declaratio musicae disciplinae, liber quintus

Incipit: Etsi in huius operis nostri primordio de excellentia atque intellectus nobilitate

File name: **UGODEC5**   Data input by: John Gray

File type: **TEXT**   Data checked by: Oliver Ellsworth & Peter Slemon

MS: Print: **X**   Data approved by: Thomas J. Mathiesen

Filelist: 15th   File size: 284K   Annotations:

Source of data: The graphics files for this treatise are
Ugolini Urbevetanis Declaratio musicae   UGODEC5 01GF-UGODEC5 30GF. See also
disciplinae, ed. Albert Seay, Corpus   UGODEC1A, UGODEC1B, UGODEC2,
scriptorum de musica, vol. 7/3 ([Rome]:   UGODEC3A, UGODEC3B, and UGODEC4.
American Institute of Musicology, 1962),
85-226. Used by permission.

Author: Ugolino Urbevetanis

Treatise: Musica disciplina

Incipit: Musici [latini] ut eam rem ad majorem nobilioremque excellentiam ducerent

File name: **UGOMUS**   Data input by: John Csonka

File type: **TEXT**   Data checked by: Bradley Jon Tucker

MS: Print: **X**   Data approved by: Thomas J. Mathiesen

Filelist: 15th   File size: 68K   Annotations:

Source of data: Based on Rome, Biblioteca Casanatense,
Adrien de la Fage, Essais de   C.II,3; fonds Baini. The text is preceded by a
dipthérographie musicale (Paris: Legouix,   complete transcription of the rubrics for Books
1864), 118-65.   I-V. The graphics files for this treatise are
     UGOMUS 01GF-UGOMUS 17GF.

Author: Ugolino Urbevetanis

Treatise: Tractatus monochordi

Incipit: Musicae disciplinae quinque partium pratice et speculative declaratione peracta

File name: **UGOTRAM**   Data input by: John Gray

File type: **TEXT**   Data checked by: Oliver Ellsworth & Peter Slemon

MS: Print: **X**   Data approved by: Thomas J. Mathiesen

Filelist: 15th   File size: 45K   Annotations:

Source of data: The graphics files for this treatise are
Ugolini Urbevetanis Declaratio musicae   UGOTRAM 01GF-UGOTRAM 06GF.
disciplinae, ed. Albert Seay, Corpus
scriptorum de musica, vol. 7/3 ([Rome]:
American Institute of Musicology, 1962),
227-53. Used by permission.

Author: Vanneo, Stephano

Treatise: Recanetum de musica aurea, liber II, capituli XX-XXXVII

Incipit: Mihi per proportionum campum qui patentissimus est

File name: **VANREC**	Data input by: Peter Slemon
File type: **TEXT**	Data checked by: Bradley Jon Tucker
MS: Print: **X**	Data approved by: Thomas J. Mathiesen

Filelist: 16th   File size: 47K   Annotations:

Source of data:

Stephano Vanneo, Recanetum de musica aurea, liber II, capituli XX-XXXVII, ed. Albert Seay, Texts/Translations, no. 2 (Colorado Springs: Colorado College Music Press, 1979). Used by permission.

The graphics files for this treatise are VANREC 01GF-VANREC 03GF.

Author: Villa Dei, Alexander de

Treatise: Carmen de musica cum glossis

Incipit: Postquam pro rudibus, fabricavi materiale, Grammatice partes reseraris cum carmine

File name: **VILCAR**	Data input by: Peter Slemon
File type: **TEXT**	Data checked by: Bradley Jon Tucker
MS: Print: **X**	Data approved by: Thomas J. Mathiesen

Filelist: 13th   File size: 35K   Annotations:

Source of data:

Alexander de Villa Dei, Carmen de musica cum glossis, ed. Albert Seay, Critical Texts, no. 5 (Colorado Springs: Colorado College Music Press, 1977), 1-25. Used by permission.

This text makes use of superscript letters to key the various glosses to specific words of phrases. In this file, superscript letters are indicated by their placement within brackets immediately following the word (i.e., without an intervening spcae) to which they pertain.

Author: Vogelsang, Johannes

Treatise: Musicae rudimenta

Incipit: Musica est ars recte canendi modulandive cognitionem administrans.

File name: **VOGMUS**	Data input by: Elisabeth Honn
File type: **TEXT**	Data checked by: Andreas Giger
MS: Print: **X**	Data approved by: Thomas J. Mathiesen

Filelist: 16th   File size: 55K   Annotations:

Source of data:

Renate Federhofer-Koenigs, "Johannes Vogelsang und sein Musiktraktat (1542): Ein Beitrag zur Musikgeschichte von Feldkirch (Vorarlberg)," Kirchenmusikalisches Jahrbuch 49 (1965): 76-113. Used by permission.

The treatise was published in Augsburg in 1542 by Valentin Otmar. The incipit is preceded by a laudatory poem, beginning: "Qui cupis in teneris, ..." and a dedicatory preface, beginning: "Cum inter alias ludi litterarii ...." The graphics files for this treatise are VOGMUS 01GF-VOGMUS 23GF.

Author: Walsingham, Thomas
Treatise: Regule Magistri. Thome Walsingham. De figuris compositis. et non compositis. et
Incipit: Cvm sit necessarium iuuenilibus ad facultatem organicam tendentibus noticiam

File name: **WALREGU**	Data input by: Peter M. Lefferts
File type: **MLBLL763**	Data checked by: Michael W. Lundell
MS: **X** Print:	Data approved by: Thomas J. Mathiesen

Filelist: 14th   File size: 24K   Annotations:

Source of data: =RISM BIII/4:87-91. The graphics files for
London, British Library, Lansdowne 763,   this treatise are WALREGU
ff. 98v-105r.   01GF-WALREGU 07GF. See also WALREG
                                               TEXT.

Author: Walsingham, Thomas
Treatise: Regulae Magistri Thomae Walsingham de figuris compositis et non compositis, et
Incipit: Cum sit necessarium iuvenilibus ad facultatem organicam tendentibus notitiam

File name: **WALREG**	Data input by: Stephen E. Hayes
File type: **TEXT**	Data checked by: Peter Lefferts & Bradley Tucker
MS: Print: **X**	Data approved by: Thomas J. Mathiesen

Filelist: 14th   File size: 25K   Annotations:

Source of data: Based on London, British Library, Lansdowne
Johannes Hothby, Opera omnia de musica   763. The graphics files for this treatise are
mensurabili; Thomas Walsingham,   WALREG 01GF-WALREG 06GF. See also
Regulae de musica mensurabili, ed.   WALREGU MLBLL763.
Gilbert Reaney, Corpus scriptorum de
musica, vol. 31 (Neuhausen-Stuttgart:
Haenssler Verlag for the American
Institute of Musicology, 1983), 74-98.
Used by permission.

Author: Weyts, Carmelite, Nicasius
Treatise: Regule
Incipit: Omnis nota in cantu mensurato Maxima figuratur quadrata

File name: **WEYREG**	Data input by: C. Matthew Balensuela
File type: **TEXT**	Data checked by: John Snyder
MS: Print: **X**	Data approved by: Thomas J. Mathiesen

Filelist: 15th   File size: 8K   Annotations:

Source of data: The graphics file for this treatise is WEYREG
Scriptorum de musica medii aevi nova   01GF.
series a Gerbertina altera, 4 vols., ed.
Edmond de Coussemaker (Paris: Durand,
1864-76; reprint ed., Hildesheim: Olms,
1963), 3:262-64.

Author: Willehelmus Hirsaugensis
Treatise: Musica
Incipit: Othlochus. Postquam donante Deo petitionibus meis et quaestionibus in astronomica

File name: **WILMU**   Data input by: Sean Ferguson
File type: **TEXT**   Data checked by: Charles M. Atkinson
  MS: Print: **X**   Data approved by: Thomas J. Mathiesen
Filelist: 9th-11t   File size: 81K   Annotations:
Source of data: The graphics files for this treatise are WILMU
  Scriptores ecclesiastici de musica sacra   01GF-WILMU 03GF. See also WILMUS and
  potissimum, 3 vols., ed. Martin Gerbert   WILMUSI.
  (St. Blaise: Typis San-Blasianis, 1784;
  reprint ed., Hildesheim: Olms, 1963),
  2:154-82.

Author: Willehelmus Hirsaugensis
Treatise: Musica
Incipit: Othlochus. Postquam donante Deo petitionibus meis et quaestionibus in astronomica

File name: **WILMUSI**   Data input by: Angela Mariani
File type: **TEXT**   Data checked by: Peter Slemon
  MS: Print: **X**   Data approved by: Thomas J. Mathiesen
Filelist: 9th-11t   File size: 80K   Annotations:
Source of data: The graphics file for this treatise is WILMUSI
  Patrologia cursus completus, series latina,   01GF. See also WILMUS and WILMU.
  ed. J. P. Migne, 221 vols. (Paris: Garnier,
  1844-1904), 150:1147-78.

Author: Willehelmus Hirsaugensis
Treatise: Musica
Incipit: Othlochus. Postquam donante Deo petitionibus meis et quaestionibus in astronomica

File name: **WILMUS**   Data input by: Stephen E. Hayes
File type: **TEXT**   Data checked by: Peter Lefferts & Angela Mariani
  MS: Print: **X**   Data approved by: Thomas J. Mathiesen
Filelist: 9th-11t   File size: 87K   Annotations:
Source of data: The incipit is preceded by a list of chapter
  Willehelmi Hirsaugensis Musica, ed.   headings. The graphics files for this treatise
  Denis Harbinson, Corpus scriptorum de   are WILMUS 01GF-WILMUS 04GF. See also
  musica, vol. 23 ([Rome]: American   WILMUSI and WILMU.
  Institute of Musicology, 1975), 11-75.
  Used by permission.

Author: Willelmus
Treatise: Breviarium regulare musice
Incipit: Multorum cantorum scripturas varias ac opera ad practicam musice laborata

File name: **WILBREV**   Data input by: John Snyder
File type: **MOBB842**   Data checked by: Bradley Jon Tucker
  MS: **X**   Print: Data approved by: Thomas J. Mathiesen
Filelist: 14th   File size: 31K   Annotations:
Source of data: =RISM BIII/4:110-15. The graphics files for
  Oxford, Bodleian Library, Bodley 842   this treatise are WILBREV 01GF-WILBREV
  (S.C. 2575), ff. 62v-73v.   07GF. Cf. WILBRE TEXT.

Author: Willelmus

Treatise: Breviarium regulare musicae

Incipit: Multorum cantorum scripturas varias ac opera ad practicam musicae laborata

File name: **WILBRE**

File type: **TEXT**

MS: Print: **X**

Filelist: 14th   File size: 30K

Data input by: Stephen E. Hayes

Data checked by: Peter Lefferts & Bradley Tucker

Data approved by: Thomas J. Mathiesen

Annotations:

Source of data:

Ms. Oxford, Bodley 842 (Willelmus), Breviarium regulare musicae; Ms. British Museum, Royal 12. C. VI., Tractatus de figuris sive de notis; Johannes Torkesey, Declaratio trianguli et scuti, Corpus scriptorum de musica, vol. 12 ([Rome]: American Institute of Musicology, 1966), 15-31. Used by permission.

Text edited from Oxford, Bodleian Library, Bodley 842. The graphics files for this treatise are WILBRE 01GF-WILBRE 06GF. Cf. WILBREV MOBB842.

Author: Wylde, John

Treatise: Musica guidonis

Incipit: Quia iuxta sapientissimum Salomonem dura est vt inferus Emulatio

File name: **WYLMUSI**

File type: **MLBLL763**

MS: **X**   Print:

Filelist: 15th   File size: 221K

Data input by: Peter M. Lefferts

Data checked by: Julie Langford-Johnson

Data approved by: Thomas J. Mathiesen

Annotations:

Source of data:

London, British Library, Lansdowne 763, ff. 3r-51v.

=RISM BIII/4:87-91. The graphics files for this treatise are WYLMUSI 01GF-WYLMUSI 34GF. Cf. WYLMUS TEXT.

Author: Wylde, Johannes

Treatise: Musica manualis cum tonale

Incipit: Quia iuxta sapientissimum Salomonem, Dura est ut infernus aemulatio

File name: **WYLMUS**

File type: **TEXT**

MS: Print: **X**

Filelist: 15th   File size: 191K

Data input by: Stephen E. Hayes

Data checked by: Peter M. Lefferts & Andreas Giger

Data approved by: Thomas J. Mathiesen

Annotations:

Source of data:

Johannis Wylde Musica manualis cum tonale, ed. Cecily Sweeney, Corpus scriptorum de musica, vol. 28 (Neuhausen-Stuttgart: American Institute of Musicology, 1982), 43-206. Used by permission.

The graphics files for this treatise are WYLMUS 01GF-WYLMUS 80GF. Cf. WYLMUSI MLBLL763.

"Cantabo Domino in vita mea." Pro huius, opusculi mei humilis, intentione tria oportet
  Author: Anonymous
    Treatise: Ars cantus mensurabilis mensurata per modos iuris
        File name: **ANO5ACM**   File type: **TEXT**

(De notulis) Sciendum est quod in notulis pro exigentia motellorum, conductorum
  Author: Anonymous
    Treatise: [Tractatus de cantu mensurabili]
        File name: **ANOCANT**   File type: **TEXT**

(M)usica est recte modulandi scientia. Et deducitur a musa vocabulo greco quod cantum
  Author: Anonymous
    Treatise: Introductorium musicae
        File name: **ANOLEIP**   File type: **TEXT**

... ascendo vel descendo, ut hic supra. Sic formantur breves plicatae
  Author: Anonymous
    Treatise: De diversis manieribus in musica mensurabili
        File name: **ANO7DDM**   File type: **TEXT**

... decem et octo. Inter sedecim et octodecim unus numerus intercidit
  Author: Anonymous
    Treatise: [De proportionibus et de intervallis]
        File name: **ANOPI**   File type: **MOBB842**

<Capitulum LXI. De litteris vel signis monocordi.> Dicunt musice doctores monocordi
  Author: Jacobus Leodiensis
    Treatise: Speculum musicae, Liber sextus
        File name: **JACSP6B**   File type: **TEXT**

A est clavis locorum A re et utriusque A la mi re. Acutae claves, acuta loca
  Author: Tinctoris, Johannes
    Treatise: Diffinitorium musicae
        File name: **TINDIF**   File type: **TEXT**

A. Proslambanosmenos, B. Hypate hypaton
  Author: Marchetus de Padua
    Treatise: Lucidarium, tractatus decimusquintus
        File name: **MARLU15**   File type: **TEXT**

A. Proslambanosmenos, [sqb]. Ypate ypaton
  Author: Marchetus de Padua
    Treatise: Lucidarium, tractatus quintus decimus
        File name: **MARLUC15**   File type: **TEXT**

Ab omni superparticulari si continuam ei superparticularem quis auferat proportionem
  Author: Anonymous III
    Treatise: Fragmentum musices
        File name: **ANO3FRA**   File type: **TEXT**

Ab omni superparticulari si continuam ei superparticularem quis auferat proportionem
  Author: Anonymous III
    Treatise: Fragmentum musices
        File name: **ANO3FRAM**   File type: **TEXT**

216

THESAURUS MUSICARUM LATINARUM: Index of Incipits

Abbas Pambo misit discipulum suum in Alexandriam, ut eorum manufacta venderet.
Author: Pambo, Abbas
Treatise: [Gerontikon]
File name: **PAMGER**   File type: **TEXT**

Actus activorum in patiente sunt et disposito si quidem dispositio ad aliquam formam
Author: Jacobus Leodiensis
Treatise: Speculum musicae, Liber secundus
File name: **JACSP2A**   File type: **TEXT**

Ad discendam artem discantandi notandum est, quod omnis discantus uno sex modorum
Author: Dietricus
Treatise: Regulae super discantum et ad discernendum ipsas notas discantus
File name: **DIEREG**   File type: **TEXT**

Ad evidentiam cantus organici est sciendum, quod cantus organicus dividitur
Author: Anonymous
Treatise: De cantu organico
File name: **AGANOCO**   File type: **TEXT**

Ad evidentiam valoris notularum, sciendum quod quotienscumque nota
Author: Anonymous II
Treatise: De musica antiqua et nova
File name: **ANO2DEM**   File type: **TEXT**

Ad evidentiam valoris notularum, sciendum quod, quotienscumque nota
Author: Anonymous
Treatise: De valore notularum tam veteris quam novae artis
File name: **ANO2DEV**   File type: **TEXT**

Ad habendam noticiam perfectam arte musice mensurabilis
Author: Torkesey, Johannes
Treatise: Trianguli et scuti declaratio
File name: **TORTRIL**   File type: **MLBL2145**

Ad habendam notitiam perfectam artis musicae mensurabilis
Author: Torkesey, Johannes
Treatise: Trianguli et scuti declaratio de proportionibus musicae mensurabilis
File name: **TORTRI**   File type: **TEXT**

Ad habendam perfectam noticiam actus musice mensurabilis
Author: Torkesey, Johannes
Treatise: Declaratio et expositio
File name: **TORKDEC**   File type: **MLBLL763**

Ad honorem et gloriam Sanctissime Trinitatis
Author: Anonymous V
Treatise: Ars cantus mensurabilis
File name: **ANO5ARS**   File type: **TEXT**

Ad honorem Sanctae et Individuae Trinitatis et intemeratae viriginis Mariae
Author: Petrus dictus Palma ociosa
Treatise: Compendium de discantu mensurabili
File name: **PETCOM**   File type: **TEXT**

THESAURUS MUSICARUM LATINARUM: Index of Incipits

Ad huius evidentiam est sciendum, quod secundum Remigium
> Author: Marchetus de Padua
>> Treatise: Lucidarium, tractatus secundus
>>> File name: **MARLU2**   File type: **TEXT**

Ad huius evidentiam est sciendum quod, secundum Remigium
> Author: Marchetus de Padua
>> Treatise: Lucidarium, tractatus secundus
>>> File name: **MARLUC2**   File type: **TEXT**

Ad musicae initiamenta quemlibet ingredientem, qui aliquam scilicet interim
> Author: Hucbald
>> Treatise: De harmonica institutione
>>> File name: **HUCHAR**   File type: **TEXT**

Ad musicae initiamenta quemlibet ingredientem, qui aliquam scilicet interim
> Author: Hucbald
>> Treatise: De harmonica institutione
>>> File name: **HUCHARM**   File type: **TEXT**

Ad sciendum artem discantus, primo est sciendum
> Author: Johannes de Muris
>> Treatise: Ars discantus
>>> File name: **MURARSD**   File type: **TEXT**

Ad videndum autem de numeris musicalibus
> Author: Marchetus de Padua
>> Treatise: Lucidarium, tractatus tertius
>>> File name: **MARLU3**   File type: **TEXT**

Ad videndum autem de numeris musicalibus
> Author: Marchetus de Padua
>> Treatise: Lucidarium, tractatus tercius
>>> File name: **MARLUC3**   File type: **TEXT**

Adsit principio Virgo Maria meo. Tibi, dilecte frater
> Author: Prosdocimo de' Beldomandi
>> Treatise: Brevis summula proportionum quantum ad musicam pertinet
>>> File name: **PROBRE1**   File type: **TEXT**

Alteratio est proprii valoris alicuius notae duplicatio. Notam etenim alterari
> Author: Tinctoris, Johannes
>> Treatise: Tractatus alterationum
>>> File name: **TINTRAL**   File type: **TEXT**

Alteratio est proprii valoris alicujus notae duplicatio. Notam enim alterari
> Author: Tinctoris, Johannes
>> Treatise: Tractatus alterationum
>>> File name: **TINTRALT**   File type: **TEXT**

Amicorum iusta et honesta petitio coactio reputatur, hac itaque me stimulante
> Author: Johannes de Muris
>> Treatise: Summa
>>> File name: **MURSUM**   File type: **TEXT**

Amicorum iusta et honesta petitio coactio reputatur. Hac itaque me stimulante
    Author: Perseus and Petrus
        Treatise: Summa musice
                File name: **PEPESUM**   File type: **TEXT**

Animaduerti quam plurimos iam pridem Adolescentulos, iucundissimae Musices
    Author: Liban, Jerzy
        Treatise: De musicae laudibus oratio
                File name: **LIBDEM**   File type: **TEXT**

Ante inventionem hujus artis, homines naturaliter cantibus utebantur
    Author: Anonymous
        Treatise: Quatuor Principalia II
                File name: **QUAPRIB2**   File type: **TEXT**

Aristobolus. Age nunc, si tibi quicquam nervorum est, musicam tueare
    Author: Gresemund, Dietrich
        Treatise: Lucubratiunculae bonarum septem artium liberalium, capitulum quintum, De
                File name: **GRELUC**   File type: **TEXT**

Aristoteles in elenchis persuadens erudiri iuvenes et assuefieri virtutibus
    Author: Ugolino Urbevetanis
        Treatise: Declaratio musicae disciplinae, liber tertius
                File name: **UGODEC3A**   File type: **TEXT**

Ars est iam utillima, a philosophis composita, ars est vocata Musica
    Author: Osbernus Cantuariensis (?)
        Treatise: De vocum consonantiis
                File name: **OSBMUS**   File type: **TEXT**

Ars pratice cantus mensurabilis duplex reperitu
    Author: Prosdocimo de' Beldomandi
        Treatise: Tractatus practice de musica mensurabili ad modum italicorum
                File name: **PROTRAP2**   File type: **TEXT**

Aurea personet lyra clara modulamina;
    Author: Anonymous
        Treatise: Fragmenta musica
                File name: **ANOFRA3**   File type: **TEXT**

Autenticus autoralis et auctoritate plenus: unde et libros antiquissimos siue firmitate
    Author: Anonymous
        Treatise: De modis musicis
                File name: **ANODM**   File type: **TEXT**

Authenticus protus constat ex prima specie diapente, et ex prima specie diatessaron
    Author: Berno Augiensis
        Treatise: Tonabius [sic]
                File name: **BERNTO**   File type: **TEXT**

Authenticus protus constat ex prima specie diapente, et ex prima specie diatessaron
    Author: Berno Augiensis
        Treatise: Tonarius
                File name: **BERNTON**   File type: **TEXT**

THESAURUS MUSICARUM LATINARUM: Index of Incipits

Beatissimo atque dulcissimo fratri Michaeli Guido, per anfractus multos dejectus
  Author: Guido d'Arezzo
    Treatise: Epistola Guidonis Michaeli monacho de ignoto cantu
      File name: **GUIEP**　　　File type: **TEXT**

Beatissimo atque dulcissimo Fratri Michaeli Guido, per anfractus multos deiectus
  Author: Guido d'Arezzo
    Treatise: Epistola Guidonis Michaeli monacho de ignoto cantu directa
      File name: **GUIEPI**　　　File type: **TEXT**

Bene res se habet: iacta sunt fundamenta vt inquit eximius orator.
  Author: Burtius, Nicolaus
    Treatise: Musices opusculum, tractatus tertius
      File name: **BURMUS3**　　　File type: **TEXT**

Binas longas maximam binasque breves longam atque brevem duas semibreves
  Author: Ramus de Pareia, Bartholomeus
    Treatise: Musica practica, tertia pars, tractatus primus
      File name: **RAMMP3T1**　　　File type: **TEXT**

Boethius, musicae doctor eximius, non ignorans quod scientia unius generis subiecti est,
  Author: Jacobus Leodiensis
    Treatise: Speculum musicae, Liber quintus
      File name: **JACSP5A**　　　File type: **TEXT**

Boetii musices disciplina quinque voluminibus comprehensa quoniam profundissimis
  Author: Ramus de Pareia, Bartholomeus
    Treatise: Musica practica, prima pars, tractatus primus
      File name: **RAMMP1T1**　　　File type: **TEXT**

Cantores quibus ars uox quoque dulcis est
  Author: Tinctoris, Johannes
    Treatise: De inventione et usu musice
      File name: **TININV2**　　　File type: **TEXT**

Cantum quem Cisterciensis ordinis ecclesiae cantare consueverant, licet gravis
  Author: Anonymous
    Treatise: Epistola Sancti Bernardi De revisione cantus Cisterciensis, et Tractatus
      File name: **BEREPI**　　　File type: **TEXT**

Cantum, a beato papa Gregorio editum, quelibet se habere fatentur ecclesie.
  Author: Abbot Guido
    Treatise: Regulae de arte musica
      File name: **ABGURAM**　　　File type: **TEXT**

Cantus dicitur autenticus melodia cuius diapente recipit inferius et dyatesseron
  Author: Anonymous
    Treatise: [Tractatulus de musica]
      File name: **ANOCADI**　　　File type: **TEXT**

Capitulum C. Instantiae contra dicta et ad illas responsio. Forsitan instabitur
  Author: Jacobus Leodiensis
    Treatise: Speculum musicae, Liber secundus
      File name: **JACSP2C**　　　File type: **TEXT**

THESAURUS MUSICARUM LATINARUM: Index of Incipits

Capitulum L. Unitatis ad binarium collatio et numeri imparis ad parem.
>Author: Jacobus Leodiensis
>>Treatise: Speculum musicae, Liber primus
>>>File name: **JACSP1B**   File type: **TEXT**

Capitulum LIII. De commatis simplicitate. Comma consonantia simplex dici potest
>Author: Jacobus Leodiensis
>>Treatise: Speculum musicae, Liber secundus
>>>File name: **JACSP2B**   File type: **TEXT**

Capitulum LXI. [De litteris vel signis monocordi.] Dicunt musice doctores monocordi
>Author: Jacobus Leodiensis
>>Treatise: Speculum musicae, Liber sextus
>>>File name: **JACSM6B**   File type: **TEXT**

Capitulum XXVII. Quod ex numeris contra se primis numeri nascuntur contra se primi.
>Author: Jacobus Leodiensis
>>Treatise: Speculum musicae, Liber tertius
>>>File name: **JACSP3B**   File type: **TEXT**

Capitulum XXXI. Ratio superius positae descriptionis. Tria tetrachorda tali nobis ratione
>Author: Jacobus Leodiensis
>>Treatise: Speculum musicae, Liber quintus
>>>File name: **JACSP5B**   File type: **TEXT**

Chromatici Generis chordae ita per tetrachorda disponuntur: ut tertia tantum chorda
>Author: Gaffurio, Franchino
>>Treatise: De harmonia musicorum instrumentorum opus, liber secundus
>>>File name: **GAFHAR2**   File type: **TEXT**

Circa artem quoque musicam hec eadam inquirenda sunt scilicet: quid sit ipsa
>Author: Gundissalinus, Dominicus
>>Treatise: De divisione philosophiae, Liber decimus, "De musica"
>>>File name: **GUNDDIV**   File type: **TEXT**

Circa modum discantandi primo attendendum est.
>Author: Anonymous
>>Treatise: [De discantu et contranota]
>>>File name: **ANOCMD**   File type: **TEXT**

Circa modum discantandi primo attendendum est.
>Author: Anonymous
>>Treatise: [De discantu et contranota]
>>>File name: **ANODDC**   File type: **MLBL2145**

Clavis est reseratio notarum in cantu quolibet signatarum
>Author: Marchetus de Padua
>>Treatise: Lucidarium, tractatus decimusquartus
>>>File name: **MARLU14**   File type: **TEXT**

Clavis est reseratio notarum in cantu quolibet signatarum
>Author: Marchetus de Padua
>>Treatise: Lucidarium, tractatus quartus decimus
>>>File name: **MARLUC14**   File type: **TEXT**

221

Cogitanti mihi viri disertissimi quod nullus est suauior animi cibus teste Lactantio.
> Author: Burtius, Nicolaus
>> Treatise: Musices opusculum, tractatus secundus
>>> File name: **BURMUS2**   File type: **TEXT**

Cognita modulatione melorum secundum viam octo troporum et secundum usum
> Author: Anonymous 4
>> Treatise: [Musica]
>>> File name: **ANO4MUS**   File type: **TEXT**

Cognita modulatione melorum, secundum viam octo troporum, et secundum usum
> Author: Anonymous 4
>> Treatise: De mensuris et discantu
>>> File name: **ANO4DEM**   File type: **TEXT**

Coniunctio in musica est dispositio sive ordinatio sonorum
> Author: Marchetus de Padua
>> Treatise: Lucidarium, tractatus nonus
>>> File name: **MARLU9**   File type: **TEXT**

Coniunctio in musica est dispositio sive ordinatio sonorum
> Author: Marchetus de Padua
>> Treatise: Lucidarium, tractatus nonus
>>> File name: **MARLUC9**   File type: **TEXT**

Consonanciarum igitur racionibus perspectis; ad species earum perspiciendas
> Author: Theinredus Doverensis
>> Treatise: Musica, liber tercius
>>> File name: **TDMUS3**   File type: **MOBB842**

Consonantie contrapuncti demonstrativi ad oculum sunt sex
> Author: Anonymous VIII
>> Treatise: Regulae de contrapuncto
>>> File name: **ANO8REG**   File type: **TEXT**

Contrapuncto daturos operam quid sit ac unde descendat scire primum oportet.
> Author: Tinctoris, Johannes
>> Treatise: Liber de arte contrapuncti, Liber primus
>>> File name: **TINCON1**   File type: **TEXT**

Contrapuncto daturos operam quid sit ac unde descendat scire primum oportet.
> Author: Tinctoris, Johannes
>> Treatise: Liber de arte contrapuncti, Liber primus
>>> File name: **TINCPT1**   File type: **TEXT**

Contrapunctus secundam tenens musicae cantandi differentiam est duorum vel plurium
> Author: Guillermus de Podio
>> Treatise: Ars musicorum liber VI
>>> File name: **GUIARS6**   File type: **TEXT**

Copiose ac luculenter mi Aaron quae ad cantum planum pertinere uidebantur
> Author: Aaron, Petrus
>> Treatise: Libri tres de institutione harmonica, liber secundus
>>> File name: **AARIH2**   File type: **TEXT**

Cum de mensurabili musica sit nostra presens intencio
    Author: Anonymous
        Treatise: [De mensurabili musica]
                File name: **ANOMM**   File type: **MLBL2145**

Cum de plana musica quidam philosophi sufficienter tractaverint
    Author: Franco
        Treatise: Ars cantus mensurabilis
                File name: **FRAACM**   File type: **TEXT**

Cum de plana musica quidam philosophi sufficienter tractaverint
    Author: Franco
        Treatise: Ars cantus mensurabilis
                File name: **FRAARSC**   File type: **TEXT**

Cum enim omnis musica de consonantiis tractet, ut Musica sillabarum refert
    Author: Ciconia, Johannes
        Treatise: Nova musica, liber secundus de speciebus
                File name: **CICNM2**   File type: **TEXT**

Cum frequenter in ecclesiae vestrae dioecesibus chorus psallentium psalmorum
    Author: Regino Prumiensis
        Treatise: De harmonica institutione
                File name: **REGDHI**   File type: **TEXT**

Cum frequenter in ecclesiae vestrae dioecesibus chorus psallentium psalmorum
    Author: Regino Prumiensis
        Treatise: Epistola de harmonica institutione
                File name: **REGHAR**   File type: **TEXT**

Cum frequenter in Ecclesiae vestrae dioecesibus chorus psallentium psalmorum
    Author: Regino Prumiensis
        Treatise: De harmonica institutione
                File name: **REGHARI**   File type: **TEXT**

Cum igitur de arte musice tractare debeamus
    Author: Johannes Verulus de Anagnia
        Treatise: Liber de musica
                File name: **VERLDM**   File type: **TEXT**

Cum igitur de arte musice tractare debeamus
    Author: Johannes Verulus de Anagnia
        Treatise: Liber de musica
                File name: **VERLIB**   File type: **TEXT**

Cum igitur humana natura scire desiderat, ideo divina clementia philosophis peritiam
    Author: Capuanus, Nicolaus
        Treatise: Compendium musicale
                File name: **NICCOM**   File type: **TEXT**

Cum in isto tractatu de figuris sive de notis, que sunt, et de earum proprietatibus
    Author: Anonymous 6
        Treatise: Tractatus de figuris sive de notis
                File name: **ANO6TRA**   File type: **TEXT**

Cum in isto tractatu de figuris sive de notis, quae sunt et de earum proprietatibus
>Author: Anonymous
>>Treatise: Tractatus de figuris sive de notis
>>>File name: **TRADEF**   File type: **TEXT**

Cum multi ueterum ac modernorum de diaphonia satis indiscrete tractassent ego
>Author: Anonymous
>>Treatise: [Ad organum faciendum]
>>>File name: **ADORFBB**   File type: **TEXT**

Cum obscuritas diaphonia multis et perplurimum tardis in ingenio difficultatem praestet
>Author: Anonymous
>>Treatise: Ad organum faciendum
>>>File name: **ADORF**   File type: **TEXT**

Cum obscuritas diaphoniae multis et perplurimum tardis ingenio difficultatem praestet
>Author: Anonymous
>>Treatise: Ad organum faciendum
>>>File name: **ADORFA**   File type: **TEXT**

Cum obscuritas diaphonie multis et perplurimum tardis in ingenio difficultatem prestet
>Author: Anonymous
>>Treatise: Ad organum faciendum
>>>File name: **ADORFAC**   File type: **TEXT**

Cum omnis institutio cuiuscunque rei a ratione suscepte de beata diffinitione proficisci:
>Author: Gaffurio, Franchino
>>Treatise: Theorica musice, liber secundus
>>>File name: **GAFTM2**   File type: **TEXT**

Cum omnis quantitas aut est continua aut discreta
>Author: Anonymous
>>Treatise: Quatuor Principalia IV
>>>File name: **QUAPRIB4**   File type: **TEXT**

Cum regularis debitaque pronunciatio vniuscuiusque vocis (que finis grammatice
>Author: Sebastianus de Felstin
>>Treatise: Modus regulariter accentuandi lectiones Matutinales, prophetias necnon
>>>File name: **FELMOD**   File type: **TEXT**

Cum sit necessarium iuvenilibus ad facultatem organicam tendentibus notitiam
>Author: Walsingham, Thomas
>>Treatise: Regulae Magistri Thomae Walsingham de figuris compositis et non
>>>File name: **WALREG**   File type: **TEXT**

Cum, in superiore libro, de consonantiis quaedam narrata sint, quaedam probata sint
>Author: Jacobus Leodiensis
>>Treatise: Speculum musicae, Liber tertius
>>>File name: **JACSP3A**   File type: **TEXT**

Cum, inquiunt, de plana musica quidam philosophi sufficienter tractaverint
>Author: Franco
>>Treatise: Ars cantus mensurabilis
>>>File name: **FRAARS**   File type: **TEXT**

THESAURUS MUSICARUM LATINARUM: Index of Incipits

Cum, inquiunt, de plana musica quidam philosophi sufficienter tractaverint
  Author: Franco
      Treatise: Ars cantus mensurabilis
              File name: **FRAARSCM**   File type: **TEXT**

Da per armoniam distanciam planetarum
  Author: Anonymous
      Treatise: [De harmonia planetarum]
              File name: **ANOHARP**   File type: **MOBB842**

Dat de psallendi metis pariterque canendi
  Author: Anonymous
      Treatise: Summula
              File name: **ANOSUM**   File type: **TEXT**

De harmonica consideratione Boetius ita disseruit quia neque solum in terminis
  Author: Anonymous
      Treatise: Alia musica
              File name: **ALIMU**   File type: **TEXT**

De harmonica consideratione Boetius ita disseruit: quia neque solum in terminis
  Author: Anonymous
      Treatise: Alia musica
              File name: **ALIMUS**   File type: **TEXT**

De harmonica consideratione Boetius ita disseruit: quia neque solum in terminis
  Author: Anonymous
      Treatise: Alia musica
              File name: **ALIMUSI**   File type: **TEXT**

De hoc autem instrumento naturali ac prestantissimo id est voce:
  Author: Tinctoris, Johannes
      Treatise: De inventione et usu musicae
              File name: **TININV**   File type: **TEXT**

De Numeris, et Proportionibus, quae ex numerorum comparationibus criuntur,
  Author: Salinas, Franciscus
      Treatise: De musica, liber secundus
              File name: **SALMUS2**   File type: **TEXT**

De origine Musice Artis quia rudem lectorem vidimus in primis tacuimus.
  Author: Anonymous
      Treatise: [De origine musice artis]
              File name: **ANODEO**   File type: **MLBLL763**

De proportionibus cantandi hoc in ultimo volumi dicturi; animadvertendum in primis
  Author: Guillermus de Podio
      Treatise: Ars musicorum liber VIII
              File name: **GUIARS8**   File type: **TEXT**

De quantitate discreta mobili est musica: est enim de sono vel est contractus
  Author: Anonymous
      Treatise: De musica
              File name: **ANOQM**   File type: **TEXT**

225

THESAURUS MUSICARUM LATINARUM: Index of Incipits

De tonorum agnicionibus singulorum et differenciarum secundum varias incepciones
Author: Anonymous
    Treatise: De tonorum agnicionibus
               File name: **ANOTON**   File type: **MLBLR12**

Debitum servitutis nostrae, qui ad ministerium laudationis deputamur, non solum
Author: Anonymous
    Treatise: Commemoratio brevis de tonis et psalmis modulandis
               File name: **ANOCOBR**   File type: **TEXT**

Debitum servitutis nostrae, qui ad ministerium laudationis deputamur, non solum
Author: Anonymous
    Treatise: Commemoratio brevis de tonis et psalmis modulandis
               File name: **ANOCOMB**   File type: **TEXT**

Decem sunt modi quorum tantum tres dicuntur consonantiae, scilicet diatesseron
Author: Anonymous
    Treatise: Liber musicae
               File name: **ANOLIBM**   File type: **TEXT**

Desiderio tuo, fili carissime, gratuito condescenderem, si rationi praeviae preces
Author: Adelboldus
    Treatise: Epistola cum tractatu de musica instrumentali humanaque ac mundana
               File name: **ADETRA**   File type: **TEXT**

Diapente et diatesseron Simphonie et intense et remisse pariter consonantia<m>
Author: Anonymous
    Treatise: [Miscellanea]
               File name: **ANOSPI**   File type: **TEXT**

Diaphonia duplex cantus est. cuius talis est diffinitio. Organum est uox sequens
Author: Anonymous
    Treatise: [Tractatus de organo]
               File name: **ANOMONT**   File type: **TEXT**

Diaphonia duplex cantus est; cuius talis est diffinitio. Organum est vox sequens
Author: Anonymous
    Treatise: [Tractatus de organo]
               File name: **ANOMON**   File type: **TEXT**

Diaphonia duplex cantus est; cuius talis est diffinitio. Organum est vox sequens
Author: Anonymous
    Treatise: [Tractatus de organo]
               File name: **ANOORG**   File type: **TEXT**

Diaphoniam seu organum constat (!) ex diatessaron symphonia naturaliter derivari.
Author: Anonymous
    Treatise: Cologne Organum Treatise
               File name: **COLORGR**   File type: **TEXT**

Diaphoniam seu organum constat ex diatessaron symphonia naturaliter dirivari.
Author: Anonymous
    Treatise: Cologne Organum Treatise
               File name: **COLORG**   File type: **TEXT**

THESAURUS MUSICARUM LATINARUM: Index of Incipits

Diaphoniam seu organum constat ex diatessaron symphonia naturaliter derivari.
    Author: Anonymous
        Treatise: Cologne Organum Treatise
                File name: **COLORGS**   File type: **TEXT**

Diatessaron alia constat ex tono et semitonio et tono, ut ab A in D; alia ex semitonio
    Author: Anonymous
        Treatise: Tractatus
                File name: **BECANO**   File type: **TEXT**

Dicamus, quae nobis Deus donare dignatur, quando fit grata et acceptabilis Deo
    Author: Nicetius, episcopus
        Treatise: De laude et utilitate spiritualium canticorum, quae fiunt in ecclesia
                File name: **NICLAU**   File type: **TEXT**

Dicendum est de prolacione proporcionis per divisionem monacordi
    Author: Anonymous
        Treatise: De divisione monacordi
                File name: **ANODIV**   File type: **MOBB842**

Dico quod postquam substancia mota fuit, accidit ei sonus, qui divisus fuit in tres species
    Author: Al-Farabi
        Treatise: De ortu scientiarum, Dictio de cognoscenda causa unde orta est ars musice
                File name: **FARORT**   File type: **TEXT**

Dictis aliquibus circa planum cantum, restat aliud dicendum de cantu
    Author: Anonymous I
        Treatise: De musica antiqua et nova
                File name: **ANO1DEM**   File type: **TEXT**

Dictis aliquibus circa planum Cantum, restat aliud dicendum de cantu
    Author: Anonymous
        Treatise: Quatuor Principalia IV
                File name: **QUAPRIA4**   File type: **MLBL4909**

Dictis autem, prout potuimus, his quibus ostendendum erat, qualiter unusquisque
    Author: Hucbald
        Treatise: De organo
                File name: **HUCORG**   File type: **TEXT**

Dicturi de tonis, primo videndum est quid sit tonus et unde dicatur.
    Author: Petrus de Cruce Ambianensis
        Treatise: Tractatus de tonis
                File name: **PETTRAC**   File type: **TEXT**

Dicturi de tonis: primo videndum est quid sit tonus et unde dicatur.
    Author: Petrus de Cruce Ambianensis
        Treatise: Tractatus de tonis
                File name: **PETTRA**   File type: **TEXT**

Differentia est inter motetos, ballados, vireletos et rondellos et fugas.
    Author: Anonymous
        Treatise: [Tractatus de musica]
                File name: **ANOTDM**   File type: **TEXT**

THESAURUS MUSICARUM LATINARUM: Index of Incipits

Dilectissimo coepiscopo e., a. divina gratia dispensante episcopus.
> Author: Anonymous
>> Treatise: Commentum super tonos
>>> File name: **ANOCST**   File type: **TEXT**

Dilectissimo coepiscopo e., a. dispensante divina gratia episcopus.
> Author: Anonymous
>> Treatise: Commentum super tonos
>>> File name: **ANOCSTO**   File type: **TEXT**

Dimidiae parti animae suae fratri et consacerdoti Rotberto, peccatis maximis
> Author: Odorannus de Sens
>> Treatise: Liber opusculorum, capitula V-VI
>>> File name: **ODOSENS**   File type: **TEXT**

Dimidium proslambanomenos est Mese, huius autem dimidium est nete hyperboleon
> Author: Bernelinus
>> Treatise: Cita et vera divisio monochordi in diatonico genere
>>> File name: **BERNDIV**   File type: **TEXT**

Dimidium proslambanomenos est Mese, hujus autem dimidium est nete hyperboleon
> Author: Bernelinus
>> Treatise: Cita et vera divisio monochordi in diatonico genere
>>> File name: **BERNDIVM**   File type: **TEXT**

Discipulus. Musica quid est? Magister. Bene modulandi scientia. D. Bene modulari
> Author: Anonymous
>> Treatise: Scholia enchiriadis de arte musica
>>> File name: **SCHEN**   File type: **TEXT**

Discipulus. Musica quid est? Magister. Bene modulandi scientia. D. Bene modulari
> Author: Anonymous
>> Treatise: Scholia enchiriadis de arte musica
>>> File name: **SCHENC**   File type: **TEXT**

Discipulus. Quid est tonus? Magister. Regula, naturam et formam cantuum regularium
> Author: Anonymous
>> Treatise: Tonale Sancti Bernardi
>>> File name: **BERTON**   File type: **TEXT**

Discipulus: Estne musica genus an species? Magister: Species est et subalternum genus
> Author: Heinricus Augustensis
>> Treatise: Musica
>>> File name: **HEIMUS**   File type: **TEXT**

Discipulus: Modo quaeritur quid est musica? Magister: Est veraciter canendi
> Author: Anonymous
>> Treatise: Jesus. Libellus musicae adiscendae valde utilis et est dialogus. Discipulus et
>>> File name: **ANOLIB**   File type: **TEXT**

Dispendiosa sub compendio tradere, facile quoniam non est, manifestum est.
> Author: Jacobus Leodiensis
>> Treatise: Compendium de musica
>>> File name: **JACCDM**   File type: **TEXT**

228

Diuturni studii lectione depraehendi musices disciplinam antiquis temporibus
    Author: Gaffurio, Franchino
        Treatise: Theorica musice, liber primus
                File name: **GAFTM1**   File type: **TEXT**

Domino et patri suo venerabili Angelorum antistiti Fulgentio
    Author: Johannes Affligemensis
        Treatise: De musica cum tonario
                File name: **JOHDEM**   File type: **TEXT**

Domino et Patri suo venerabili Anglorum antistiti Fulgentio
    Author: Johannes Affligemensis
        Treatise: Musica
                File name: **JOHMU**   File type: **TEXT**

Domino et patri suo venerabili Angelorum antistiti Fulgentio
    Author: Johannes Affligemensis
        Treatise: Musica
                File name: **JOHMUS**   File type: **TEXT**

Domno suo Ellenhardo praesulum dignissimo, in universa morum honestate praeclaro
    Author: Aribo
        Treatise: De musica
                File name: **ARIDEM**   File type: **TEXT**

Domno suo Ellenhardo praesulum dignissimo in universa morum honestate praeclaro
    Author: Aribo
        Treatise: Musica
                File name: **ARIMU**   File type: **TEXT**

Domno suo Ellenhardo praesulum dignissimo in universa morum honestate praeclaro
    Author: Aribo
        Treatise: Musica
                File name: **ARIMUS**   File type: **TEXT**

Dubitare multae eruditionis documentum est. Etenim indubiae cognitionis initium quidam
    Author: Critopulus, hieromonachus, Metrophanes
        Treatise: Epistola de vocibus in musica liturgica Graecorum usitatis
                File name: **CRIEPI**   File type: **TEXT**

Dulce ingenium artis musicae, quamvis plurimis instrumentis vigeat
    Author: Anonymous
        Treatise: Dulce ingenium (Versio Pragensis)
                File name: **ANODUL2**   File type: **TEXT**

Dulce ingenium musicae, quamvis instrumentis plurimis vigeat
    Author: Anonymous
        Treatise: Dulce ingenium (Versio Parisiensis et Brugensis)
                File name: **ANODUL**   File type: **TEXT**

Dulcis celebs, Urania, annue auspicio;
    Author: Ciconia, Johannes
        Treatise: Nova musica
                File name: **CICNM**   File type: **TEXT**

Dum Domino psalles. psallendo tu tria serves.
Author: Anonymous
Treatise: [Versus de musica]
File name: **ANOVER**   File type: **TEXT**

Dum quidam mihi carus ac uti frater intimus lucas nomine de castro lendenarie policinii
Author: Prosdocimo de' Beldomandi
Treatise: Tractatus musice speculative
File name: **PROSPE**   File type: **TEXT**

Duo semisphaeria, quas magadas vocant, concavo instrumento hinc et hinc superponuntur
Author: Anonymous I
Treatise: Musica
File name: **ANO1MU**   File type: **TEXT**

Duo semisphaeria, quas magadas vocant, concavo instrumento hinc et hinc superponuntur
Author: Anonymous I
Treatise: Musica
File name: **ANO1MUS**   File type: **TEXT**

Duplex est notula, ligata scilicet et non ligata. Notularum non ligatarum
Author: Anonymous
Treatise: De figuris
File name: **ANODEF**   File type: **TEXT**

Dvo tantum genera proportionum ueteres et praesertim Pythagorici: ad musicas
Author: Folianus, Ludovicus
Treatise: Musica theorica, sectio secunda
File name: **FOLMUS2**   File type: **TEXT**

Effectus primus est iste: Musica Deum delectat. Proprium etenim est cujuslibet artificis
Author: Tinctoris, Johannes
Treatise: Complexus effectuum musices
File name: **TINCOM**   File type: **TEXT**

Effectus primus est iste: Musica Deum delectat.--Proprium etenim est: cujuslibet
Author: Tinctoris, Johannes
Treatise: Complexus viginti effectuum nobilis artis musices
File name: **TINCOM2**   File type: **TEXT**

Eodem etiam modo se habent ad invicem numerus de quo arithmetica et numerus
Author: Kilwardby, Robert
Treatise: De ortu scientiarum
File name: **KILDOS**   File type: **TEXT**

Est autem unisonus quando due voces manent in uno et eodem loco
Author: Anonymous 5
Treatise: De discantu
File name: **ANO5DED**   File type: **TEXT**

Est musica humana mundana et instrumentalis De instrumentali agit Boecius
Author: Anonymous
Treatise: [Tractatulus de musica]
File name: **ANOTRDM**   File type: **MMBS2818**

Est musica mundana, humana et instrumentalis. De instrumentali agit Boethius

    Author: Anonymous

        Treatise: [Tractatulus de musica]

                File name: **ANOTRDM**   File type: **TEXT**

Est musica mundana. humana et instrumentalis. De instrumentali agit Boecius

    Author: Anonymous

        Treatise: [Tractatulus de musica]

                File name: **ANOTRDMK** File type: **MKBJ754**

Est tonus sic Vt Re Vt. vel Re My Re. vel Fa Sol Fa. vel Sol. La Sol.

    Author: Anonymous

        Treatise: Est tonus sic

                File name: **ANOEST**   File type: **MLBLL763**

Et dixit <Guido>: Qui nescit palmam, in uanum tendit ad musicam.

    Author: Anonymous

        Treatise: Cartula de cantu plano

                File name: **ANOCAR**   File type: **TEXT**

Et quia superius, cum de inventione musicae loqueremur

    Author: Johannes de Muris

        Treatise: De numeris, qui musicas retinent consonantias, secundum Ptolomaeum de

                File name: **MURDEN**   File type: **TEXT**

Et si harmonicam scientiam plerique cessante usu

    Author: Gaffurio, Franchino

        Treatise: Practica musice

                File name: **GAFPM1**   File type: **TEXT**

Etiam nunc voces musicas distinguamus. Vox est aeris repercussio indissoluta

    Author: Ramus de Pareia, Bartholomeus

        Treatise: Musica practica, prima pars, tractatus secundus

                File name: **RAMMP1T2** File type: **TEXT**

Etsi facile sit inventis addere

    Author: Prosdocimo de' Beldomandi

        Treatise: Libellus monocordi

                File name: **PROLIB**   File type: **TEXT**

Etsi facile sit inventis addere

    Author: Prosdocimo de' Beldomandi

        Treatise: Parvus tractatulus de modo monacordum dividendi

                File name: **PROPAR**   File type: **TEXT**

Etsi in huius operis nostri primordio de excellentia atque intellectus nobilitate

    Author: Ugolino Urbevetanis

        Treatise: Declaratio musicae disciplinae, liber quintus

                File name: **UGODEC5**   File type: **TEXT**

Etsi multi musici his tribus vocabulis: tropus, modus et tonus, quasi sinonimis

    Author: Monachus Carthusiensis

        Treatise: Tractatus de musica plana

                File name: **CARTRA**   File type: **TEXT**

Etsi Musica humanum inventum est, cantus tamen nonnullos usque adeo suaves
>> Author: Ancina Fossaniensis, Juvenal
>>> Treatise: De musica
>>>> File name: **ANCMUS**   File type: **TEXT**

Etsi non parvum auribus humanis afferre soleant modi musici per ruritum
>> Author: Johannes Gallicus dictus Carthusiensis seu de Mantua
>>> Treatise: Incipit praefationcula in tam admirabilem quam tacitam et quietissimam
>>>> File name: **GALTRA**   File type: **TEXT**

Etsi omnia quae demonstranda erant superioris libri tractatione digessimus
>> Author: Boethius, Anicius Manlius Severinus
>>> Treatise: De institutione musica, liber quartus
>>>> File name: **BOEDIM4**   File type: **TEXT**

Etsi omnia, quae demonstranda est superioris libri tractatione digressimus
>> Author: Boethius, Anicius Manlius Severinus
>>> Treatise: De institutione musica, liber quartus
>>>> File name: **BOEMUS4**   File type: **TEXT**

Ex altera parte secuntur versus mistici huic gamme pertinente
>> Author: Anonymous
>>> Treatise: Monachus quidam de Sherbourn talem musicam profert de Sancta Maria
>>>> File name: **ANODESA**   File type: **MLBLL763**

Ex omni innumera varietate numerorum pauci et numerabiles inventi sunt
>> Author: Anonymous
>>> Treatise: De musica et tonis tractatus
>>>> File name: **METANO1**   File type: **TEXT**

Existimo, quod nunc temporis quatuor principales sunt differentiae cantorum.
>> Author: Arnulphus de Sancto Gilleno
>>> Treatise: Tractatulus de differentiis et generibus cantorum
>>>> File name: **ARNTRA**   File type: **TEXT**

Experimento multiplici colligi potest, quod musica promoveat affectiones animae
>> Author: Johannes de Muris
>>> Treatise: Tractatus de musica
>>>> File name: **MURMUS**   File type: **TEXT**

Fac tibi fistulam secundum aestimationem, utpote unius ulnae et dimidiae langam
>> Author: Anonymous
>>> Treatise: De mensura fistularum in organis
>>>> File name: **ANOFIS**   File type: **TEXT**

Figura est repraesentatio vocis in aliquo modorum ordinatae.
>> Author: Anonymous
>>> Treatise: Ars musicae mensurabilis secundum Franconem
>>>> File name: **ANOFIG**   File type: **TEXT**

Figura est repraesentatio vocis in aliquo modorum ordinatae.
>> Author: Anonymous
>>> Treatise: Quaedam de arte discantandi
>>>> File name: **ANOQUA**   File type: **TEXT**

THESAURUS MUSICARUM LATINARUM: Index of Incipits

Figurae cantus figurati sunt octo, videlicet maxima, longa, brevis, semibrevis
    Author: Hothby, Johannes
        Treatise: Regulae Magistri Johannis Hoctobi anglici cantus figurati
                File name: **HOTDCF2**   File type: **TEXT**

Figurae enim cantus choralis sunt 8, sed proprie 5 dumtaxat
    Author: Hothby, Johannes
        Treatise: Regulae cantus mensurati secundum Johannem Otteby
                File name: **HOTRCM2**   File type: **TEXT**

Finitis tribus partibus huius tractatus nostri de Musica, ad quartam partem
    Author: Engelbertus Admontensis
        Treatise: De musica, tractatus quartus
                File name: **ENGDEM4**   File type: **TEXT**

Flaminius. Non possem mi Aaron verbis assequi, quanta te de hisce rebus
    Author: Aaron, Petrus
        Treatise: Libri tres de institutione harmonica, liber tertius
                File name: **AARIH3**   File type: **TEXT**

Gaudent breuitate moderni. Quandoque punctus quadratus, aut nota quadrata
    Author: Anonymous
        Treatise: Compendium breve artis musicae
                File name: **ANOCBA**   File type: **MBAV5320**

Gaudent brevitate moderni. Quandocunque punctus quadratus, vel nota quadrata
    Author: Anonymous 2
        Treatise: Tractatus de discantu
                File name: **ANO2TRA**   File type: **TEXT**

Gaudent brevitate moderni. Quandocunque nota quadrata, vel punctus quadratus
    Author: Anonymous 3
        Treatise: De cantu mensurabili
                File name: **ANO3DEC**   File type: **TEXT**

Gaudent brevitate moderni. Quandocumque punctus quadratus vel nota quadrata
    Author: Anonymous
        Treatise: Compendium musicae mensurabilis artis antiquae
                File name: **ANOCOM**   File type: **TEXT**

Gaudent brevitate moderni. Quandocumque nota quadrata vel punctus quadratus
    Author: Anonymous
        Treatise: Compendium musicae mensurabilis artis antiquae
                File name: **ANOCOMM**   File type: **TEXT**

Gaudent brevitate moderni. Quandocunque punctus quadratus seu nota quadrata
    Author: Anonymous
        Treatise: Practica musicae artis mensurabilis
                File name: **ANOPRA**   File type: **TEXT**

Gaudent brevitate moderni. Quandocumque punctus quadratus vel nota quadrata
    Author: Anonymous II
        Treatise: Tractatus de discantu
                File name: **ANOTDD**   File type: **TEXT**

Gaudent brevitate moderni. Quandocunque punctus quadratus
   Author: Johannes dictus Balloce
      Treatise: Abreviatio Magistri Franconis
         File name: **BALABM**   File type: **TEXT**

Gaudent brevitate moderni. Quandocunque punctus quadratus
   Author: Johannes dictus Ballox
      Treatise: Abreviatio Magistri Franconis
         File name: **BALABR**   File type: **TEXT**

Gaudent musicorum discipuli, quod Henricus de Zeelandia
   Author: Henricus de Zelandia
      Treatise: Tractatus de cantu perfecto et imperfecto
         File name: **ZELTRA**   File type: **TEXT**

Gaudentius quidam de Musica scribens, Pythagoram dicit huius rei invenisse
   Author: Cassiodorus, Aurelius
      Treatise: Institutiones musicae, seu excerpta ex eiusdem libro, de artibus ac disciplinis
         File name: **CASINS**   File type: **TEXT**

Gaudentius quidam, de musica scribens, Pythagoram dicit hujus rei invenisse
   Author: Cassiodorus, Aurelius
      Treatise: Institutiones musicae, seu excerpta ex eiusdem libro, de artibus ac disciplinis
         File name: **CASIM**   File type: **TEXT**

Gaudentius quidam, de musica scribens, Pythagoram dicit huius rei invenisse
   Author: Cassiodorus, Aurelius
      Treatise: Institutionum liber secundus saecularium litterarum
         File name: **CASINST**   File type: **TEXT**

Genera inaequalitatis quinque sunt, scilicet multiplex
   Author: Marchetus de Padua
      Treatise: Lucidarium, tractatus septimus
         File name: **MARLU7**   File type: **TEXT**

Genera inequalitatis quinque sunt, scilicet multiplex
   Author: Marchetus de Padua
      Treatise: Lucidarium, tractatus septimus
         File name: **MARLUC7**   File type: **TEXT**

Grecam litteram ideo moderni maluerunt ponere quam latinam, ut Greci per hoc
   Author: Anonymous
      Treatise: De musica et de transformatione specialiter
         File name: **ANODMT**   File type: **TEXT**

Gymnasio musas placuit reuocare solutas.
   Author: Guido d'Arezzo
      Treatise: Micrologus
         File name: **GUIMICB**   File type: **MBBR2784**

Gymnasio musas placuit revocare solutas,
   Author: Guido d'Arezzo
      Treatise: Micrologus
         File name: **GUIMIC**   File type: **TEXT**

THESAURUS MUSICARUM LATINARUM: Index of Incipits

Gymnasio musas placuit revocare solutas,
  Author: Guido d'Arezzo
    Treatise: Micrologus
                  File name: **GUIMICR**   File type: **TEXT**

Gymnasio musas placuit revocare solutas.
  Author: Guido d'Arezzo
    Treatise: Micrologus
                  File name: **GUIMICRO**   File type: **TEXT**

Habitis itaque atque utcumque enucleatis musices rudimentis quibus pueri
  Author: Rossetti, Biagio
    Treatise: Libellus de rudimentis musices: De choro et organo compendium
                  File name: **ROSLIB2**   File type: **TEXT**

Habito de ipsa plana musica que immensurabilis dicitur
  Author: Johannes de Garlandia
    Treatise: De musica mensurabili
                  File name: **GARDEM**   File type: **TEXT**

Habito de ipsa plana musica, quae immensurabilis dicitur
  Author: Johannes de Garlandia
    Treatise: De mensurabili musica
                  File name: **GARDMM**   File type: **TEXT**

Habito, inquit Johannes, de cognitione plane musice et omnium specierum soni
  Author: Johannes de Garlandia
    Treatise: De musica mensurabili positio
                  File name: **GARDEMP**   File type: **TEXT**

Habito, inquit Johannes, de cognitione planae musicae et omnium specierum soni
  Author: Johannes de Garlandia
    Treatise: De musica mensurabili positio
                  File name: **GARDMMP**   File type: **TEXT**

Hactenus idem fere facere studui, quod probat pictores erga discipulos suos solent
  Author: Heyden, Sebaldus
    Treatise: De arte canendi, ac vero signorum in cantibus usu, liber secundus
                  File name: **HEYDAC2**   File type: **TEXT**

Hactenus omnia, quae uisa sunt necessaria, huius scientiae principia
  Author: Glareanus, Henricus
    Treatise: Dodecachordum, Liber secundus
                  File name: **GLADOD2**   File type: **TEXT**

Hactenus omnia, quae uisa sunt necessaria, huius scientiae principia
  Author: Glareanus, Henricus
    Treatise: Dodecachordum, Liber tertius
                  File name: **GLADOD3**   File type: **TEXT**

Harmonici modulaminis Genus auctore Baccheo est
  Author: Gaffurio, Franchino
    Treatise: Practica musice
                  File name: **GAFPM3**   File type: **TEXT**

Hic incipit musica magistri Franconis cum additionibus et opinionibus diversorum.

   Author: Hanboys, Johannes

      Treatise: Summa

           File name: **HANSUM**   File type: **TEXT**

Hic incipit musica magistri Franconis cum additionibus et opinionibus diversorum.

   Author: Hanboys, Johannes

      Treatise: Summa

           File name: **HANSUMA**   File type: **TEXT**

His ista rite peractis ac quindecim philosophorum cordis in unum collectis

   Author: Johannes Gallicus dictus Carthusiensis seu de Mantua

      Treatise: Ritus canendi vetustissimus et novus, liber tertius

           File name: **GALRIT3**   File type: **TEXT**

His litteris et hac supputatione plena calculatio est cognita.

   Author: Anonymous

      Treatise: Fragmentum

           File name: **ANOFRA7**   File type: **TEXT**

Hoc expleto primo libro volens implere promissus ac in monocordo

   Author: Johannes Gallicus dictus Carthusiensis seu de Mantua

      Treatise: Ritus canendi vetustissimus et novus, liber secundus

           File name: **GALRIT2**   File type: **TEXT**

Homo dicitur esse liber qui sui ipsius causa est et in ratione causae moventis

   Author: Ugolino Urbevetanis

      Treatise: Declaratio musicae disciplinae, liber secundus

           File name: **UGODEC2**   File type: **TEXT**

Huius artis (musicae) experienciam querere cupientibus a figuram manus inchoandum

   Author: Anonymous

      Treatise: Ars musica

           File name: **METANO3**   File type: **TEXT**

Huius artis experientiam quaerere cupientibus, a figura manus inchoandum est

   Author: Anonymous

      Treatise: [Ars musica]

           File name: **ANOARSMU**   File type: **TEXT**

Iam facibus lassos spectans marcentibus ignes instaurare iubet tunc hymenea Venus

   Author: Martianus Capella

      Treatise: De nuptiis Philologiae et Mercurii, Liber IX, De harmonia

           File name: **MARDEN9**   File type: **TEXT**

Iam facibus lassos spectans marcentibus ignes instaurare jubet. tunc hymenea Venus;

   Author: Martianus Capella

      Treatise: De nuptiis Philologiae et Mercurii, Liber IX, De musica

           File name: **MARDNP9**   File type: **TEXT**

Iam sequitur de valoribus notarum et hoc iam dictatur.

   Author: Anonymous

      Treatise: Modus cantandi in mensuralibus

           File name: **ANOMOD**   File type: **TEXT**

Iam vero telam nobis (ut aiunt) exordientibus, non suppetet facultas
    Author: Frosch, Johannes
        Treatise: Rerum musicarum opusculum rarum ac insigne
            File name: **FRORER**   File type: **TEXT**

Ibi incipere debet musice practica: ubi desinit eius theorica.
    Author: Dionysius Lewis de Ryckel
        Treatise: De arte musicali, secunda pars: Musica practica
            File name: **GENTPRA**   File type: **MGRU70**

Igitur octo tonis manifestum est musicam consistere, per quos musicae modulationis
    Author: Berno Augiensis
        Treatise: De consona tonorum diversitate
            File name: **BERNDCT**   File type: **TEXT**

Igitur octo tonis manifestum est musicam consistere, per quos musicae modulationis
    Author: Berno Augiensis
        Treatise: De consona tonorum diversitate
            File name: **BERNDEC**   File type: **TEXT**

Ignatius Antiochie Syrie tertius post apostolum Petrum Episcopus,
    Author: Regino Prumiensis
        Treatise: Tonarius
            File name: **REGTON**   File type: **TEXT**

In consideranda monochordi positione ea prima speculatio occurrit
    Author: Hermannus Contractus
        Treatise: Musica
            File name: **HERMUS**   File type: **MRSL1496**

In consideranda monochordi positione ea prima speculatio occurrit
    Author: Hermannus Contractus
        Treatise: Musica
            File name: **HERMUSB**   File type: **TEXT**

In consideranda monochordi positione ea prima speculatio occurrit
    Author: Hermannus Contractus
        Treatise: Musica
            File name: **HERMUSE**   File type: **TEXT**

In consideranda monochordi positione ea prima speculatio occurrit
    Author: Hermannus Contractus
        Treatise: Musica
            File name: **HERMUSG**   File type: **TEXT**

In consideranda monochordi positione ea prima speculatio occurrit
    Author: Hermannus Contractus
        Treatise: Musica
            File name: **HERMUSP**   File type: **TEXT**

In defectionibus hujusmodi solet necessario synemenon in superibus aliquando
    Author: Anonymous
        Treatise: De cantibus quae supra modum intenduntur vel remittuntur
            File name: **ANOCAN**   File type: **TEXT**

237

In laudem pulcherrime artis musicae assummo dictum diuini Dauid
> Author: Sebastianus de Felstin
>> Treatise: Opusculum musice
>>> File name: **FELOP**   File type: **TEXT**

In manus meas incidit liber quidam tuus quem de arte musica conscriptsisti
> Author: Hothby, Johannes
>> Treatise: Excitatio quaedam musicae artis per refutationem
>>> File name: **HOTEXC**   File type: **TEXT**

In monocordo, quod dicitur Fortunatiani, illa mensura tenenda est
> Author: Anonymous
>> Treatise: Mensura monocordi
>>> File name: **ANOMMON**   File type: **TEXT**

In nomine domini incipit Michrologus id, est brevis sermo de Musica.
> Author: Joannes Presbyter
>> Treatise: De musica antica et moderna
>>> File name: **JOAMUS**   File type: **TEXT**

In nomine sancte et indiuidue Trinitatis incipit. de plana musica id est breuis sermo.
> Author: Anonymous
>> Treatise: Metrologus liber
>>> File name: **ANOMET**   File type: **MLBLL763**

In prephatione Nove Musice nobis placuit de eius magnitudine intimare
> Author: Ciconia, Johannes
>> Treatise: Nova musica, liber primus de consonantiis
>>> File name: **CICNM1**   File type: **TEXT**

In primis a capite iuxta primum plectrum, infra usque ad aliud plectrum
> Author: Odo
>> Treatise: Quomodo organistrum construatur
>>> File name: **ODOORG**   File type: **TEXT**

In primis a capite juxta primum plectrum, infra usque ad aliud plectrum
> Author: Odo
>> Treatise: Quomodo organistrum construatur
>>> File name: **ODOOR**   File type: **TEXT**

In primis. [Gamma], a, b, c, d, e, f, g, a, b, [sqb], c, d, e, f, g, a, b, [sqb], c, d.
> Author: Anonymous
>> Treatise: Regula de monocordo
>>> File name: **REGDEML**   File type: **MLBL2145**

In primo dico quod contrapunctum requirit habere quatuor res
> Author: Hothby, Johannes
>> Treatise: [De arte contrapuncti]
>>> File name: **HOTDAC**   File type: **TEXT**

In superioribus particulis dictum est de divisione Musicae
> Author: Anonymous
>> Treatise: Quatuor Principalia III
>>> File name: **QUAPRIA3**   File type: **MLBL4909**

In superioribus particulis dictum est de divisione musicae
    Author: Anonymous
        Treatise: Quatuor Principalia III
            File name: **QUAPRIB3**   File type: **TEXT**

Incipit brevis collectio artis musicae, tam ex determinationibus antiquorum
    Author: Bonaventura da Brescia
        Treatise: Brevis collectio artis musicae
            File name: **BONBRE**   File type: **TEXT**

Incipit dialogus de musica:--Interrogatio. Musica a quo inventa?
    Author: Anonymous
        Treatise: Fragmenta musica
            File name: **ANOFRA2**   File type: **TEXT**

Incipit formula super tonos, qualiter unusquisque cantor in ecclesia agere debeat.
    Author: Odo
        Treatise: Tonarium
            File name: **ODOTO**   File type: **TEXT**

Incipit formula super tonos, qualiter unusquisque cantor in Ecclesia agere debeat.
    Author: Odo
        Treatise: Tonarium
            File name: **ODOTON**   File type: **TEXT**

Incipit intonarium a Domno Octone abbate diligenter examinatum et ordinatum
    Author: Odo
        Treatise: Intonarium
            File name: **ODOINT**   File type: **TEXT**

Incipit lectura per Petrum Tallanderii ordinata tam super cantu mensurabili
    Author: Tallanderius, Petrus
        Treatise: Lectura
            File name: **TALLEC**   File type: **TEXT**

Incipit tractatus figurarum per quas diversimode discantatur
    Author: Anonymous
        Treatise: Tractatus figurarum
            File name: **TRAFIG**   File type: **TEXT**

Incipit tractatus fratris Petri de Sancto Dionysio, qui est in duas partes divisus
    Author: Petrus de Sancto Dionysio
        Treatise: Tractatus de Musica
            File name: **PSDTRA**   File type: **TEXT**

Incipiunt octo toni musicae artis cum suis differentiis authenticus protus
    Author: Regino Prumiensis
        Treatise: Tonarius
            File name: **REGTONA**   File type: **TEXT**

Incipiunt regule cum maximis magistri Franconis cum additionibus aliorum musicorum
    Author: Robertus de Handlo
        Treatise: Regule
            File name: **HANREG**   File type: **TEXT**

THESAURUS MUSICARUM LATINARUM: Index of Incipits

Incipiunt regule cum maximis magistri Franconis, cum additionibus aliorum musicorum
   Author: Robertus de Handlo
      Treatise: Regulae
            File name: **HANREGU**   File type: **TEXT**

INtendentes sciencie musicalis exquirere cognicionem ad sonum applicatum
   Author: Anonymous
         Treatise: Regule Magistri Johannis de Muris incipiunt
            File name: **MURREG**   File type: **MLBLL763**

Inter caeteras praeclaras artes quae uere dei dona sunt, non infimum locum
   Author: Finck, Hermann
         Treatise: Practica musica
            File name: **FINPRA**   File type: **TEXT**

Inter omnium animantium voces merito vox humana principem locum obtinere
   Author: Salinas, Franciscus
         Treatise: De musica, liber primus
            File name: **SALMUS1**   File type: **TEXT**

Interuallum est soni grauis, acutique spaciorum habitudo. Spacium vocamus neruum
   Author: Faber Stapulensis, Jacobus
         Treatise: Elementa musicalia
            File name: **STAPMUS**   File type: **TEXT**

Introductiones in arte musice. Primo videndum est quod sit introductio
   Author: Magister de Garlandia
         Treatise: Introductio musice
            File name: **GARINT**   File type: **TEXT**

Isidora. Musica est ars modulandi sono cantuque consistens
   Author: Anonymous
         Treatise: [Fragmenta]
            File name: **ANOFRAG**   File type: **MOBB842**

Isti versus sunt scripti in scrinio corporis sancti Remigii in linea superiori
   Author: Anonymous
         Treatise: Vita Sancti Remigii
            File name: **REMVIT**   File type: **TEXT**

Item de fistulis Gerlandus. Si fistulae aequalis grossitudinis fuerint, et maior minorem
   Author: Gerlandus
         Treatise: Fragmenta de musica
            File name: **GERFRA**   File type: **TEXT**

Item diceres, quare musica studetur? Respondetur quod illo modo: quod cultus divinus
   Author: Anonymous XI
         Treatise: [Tractatus de musica plana et mensurabili]
            File name: **ANO11TDM**   File type: **TEXT**

Item notandum quod notularum species quantum plures
   Author: Anonymous X
         Treatise: De minimis notulis
            File name: **ANO10DEM**   File type: **TEXT**

THESAURUS MUSICARUM LATINARUM: Index of Incipits

Item notandum quod septem sunt reformationes in manu videlicet:
    Author: Anonymous
        Treatise: Tractatus de musica figurata et de contrapuncto ab anonymo auctore
            File name: **TRADEM**   File type: **TEXT**

Iunior quidam monachus, D. Antonii Abbatis discipulus, missus est aliquando
    Author: Anonymous
        Treatise: Monacho qua mente sit psallendum
            File name: **MONPSAL**   File type: **TEXT**

Jam tempus est de ortu aliarum mathematicarum aliquid dicere
    Author: Kilwardby, Robert
        Treatise: De ortu et divisione philosophiae, Capitulum XVIII, De ortu et subiecto et
            File name: **KILDEO**   File type: **TEXT**

Jam vero quisquis inquirere cupit a primis numeris
    Author: Johannes Gallicus dictus Carthusiensis seu de Mantua
        Treatise: Tacita nunc inchoatur stupendaque numerorum musica
            File name: **GALLIB**   File type: **TEXT**

Libet post editum de divino cantu quod pauperi clero sponte devoveram
    Author: Johannes Gallicus dictus Carthusiensis seu de Mantua
        Treatise: Incipit liber tertius de contrapuncto praefationcula
            File name: **GALRITS3**   File type: **TEXT**

Libro superiore satis atque abunde de consonantijs, et minoribus interuallis
    Author: Salinas, Franciscus
        Treatise: De musica, liber tertius
            File name: **SALMUS3**   File type: **TEXT**

Libro tercio de phylosophica consolatione boethius uolens reddere causam
    Author: Johannes de Muris
        Treatise: Speculum musicae, Liber primus
            File name: **MURSPE**   File type: **TEXT**

Libro tertio de Philosophica Consolatione, Boethius, volens reddere causam
    Author: Jacobus Leodiensis
        Treatise: Speculum musicae, Liber primus
            File name: **JACSP1A**   File type: **TEXT**

Licet michi ipsi in omni sciencia nimis sim insufficiens de ipsius auxilio qui dat
    Author: Amerus
        Treatise: Practica artis musice
            File name: **AMEPRA**   File type: **TEXT**

M. Attende igitur diligenter, et nunc demum accipe quasi alterum nostrae disputationis
    Author: Augustinus, Aurelius
        Treatise: De musica, liber secundus
            File name: **AUGDEM2**   File type: **TEXT**

M. Quid sit versus, inter doctos veteres non parva luctatione quaesitum est
    Author: Augustinus, Aurelius
        Treatise: De musica, liber quintus
            File name: **AUGDEM5**   File type: **TEXT**

M. Redeamus ergo ad metri considerationem, propter cujus progressum ac longitudinem
    Author: Augustinus, Aurelius
        Treatise: De musica, liber quartus
                File name: **AUGDEM4**   File type: **TEXT**

M. Satis diu pene atque adeo plane pueriliter per quinque libros in vestigiis numerorum
    Author: Augustinus, Aurelius
        Treatise: De musica, liber sextus
                File name: **AUGDEM6**   File type: **TEXT**

M. Tertius hic sermo postulat, ut quoniam de pedum amicitia quadam concordiaque
    Author: Augustinus, Aurelius
        Treatise: De musica, liber tertius
                File name: **AUGDEM3**   File type: **TEXT**

Magister: Modus, qui pes est? Discipulus: Pyrrhichius. M. Quot temporum est?
    Author: Augustinus, Aurelius
        Treatise: De musica, liber primus
                File name: **AUGDEM1**   File type: **TEXT**

Magnum est Flamini quod heri sum pollicitus nec me quidem poenitet aut sententiam
    Author: Aaron, Petrus
        Treatise: Libri tres de institutione harmonica, liber primus
                File name: **AARIH1**   File type: **TEXT**

Manus est brevis et utilis doctrina ostendens compendiose qualitates vocum musicae
    Author: Tinctoris, Johannes
        Treatise: Expositio manus
                File name: **TINEM**   File type: **TEXT**

Manus est brevis et utilis doctrina ostendens compendiose qualitates vocum musicae
    Author: Tinctoris, Johannes
        Treatise: Expositio manus
                File name: **TINEXP**   File type: **TEXT**

Mensura in musica est ordo cantuum mensuratorum
    Author: Marchetus de Padua
        Treatise: Lucidarium, tractatus decimus
                File name: **MARLU10**   File type: **TEXT**

Mensura in musica est ordo cantuum mensuratorum
    Author: Marchetus de Padua
        Treatise: Lucidarium, tractatus decimus
                File name: **MARLUC10**   File type: **TEXT**

Mensurabilis musica est cantus longis brevibusque temporibus mensuratus.
    Author: Anonymous
        Treatise: Ars musicae mensurabilis secundum Franconem
                File name: **ANOARSM**   File type: **TEXT**

Mensuralis musicae haec est descriptio, cuius figurae in signis positivis possunt
    Author: Adamus de Fulda
        Treatise: Musica, pars tertia
                File name: **FULMUS3**   File type: **TEXT**

Mensuram fistularum dicturi pauca praemittere volumus
Author: Eberhardus Frisingensis
Treatise: Tractatus de mensura fistularum
File name: **EBETRA**   File type: **TEXT**

Micros graece, brevis latine; logos sermo, inde micrologus Guidonis
Author: Anonymous
Treatise: Commentarius in Micrologum Guidonis Aretini
File name: **GUICOM**   File type: **TEXT**

Mihi per proportionum campum qui patentissimus est
Author: Vanneo, Stephano
Treatise: Recanetum de musica aurea, liber II, capituli XX-XXXVII
File name: **VANREC**   File type: **TEXT**

Modo iam in duabus partibus huius tractatus praehabitis et praedeclaratis aliquibus
Author: Engelbertus Admontensis
Treatise: De musica, tractatus tertius
File name: **ENGDEM3**   File type: **TEXT**

Modos apud ueteres de mente Aristotelis trigesimi luciditate Problematis Petrus
Author: Gaffurio, Franchino
Treatise: De harmonia musicorum instrumentorum opus, liber quartus et ultimus
File name: **GAFHAR4**   File type: **TEXT**

Modus in musica est debita mensuratio temporis, scilicet per longas et breves
Author: Anonymous 7
Treatise: De musica libellus
File name: **ANO7DEM**   File type: **TEXT**

Monochordum Encheriadis constat in X et VIII cordis, ex quatuor videlicet gravibus
Author: Anonymous
Treatise: Monochordum Encheriadis
File name: **ANOMONEN**   File type: **TEXT**

Mos fuit apud Antiquos uir Amplissime: quem posteriores per manus traditum
Author: Gaffurio, Franchino
Treatise: De harmonia musicorum instrumentorum opus, liber primus
File name: **GAFHAR1**   File type: **TEXT**

Multorum cantorum scripturas varias ac opera ad practicam musicae laborata
Author: Willelmus
Treatise: Breviarium regulare musicae
File name: **WILBRE**   File type: **TEXT**

Multorum considerans errorem coactus sum Gregorii cantum, quem multis in locis
Author: Guido d'Arezzo [Ps.]
Treatise: Tractatus Guidonis correctorius multorum errorum, qui fiunt in cantu
File name: **ANOTRA2**   File type: **TEXT**

Multorum considerans errorem coactus sum Gregorii cantum, quem multis in locis
Author: Guido d'Arezzo [Ps.]
Treatise: Tractatus Guidonis correctorius multorum errorum, qui fiunt in cantu
File name: **ANOTRAC2**   File type: **TEXT**

THESAURUS MUSICARUM LATINARUM: Index of Incipits

Musica ars a nobis sub arboris figura visa est. Nam arbor musice magnitudo eius est.
  Author: Ciconia, Johannes
    Treatise: Nova musica, liber tertius de proportionibus
      File name: **CICNM3**   File type: **TEXT**

Musica disciplina est, quae de numeris loquitur, qui ad aliquid sunt his, qui inveniuntur
  Author: Anonymous
    Treatise: [Musica disciplina]
      File name: **ANOMUSD**   File type: **TEXT**

Musica duplex est, Theorice ac pratice. Theorice circa rerum musicarum
  Author: Glareanus, Henricus
    Treatise: Dodecachordum, Liber primus
      File name: **GLADOD1**   File type: **TEXT**

Musica est ars Deo placens ac hominibus, omne quod canitur discernens
  Author: Rossetti, Biagio
    Treatise: Libellus de rudimentis musices: Compendium musicae
      File name: **ROSLIB1**   File type: **TEXT**

Musica est ars recte canendi modulandive cognitionem administrans.
  Author: Vogelsang, Johannes
    Treatise: Musicae rudimenta
      File name: **VOGMUS**   File type: **TEXT**

Musica est ars recte canendi sono cantuque consistens.
  Author: Anonymous
    Treatise: Tractatus de musica plana et organica
      File name: **ANOMUPO**   File type: **TEXT**

Musica est ars spectabilis et suavis, ut in primo libro rettulimus
  Author: Ciconia, Johannes
    Treatise: Nova musica, liber quartus de accidentibus
      File name: **CICNM4**   File type: **TEXT**

Musica est enim scientia regularem docens notitiam ad canendi perfectionem
  Author: Johannes de Olomons
    Treatise: Palma choralis
      File name: **JOHPAL**   File type: **TEXT**

Musica est motus vocum rationabilium in arsim et a thesim, id est in elevatione
  Author: Anonymous
    Treatise: [Tractatus de musica]
      File name: **ANOMIC**   File type: **TEXT**

Musica est motus vocum rationabilium in arsim item thesim, idest inclinationem
  Author: Anonymous
    Treatise: [Tractatus de musica]
      File name: **ANOPHIL**   File type: **TEXT**

Musica est motus vocum, id est, per arsyn et thesyn. Est etiam veraciter canendi scientia
  Author: Roffredi, Guglielmo
    Treatise: Summa musicae artis
      File name: **ROFFSUM**   File type: **TEXT**

Musica est peritia modulationis sono cantuque consistens; et dicta musica
> Author: Isidorus Hispalensis
>> Treatise: De musica
>>> File name: **ISIDEM**   File type: **TEXT**

Musica est peritia modulationis sono cantuque consistens. Et dicta musica
> Author: Isidorus Hispalensis
>> Treatise: De musica
>>> File name: **ISIDEMU**   File type: **TEXT**

Musica est peritia modulationis sono cantuque consistens, et dicta Musica
> Author: Isidorus Hispalensis
>> Treatise: Sententiae de musica
>>> File name: **ISISEN**   File type: **TEXT**

Musica est peritia modulationis sono cantuque consistens; et dicta musica
> Author: Rabanus Maurus
>> Treatise: De universo, liber XVIII, caput IV
>>> File name: **MAUDEU**   File type: **TEXT**

Musica est peritia modulationis sono cantuque consistens et dicta musica
> Author: Rabanus Maurus
>> Treatise: De origine rerum
>>> File name: **MAUMUS**   File type: **TEXT**

Musica est scientia recte canendi, sive scientia de numero relato ad sonum.
> Author: Anonymous
>> Treatise: De origine et effectu musicae
>>> File name: **ANOOREF**   File type: **TEXT**

Musica est vna de septem artibus, quas liberales appelamus
> Author: Anonymous
>> Treatise: Ars musice
>>> File name: **ANOAM**   File type: **TEXT**

Musica omnibus temporibus apud bonos et doctos in magno precio fuit.
> Author: Dresseler, Gallus
>> Treatise: Praecepta musicae poeticae
>>> File name: **DREPRA**   File type: **TEXT**

Musica, secundum Augustinum, est bene modulandi scientia.
> Author: Agricola, Martinus
>> Treatise: Rudimenta musices
>>> File name: **AGRRUD**   File type: **TEXT**

Musicae artis disciplina summo studio appetenda est, et maxime his qui communi
> Author: Odo
>> Treatise: De musica
>>> File name: **ODOMU**   File type: **TEXT**

Musicae artis disciplina summo studio appetenda est, et maxime his, qui communi
> Author: Odo
>> Treatise: De musica
>>> File name: **ODOMUS**   File type: **TEXT**

THESAURUS MUSICARUM LATINARUM: Index of Incipits

Musicae artis non unum tantum, sed plures diversis saeculis et coeli plagis
    Author: Saess, Heinrich
        Treatise: Musica plana atque mensurabilis una cum nonnullis solmisationis regulis
            File name: **SAEMUS**   File type: **TEXT**

Musicae artis plures fuisse legimus inventores, secundum varias opiniones
    Author: Aegidius Zamorensis, Iohannes
        Treatise: Ars musica
            File name: **ZAMLAM**   File type: **TEXT**

Musicae artis plures fuisse legimus inuentores, secundum uarias opiniones
    Author: Aegidius Zamorensis, Iohannes
        Treatise: Liber artis musicae
            File name: **ZAMLIB**   File type: **TEXT**

Musicae disciplinae quinque partium pratice et speculative declaratione peracta
    Author: Ugolino Urbevetanis
        Treatise: Tractatus monochordi
            File name: **UGOTRAM**   File type: **TEXT**

Musicae tria sunt genera: mundanum, humanum et instrumentale
    Author: Philippe de Vitry
        Treatise: Ars nova
            File name: **VITARN**   File type: **TEXT**

Musicae tria sunt genera: mundanum, humanum et instrumentale
    Author: Philippe de Vitry
        Treatise: Ars nova
            File name: **VITARNO**   File type: **TEXT**

Musicalis scientia, que sonorum respicit intervalla et de proportionibus gravis
    Author: Boen, Johannes
        Treatise: Musica
            File name: **BOENMUS**   File type: **TEXT**

Musicam artem multis retro seculis floruisse, nemo est qui neget.
    Author: Rhau, Georg
        Treatise: Enchiridion utriusque musicae practicae
            File name: **RHAENC**   File type: **TEXT**

Musicam disciplinam non esse contempnendam, multa et antiquorum gentilium
    Author: Aurelianus Reomensis
        Treatise: Musica disciplina
            File name: **AURMD**   File type: **TEXT**

Musicam disciplinam non esse contemnendam, multa et antiquorum, gentilium
    Author: Aurelianus Reomensis
        Treatise: Musica disciplina
            File name: **AURMUS**   File type: **TEXT**

Musicam disciplinam non esse contempnendam, multa et antiquorum gentilium
    Author: Aurelianus Reomensis
        Treatise: Musica disciplina
            File name: **AURMUSD**   File type: **TEXT**

Musicam triphariam doctores quidam esse dixerunt, scilicet, armonicam, organicam
   Author: Carlerius, Egidius
      Treatise: De cantu iubiliationis armonicae et utilitate eius
         File name: **CARLCAN**   File type: **TEXT**

Musicam triplicem esse ferunt sapientes, metricam unam, rhythmicam alteram
   Author: Keck, Ioannes
      Treatise: Introductorium musicae
         File name: **KECKINMU**   File type: **TEXT**

Musicam vocis actionem quam superiori volumine
   Author: Gaffurio, Franchino
      Treatise: Practica musice
         File name: **GAFPM2**   File type: **TEXT**

Musice tria sunt genera Mundanum humanum et instrumentalem
   Author: Philippe de Vitry
      Treatise: Ars nova
         File name: **VITANV**   File type: **MBAVB307**

Musice tria sunt genera: mundanum, humanum, et instrumentale
   Author: Philippe de Vitry
      Treatise: Ars nova
         File name: **VITARSN**   File type: **TEXT**

Musici [latini] ut eam rem ad majorem nobilioremque excellentiam cucerent
   Author: Ugolino Urbevetanis
      Treatise: Musica disciplina
         File name: **UGOMUS**   File type: **TEXT**

Musicorum et cantorum magna est distantia. Isti dicunt, illi sciunt, quae componit
   Author: Guido d'Arezzo
      Treatise: Regulae rhythmicae
         File name: **GUIREG**   File type: **TEXT**

Musicorum et cantorum magna est distantia, Isti dicunt, illi sciunt, quae componit
   Author: Guido d'Arezzo
      Treatise: Regulae rhythmicae in antiphonarii sui prologum prolatae
         File name: **GUIRR**   File type: **TEXT**

Musicorum et cantorum magna est distantia. Isti dicunt, illi sciunt, quae componit
   Author: Guido d'Arezzo
      Treatise: Regulae rhythmicae in antiphonarii sui prologum prolatae
         File name: **GUIRRH**   File type: **TEXT**

Musicus dicitur ille, testante Boetio, cui adest facultas
   Author: Marchetus de Padua
      Treatise: Lucidarium, tractatus decimussextus
         File name: **MARLU16**   File type: **TEXT**

Musicus dicitur ille, testante Boetio, cui adest facultas
   Author: Marchetus de Padua
      Treatise: Lucidarium, tractatus sextus decimus
         File name: **MARLUC16**   File type: **TEXT**

THESAURUS MUSICARUM LATINARUM: Index of Incipits

Mutetus est cantus mensuralis per triplum vadens in quo discantus habet textum
  Author: Paulirinus, Paulus
    Treatise: Tractatus de musica
      File name: **PAUTRA**   File type: **TEXT**

MVsica. est sciencia recte canendi. siue sciencia de numero relato ad sonum.
  Author: Anonymous
    Treatise: De origine et effectu musice
      File name: **ANOORI**   File type: **MLBLL763**

Mvsicae facvltatis svbiectvm: Quod: Numerus sonorus: appellatur: nihil aliud est:
  Author: Folianus, Ludovicus
    Treatise: Musica theorica, sectio prima
      File name: **FOLMUS1**   File type: **TEXT**

Nos te nostrum carmen facile intellexisse fatemur cum picturae
  Author: Hothby, Johannes
    Treatise: Dialogus in arte musica
      File name: **HOTDIA**   File type: **TEXT**

Nota quod contrapunctus semper debet incipi et finiri per consonantias
  Author: Hothby, Johannes
    Treatise: Regulae contrapuncti
      File name: **HOTRC**   File type: **TEXT**

Nota quod duplex est prolatio, scilicet major et minor.
  Author: Guilielmus monachus
    Treatise: De preceptis artis musice et pratice compendiosus libellus
      File name: **MONPRE**   File type: **TEXT**

Nota quod duplex est prolatio, scilicet, maior et minor.
  Author: Guilielmus monachus
    Treatise: De preceptis artis musice et pratice compendiosus libellus
      File name: **MONPREC**   File type: **TEXT**

Nota quod omnes uoces totius organi tam toni quam semitoni possunt esse
  Author: Anonymous
    Treatise: Ars et modus pulsandi organa secundum modum novissimum inventum per
      File name: **ANOAMP**   File type: **TEXT**

Notandum est quod omnis ars in ratione continetur. Musica quoque in ratione numerorum
  Author: Beda [Ps.]
    Treatise: Musica theorica
      File name: **BEDMUST**   File type: **TEXT**

Notandum est quod regula subscripta debet doceri per magistros omnibus illis qui
  Author: Anonymous
    Treatise: De musica
      File name: **ANOMUS2**   File type: **TEXT**

Notandum primo, quod quatuor sunt uoces supra tenorem consonantiam facientes
  Author: Nicolaus de Senis
    Treatise: Tractatus de musica
      File name: **NICTRA**   File type: **TEXT**

THESAURUS MUSICARUM LATINARUM: Index of Incipits

Notandum quod, muteto vel conducto qui mensurabiliter cantantur
>   Author: Anonymous
>> Treatise: Tractatus artis antiquae cum explicatione mensurae binariae
>>> File name: **ANOTAA**   File type: **TEXT**

Numerus sexdecim. est numerus perfectissimus. quia semper potest diuidi in duas partes
>   Author: Anonymous
>> Treatise: Distinccio inter colores musicales, et armorum heroum
>>> File name: **ANODIST**   File type: **MLBLL763**

Nunc vero de cantu ecclesiastico, secundum scilicet quod discantus subjicitur
>   Author: Anonymous
>> Treatise: Discantus vulgaris positio
>>> File name: **DISVUL**   File type: **TEXT**

Nvnctis iam quae mihi ante monochordi diuisionem: expedienda uidebantur: expeditis:
>   Author: Folianus, Ludovicus
>> Treatise: Musica theorica, sectio tertia
>>> File name: **FOLMUS3**   File type: **TEXT**

Occasionem dicendi de te prebes Ioannes Spatarie qui in alios dicere solitus es.
>   Author: Gaffurio, Franchino
>> Treatise: Apologia adversus Ioannem Spatarium et complices musicos Bononienses
>>> File name: **GAFAPO**   File type: **TEXT**

Ociosum me nec gravioribus additum studiis
>   Author: Stoquerus, Gaspar
>> Treatise: De musica verbali libri duo
>>> File name: **STODEM**   File type: **TEXT**

Octo sunt figure mensurabilis cantus, videlicet maxima, longa, brevis, semibrevis
>   Author: Hothby, Johannes
>> Treatise: De cantu figurato secundum eundem fratrem Johannem Hothbi Carmelitam
>>> File name: **HOTDCF1**   File type: **TEXT**

Octo sunt figure mensurabilis cantus, videlicet maxima, longa, brevis, semibrevis
>   Author: Hothby, Johannes
>> Treatise: De cantu figurato
>>> File name: **HOTDEC**   File type: **TEXT**

Octo sunt partes prolationis sive figurae cantus simpliciter mensurabilis sive cantus
>   Author: Hothby, Johannes
>> Treatise: Sequuntur regulae cantus mensurati eiusdem Ottobi
>>> File name: **HOTRCM1**   File type: **TEXT**

Octo tonos in Musica consistere musicus scire debet, per quos omnis modulatio
>   Author: Alcuinus, Flaccus
>> Treatise: Musica
>>> File name: **ALCMUS**   File type: **TEXT**

Omnem ob sex sillabas et quinque vel sex modici decoris figuras
>   Author: Johannes Gallicus dictus Carthusiensis seu de Mantua
>> Treatise: Incipit liber secundus de sex, ut, re, mi, fa, sol, la, sillabis
>>> File name: **GALRITS2**   File type: **TEXT**

Omnem sapientiam omnemque naturam philosophiam credimus procedere
    Author: Ciconia, Johannes
        Treatise: De proportionibus
                File name: **CICPROP**   File type: **TEXT**

Omnem scientiam omnemque philosophiam credimus et profitemur de externo fonte
    Author: Sadze de Flandria, Christianus
        Treatise: Tractatus modi, temporis et prolationis
                File name: **FLATRA**   File type: **TEXT**

Omnes homines, sicut dicit philosophus, naturaliter scire desiderant
    Author: Ludovicus Sanctus
        Treatise: Sentencia in musica sonora subiecti
                File name: **LUDSEN**   File type: **TEXT**

Omni desideranti notitiam artis mensurabilis tam noue quam ueteris obtinere
    Author: Anonymous
        Treatise: Tractatus de musica
                File name: **AGANONT**   File type: **TEXT**

Omni desideranti notitiam artis musicae mensurabilis tam novae quam veteris obtinere
    Author: Anonymous
        Treatise: Sub brevissimo compendio Philippus de Vitriaco in musica incipit
                File name: **ANOOMD**   File type: **TEXT**

Omni desideranti notitiam artis musice mensurabilis tam noue quam ueteris obtinere
    Author: Anonymous
        Treatise: Sub breuissimo compendio Philippo de Vitriaco in musica incipit
                File name: **ANOOMDE**   File type: **MSBCLV30**

Omnibus ecce modis descripta relatio vocis. Est tonus, in numeris superantur
    Author: Guido d'Arezzo
        Treatise: De sex motibus vocum ad se invicem et dimensione earum
                File name: **GUISEX**   File type: **TEXT**

Omnis ars Musica proportionibus constat, id est consonantiis. (Dico, quidquid recte
    Author: Remigius Altisiodorensis
        Treatise: Musica
                File name: **REMMUS**   File type: **TEXT**

Omnis ars musica proportionibus constat, id est consonantiis. (Dico, quidquid recte
    Author: Remigius Altisiodorensis
        Treatise: Musica
                File name: **REMMUSI**   File type: **TEXT**

Omnis ars sive doctrina honorabiliorem habet rationem
    Author: Anonymous
        Treatise: De musica mensurabili
                File name: **ANODEM** ·   File type: **TEXT**

Omnis ars sive doctrina honorabiliorem habet rationem
    Author: Theodoricus de Campo
        Treatise: De musica mensurabili
                File name: **CAMDEM**   File type: **TEXT**

THESAURUS MUSICARUM LATINARUM: Index of Incipits

Omnis igitur regularis monochordi constitutio, secundum praeclaram disertissimi viri
   Author: Berno Augiensis
      Treatise: Musica seu Prologus in Tonarium
            File name: **BERNMUS**   File type: **TEXT**

Omnis igitur regularis monochordi constitutio secundum praeclaram disertissimi viri
   Author: Berno Augiensis
      Treatise: Musica seu Prologus in Tonarium
            File name: **BERNPRO**   File type: **TEXT**

Omnis nota in cantu mensurato Maxima figuratur quadrata
   Author: Weyts, Carmelite, Nicasius
      Treatise: Regule
            File name: **WEYREG**   File type: **TEXT**

Omnis numerus habet tot partes quot sub se sunt unitates
   Author: Hothby, Johannes
      Treatise: Regulae super proportionem
            File name: **HOTREGP**   File type: **TEXT**

Omnium humanarum actionum seu studiorum que moderantur ... sicut dicit Hugo
   Author: Anonymous
      Treatise: [Regulae de musica]
            File name: **METANO2**   File type: **TEXT**

Omnium quidem artium, etsi varia sit introductio
   Author: Johannes Gallicus
      Treatise: Ritus canendi [Pars prima]
            File name: **GALRC1**   File type: **TEXT**

Omnium quidem artium, etsi varia sit introductio
   Author: Johannes Gallicus dictus Carthusiensis seu de Mantua
      Treatise: Ritus canendi vetustissimus et novus, liber primus
            File name: **GALRIT1**   File type: **TEXT**

Omnium quidem perceptio sensuum ita sponte ac naturaliter quibusdam viventibus adest
   Author: Boethius, Anicius Manlius Severinus
      Treatise: De institutione musica, liber primus
            File name: **BOEMUS1**   File type: **TEXT**

Omnium quidem perceptio sensuum, ita sponte ac naturaliter quibusdam viventibus adest
   Author: Boethius, Anicius Manlius Severinus
      Treatise: De institutione musica, liber primus
            File name: **BOEDIM1**   File type: **TEXT**

Ordo poscit naturalis ut absoluta rei cognitio collativam antecedat.
   Author: Jacobus Leodiensis
      Treatise: Speculum musicae, Liber quartus
            File name: **JACSP4**   File type: **TEXT**

Organum est cantus subsequens precedentem, quia cantor debet precedere
   Author: Anonymous
      Treatise: Ars organi
            File name: **ARSORG**   File type: **TEXT**

251

THESAURUS MUSICARUM LATINARUM: Index of Incipits

Ostenso superius de tonis quomodo per species formentur
Author: Marchetus de Padua
Treatise: Lucidarium, tractatus duodecimus
File name: **MARLUC12**   File type: **TEXT**

Ostenso superius de tonis, quomodo per species formentur
Author: Marchetus de Padua
Treatise: Lucidarium, tractatus duodecimus
File name: **MARLU12**   File type: **TEXT**

Othlochus. Postquam donante Deo petitionibus meis et quaestionibus in astronomica
Author: Willehelmus Hirsaugensis
Treatise: Musica
File name: **WILMU**   File type: **TEXT**

Othlochus. Postquam donante Deo petitionibus meis et quaestionibus in astronomica
Author: Willehelmus Hirsaugensis
Treatise: Musica
File name: **WILMUS**   File type: **TEXT**

Othlochus. Postquam donante Deo petitionibus meis et quaestionibus in astronomica
Author: Willehelmus Hirsaugensis
Treatise: Musica
File name: **WILMUSI**   File type: **TEXT**

Partem primam agressurus cogitavi mecum, perficiendum fore, nisi divini auxilii
Author: Adamus de Fulda
Treatise: Musica, pars prima
File name: **FULMUS1**   File type: **TEXT**

Partes prolationis quot sunt? Quinque. Quae? Maxima, longa, brevis, semibrevis
Author: Johannes de Muris
Treatise: Compendium musicae practicae
File name: **MURCOM**   File type: **TEXT**

Partes prolationis quot sunt? Quinque. Quae? maxima, longa, brevis, semibrevis
Author: Johannes de Muris
Treatise: Quaestiones super partes musicae
File name: **MURQUAE**   File type: **TEXT**

Patrum nostrorum memoria et Alphonsus, splendidissimus ille Aragonum rex
Author: Lippus, junior, Raphael Brandolinus
Treatise: De musica et poetica opusculum in quo Conradolum Stangam
File name: **LIPDEM**   File type: **TEXT**

Pauli III. Pontificis maximi anno undecimo 1545. Cantorum pontificii systematis
Author: Anonymous
Treatise: Constitutiones capellae pontificiae
File name: **ANOCON**   File type: **TEXT**

Pauperibus ecclesiae Dei clericis, ac religiosis Deo laudes concinere
Author: Johannes Gallicus
Treatise: Ritus canendi [Pars secunda]
File name: **GALRC2**   File type: **TEXT**

THESAURUS MUSICARUM LATINARUM: Index of Incipits

Pauperibus ecclesiae Dei clericis, ac religiosis Deo laudes concinere
    Author: Johannes Gallicus dictus Carthusiensis seu de Mantua
        Treatise: Vera quamque facilis ad cantandum atque brevis introductio
            File name: **GALRITS1**   File type: **TEXT**

Pes est syllabarum et temporum certa dinumeratio ... pedes disyallabi sunt quattuor
    Author: Anonymous
        Treatise: [Rhythmica]
            File name: **ANOPES**   File type: **TEXT**

Petistis obnixe, Carissimi Fratres! quatenus paucas vobis de Musica regulas traderem
    Author: Odo
        Treatise: Dialogus de musica
            File name: **ODODIA**   File type: **TEXT**

Petistis obnixe, charissimi fratres, quatenus paucas vobis de Musica regulas traderem
    Author: Odo
        Treatise: Dialogus de musica
            File name: **ODODI**   File type: **TEXT**

Plura quam digna de musicae speculatione et musicae speculatoribus perutilia brevi
    Author: Odington, Walter
        Treatise: Summa de speculatione musice
            File name: **ODISUM**   File type: **TEXT**

Plura quam digna de musice speculatione et musice speculatoribus perutilia brevi
    Author: Odington, Walter
        Treatise: De speculatione musice
            File name: **ODIDES**   File type: **TEXT**

Post monochordi regularis divisionem adjicienda arbitror esse ea in quibus veteres
    Author: Boethius, Anicius Manlius Severinus
        Treatise: De institutione musica, liber quintus
            File name: **BOEDIM5**   File type: **TEXT**

Postquam in precedenti capitulo dictum est de partibus et consideracione
    Author: Anonymous
        Treatise: [Capitulum de vocibus applicatis verbis]
            File name: **ANOCAP**   File type: **TEXT**

Postquam in prima parte huius tractatus circa voces et sonos musicos pro introductionis
    Author: Engelbertus Admontensis
        Treatise: De musica, tractatus secundus
            File name: **ENGDEM2**   File type: **TEXT**

Postquam pro rudibus, fabricavi materiale, Grammatice partes reseraris cum carmine
    Author: Villa Dei, Alexander de
        Treatise: Carmen de musica cum glossis
            File name: **VILCAR**   File type: **TEXT**

Postquam superiori libro de concordantiis tractatum est, ut nunc de discordantiis
    Author: Tinctoris, Johannes
        Treatise: Liber de arte contrapuncti, Liber secundus
            File name: **TINCON2**   File type: **TEXT**

Postquam superiori libro de concordantiis tractatum est, ut nunc de discordantiis
    Author: Tinctoris, Johannes
        Treatise: Liber de arte contrapuncti, Liber secundus
            File name: **TINCPT2**   File type: **TEXT**

Postquam tribus superioribus libris absoluimus omnia, quae ad compositionem
    Author: Salinas, Franciscus
        Treatise: De musica, liber quartus
            File name: **SALMUS4**   File type: **TEXT**

Potentiarum animae nobilissima esse noscitur intellectiva potentia, nam anima
    Author: Ugolino Urbevetanis
        Treatise: Declaratio musicae disciplinae, liber primus
            File name: **UGODEC1A**   File type: **TEXT**

Praesens compendium secundum famosiores musicos in quindecim capitula
    Author: Anonymous
        Treatise: Tractatus de musica compendium cantus figurati
            File name: **ANOCOMP**   File type: **TEXT**

Prima conclusio quod longa possit inperfecta per breuem probatur
    Author: Anonymous
        Treatise: Diverse conclusiones
            File name: **ANODC**   File type: **MOBB842**

Primo accipe tenorem alicujus antiphone vel responsorii
    Author: Aegidius de Murino
        Treatise: Tractatus cantus mensurabilis
            File name: **AEGTRA**   File type: **TEXT**

Primo nota quod omnes notulae sunt aequivocae: sic tempus ac semibrevis
    Author: Anonymous
        Treatise: De semibrevibus caudatis
            File name: **ANOSEM**   File type: **TEXT**

Primo punctus quadratus vel nota quadrata est duplex, vel est caudatus vel non.
    Author: Anonymous
        Treatise: Compendium totius artis motetorum
            File name: **WFANON3**   File type: **TEXT**

Primo vero notandum tredecim esse species consonantiarum et dissonantiarum
    Author: Franco
        Treatise: Compendium discantus
            File name: **FRACOM**   File type: **TEXT**

Primo videndum est quid sit introductio et unde dicatur. Secundo quot modis dividitur.
    Author: Anonymous
        Treatise: Quaestiones et solutiones advidendum tam mensurabilis cantus quam
            File name: **ANOQS**   File type: **TEXT**

Primo, Musica Deum delectat. Proprium etenim est cujuslibet artificis
    Author: Tinctoris, Johannes
        Treatise: Complexus effectuum musices
            File name: **TINCOM1**   File type: **TEXT**

THESAURUS MUSICARUM LATINARUM: Index of Incipits

Primum igitur de notis, postmodum de pausis tractemus. Nota est signum vocis certi
　　Author: Tinctoris, Johannes
　　　　Treatise: Tractatus de notis et pausis
　　　　　　　　File name: **TINTDN**　　　　File type: **TEXT**

Primum igitur de notis, postmodum de pausis tractemus. Nota est signum vocis certi
　　Author: Tinctoris, Johannes
　　　　Treatise: Tractatus de notis et pausis
　　　　　　　　File name: **TINTRAN**　　　　File type: **TEXT**

Primum tractatum huius voluminis de symphonia id est vocum motione prosecuti
　　Author: Anonymous
　　　　Treatise: De tractatu tonorum
　　　　　　　　File name: **SCHANO**　　　　File type: **TEXT**

Primus est tonus Re La. Re Fa. quoque secundus.
　　Author: Anonymous
　　　　Treatise: Et octo tonorum incipit tractatus metricus
　　　　　　　　File name: **ANOOCTT**　　　　File type: **MLBLL763**

Primus gradus incipit in diapason hoc est in octaua nota.
　　Author: Anonymous
　　　　Treatise: Regula discantus
　　　　　　　　File name: **ANORD**　　　　File type: **MLBL2145**

Primus habet m .ne. sic sextus tercius atque septimus octauus fieri dicit
　　Author: Anonymous
　　　　Treatise: [De proportione]
　　　　　　　　File name: **ANOPROP**　　　　File type: **MOBB842**

Princeps philosophorum Aristoteles ait in prooemio metaphysicae suae:
　　Author: Johannes de Muris
　　　　Treatise: Ars discantus data a Magistro Iohanne de Muris abbreviando
　　　　　　　　File name: **MURAD**　　　　File type: **TEXT**

Princeps philosophorum Aristoteles ait in prooemio Metaphysicae suae: Omnino scientis
　　Author: Johannes de Muris
　　　　Treatise: Notitia artis musicae
　　　　　　　　File name: **MURNOT**　　　　File type: **TEXT**

Pro aliquali notitia de Musica habenda. Primo, videndum est quid sit Musica
　　Author: Anonymous
　　　　Treatise: Quatuor Principalia I
　　　　　　　　File name: **QUAPRIA1**　　　　File type: **MLBL4909**

Pro facili informatione eorum, qui ad culmen artis musicae scientiae pervenire
　　Author: Anonymous
　　　　Treatise: [De musica mensurata]
　　　　　　　　File name: **ANOBRI**　　　　File type: **TEXT**

Pro themate praesentis operis assigno Cassiodorum in quadam epistola sic inquirentum:
　　Author: Ladislaus de Zalka
　　　　Treatise: [Musica]
　　　　　　　　File name: **SZAMUS**　　　　File type: **TEXT**

THESAURUS MUSICARUM LATINARUM: Index of Incipits

Pro themate presentis operis assummo Cassiodorum in quadam epistola
>   Author: Anonymous
>>   Treatise: [Tractatus de musica]
>>>   File name: **ANOPRO**   File type: **TEXT**

Proemium. Post monochordi regularis divisionem adicienda esse arbitror ea
>   Author: Boethius, Anicius Manlius Severinus
>>   Treatise: De institutione musica, liber quintus
>>>   File name: **BOEMUS5**   File type: **TEXT**

Proemium. Superius volumen cuncta digessit, quae nunc diligentius demonstranda esse
>   Author: Boethius, Anicius Manlius Severinus
>>   Treatise: De institutione musica, liber secundus
>>>   File name: **BOEMUS2**   File type: **TEXT**

Prooemium. Superius volumen cunctas digessit, quae nunc diligentius explicanda esse
>   Author: Boethius, Anicius Manlius Severinus
>>   Treatise: De institutione musica, liber secundus
>>>   File name: **BOEDIM2**   File type: **TEXT**

Propitia divinitatis gratia nutuque favente divino, tonorum sive ut nonnulli tenorum
>   Author: Aurelianus Reomensis
>>   Treatise: Musica disciplina, cap. VIII-XVI
>>>   File name: **AURMDAP**   File type: **TEXT**

Proporcio. est duarum rerum equalium vel inequalium adinuicem habitudo
>   Author: Anonymous
>>   Treatise: Proportio est duarum rerum
>>>   File name: **ANODUA**   File type: **MLBLL763**

Proportio apud Euclidem est duarum quamcaecumque
>   Author: Gaffurio, Franchino
>>   Treatise: Practica musice
>>>   File name: **GAFPM4**   File type: **TEXT**

Proportio est divisarum rerum ad se invicem comparabilis collatio.
>   Author: Anonymous
>>   Treatise: Fragmenta musica
>>>   File name: **ANOFRA**   File type: **TEXT**

Proportio est duorum numerorum inaequalitas, Boetio teste. Ex hac definitione
>   Author: Adamus de Fulda
>>   Treatise: Musica, pars quarta
>>>   File name: **FULMUS4**   File type: **TEXT**

Proportio est duorum terminorum ad invicem habitudo. Haec autem diffinitio generalis
>   Author: Tinctoris, Johannes
>>   Treatise: Proportionale musices
>>>   File name: **TINPRO**   File type: **TEXT**

Proportio est duorum terminorum ad invicem habitudo. Haec autem diffinitio generalis
>   Author: Tinctoris, Johannes
>>   Treatise: Proportionale musices
>>>   File name: **TINPROM**   File type: **TEXT**

THESAURUS MUSICARUM LATINARUM: Index of Incipits

Proportio est quaedam habitudo duorum terminorum
  Author: Marchetus de Padua
    Treatise: Lucidarium, tractatus quartus
        File name: **MARLU4**   File type: **TEXT**

Proportio est quedam habitudo duorum terminorum
  Author: Marchetus de Padua
    Treatise: Lucidarium, tractatus quartus
        File name: **MARLUC4**   File type: **TEXT**

Proportionum adipisci musicalium a venerandae memoriae magistro Iohanne de Muris
  Author: Johannes de Muris
    Treatise: Tractatus de proportionibus
        File name: **MURDEP**   File type: **TEXT**

Proprietas in musica est derivatio plurium vocum, ab uno eodemque principio.
  Author: Anonymous
    Treatise: Compendium musices
        File name: **ANOCMU**   File type: **TEXT**

Propter amicorum et familiarium dilectionem et complacentiam, quibus totum volo
  Author: Engelbertus Admontensis
    Treatise: De musica, tractatus primus
        File name: **ENGDEM1**   File type: **TEXT**

Punctus est minimum signum quod notae appositum eam dividit, aut augmentat
  Author: Tinctoris, Johannes
    Treatise: Tractatus de punctis
        File name: **TINTDP**   File type: **TEXT**

Punctus est minimum signum quod notae appositum eam dividit, aut augmentat
  Author: Tinctoris, Johannes
    Treatise: Tractatus super punctis musicalibus
        File name: **TINTRAP**   File type: **TEXT**

Pythagoras philosophus primus apud Graecos musicae artis repertor legitur.
  Author: Theogerus Metensis
    Treatise: Musica
        File name: **THEMUS**   File type: **TEXT**

Pythagoras philosophus primus apud Graecos musicae artis repertor legitur.
  Author: Theogerus Metensis
    Treatise: Musica
        File name: **THEMUSI**   File type: **TEXT**

Quae nominibus tria proponuntur, re vera quatuor sunt.
  Author: Stoquerus, Gaspar
    Treatise: De modo, tempore, et prolatione
        File name: **STOMTP**   File type: **MMBN6486**

Quae pars harmonica? Harmonica pars est de sonorum inflexione ad bene canendum
  Author: Beurhusius, Fredericus
    Treatise: Erotematum musicae liber secundus
        File name: **BEUERO2**   File type: **TEXT**

257

Quae pars harmonica? Harmonica pars est de sonorum inflexione ad bene canendum
  Author: Beurhusius, Fredericus
    Treatise: Musicae rudimenta e pleniore eius descriptione itemque exempla quaedam
        File name: **BEUMUS2**   File type: **TEXT**

Quae superiori libro diximus, non solum illa quidem ad planam musicam spectant
  Author: Kromer, Marcin
    Treatise: De musica figurata
        File name: **KRODEM**   File type: **TEXT**

Quaedam lector humanissime in nostris institutionibus obscuriora quibusdam
  Author: Aaron, Petrus
    Treatise: Libri tres de institutione harmonica; Petrus Aaron Florentinus ad Lectorem
        File name: **AARIHCOR**   File type: **TEXT**

Quaeritur, quare una consonantia magis concordet quam altera
  Author: Marchetus de Padua
    Treatise: Lucidarium, tractatus sextus
        File name: **MARLU6**   File type: **TEXT**

Quaesivit quidam devotus, quid est quod in multis ecclesiis tam cathedralibus
  Author: Carlerius, Egidius
    Treatise: Tractatus de duplici ritu cantus ecclesiastici in divinis officiis et primo de
        File name: **CARLTRA**   File type: **TEXT**

Qualiter in arte practica mensurabilis cantus erudiri mediocriter affectans
  Author: Antonius de Luca
    Treatise: Ars cantus figurati
        File name: **LUCARS**   File type: **TEXT**

Qualiter Pytagoras adinvenit musicam, memorat Macrobius
  Author: Marchetus de Padua
    Treatise: Lucidarium, tractatus primus
        File name: **MARLU1**   File type: **TEXT**

Qualiter Pytagoras adinvenit musicam memorat Macrobius
  Author: Marchetus de Padua
    Treatise: Lucidarium, tractatus primus
        File name: **MARLUC1**   File type: **TEXT**

Quam stulte faciant, qui Solfizandi rationem pueros ex Guidonis scala docere conantur
  Author: Stoquerus, Gaspar
    Treatise: De vera solfizationis
        File name: **STOVERA**   File type: **MMBN6486**

Quamquam in plerisque opusculis nostris quot et quae notae sint explicaverimus
  Author: Tinctoris, Johannes
    Treatise: Tractatus de regulari valore notarum
        File name: **TINTDR**   File type: **TEXT**

Quamquam in plerisque opusculis nostris quot et quae notae sint explicaverimus
  Author: Tinctoris, Johannes
    Treatise: Tractatus de regulari valore notarum
        File name: **TINTRAR**   File type: **TEXT**

Quamvis inter artes liberales musica sit digne numerata, ipsa tamen quorundam
  Author: Person, Gobelinus
    Treatise: Tractatus musicae scientiae
      File name: **PERTRA**   File type: **TEXT**

Quamvis species sive consonantiae discantus infinitae sint
  Author: Hothby, Johannes
    Treatise: Regulae supra contrapunctum
      File name: **HOTRSC**   File type: **TEXT**

Quamvis species sive consonantie discantus infinite sint
  Author: Hothby, Johannes
    Treatise: Regulae supra contrapunctum
      File name: **HOTREGC**   File type: **TEXT**

Quando duae notae sunt in unisono et tertia ascendit, prima debet esse in quinto
  Author: Anonymous
    Treatise: De arte discantandi
      File name: **ARTDIS**   File type: **TEXT**

Quantitatem duplicem esse Mathematici asserunt Continuam scilicet et discretam
  Author: Gaffurio, Franchino
    Treatise: Theorica musice, liber tertius
      File name: **GAFTM3**   File type: **TEXT**

Quare musica studetur? Respondetur quod illo modo: quod cultus divinus
  Author: Anonymous XI
    Treatise: Tractatus de musica plana et mensurabili
      File name: **ANO11TRA**   File type: **TEXT**

Quare non possint esse plura quam septem vocum discrimina. Natura omnium rerum
  Author: Rudolf of St. Trond
    Treatise: Quaestiones in musica
      File name: **RUDQUA**   File type: **TEXT**

Quartam vtilitatem, Ecclesiae ministris noticia accentuum conferat.
  Author: Liban, Jerzy
    Treatise: De accentuum ecclesiasticorum exquisita ratione
      File name: **LIBDEA**   File type: **TEXT**

Quatuor ecce tropi natura matre creati
  Author: Anonymous
    Treatise: Ars musice
      File name: **WFANON2**   File type: **TEXT**

Quatuor sunt signa per que facile cognosci potest omnis cantus
  Author: Anonymous
    Treatise: [De prolatione]
      File name: **ANOPROL**   File type: **MOBB842**

Quatuor ut reges infra sua regna sedentes;
  Author: Anonymous
    Treatise: Ars musica
      File name: **ANOFRA6**   File type: **TEXT**

Quem enim a teneris unguiculis, ut aiunt greci, contrapunctum didicerim vobis
   Author: Burtius, Nicolaus
      Treatise: Musices opusculum, tractatus secundus, capitulum VI
            File name: **BURMUSX**   File type: **TEXT**

Quemadmodum inter triticum et zizania quamdiu herba est
   Author: Anonymous
      Treatise: Quatuor Principalia I
            File name: **QUAPRIB1**   File type: **TEXT**

Quemodmodum, ut ait ille venerabilis doctor Ambrosius, in quodam sermone
   Author: Anonymous
      Treatise: Musicae liber
            File name: **ANOMUS**   File type: **TEXT**

Queritur quare una consonantia magis concordet quam altera
   Author: Marchetus de Padua
      Treatise: Lucidarium, tractatus sextus
            File name: **MARLUC6**   File type: **TEXT**

Quia iuxta sapientissimum Salomonem, Dura est ut infernus aemulatio
   Author: Wylde, Johannes
      Treatise: Musica manualis cum tonale
            File name: **WYLMUS**   File type: **TEXT**

Quia iuxta sapientissimum Salomonem dura est vt inferus Emulatio
   Author: Wylde, John
      Treatise: Musica guidonis
            File name: **WYLMUSI**   File type: **MLBLL763**

Quia omnes septem sciencie liberales .a. septiformi gracia spiritus sancti procedentes
   Author: Anonymous
      Treatise: Speculum cantancium. siue psallencium
            File name: **ANOSPEC**   File type: **MLBLL763**

Quicumque aliquod sibi artificium inchoat: semper ad eventum festinat
   Author: Berno Augiensis
      Treatise: De mensurando monochordo
            File name: **BERNDEM**   File type: **TEXT**

Quid est cantus? peritia musicae, artis, inflexio vocis et modulatio.
   Author: Anonymous
      Treatise: Quid est cantus?
            File name: **ANOQUID**   File type: **TEXT**

Quid est Musica mensuralis? Quae in suis notis secundum signorum ac figurarum
   Author: Cochlaeus, Johannes
      Treatise: Tetrachordum musices, tractatus quartus
            File name: **COCTET4**   File type: **TEXT**

Quid est musica plana? Quae in suis notis aequam seruat mensuram absque incremento
   Author: Cochlaeus, Johannes
      Treatise: Tetrachordum musices, tractatus secundus
            File name: **COCTET2**   File type: **TEXT**

Quid est musica. Musica est ars bene canendi. Unde dicta est musica. Musica a Musis
    Author: Beurhusius, Fredericus
        Treatise: Erotematum musicae liber primus
                File name: **BEUERO1**   File type: **TEXT**

Quid est musica? Est bene modulandi scientia. Augustinus. Vel est facultas
    Author: Cochlaeus, Johannes
        Treatise: Tetrachordum musices, tractatus primus
                File name: **COCTET1**   File type: **TEXT**

Quid est musica? Musica est ars bene canendi. Quot sunt partes musicae?
    Author: Beurhusius, Fredericus
        Treatise: Musicae rudimenta e pleniore eius descriptione itemque exempla quaedam
                File name: **BEUMUS1**   File type: **TEXT**

Quid est tonus? Est regula per ascensum et descensum quemuis cantum in fine diiudicans.
    Author: Cochlaeus, Johannes
        Treatise: Tetrachordum musices, tractatus tertius
                File name: **COCTET3**   File type: **TEXT**

Quid singulae litterae in superscriptione significent cantilenae
    Author: Notker
        Treatise: De musica
                File name: **NOTDEM**   File type: **TEXT**

Quid singulae litterae in superscriptione significent cantilenae
    Author: Notker
        Treatise: [De musica]
                File name: **NOTDEMU**   File type: **TEXT**

Quid sit lyra populariter leutum dicta: quid etiam quelibet instrumentalis species
    Author: Tinctoris, Johannes
        Treatise: De inventione et usu musicae
                File name: **TININV4**   File type: **TEXT**

Quilibet affectans scire contrapunctum ea scribat diligenter
    Author: Johannes de Muris
        Treatise: Ars contrapuncti
                File name: **MURARSC**   File type: **TEXT**

Quilibet in arte pratica mensurabilis cantus erudiri
    Author: Johannes de Muris
        Treatise: Libellus cantus mensurabilis
                File name: **MURLIBF**   File type: **MFAB1119**

Quilibet in arte pratica mensurabilis cantus erudiri
    Author: Johannes de Muris
        Treatise: Libellus cantus mensurabilis
                File name: **MURLIBV**   File type: **MVBM8-85**

Quindecim chordae habentur in monochordo secundum Boetium.
    Author: Anonymous
        Treatise: Tractatus cuiusdam monachi de musica
                File name: **WFANON1**   File type: **TEXT**

Quinque sunt consonantiae musicae, diatessaron, quae et sesquitertia dicitur
Author: Anonymous II
Treatise: Tractatus de musica
File name: **ANO2TDM** File type: **TEXT**

Quinque sunt consonantiae musicae, Diatessaron, quae et sesquitertia dicitur
Author: Anonymous II
Treatise: Tractatus de musica
File name: **ANO2TRDM** File type: **TEXT**

Quinque sunt in Arithmetica inaequalitatis genera. Ex quibus tria postrema respuens
Author: Anonymous
Treatise: Quomodo de arithmetica procedit musica
File name: **ANOQUO** File type: **TEXT**

Quinque sunt in Arithmetica inaequalitatis genera. Ex quibus tria postrema respuens
Author: Anonymous
Treatise: Quomodo de arithmetica procedit musica
File name: **ANOQUOM** File type: **TEXT**

Quisquis hoc legerit magno cum jure patratum
Author: Aurelianus Reomensis
Treatise: Musica disciplina
File name: **AUREPI** File type: **TEXT**

Quod punctus per sui additionem possit facere brevem alterari.
Author: Anonymous OP
Treatise: Tractatus de musica
File name: **ANOPTRA** File type: **TEXT**

Quoniam autem huc usque de usu concordantiarum permissuque discordantiarum
Author: Tinctoris, Johannes
Treatise: Liber de arte contrapuncti, Liber tertius
File name: **TINCPT3** File type: **TEXT**

Quoniam autem hucusque de usu concordantiarum praemissuque discordantiarum
Author: Tinctoris, Johannes
Treatise: Liber de arte contrapuncti, Liber tertius
File name: **TINCON3** File type: **TEXT**

Quoniam autem sic cantus, ut jam diximus, firmus sive planus, precipue ecclesiasticus
Author: Ieronimus de Moravia
Treatise: Tractatus de musica
File name: **IERTRA2** File type: **TEXT**

Quoniam cantum mensuralem seu figuratum musice artis multi ignorantes solent
Author: Anonymous
Treatise: Tractatulus de cantu mensurali seu figurativo musice artis
File name: **ANOTRA** File type: **TEXT**

Quoniam circa artem musicalis sciencie hodiernis temporibus cantando delyrant
Author: Anonymous
Treatise: Tractatus de musica mensurabili
File name: **WFANON4** File type: **TEXT**

THESAURUS MUSICARUM LATINARUM: Index of Incipits

Quoniam circa artem musicam necessaria quedam ad utilitatem constantium
    Author: Aristotle
        Treatise: Tractatus de musica
                File name: **ARITRA**   File type: **TEXT**

Quoniam circa artem musicam necessaria quaedam ad utilitatem cantantium tractare
    Author: Beda [Ps.]
        Treatise: Musica quadrata seu mensurata
                File name: **BEDMUS**   File type: **TEXT**

Quoniam circa artem musicam necessaria quedam ad utilitatem cantantium tractare
    Author: Anonymous
        Treatise: [Tractatus de musica]
                File name: **LAMTRAC**   File type: **MSBCLV30**

Quoniam de arte mensurabili tractare proponimus
    Author: Philippe de Vitry
        Treatise: Liber musicalium
                File name: **VITLIBM**   File type: **TEXT**

Quoniam de plana musica sive de compositione gammatis breviter
    Author: Anonymous
        Treatise: De plana musica breve compendium
                File name: **ANODMP**   File type: **TEXT**

Quoniam dicente philosopho inde omnia accidentia multum conferunt
    Author: Marchetus de Padua
        Treatise: Pomerium
                File name: **MARPOM**   File type: **TEXT**

Quoniam homine senescente senescunt et ea, que hominis sunt, et deteriorantur
    Author: Anonymous
        Treatise: Contrapunctus
                File name: **ANOVIC**   File type: **TEXT**

Quoniam in antelapsis temporibus quamplures de cantibus
    Author: Anonymous
        Treatise: Berkeley Manuscript
                File name: **BERMAN**   File type: **TEXT**

Quoniam in antepositis sermonibus theoricam musicae leniter tetigimus et in brevi
    Author: Johannes de Muris
        Treatise: De practica musica, seu de mensurabili
                File name: **MURPRA**   File type: **TEXT**

Quoniam inter cetera mortalium nichil dignius esse constat scientiarum liberalium
    Author: Guerson, Guillaume
        Treatise: Utillissime musicales regule
                File name: **GUEUT**   File type: **TEXT**

Quoniam inter septem artes liberales primatum optinet musica. testante Boetio.
    Author: Anonymous
        Treatise: [Tractatus de musica]
                File name: **ANOTRAC**   File type: **MCBOLT1**

THESAURUS MUSICARUM LATINARUM: Index of Incipits

Quoniam multitudo scripture lectoris animo sepius fastidium non parum infert
  Author: Prosdocimo de' Beldomandi
    Treatise: Tractatus practice de musica mensurabili
                    File name: **PROTRAP1**   File type: **TEXT**

Quoniam musicorum de hijs cantibus frequens est dissensio. qui in uno octo chordo
  Author: Theinredus Doverensis
    Treatise: Musica, liber primus
                    File name: **TDMUS1**   File type: **MOBB842**

Quoniam nonnulli maxime novi auditores compendiosa brevitate letantur
  Author: Petrus Picardus
    Treatise: Musica mensurabilis
                    File name: **PETMUS**   File type: **TEXT**

Quoniam nonnulli, maxime novi auditores, compendiosa brevitate letantur
  Author: Petrus Picardus
    Treatise: Ars motettorum compilata breviter
                    File name: **PETARS**   File type: **TEXT**

Quoniam nonnulli, maxime novi auditores, compendiosa brevitate laetantur
  Author: Petrus Picardus
    Treatise: Musica mensurabilis
                    File name: **PETMUSM**   File type: **TEXT**

Quoniam omnis cantus mesuratus dicitur eo quod tempore mensuratur
  Author: Marchetus de Padua
    Treatise: Brevis compilatio in arte musicae mensuratae
                    File name: **MARBRE**   File type: **TEXT**

Quoniam omnis tonus et semitonium in voce consistit
  Author: Marchetus de Padua
    Treatise: Lucidarium, tractatus octavus
                    File name: **MARLU8**   File type: **TEXT**

Quoniam omnis tonus et semitonium in voce consistit
  Author: Marchetus de Padua
    Treatise: Lucidarium, tractatus octavus
                    File name: **MARLUC8**   File type: **TEXT**

Quoniam omnium uarietate numerorum Macrobius: ac Boetius coeterique Musici
  Author: Gaffurio, Franchino
    Treatise: Theorica musice, liber quartus
                    File name: **GAFTM4**   File type: **TEXT**

Quoniam per ignorantiam artis musice multi, et maxime temporibus moderni,
  Author: Anonymous III
    Treatise: Compendiolum artis veteris ac novae
                    File name: **ANO3COM**   File type: **TEXT**

Quoniam per ignorantiam artis musicae multi, et maxime temporibus modernis
  Author: Anonymous
    Treatise: De arte musicae
                    File name: **ANOART**   File type: **TEXT**

THESAURUS MUSICARUM LATINARUM: Index of Incipits

Quoniam per magis noti notitiam ad ignoti facilius devenitur notitiam
    Author: Anonymous
        Treatise: Tractatus cantus figurati
                File name: **ANO12TCF**   File type: **TEXT**

Quoniam per magis noti notitiam ad ignoti facilius devenitur notitiam
    Author: Anonymous XII
        Treatise: Tractatus de musica
                File name: **ANO12TRA**   File type: **TEXT**

Quoniam prosam artis musicae mensurabilis ab excellentibus in arte musicis
    Author: Anonymous
        Treatise: De musica mensurata
                File name: **ANODMM**   File type: **TEXT**

Quoniam prosam artis musice mensurabilis ab excellentibus in arte musicis
    Author: Anonymous
        Treatise: De expositione musice
                File name: **ANO1279**   File type: **TEXT**

Quoniam quidam iuvenum, amici mei, me cum affectu rogaverunt, quatenus eis aliquid
    Author: Johannes de Grocheo
        Treatise: De musica
                File name: **GRODEM**   File type: **TEXT**

Quoniam quidam iuvenum, amici mei, me cum affectu rogaverint, quatenus eis aliquid
    Author: Johannes de Grocheo
        Treatise: Theoria
                File name: **GROTHE**   File type: **TEXT**

Quoniam sicut domino placuit scientiam musice
    Author: Philippus de Caserta
        Treatise: Tractatus de diversis figuris
                File name: **CASTRA**   File type: **TEXT**

Quoniam vt inquit Cicero: in libello qui de vniuersitate nuncupatur: circa finem.
    Author: Burtius, Nicolaus
        Treatise: Musices opusculum, tractatus primus
                File name: **BURMUS1**   File type: **TEXT**

Quoniam, dicente Philosopho in prooemio de Anima, accidentia multum conferunt
    Author: Marchetus de Padua
        Treatise: Pomerium
                File name: **MARPOME**   File type: **TEXT**

Quoniam, ut dicit Boetius in prohemio super musicam, sicut in visu non sufficit
    Author: Ieronimus de Moravia
        Treatise: Tractatus de musica
                File name: **IERTDM1**   File type: **TEXT**

Quoniam, ut dicit Boetius in prohemio super musicam, sicut in visu non sufficit
    Author: Ieronimus de Moravia
        Treatise: Tractatus de musica
                File name: **IERTDM2**   File type: **TEXT**

THESAURUS MUSICARUM LATINARUM: Index of Incipits

Quoniam, ut dicit Boetius in prohemio super musicam
  Author: Ieronimus de Moravia
    Treatise: Tractatus de musica
      File name: **IERTRA1**   File type: **TEXT**

Quum dictum sit musicam in numero ternario sumere perfectionem
  Author: Anonymous VI
    Treatise: De musica mensurabili
      File name: **ANO6DEM**   File type: **TEXT**

Qvatuor superioribus libris a nobis tractatum est de priore Musicae parte
  Author: Salinas, Franciscus
    Treatise: De musica, liber quintus
      File name: **SALMUS5**   File type: **TEXT**

Raciones autem musicarum consonanciarum hee sunt uniuersi generis arithmetici
  Author: Theinredus Doverensis
    Treatise: Musica, liber secundus
      File name: **TDMUS2**   File type: **MOBB842**

Rationem extremorum sonorum in harmonia inuicem consonantium harmonica
  Author: Gaffurio, Franchino
    Treatise: De harmonia musicorum instrumentorum opus, liber tertius
      File name: **GAFHAR3**   File type: **TEXT**

Redeamus igitur ad ipsam musicae speciem, quae totam harmoniae vim dicitur
  Author: Ramus de Pareia, Bartholomeus
    Treatise: Musica practica, prima pars, tractatus tertius
      File name: **RAMMP1T3**   File type: **TEXT**

Refert Nicomachus canendi disciplinam primitus adeo simplicem fuisse
  Author: Gaffurio, Franchino
    Treatise: Theorica musice, liber quintus
      File name: **GAFTM5**   File type: **TEXT**

Sancti Patres nostri antiqui docuerunt et instituerunt subditos suos, praecipientes
  Author: Anonymous
    Treatise: Instituta patrum de modo psallendi sive cantandi
      File name: **PATPSAL**   File type: **TEXT**

Sciendum est, quod ars musicae septenario numero litterarum contenta est
  Author: Salomo, Elias
    Treatise: Scientia artis musicae
      File name: **SALSCI**   File type: **TEXT**

Scientia uero musice, comprehendit in summa, cognitionem specierum armoniarum
  Author: Al-Farabi
    Treatise: De scientiis
      File name: **FARSCIE**   File type: **TEXT**

Scientia vero musice comprehendit in summa cognitionem specierum armoniarum
  Author: Al-Farabi
    Treatise: De scientiis
      File name: **FARSCI**   File type: **TEXT**

Scribit Aristoteles, secundo Elencorum capitulo ultimo
    Author: Prosdocimo de' Beldomandi
        Treatise: Tractatus de contrapuncto
                File name: **PROTRAC**   File type: **TEXT**

Scribit Aristotiles secundo Elenchorum, capitulo ultimo
    Author: Prosdocimo de' Beldomandi
        Treatise: Contrapunctus
                File name: **PROCON**   File type: **TEXT**

Secundo. Principaliter videndum est, primo, de Arte Musicae
    Author: Anonymous
        Treatise: Quatuor Principalia II
                File name: **QUAPRIA2**   File type: **MLBL4909**

Secundum Ciceronis praeceptum in eo libro quem de officiis inscripsit
    Author: Tinctoris, Johannes
        Treatise: Liber de natura et proprietate tonorum
                File name: **TINLDN**   File type: **TEXT**

Secundum Ciceronis praeceptum in eo libro quem de Officiis inscripsit
    Author: Tinctoris, Johannes
        Treatise: Liber de natura et proprietate tonorum
                File name: **TINNAT**   File type: **TEXT**

Semidictonus est inaequalium notarum consonantia, tonum perfectum cum semitonio
    Author: Anonymous
        Treatise: De musica
                File name: **ANOFRA4**   File type: **TEXT**

Septem orbes septem planetarum cum dulcissima armonia voluuntur
    Author: Anonymous
        Treatise: De octo tonis vbi nascuntur et oriuntur aut efficiuntur
                File name: **ANOOCT**   File type: **MLBLL763**

Septem sunt concordancie in discantu, videlicet unisonus. tercia, quinta, sexta
    Author: Anonymous
        Treatise: [De discantu et contranota]
                File name: **ANODDCS**   File type: **TEXT**

Septem sunt species consonantiarum in discantu
    Author: Philippe de Vitry
        Treatise: Ars perfecta in musica
                File name: **VITARSP**   File type: **TEXT**

Septem sunt species discantus secundum modernos, videlicet unisonus
    Author: Torkesey, Johannes
        Treatise: Septem sunt species
                File name: **TORKSEP**   File type: **TEXT**

Sequitur de alteratione unde alteratio in musica est proprii valoris secundum notae
    Author: Ugolino Urbevetanis
        Treatise: Declaratio musicae disciplinae, liber tertius
                File name: **UGODEC3B**   File type: **TEXT**

Sequitur de sinemenis sic: b c, cujus medium erit [sqb] parvum.

    Author: Anonymous

        Treatise: De sinemenis

                File name: **ANODES**   File type: **TEXT**

Sequitur videre de consonantia, de qua primo videbimus

    Author: Marchetus de Padua

        Treatise: Lucidarium, tractatus quintus

                File name: **MARLU5**   File type: **TEXT**

Sequitur videre de consonantia, de qua primo videbimus

    Author: Marchetus de Padua

        Treatise: Lucidarium, tractatus quintus

                File name: **MARLUC5**   File type: **TEXT**

Sequitur videre de pausis, scilicet quo modo in cantu plano

    Author: Marchetus de Padua

        Treatise: Lucidarium, tractatus decimustertius

                File name: **MARLU13**   File type: **TEXT**

Sequitur videre de pausis, scilicet quomodo in cantu plano

    Author: Marchetus de Padua

        Treatise: Lucidarium, tractatus tercius decimus

                File name: **MARLUC13**   File type: **TEXT**

Sequuntur numeri proportionales secundum Macrobium, qui quidem numeri

    Author: Johannes de Muris

        Treatise: De tonis

                File name: **MURTON**   File type: **TEXT**

Sesquialtera proportio est, quando numerus major continet in se totum numerum

    Author: Odo

        Treatise: Regulae de rhythmimachia

                File name: **ODORH**   File type: **TEXT**

Sesquialtera proportio est, quando numerus maior continet in se totum numerum

    Author: Odo

         Treatise: Regulae de rhythmimachia

                File name: **ODORHY**   File type: **TEXT**

Sex sunt species principales sive concordantie discantus: unisonus, semiditonus

    Author: Anonymous

        Treatise: Ars mensurandi motetos

                File name: **ANOARS**   File type: **TEXT**

Si cantus ascendit duas voces et organum incipit in duplici voce

    Author: Gui de Chalis

        Treatise: Musica

                File name: **GUICHA**   File type: **TEXT**

Si cantus ascendit duas voces, et organum incipit in dupplici voce

    Author: Abbot Guido

        Treatise: Regulae organi

                File name: **ABGUREG**   File type: **TEXT**

Si quis artem musicae mensurabilis tam veterem quam novam
    Author: Anonymous
        Treatise: Compendium musicae mensurabilis tam veteris quam novae artis
               File name: **ANO4CMM**   File type: **TEXT**

Si quis artem musice mensurabilis tam veterem quam novam
    Author: Anonymous IV
        Treatise: Compendium artis mensurabilis tam veteris quam novae
               File name: **ANO4COM**   File type: **TEXT**

Si quis concordiam organorum scire uoluerit ita inchoare studeat.
    Author: Anonymous
        Treatise: Qualiter debeant fieri organa
               File name: **ANOQUAL**   File type: **MPBN7400**

Si quis notitiam abaci habere desiderat, necesse est ut in consideratione numeri
    Author: Odo
        Treatise: Regulae super abacum
               File name: **ODORE**   File type: **TEXT**

Si quis notitiam abaci habere desiderat, necesse est, ut in consideratione numeri
    Author: Odo
        Treatise: Regulae super abacum
               File name: **ODOREG**   File type: **TEXT**

Sic formantur breves plicate:
    Author: Anonymous VII
        Treatise: De diversis maneriebus in musica mensurabili
               File name: **ANO7DED**   File type: **TEXT**

Sicut igitur ex numerorum multiplicatione relata proportionum genera redundarunt
    Author: Ramus de Pareia, Bartholomeus
        Treatise: Musica practica, tertia pars, tractatus secundus
               File name: **RAMMP3T2**   File type: **TEXT**

Sicut notatores Antiphonarium praemunivimus, ita et eos qui gradualia notaturi sunt
    Author: Anonymous
        Treatise: Tractatus cantandi graduale. Graduali Cisterciensi prologi instar praemissus
               File name: **ANOCIST**   File type: **TEXT**

Sicut vocis articulatae elementariae atque individuae partes sunt litterae
    Author: Anonymous
        Treatise: Musica enchiriadis
               File name: **MUSENC**   File type: **TEXT**

Sicut vocis articulatae elementariae atque individuae partes sunt litterae
    Author: Anonymous
        Treatise: Musica enchiriadis
               File name: **MUSENCH**   File type: **TEXT**

Significatum organi aliud naturale aliud remotum a natura. Naturale est illud
    Author: Anonymous
        Treatise: [Ad organum faciendum]
               File name: **ADORFBR**   File type: **TEXT**

THESAURUS MUSICARUM LATINARUM: Index of Incipits

Simplicius in commento suo super Aristotelis pedicamenta in commendationem
Author: Jacobus Leodiensis
Treatise: Speculum musicae, Liber septimus
File name: **JACSM7**   File type: **TEXT**

Simplicius, in <commentario> suo super Aristotelis predicamenta, in commendationem
Author: Jacobus Leodiensis
Treatise: Speculum musicae, Liber septimus
File name: **JACSP7**   File type: **TEXT**

Sunt autem imprimis septem consideranda, per quae tamquam per magis principalia
Author: Adamus de Fulda
Treatise: Musica, pars secunda
File name: **FULMUS2**   File type: **TEXT**

Superiore volumine demonstratum est diatessaron consonantiam ex duobus tonis
Author: Boethius, Anicius Manlius Severinus
Treatise: De institutione musica, liber tertius
File name: **BOEDIM3**   File type: **TEXT**

Superiore volumine demonstratum est diatessaron consonantiam ex duobus tonis
Author: Boethius, Anicius Manlius Severinus
Treatise: De institutione musica, liber tertius
File name: **BOEMUS3**   File type: **TEXT**

Svperest nunc vt de metris ac versibus ac eorum canoris differentijs dicamus
Author: Salinas, Franciscus
Treatise: De musica, liber sextus
File name: **SALMUS6**   File type: **TEXT**

Taliter hucusque prosecuti fuimus, ut tantum de vocibus successive prolatis
Author: Ramus de Pareia, Bartholomeus
Treatise: Musica practica, secunda pars, tractatus primus
File name: **RAMMP2**   File type: **TEXT**

Temporibus nostris . super omnes homines (:) fatui sunt cantores!
Author: Guido d'Arezzo
Treatise: Prologus in antiphonarium
File name: **GUIPRO**   File type: **TEXT**

Temporibus nostris super omnes homines fatui sunt cantores
Author: Guido d'Arezzo
Treatise: Prologus in antiphonarium
File name: **GUIPRAN**   File type: **TEXT**

Temporibus nostris super omnes homines fatui sunt cantores
Author: Guido d'Arezzo
Treatise: Prologus in antiphonarium
File name: **GUIPROL**   File type: **TEXT**

Tertia differentia huius quarti tropi cum secunda conformem habet modum
Author: Ugolino Urbevetanis
Treatise: Declaratio musicae disciplinae, liber primus
File name: **UGODEC1B**   File type: **TEXT**

THESAURUS MUSICARUM LATINARUM: Index of Incipits

Tibi, dilecte frater, tuus Prosdocimus de Beldemandis
    Author: Prosdocimo de' Beldomandi
        Treatise: Brevis summula proportionum
                File name: **PROBRE2**   File type: **TEXT**

Tonus dicitur a tonando quia prima uox est qui naturaliter tonat.
    Author: Anonymous
        Treatise: [De intervallis]
                File name: **ANOINT**   File type: **MLBLH978**

Tonus est regula quo de omni cantu in fine diiudicat
    Author: Anonymous
        Treatise: [De intervallis]
                File name: **ANOIN**   File type: **MOBB842**

Tonus primus NONANOEANE, qui graece dicitur autentos protos
    Author: Anonymous
        Treatise: Alia musica
                File name: **ALIAMU**   File type: **TEXT**

Tonus prout antiphona vel alter cantus totus alicuius toni dicitur, est plurium
    Author: Jacobus Leodiensis
        Treatise: Tractatus de intonatione tonorum
                File name: **JACDIT**   File type: **TEXT**

Tonus, tropus, sive modus, secundum dicta Boetii
    Author: Marchetus de Padua
        Treatise: Lucidarium, tractatus undecimus
                File name: **MARLU11**   File type: **TEXT**

Tonus, tropus, sive modus, secundum dicta Boetii
    Author: Marchetus de Padua
        Treatise: Lucidarium, tractatus undecimus
                File name: **MARLUC11**   File type: **TEXT**

Totum monochordum partire in primis in quatuor, et in initio monochordi pone F.
    Author: Anonymous
        Treatise: Mensura monochordi Boetii
                File name: **ANOMMB**   File type: **TEXT**

Totum monochordum partire inprimis in quatuor, et in initio monochordi pone F.
    Author: Anonymous
        Treatise: Mensura monochordi Boetii
                File name: **ANOMEN**   File type: **TEXT**

Tractaturus autem de ipsis notarum musicalium imperfectionibus
    Author: Tinctoris, Johannes
        Treatise: Liber imperfectionum notarum musicalium
                File name: **TINLIB**   File type: **TEXT**

Tractaturus autem de ipsis notarum musicalium imperfectionibus
    Author: Tinctoris, Johannes
        Treatise: Liber imperfectionum notarum musicalium
                File name: **TINLIMP**   File type: **TEXT**

THESAURUS MUSICARUM LATINARUM: Index of Incipits

Traditis iam et expositis, quae ad rhythmorum et metrorum compositionem visa sunt
    Author: Salinas, Franciscus
       Treatise: De musica, liber septimus
           File name: **SALMUS7**   File type: **TEXT**

Tredecim consonantiae sunt quibus omnis ecclesiasticus cantus contexitur
    Author: Jacobus Leodiensis
       Treatise: Tractatus de consonantiis musicalibus
           File name: **JACDCM**   File type: **TEXT**

Tredecim consonantie sunt quibus omnis cantus ecclesiaticus contexitur.
    Author: Anonymous 1
       Treatise: Tractatus de consonantiis musicalibus
           File name: **ANO1TRA**   File type: **TEXT**

Tres esse musicas, mundanam, scilicet, humanam et instrumentalem, ex prioris
    Author: Ugolino Urbevetanis
       Treatise: Declaratio musicae disciplinae, liber quartus
           File name: **UGODEC4**   File type: **TEXT**

Unumquodque opus tanto laudabilius est necnon utilius, quanto per illud ad bonum aliquod
    Author: Jacobus Leodiensis
       Treatise: Speculum musicae, Liber sextus
           File name: **JACSM6A**   File type: **TEXT**

Unumquodque opus tanto laudabilius est necnon utilius, quanto per illud ad bonum aliquod
    Author: Jacobus Leodiensis
       Treatise: Speculum musicae, Liber sextus
           File name: **JACSP6A**   File type: **TEXT**

Usu comperimus, longe alium institutionis modum requiri, si quis pueros adhuc
    Author: Heyden, Sebaldus
       Treatise: De arte canendi, ac vero signorum in cantibus usu, liber primus
           File name: **HEYDAC1**   File type: **TEXT**

Ut enim maiorum firmat auctoritas, omnis veteris testamenti scriptura inprimis
    Author: Berno Augiensis
       Treatise: De varia psalmorum atque cantuum modulatione
           File name: **BERNVAR**   File type: **TEXT**

Ut enim majorum firmat auctoritas, omnis Veteris Testamenti Scriptura inprimis
    Author: Berno Augiensis
       Treatise: De varia psalmorum atque cantuum modulatione
           File name: **BERNVARP**   File type: **TEXT**

Ut pateat euidenter monochordi. quot et quibus pleri licet nescienter diuersis
    Author: Anonymous
       Treatise: [Opusculum musicum]
           File name: **MUSICAO**   File type: **MOBB842**

Ut vero indubitanter consonantiarum ratio colligatur, tali brevissimo ac simplici effici
    Author: Adelboldus
       Treatise: Musica
           File name: **ADEMUS**   File type: **TEXT**

THESAURUS MUSICARUM LATINARUM: Index of Incipits

Ut vero indubitanter consonantiarum ratio colligatur, tali brevissimo ac simplici effici
    Author: Adelboldus
        Treatise: Musica
                File name: **ADEMUSI**   File type: **TEXT**

Utilis in multis ars musica rebus habetur;
    Author: Bertrandus Prudentius
        Treatise: De arte musica
                File name: **BERTARM**   File type: **TEXT**

Utilitas huius scientie musicalis magna est et mirabilis atque virtuosa ualde.
    Author: Dionysius Lewis de Ryckel
        Treatise: De arte musicali, prima pars: Musica speculativa
                File name: **GENTSPE**   File type: **MGRU70**

Veror nimirum magnifice domine Rector, Doctores Celebres, Magistri insignes
    Author: Liban, Jerzy
        Treatise: De philosophiae laudibus oratio
                File name: **LIBDEP**   File type: **TEXT**

Versus atque notas Herimannus protulit istas,
    Author: Hermannus Contractus
        Treatise: Versus ad discernendum cantum
                File name: **HERVER**   File type: **TEXT**

Versus atque notas Herimannus protulit istas,
    Author: Hermannus Contractus
        Treatise: Versus ad discernendum cantum
                File name: **HERVERP**   File type: **TEXT**

Versus Post octavam quinta, si note tendunt
    Author: Phillipotus Andrea
        Treatise: De contrapuncto quaedam regulae utiles
                File name: **ANDCON**   File type: **TEXT**

Viso de gravibus ordine ad acutas, notatoque quomodo ex speciebus diatessaron
    Author: Anonymous
        Treatise: Tractatus de musica
                File name: **ANOFRA5**   File type: **TEXT**

Viso igitur quid sit discantus, quedam precogniciones sunt videnlde.
    Author: Anonymous
        Treatise: Discantus positio vulgaris
                File name: **DISPOS**   File type: **TEXT**

Viso igitur, quid sit discantus, quaedam precognitiones sunt videndae.
    Author: Anonymous
        Treatise: Discantus positio vulgaris
                File name: **DISPOVU**   File type: **TEXT**

Vnisonus. Semitonus. Tonus. Semiditonus. Ditonus. Diateseron. Tritonus. Diapente.
    Author: Anonymous
        Treatise: Species plani cantus sunt terdecim
                File name: **ANOSPE**   File type: **TEXT**

Vocum copulationes dicuntur. omni symphonia et de omni cantu dicatur.
>   Author: Anonymous
>   Treatise: [Ad organum faciendum]
>   File name: **ADORFBA**   File type: **TEXT**

Volentibus introduci in arte contrapunctus
>   Author: Johannes de Garlandia
>   Treatise: Optima introductio in contrapunctum pro rudibus
>   File name: **GAROPT**   File type: **TEXT**

Volentibus introduci in artem contrapuncti
>   Author: Philippe de Vitry
>   Treatise: Ars contrapunctus
>   File name: **VITARSC**   File type: **TEXT**

Vox est aer ictus auditu sensibilis quantum in ipso est. Omnis autem vox aut est
>   Author: Guido d'Arezzo
>   Treatise: De modorum formulis et cantuum qualitatibus
>   File name: **GUIMOD**   File type: **TEXT**

[Gamma], A, B, C, D, E, F, G, a, b, h [sqb], c, d, e, f, g, aa, bb, hh [sqb][sqb], cc, dd.
>   Author: Anonymous
>   Treatise: Regula de monocordo
>   File name: **REGDEM**   File type: **TEXT**

[L,B,S,M] Hec sunt quatuor note, quibus omnis mensurabilis contexitur cantelena.
>   Author: Boen, Johannes
>   Treatise: Ars (musicae)
>   File name: **BOENMU**   File type: **TEXT**

[See annotations below]
>   Author: Marchetus de Padua, Ciconia, and Anonymous
>   Treatise: Lucidarium, Regulae de tonis, Tractatus figurarum, and Nova musica
>   File name: **LAFVAR**   File type: **TEXT**

[Varia]
>   Author: Anonymous
>   Treatise: [Mensura cymbalorum]
>   File name: **ANOCYM**   File type: **TEXT**

[varia]
>   Author: Anonymous
>   Treatise: Tractatuli
>   File name: **ANOTRA17**   File type: **TEXT**

[varia]
>   Author: Berno Augiensis
>   Treatise: Interpolationen
>   File name: **BERNINT**   File type: **TEXT**